T0366907

The Accidental Republic

THOMAS J. WILSON PRIZE

The Board of Syndics of Harvard University Press has awarded this book the thirty-third annual Thomas J. Wilson Prize, honoring the late director of the Press. The Prize is awarded to the book chosen by the Syndics as the best first book accepted by the Press during the calendar year.

The Accidental Republic

Crippled Workingmen,
Destitute Widows, and the
Remaking of American Law

John Fabian Witt

Harvard University Press

Cambridge, Massachusetts, and London, England

First Harvard University Press paperback edition, 2006

Library of Congress Cataloging-in-Publication Data

Witt, John Fabian.
    The accidental republic : crippled workingmen, destitute widows, and the
remaking of American law / John Fabian Witt.
      p. cm.
    Includes bibliographical references and index.
    ISBN13 978-0-674-01267-7 (cloth)
    ISBN10 0-674-01267-4 (cloth)
    ISBN13 978-0-674-02261-4 (pbk.)
    ISBN10 0-674-02261-0 (pbk.)
    1. Workers' compensation—Law and legislation—United States—History.
2. Accident law—United States—History. I. Title.

KF3615.W58 2004
344.7302'1—dc22   2003056684

For my parents,
Loretta Cooper Witt
and
Thomas Powell Witt

Contents

The Accidental Republic

Introduction

On June 10, 1907, President Theodore Roosevelt traveled south from Washington for a speaking engagement at the Jamestown Exposition in Norfolk, Virginia. The exposition, which had begun in April of that year, was one of the era's great world's fairs, held in celebration of the tercentennial of Jamestown's founding just a few miles up the James River. The occasion of Roosevelt's speech was Georgia Day, a day of ceremony at the exposition in honor of the state of Georgia, its traditions, and its contributions to the nation. Roosevelt was an ideal keynote speaker. His mother was a native of Georgia, and his great-great-grandfather had served as the state's first governor. Roosevelt's maternal lineage made him the first elected president since the Civil War (and indeed the first since Kentucky-born Abraham Lincoln) to have such close ties to the South. He was, journalists noted that day, a "son of Georgia"—a man "teeming with virility and conviction, Georgia tradition and Georgia blood."[1]

Georgia Day's intended message was one of sectional reconciliation. As Roosevelt's commingling of northern and southern blood symbolized, the North and the South had put aside their differences to come together once more. Indeed, the bitter contests over slavery and freedom for which the Civil War had been fought appeared to have been forgotten.[2] Seated on the reviewing stand alongside Roosevelt was General Stephen D. Lee, veteran of the Confederate army and commander-in-chief of the United Confederate Veterans. Lee's presence made concrete the racial politics of sectional reconciliation. Elected as a state senator allied with white "redemption" forces in Mississippi in 1878, Lee had served as a delegate to the infamous Mississippi Constitutional Convention of 1890, the first of a series of southern constitutional conventions that successfully disfranchised the region's black population. In the year of the Mississippi convention, Lee had also helped found the Mississippi Historical Society, an organization dedicated to mythologizing the past of the Old South as a place of chivalry, honor, and harmonious racial hierarchy.[3] At the Jamestown Exposition itself, the voices of black Americans, represented in a cobbled-together exhibition that had not yet been finished by the time of the Georgia Day celebrations, had largely been silenced. African American protests of the Jamestown tercentennial, led by W. E. B. Du Bois, went virtually unnoticed outside the black press.[4]

When Roosevelt got up to speak to the estimated crowd of between thirty and fifty thousand Georgia Day participants, he began where white men like Lee had left off. Georgia's sons, he declared, "have stood high in every field of activity, intellectual or physical; and rapid though her progress has been in the past, it bids fair to be even greater in the wonderful new century which has now fairly opened." Noting that he was himself "half Southern and half Northern in blood," Roosevelt told the assembled crowd that what "struck him most" was the "essential oneness, the essential unity of our people." A half-son of the South had come back as president to celebrate renewed bonds of national identity at a place of the nation's founding. "The occasion," crowed the editors of the *Atlanta Constitution*, "became one which could not but loom large in the mind of the historian."[5]

Yet sectional harmony and the creative forgetting of the Civil War were not the messages for which Roosevelt's address would be remembered in the months and years ahead. With ships from the modern fleets of the world's great industrializing nations anchored behind him, Roosevelt chose the occasion of the Georgia Day address to mark the rise of a new kind of peril, unforeseen by either the nation's founders or those who had fought in the Civil War. Roosevelt's chief subject was the problem of industrial accidents. His speech quickly turned from the traditions of his mother's home state to the problems of industrialization in a nation fast leaving behind nineteenth-century troubles for new dilemmas. Inequalities of wealth seemed to have created new conditions of distrust between rich and poor. Steamships daily brought waves of new immigrants. And the evils of child labor and women in the paid industrial workforce seemed to threaten what Roosevelt called "the nation's most valuable asset," its children. Each of these issues pointed to ever more pressing conditions of "mutual interdependence" among a people long used to "self-reliant individualism." But of all of these issues, industrial accidents most captured Roosevelt's attention, and it was on the industrial accident that his address focused.

"The great increase in mechanical and manufacturing operations," Roosevelt told his audience, "means a corresponding increase in the number of accidents to the wage-workers employed therein."[6] Indeed, even as Roosevelt spoke, the United States was in the fifth decade of an accident crisis like none the world had ever seen and like none any Western nation has witnessed since. At the turn of the century, one worker in fifty was killed or disabled for at least four weeks each year because of a work-related accident. Among the population as a whole, roughly one in every thousand Americans died in an accident each year.[7] For those who worked in dangerous industries, accident rates were considerably higher. In 1890 alone, one railroad worker in every three hundred was killed on the job; among freight railroad brakemen, one out of a hundred died in work accidents.[8] Nonfatal accident rates, though more difficult to estimate, appear to have been much higher. By one contemporary estimate, no fewer than 42 percent of railroad workers involved in the day-to-day operation of trains in the state of Colorado were injured on the job each year.[9]

The most extraordinary rates of death and injury appear to have occurred in the anthracite coal mines of eastern Pennsylvania during the 1850s and 1860s, where each year 6 percent of the workforce was killed, 6 percent permanently crippled, and 6 percent seriously but temporarily disabled.[10] But by some measures, accident rates in many industries had increased in the intervening half-century. Indeed, the year of the Jamestown Exposition was, according to a leading historian of mining safety, "the worst year in the history of industrial accidents." Eighteen disasters, including an explosion in a West Virginia mine that December (which killed 361 miners), produced a total of 918 mining fatalities for the year. And by comparison to the early twenty-first century, accidental death rates for the population as a whole were astronomical. In 1900 the annual U.S. accidental-death rate of 1 in 1,000 was as great as that of the most dangerous occupations a century later.[11]

In Roosevelt's view, as he explained that June day in 1907, the mounting toll of industrial accidents required bold changes in the nation's laws. For "the ordinary wage-worker's family," he reminded his audience, "such a calamity means grim hardship." Given that the work out of which such accidents arose was "done for the employer, and therefore ultimately for the public, it is a bitter injustice that it should be the wage-worker himself and his wife and children who bear the whole penalty." The relevant law, Roosevelt explained, made it exceedingly difficult for employees to recover damages from their employers. The governing common law principles, which generally required an injured employee to prove that an injury was caused by the employer's negligence, had been created some seventy years before when judges had decided that workers rather than their employers ought to assume the risks characteristic of their occupations. Echoing a proposal he had put on the nation's agenda just a few months before, the president envisioned a very different way of dealing with such accidents: "Workmen should receive," he said, "a certain definite and limited compensation for all accidents" arising "as an incident of the performance of their duties," whether or not they were able to prove the employer negligence required for recovery under existing law. Such a regime of workmen's compensation for industrial accidents would induce employers to take greater care, and thereby reduce the number of accidents. Moreover, it would represent a "step toward the goal of securing, so far as human wisdom can secure, fair and equitable treatment for every one of our people." Roosevelt insisted that workmen's compensation would do so with no more than a "temporary burden" for the nation's industries. Employers would "gain a desirable certainty of obligation" and "get rid of" burdensome and costly litigation, while the "workman and the workman's family would be relieved from a crushing load." It seemed, then, that "from every standpoint, the change would be a benefit."[12]

The president's Georgia Day speech was not simply about putting to rest the conflicts of the Civil War. It was about defining the central dilemmas of the new century. The first line of the next day's *Washington Post* headline about the speech looked backward on the eclipse of sectional conflict: "Proud of His Georgian Ancestry," it read, "Roosevelt Pays Glowing Tribute to South and Its Marvelous Progress." But the subhead struck a different, distinctly modern chord: "Automatic Indemnity for Personal Injury," it announced.[13] In place of the concerns that had led the nation to a war over slave labor, Roosevelt raised questions about new risks in the ostensibly free labor society that the Civil War had helped to usher in. Though the president faced them with characteristically forceful bravado, these risks and others like them (even as Roosevelt spoke) were coming to preoccupy a generation of Americans, from labor leaders and progressive reformers, to lawyers, judges, and legislators, to engineers and the leaders of the nation's most important industries.

This book is about the American industrial-accident crisis and the transformations it occasioned in American law. Beginning soon after the Civil War, industrial accidents gave rise to a series of large-scale experiments in social, institutional, and legal reform. Judges and jurists developed an entire field of law known as the law of torts. Millions of Americans joined newly organized life insurance programs. Leading employers developed new approaches to relations with workers and to the employment contract. And by the first decade of the twentieth century, special commissions of lawyers, legislators, social insurance experts, labor leaders, and employers sponsored dozens of studies of the social consequences of work accidents, considering an array of innovative options for reform. Between 1909 and 1913, twenty-eight state and federal commissions (representing virtually every important industrial state in the nation) studied the industrial-accident problem. By the beginning of 1920, compensation systems like the one advocated by Roosevelt in 1907 were in place in forty-two states and three U.S. territories, replacing a wide swath of nineteenth-century common law with compulsory state-administered insurance regimes. Along the way, the accident problem became the center of formative (and often highly controverted) debates over such issues as the relationship between workingmen's organizations and the state; the rise of statistical strategies in law and policy; judicial review of reform legislation; and even the meaning of free labor.[14]

The book advances three interrelated arguments. First, the book provides an account of the creation of twentieth- and twenty-first-century accident law in the United States, the foundations of which were put in place during the industrial-accident crisis of the late nineteenth and early twentieth centuries. The second strand of this book connects the making of modern American systems of accident law to some of the basic features of social policy in the modern American state. Industrial accidents constituted one of the nation's chief early encounters with the kinds of dilemmas that would preoccupy lawyers, legislators, and policymakers throughout the next century. The outcomes of experiments in industrial-accident law created patterns for the thinking of subsequent generations of social policymakers. Third, as Theodore Roosevelt's Georgia Day address suggested, the industrial-accident crisis and its attendant experimentation in new legal and social institutions signaled a paradigm shift in the animating concerns of many American lawyers, judges, and lawmakers. Where the Civil War's legacy had been a series of questions about the meaning of free labor and about the distinctions between a free labor society and a slave society, the industrial-accident crisis introduced to the American legal system new ideas and institutions organized around risk, security, and the actuarial categories of insurance—ideas and institutions that to this day remain at the heart of much of our law.

Accident-law institutions play vitally important roles in American governance. The costs of accidents in the United States at the beginning of the twenty-first century amount to $500 billion each year. Although accident rates are far lower than they were at the turn of the twentieth century, close to 100,000 Americans are killed in accidents each year. Tort cases make up a substantial share of the nation's court dockets—as much as 10 percent of all civil lawsuits filed in state courts, according to one recent study. And among policymakers, lobbyists, and academics, accident law generates heated and continuing controversies over such issues as whether it deters unreasonable hazards or inhibits the development of valuable new technologies, whether it compensates victims or bankrolls the plaintiffs' bar, and whether it effectively spreads risk or has caused an unwarranted explosion in liability.[15]

The first argument of this book is that the history of American accident law is a story of widespread experimentation at the turn of the twentieth century with a number of very different legal and institutional approaches to the industrial-accident problem. In historical terms, accident law as we know it today is a remarkably recent development. Indeed, the field of accident law is almost entirely a product of a period of experimentation that began in the middle of the nineteenth century, when the accident rates of industrializing economies gave rise to new institutions to deal with the fallout from unintentional injury and death.

Eighteenth-century lawyers and judges in England and in the American colonies paid little attention to the problem of unintentional injury. William Blackstone's monumental four-volume treatise on the English common law, published between 1765 and 1769, was largely concerned with the technicalities of real property law. Blackstone's treatment of "private wrongs" was cursory and wholly unconcerned with the substantive law of unintentional harms.[16] Early- and mid-nineteenth-century lawyers and judges in the American North, in turn, sought increasingly to organize important areas of the law around the principle of contract. Private contractual relations became the framework with which common law lawyers and judges approached many legal problems. Lawyers thus treated as contracts cases many disputes that today are often considered torts cases.[17] To be sure, wide swaths of the mid-nineteenth-century common law were inconsistent with contractual theories of social relations. Noncontractual status relationships, for example, characterized the relations of husband and wife and of master and servant. At the same time, a robust tradition of public regulation of social life persisted alongside the rhetoric of contractualization. States and municipalities governed communities through the power of eminent domain, the regulation of marriage and sexuality, the policing of labor relations, the regulation of public markets via the police power, and innumerable other spheres of regulation, ranging from usury to bankruptcy to corporations to the common law of competition.[18] Nonetheless, many leading early- and mid-nineteenth-century judges, lawyers, and legal scholars sought to marginalize these noncontractual aspects of American law in favor of the organizing principle of contract.

Of course, to say that the categories of property and contract dominated American legal discourse prior to the late nineteenth century is not to say that there was no concept of civil remedies for noncontractual personal wrongs. Basic legal principles of recompense for injury have ancient roots. Sociologists in the Weberian tradition, for instance, have long argued that the state originated not in contract, as Locke and Hobbes argued, but rather in tort. On this account, payment of damages through a centralized institution (the state) replaced clan vengeance as the mechanism for making amends for injury. The Code of Hammurabi, written sometime around the year 2000 B.C.E., included a schedule of damages that an injurer had to pay to the injured. So did the early Roman Twelve Tables. Aristotle's account of corrective justice and the law in the *Nicomachean Ethics* required the restoration of the status quo ante in the event of wrongful acts that he called "involuntary" transactions. Classical Roman law had an ad hoc collection of rules for compensatory justice in instances of bodily injury, rules that had evolved (as in the Weberian account) out of an earlier practice of buying off family vengeance. A similar line of development is apparent in England, where medieval Anglo-Saxon law provided for a statutory sum known as a *wergild*, by which one kin group could atone for the slaughter of a member of another kin group. By the fourteenth century the Anglo-Saxon *wergild* had been routinized into the common law action for personal injury pleaded under the writ of trespass and adjudicated by a common law jury. And by the early modern period, civil law scholars on the Continent had distilled from the Roman law a single standard of civil liability for "fault," which scholars took to mean action or inaction "in conflict with what men ought to do."[19]

But if Western legal systems had dealt with wrongful harms for centuries, the problem of compensation for unintentional human injuries generated on a mass scale by the regular operations of economic life was largely new to Western legal systems in the mid to late nineteenth century. Aristotle had discussed his conception of corrective justice not in relation to unintentional accidental injury but in relation to intentional acts such as violent assault, false imprisonment, and insult.[20] Even as late as the 1880s, the future U.S. Supreme Court justice Oliver Wendell Holmes Jr., like Aristotle more than 2,000 years before, had little conception of the special problems raised for the law in a society facing the inevitability of unintentional injury from economic activity. Holmes developed his theory of torts not around industrial injury cases but around personal interactions. For Holmes—or at least for the Holmes who wrote *The Common Law* in 1881—the case of *Brown v. Kendall*, in which one man accidentally struck another with a stick while separating two fighting dogs, became the paradigm case for his theory of tort law.[21]

Yet even as Holmes formulated his early ideas about torts in the 1870s and 1880s, industrialization and the growth of the railroads were transforming the kinds of injury cases that occupied jurists. Accident rates increased dramatically. Personal injury litigation developed and litigation rates skyrocketed. For the first time, middle- and working-class people purchased life insurance policies on a widespread basis. Newly established accident-insurance companies wrote a new kind of policy for railway passengers. And legal scholars developed a discrete category of legal rules and principles known as "tort law." Boston lawyer Francis Hilliard's 1859 treatise on torts, though still framed in Blackstone's terms as a treatise on "private wrongs," was, as Hilliard observed in his preface, the first work exclusively devoted to the law of torts.[22] Though a decade later Holmes still believed that torts was "not a proper subject for a law book," law libraries swelled with new treatises on torts and related fields like railroad and insurance law.[23] Harvard Law School added a course on torts to its curriculum, with a book on torts published specifically for the course in 1870.[24] And within two decades of his 1881 lectures on the common law, Holmes was compelled to rethink his ideas about torts in light of the apparent inevitability of accidents in modern life. In 1881 he had been preoccupied with interpersonal torts resulting from chance occurrences. By 1897 he observed that the "torts with which our courts are kept busy to-day are mainly the incidents of certain well known businesses. They are injuries to person or property by railroads, factories, and the like."[25] These injuries, produced by the seemingly inexorable progress of industry, created the accident-law dilemmas of the late nineteenth and early twentieth centuries.

Historians' accounts of how American accident law developed in these years have proceeded along two lines: materialist and idealist. Materialist accounts explain changes in the law of personal injury as responses to the processes of economic development. The standard story in the historical literature begins in a pre-industrial era often supposed to have been characterized by strict liability to injurers for harm inflicted on victims.[26] The old common law writ of trespass, in this view, provided victims of personal injury (as well as victims of any number of different kinds of injury to personal or real property) a means to recover for harm inflicted, whether or not the injurer acted negligently. Trespass thus protected a static conception of the social order by requiring corrective justice for violations of the status quo.[27] This conventional materialist story continues into the dawn of the industrial era, when the strict-liability standard of the writ of trespass is said to have given way to a relatively restrictive standard of liability only on a showing of the defendant's negligence, a principle that underwrote industrial development by shifting some of the cost of injury-producing activity onto workers, passengers, and neighboring property owners.[28] Then, in the last years of the nineteenth century and the first years of the twentieth, growth in the rate of accidents and the new maturity of the nation's industrialized economy gave rise to an expansion in tort liability.[29] In the final stage of the materialist account, when tort liability threatened to become too great, states adopted workmen's compensation statutes at the behest of employers to limit employee recovery in work-accident cases.[30]

Idealist accounts of the development of accident law tend to agree with materialist histories on the broad outlines of the story, but the idealists explain historical change by reference to developments in the history of ideas, the sociology of knowledge, or deeply rooted individualist traditions, rather than developments in the economy. Under these approaches, for example, it has been argued that the crystallization of the negligence principle in nineteenth-century tort law arose not out of the developmental imperatives of an industrializing economy, but out of efforts in the late-nineteenth-century American legal profession to reconceptualize legal rules as a set of ordered and scientific principles.[31] Jurists like Holmes took it upon themselves during these years to bring conceptual order and theoretical cohesion to the jumble of legal doctrines that had constituted the early-nineteenth-century law of torts. The negligence principle suggested itself to doctrinal conceptualists like Holmes because it satisfied the conceptualist desire to unify and synthesize tort law at a high level of generality around a single abstract principle.[32] Thus, rather than an ad hoc collection of relational standards, the law of torts would instead consist of one duty of care—"reasonable" care—that each individual owed to all the world.[33] Idealist approaches attribute later shifts toward a twentieth-century regime of liberalized liability to such intellectual developments as widening conceptions of causation, responsibility, and interdependence, all of which (the story goes) prompted lawyers and judges to expand the scope of liability in tort.[34]

Neither of the prevailing historical accounts recognize the extent to which the late nineteenth century presented a moment of possibility for alternate paths of development. Neither the materialist nor the idealist approach, in other words, adequately grasps the contingency of the American accident-law regime.[35] Both interpretations are almost exclusively concerned with the doctrinal and institutional history of the law of torts. Moreover, although recent scholarship foreshadows the beginnings of new approaches, both of the conventional historical accounts tacitly assume a determinate relation between a particular course of social change (industrialization) or a new intellectual development (changing ideas about causation) and a particular regime or doctrinal structure in accident law.[36] Such assumptions might be plausible within the relatively narrow confines of tort law; wider conceptions of causation, for example, might expand the number of persons who could be said to have caused a particular injury.[37] But by focusing almost exclusively on tort doctrine and tort cases, scholars have diverted attention from the dynamic character of American accident law at the turn of the twentieth century.

In fact, the United States experimented in the late nineteenth and early twentieth centuries with an array of policy alternatives to address industrial accidents. Policymakers and academics during these decades participated in a vibrant transatlantic dialogue on the problem.[38] During the 1870s and 1880s, labor leaders studied the apparently more favorable liability rules in European jurisdictions, often framing arguments for liberalized American employers' liability laws in comparative terms.[39] Scholars and government officials studied German approaches to industrial-accident policy.[40] And beginning with a report by the Massachusetts Bureau of Statistics of Labor in 1872, prepared under the direction of future U.S. commissioner of labor Carroll D. Wright, government agencies at the state and federal levels compiled in-depth reports on comparative accident law.[41] In the first decade of the twentieth century, as workmen's compensation legislation became a topic of serious discussion in American legislatures, teams of reformers and academics traveled to Europe under the aegis of such organizations as the Russell Sage Foundation, the National Association of Manufacturers, and the U.S. Department of Labor to see for themselves how other nations dealt with accident compensation.[42] Moreover, transatlantic policy exchange went both ways. German social scientists commissioned studies of insurance systems among American workingmen, and even came to the United States to study American cooperative insurance societies.[43]

Late-nineteenth-century Americans built on these transatlantic exchanges to develop an eclectic array of experimental alternatives for adapting American institutions to the industrial-accident crisis. In particular, four leading approaches to the accident problem emerged in the United States in the second half of the nineteenth century. In the nation's courts, lawyers and judges created the common law of torts, repackaging a formerly ad hoc jumble of rules and standards into a common law accident regime. Workers organized widespread but remarkably little-known cooperative insurance societies. Sophisticated employers and the first generation of scientific managers developed private employer compensation programs. And social insurance advocates proposed the compulsory accident-compensation schemes that were enacted in the decade after 1910. By the end of our period, in the 1920s and 1930s, the basic allocations of labor between workmen's compensation systems for work accidents, on one hand, and tort for virtually the rest of the field, on the other, had been set in place. But in the preceding half-century, the proliferation of alternatives in American accident law had occasioned a highly plastic moment in which the institutions that make up our contemporary accident-law regime might have developed in any number of different ways.

Experiments in accident law in the first two decades of the twentieth century had important consequences for the future of American social policy. The industrial-accident crisis and Americans' responses to it were among the nation's first sustained encounters with social policy for a modern industrial economy. Alternative approaches to dealing with the accident problem advanced not just discrete models for dealing with the problem of industrial accidents, but also broader agendas for dealing with an array of modern social policy problems that were beginning to emerge on the American political scene.

Indeed, the accident crisis set in place patterns that would characterize a number of subsequent developments in American social policy. By the time of the New Deal, the American state was dominated by figures who had come of age around the problem of work-accident law reform. Franklin Roosevelt had been actively involved in the nation's work-accident law as a young state legislator in New York. Charles Evans Hughes, chief justice of the U.S. Supreme Court during the New Deal, signed into law the nation's first work-accident compensation statute in 1910 as the last major act of his term as governor of the state of New York. George Sutherland, one of the conservative "Four Horsemen" on the New Deal Supreme Court, chaired an important 1912 federal commission recommending enactment of workmen's compensation legislation for interstate railroad workers. Pierce Butler (a conservative ally of Sutherland's on the Court) wrote an influential brief in favor of workmen's compensation for the Minnesota Bar Association. Frances Perkins, New Deal secretary of labor, worked closely with the New York State Factory Inspection Commission in the wake of the 1911 Triangle Shirtwaist Fire that killed 146 people, and later oversaw the administration of the New York State workmen's compensation scheme in the early 1920s. Harry Hopkins, FDR's influential aide, got his start in social work in the 1910s assisting New York workingmen and widows with workmen's compensation claims. And Huey Long, the populist Louisiana governor and senator who helped push the New Deal to the left, began his career as a plaintiffs' lawyer in cases brought under Louisiana's then-new compensation statute. These crucially important figures came to know the capacities and limitations of the modern American state through their experiences with workmen's compensation programs.[44]

Leading supporters and opponents of the New Deal were not alone in experiencing work-accident law as formative of many of their understandings of the twentieth-century state. The number of Americans touched by the workmen's compensation statutes alone suggests the massive transformations wrought by the work-accident crisis in relationships between everyday working-class families and the institutions of American law. By 1917, 68 percent of the nation's wage-earning workforce—some 13 million wage earners—was covered by the still newly enacted statutes. By 1930, workers in New York State alone were filing 200,000 new claims per year. Work-accident law reform, in short, touched the lives of millions upon millions of Americans, from presidents to Supreme Court justices to countless working men and women across the nation.[45]

Not surprisingly, then, innovations in work-accident law exerted strong pull on the development of social policy during the first four decades of the twentieth century. Leading New Deal students of unemployment insurance borrowed from workmen's compensation the idea of cost internalization:

that employers could be made to minimize unemployment (just as they could be made to minimize work accidents) if layoffs generated costs in the form of higher unemployment insurance rates. Drafters of the Social Security Act's old-age pensions adopted a model for supporting wage-earning families that they drew virtually word for word from the American wrongful death statutes of the 1840s and the workmen's compensation statutes of the 1910s. And the actuaries whose expertise was critical to the success of both unemployment insurance and old-age pensions had introduced their techniques to American audiences largely through descriptions of the seemingly inevitable onslaught of industrial accidents.

Nor were the consequences of work-accident reform limited to government programs. Early twentieth-century firms organized new human resources bureaucracies around the management of work-accident benefits. Workingmen's organizations and employees, in turn, began in claims cases before workmen's compensation commissions to learn new skills of entitlement-claiming in the administrative state.

Perhaps most important, political lobbies and powerful interest groups were still in the process of formation in the early years of accident-law reform. Just a few decades into the twentieth century, these constituencies would come to dominate and often calcify policymaking processes in areas such as accident law and health insurance reform. As historian Daniel Rodgers has written, the result would be the preclusion of policy options in a "field too thick with claimants"; the "territory of action" had "already . . . been preempted" by the presence of strong interests.[46] By comparison, American lawyers, judges, reformers, and legislators first encountered the accident problem in a relatively open field and in a moment of relatively indeterminate beginnings. The era of accident-law reform thus stood as one of those seminal moments of possibility in American politics, one of those punctuations in the equilibria of normal politics: a critical juncture in which the future of American law and policy was open to a number of different possible lines of development.[47] Its outcomes helped shape the developmental path for American social policy in the century to come.

The immersion of a generation of lawmakers in the problem of industrial-accident law signaled a sea change in important areas of American law. In the middle decades of the nineteenth century, contractualization of broad swaths of the law had adherents on both sides of the Atlantic. In England, John Stuart Mill wrote in 1848 that the purpose of the state was "enforcing contracts." Several decades later, the American social Darwinist William Graham Sumner would affirm that "the social structure is based on contract"; indeed, Sumner would add that this was so "in the United States more than anywhere else." Society was constituted by free agents entering into consensual relations for mutual advantage. The function of the state was to enforce the contract rights created in such relations.[48]

In both Britain and the United States, contract ideas were expressed powerfully in the law of industrial accidents. In the 1837 case *Priestley v. Fowler,* the English Court of Exchequer announced that only where the employer himself was negligent could an employee recover damages from his employer for injuries suffered at work. The opinion's author, Lord Abinger, had long supported reform in the English Poor Law along the lines advocated by classical economists Malthus and Ricardo, on the theory that state-provided material support undermined incentives to work and led to pauperism. Accordingly, in *Priestley,* Abinger held that the law of industrial accidents would turn not on state-mandated standards but rather on the private contractual arrangements of the parties. In Abinger's view, employees consented by implied contract to take the risk of injuries other than those caused by the negligence of their employer.[49]

Five years later, in the famous case of *Farwell v. Boston and Worcester Rail Road,* the great Massachusetts chief justice Lemuel Shaw would set the American law of work accidents down a similar path, holding that responsibility for accidental employee injuries was controlled by the terms of the contract between employer and employee. In Shaw's view, employment contracts generally allocated to the employee responsibility for the "natural and ordinary risks and perils incident to the performance of [the] services," including the "carelessness and negligence of those who are in the same employment." Such a rule, Shaw insisted, would "best promote the safety and security of all parties concerned" because the employee was "as likely to know" of dangers as the employer and could "as effectually guard" against them. In any event, Shaw ruled, the law presumed that the employee's "rate of compensation" would be "adjusted" so as to "provide[] for" the risks assumed by the employee.[50]

Although there were strong parallels between English and American contractarian thinking, the United States developed its own distinctive brand of contractarian ideas organized around what historians have come to call the ideology of free labor. By "ideology," I do not mean the rigid worldview of the ideologue, who blindly advocates a set of abstract ideas regardless of their truth value. Rather, I use the term "ideology" in the sense that has become familiar over the past several decades in the historical literature on social and political thought: as a loose collection of interrelated ways of understanding and mentally organizing human experience.[51] I mean, in other words, a kind of rough-hewn paradigm for thinking about social relationships, similar (though typically less internally rigorous) to the idea of a scientific paradigm in the history of science. A scientific paradigm sets the common agenda of a field of inquiry, shaping its questions and methods.[52] Similarly, ideologies loosely organize a common set of concerns and values shared by a group of human beings. An ideology or paradigm need not command perfect agreement among the women and men who work from within its categories. Indeed, as we shall see, there was as much disagreement over the meanings of free labor as there was disagreement over the best way to deal with industrial accidents. But to count as an ideology or a paradigm, a body of ideas must exert a common shaping influence on the ways in which some group of women and men think about the world around them. In this sense, free labor ideology in the mid-nineteenth century organized important areas of American political and legal thought around the polar opposition of free labor to slave labor, marking out a diverse array of virtues that were said to distinguish the former from the latter—virtues such as autonomy, independence, efficiency, and domesticity.

As an ideology, as a system for thinking about the world, free labor came by the middle of the nineteenth century to influence powerfully the politics and law of the United States. It served as the centerpiece of Abraham Lincoln's extraordinary speeches in the fall of 1859, where he described free labor as "the inspiration of hope," promising opportunity for "advancement" and "improvement in condition," and ensuring that there would be no "permanent class" of laborers, either slave or hireling. Indeed, the Civil War itself was said by many on the Union side to be "a war for the establishment of free labor."[53] In turn, the Thirteenth Amendment that followed on the heels of the war enshrined free labor in the nation's fundamental law by prohibiting "slavery" and "involuntary servitude, except as a punishment for crime."

Ideologies focus their adherents' attention on certain phenomena. But as historian David Brion Davis writes, they do so by "screening out other phenomena."[54] Of special significance to us here, free labor ideas exhibited a kind of systemic disregard for the phenomenon of risk. Consider one of Lincoln's most famous encomiums to the system of free labor, given in his address to the Wisconsin State Agricultural Society in September 1859, on the eve of the Civil War. "Free labor," Lincoln announced, was "the just and generous, and prosperous system" that "gives hope to all, and energy, and progress, and improvement of condition to all." He continued, "If any continue through life in the condition of the hired laborer, it is not the fault of the system, but because of either a dependent nature which prefers it, or improvidence, folly, or *singular misfortune*."[55] "Singular misfortune," it seemed, was not the responsibility of what Lincoln called "the system." It was a phenomenon that he recognized, but not one that drew his attention, nor apparently the attention of his audience.

In this, Lincoln was hardly alone. Just a few years earlier, the influential essayist, lecturer, outspoken opponent of slavery, and avatar of self-reliance Ralph Waldo Emerson had written an essay titled "Compensation." If written half a century later, the title would have connoted the workmen's compensation systems then being enacted in Europe and being discussed in the United States. But in the 1840s, Emerson meant to suggest almost the opposite: a kind of universal rule of natural compensations—a "law of Compensation" he called it—under which all action was matched by reaction, and in which no human law was needed to ensure the universe's unalterable harmony. Even "calamity" had its "compensations." "A fever, a mutilation," or "a cruel disappointment," Emerson suggested, all seemed to represent "unpaid loss." But Emerson contended that calamity inevitably gave rise to corresponding (and compensating) benefits, even if unforeseen at the moment. This was the "deep remedial force" of the natural law of compensation. And indeed, with Chief Justice Shaw in *Farwell*, Emerson suggested that it could not be otherwise. The natural law of compensation, he argued, "writes the laws of cities of nations"; "[i]t is in vain to build or plot or combine against it." "Human labor," like everything in life, "has its price—and if that price is not paid, not that thing but something else is obtained, and it is impossible to get anything without its price." As Lemuel Shaw might have redescribed Emerson's idea, no one could hire human labor without paying for its attendant risks, for risk would inevitably be washed away in the price term of the employment contract.[56]

In the decades after the Civil War, industrial accidents made it increasingly difficult for free labor thinking to screen out the problem of risk. By the first decade of the twentieth century, Theodore Roosevelt would warn that though the nation had outgrown the perils confronted by its forefathers, "[w]e now face other perils, the very existence of which it was impossible that they should foresee." "Modern life," he continued at his 1905 Inaugural Address, "is both complex and intense, and the tremendous changes wrought by the extraordinary industrial development of the last half-century are felt in every fibre of our social and political being." And by the 1930s, Theodore's distant cousin Franklin Delano would place security from risk at the center of the New Deal. The hazards of modern wage-earning had replaced free labor as the centerpiece of lawmakers' ideas about the regulation of labor. In this new paradigm of risk and insurance, the salient categories were not those of free labor, the independent and autonomous workingman chief among them. They were the categories of modern statistics, the categories of the actuary and the social scientist. And therein lay a profoundly important force in the demise of the free labor paradigm.[57]

The story that follows describes the nation's leading attempts to do what

Shaw, Lincoln, and Emerson had not: to adapt the values of free labor thinking to the problems of risk in a modern wage-earning economy. For five decades after the end of the Civil War, jurists and lawmakers, workingmen and labor union leaders, employers and managers all sought to remake free labor ideas and institutions in a new era in which risks could no longer be ignored. Their experiments, in turn, transformed the free labor values with which they had begun. By the end of the period, "free labor" no longer served as a kind of catch-all label for the just society. Moreover, such integral free labor values as autonomy and independence no longer held the kind of sway they had held in the years surrounding the Civil War, even as other free labor values persisted under new guises.

It would be easy to overstate the nature of the shift I seek to describe. Risk regulation and insurance are not all that our contemporary government does, nor even what it principally does. Federal and state officials act in myriad ways, ranging from highway construction to criminal law enforcement to public education to the regulation of social castes based on race, gender, and sexual orientation. In many areas, moreover, American law continues to this day to resist the actuarial categories of risk management and insurance. And it goes without saying that contracts remain one of the core mechanisms of our legal and governmental institutions. (Some might even say that contract has undergone a revival of sorts in the last two decades of the twentieth century, decades during which "deregulation" became a watchword in American politics and law.) By the same token, it would be misleading to suggest that Americans before the late nineteenth century did not think about risk and insurance. Merchants had long dealt in insurance for shipping risks on the high seas. The maritime, fire, and life insurance industries had their beginnings at the end of the eighteenth century.[58] And from its very beginnings, the federal government created insurance-benefit systems for seamen and provided ad hoc disaster relief to the victims of natural disasters.[59] The paradigm shift from free labor to risk and insurance, then, was not so much a clean break as a halting, inevitably partial, and often barely perceptible change in emphasis.

Identifying paradigm shifts in systems of legal ordering can be an especially difficult task. Law is not a discipline in the sense of being bound tightly together by a common set of questions and methodological premises. A legal system is far too vast and unwieldy to undergo the kinds of paradigm shifts that have been plausibly (if controversially) identified in the history of the natural sciences. There are too few agreed upon starting points, and even fewer agreed upon ends. Law is thus not susceptible to relatively clean revolutions in which one paradigm is replaced by another across the sharp divide of a particular transformative crisis.

At most, legal systems tend to experience what, in a 1969 postscript to his influential theory of scientific revolutions, Thomas Kuhn referred to as paradigm shifts in a "subcommunity" of specialists. In the law of industrial accidents, this book describes a paradigm shift from the categories of free labor to the problems of risk and insurance within the subcommunity of industrial-accident specialists. One of the central arguments of the final two chapters of this book is that transformations in the law of work accidents radiated out from the subcommunity of industrial-accident specialists into other areas of American law. And yet this process of diffusion quickly experienced limits. Deeply entrenched legal institutions, influential bodies of constitutional law, and powerful interest group pressures all served to contain the scope of the dramatic shifts that took place within the sphere of industrial accidents.

The legal transformations in the law of work injuries are thus perhaps best described as ushering in a kind of halfway revolution. As such, however, the halfway revolution described here may better capture the full sense of the term "revolution." A revolution is often as much a coming-full-circle—a revolution in the sense of the earth around the sun, or a wheel around its axle—as a clean break with what has gone before. In this sense, legal paradigm shifts (especially, perhaps, those taking place in backward-looking common law systems oriented around precedent) maintain the palpable traces of their predecessors.[60]

Yet with these caveats in mind, it remains true that between the time of Lincoln and the era of Franklin Roosevelt, important elements of American governance shifted from contests over the meaning and scope of contract freedoms and self-ownership, to debates over how to allocate the risks accompanying those contract freedoms. This book is about this transformation in American law and politics—halting and partial though it was—from the poles of freedom and slavery to the oppositions of freedom and risk. It aims to account for the processes by which, in the words of the great mid-twentieth-century lawyer Grant Gilmore, tort "swallowed up" contract.[61] The pivot on which this remaking of American law took place was the great and horrible industrial-accident crisis of the turn of the twentieth century.

A few points are worth clarifying at the outset. First, this is emphatically a *legal* history of the U.S. experience of industrial accidents in the late nineteenth and early twentieth centuries. In many parts of the book, this will be readily apparent. I am concerned in Chapters 2 and 6, for example, with the classic stuff of histories of law: courts, judges, lawyers, constitutions, and cases. Chapter 5 describes the workmen's compensation statutes, which have long been the shared jurisdiction of lawyers and social scientists.

In other parts of the book, I concentrate on institutions and practices that traditionally lie outside the purview of the historian of law. Among other things, I describe the cooperative insurance societies organized by American workingmen in the decades after the Civil War, as well as developments in the employment practices of certain sophisticated turn-of-the-century employers. But these, too, were legal phenomena. In recent years, legal historians have exuberantly burst through the artificial boundaries that once separated law from society.[62] At the same time, legal scholars in a variety of disciplines have broadened their agenda to include informal as well as formal systems of social ordering.[63] This book proceeds in the same spirit. It is concerned principally with the ways in which people ordered their relations with one another in dealing with the problem of industrial accidents.[64] Indeed, even such informal mechanisms of social order as the workingmen's cooperatives were themselves thickly constituted by legal rules and institutions. Workingmen's insurance societies were, like corporations and partnerships, legal forms; they benefitted from certain legal privileges and were subject to certain legal restraints. Employers' labor relations practices were largely pursued through the execution of contracts drafted in the shadow of the law of employment. It is not, then, simply that developments in the formal law of accidents—the law of torts, for example, or the doctrines of insurance law—are best understood alongside institutions usually outside the jurisdiction of legal-historical study, though they are. The point I seek to make here is that such institutions, together with more formal features of our accident law, constitute a complex and decentralized set of interrelated legal systems.[65] Their history, alongside such traditional objects of study as the landmark decisions of Holmes, Benjamin Cardozo, and Learned Hand, make up the history of the important field lawyers have come to know as accident law.

The close reader will note that notwithstanding the inclusion of subjects traditionally left out of histories of tort and accident law, the book also excludes subjects that are part of the history of accident law in the United States. I touch on the law of slavery, for example, only in passing, even though the problem of injuries to slaves created an important body of slave law in the American South. Legend even has it that the first steam railroad fatality in the United States was a black slave killed in a boiler explosion in South Carolina in 1831.[66] Nonetheless, the law of slavery exists in my account as little more than a foil against which the law of free labor work accidents developed. Indeed, the South as a whole plays relatively little role in the story I set out here. Industrial accidents first drew sustained attention in northern states. And despite interesting early developments in states such as Georgia, which enacted reform legislation liberalizing its law of employers' liability on the railroads as early as 1856, southern states tended to be laggards in the development of work-accident law reform, following paths charted by northern states. Moreover, as a result of the small role for the South in this narrative, there is also little about African Americans. Although immigrant workers from southern and eastern Europe played central roles in the problem of industrial accidents (as both victims and designers of institutional responses), there were very few blacks in the North prior to the first wave of northward migration in and around World War I. A history of accidents and the law in the nineteenth- and early -twentieth-century South would doubtless form a fascinating story, and problems relating to race would likely play a central role. But such a history would be a different project from the one on which I have embarked here.

This book also spends relatively little time on the development of command-and-control state factory regulations, or on the development of state factory inspection offices, mine safety laws, and railroad safety legislation. I am principally concerned here with legal institutions designed to compensate injured employees and their families. Moreover, factory regulations went famously underenforced during the period that occupies this study. Factory inspectors were understaffed, overworked, frequently incompetent, and sometimes corrupt. Sanctions for violations tended to be paltry. The failings of state factory regulation and inspection play an important role in Chapter 3, where I describe the decline of the workingmen's cooperative insurance associations. But those failings virtually ruled out the possibility that factory inspections and command-and-control regulations would become a promising avenue for the development of new accident-law institutions in the late nineteenth and early twentieth centuries. The structure of the institutions of state and federal government in the United States—especially the absence of a professional civil service—meant that effective factory inspection was generally not a viable option for those who sought to enact legal reform in the area of industrial accidents. I have chosen in this book to follow the leading experiments in dealing with industrial accidents, by which I mean those that for women and men at the time (and for historians today) constituted plausible alternative paths of development for the American law of accidents. With the important exception of Chapter 3, factory inspection's role in this story is therefore limited.

Throughout this book, I use the gendered terminology of the period. Wage earners in the industries on which students of industrial accidents tended to focus their attention were almost exclusively male. To be sure, women—often young and single women—frequently worked in textile mills whose whirring shuttles and fast-moving belts could pose real dangers to fingers and hands, and worse. Early students of industrial diseases studied industries such as match-making, in which many women worked. Moreover, the infamous Triangle Fire of 1911 killed more than a hundred young female wage earners.[67] Yet the central preoccupation of those who sought to address the industrial-accident crisis was injury to the male wage earner with a dependent wife and children. As Chapter 1 begins to demonstrate, this model of the family—the so-called family wage—played an influential role in the development of the American law of accidents. And so I often generically refer to *workmen* or *workingmen* rather than workers, and to *workmens* compensation (its gender specificity no coincidence) rather than workers' compensation. The gendered nature of all these terms, and of the institutions to which they referred, constituted critically important parts of the industrial-accident crisis and of the responses to it.

Finally, a word on the book's title. By the phrase "accidental republic," I mean to make two related gestures. The first is to suggest, simply, the extent to which developments in accident law contributed to the foundations of the twentieth- and twenty-first-century American republic. Many features of our modern state, ranging from its social insurance systems to its federalism principles and beyond, cannot be understood without reference to the story I tell here.

The second meaning of the phrase suggests something more abstract—namely, that the developments in accident law (and thus in part the foundations of the modern republic) were themselves accidental. In law, as in philosophy, the term "accident" has long defied precise definition. Tort lawyers distinguish injuries that are accidental from injuries that are intentional. But this distinction almost immediately bogs down in tortured definitions of intentionality.[68] In the law of insurance, courts construe the term to mean something unforeseen or unexpected.[69] But here, too, we quickly run into difficulty, for to determine whether something is unforeseen we must first decide on a perspective and level of generality. An automobile accident may be unforeseen by the driver of the car about to turn the corner into the back of the garbage truck, but the collision is plainly no accident from the perspective of the window washer above, who has watched the traffic pattern unfold. And at a more abstract level of generality, it is surely not unexpected, even to the driver of the car, that her driving will raise the risk of being in a car accident.[70]

What, then, do I mean when I say that American accident law and the institutions in American law to which it contributed are themselves accidental? In part, I mean to invoke each of the two legal senses of the term: unintended and unforeseen. Our contemporary law of accidents exhibits features drawn from any number of the many reform projects with which turn-of-the-century Americans experimented, mixing them together into a patchwork of systems that no single individual or group of individuals either intended or foresaw. But I also want to suggest that our accident law is accidental in the still more abstract sense of being undetermined. Cardozo once warned that to grapple with whether events are determined or rather the outcome of contingent and accidental forces was inevitably to become mired in what, drawing on Milton's account of hell, he called the "Serbonian bog" of determinism and chance. Cardozo himself was a historical determinist, at least with respect to natural phenomena: "Probably it is true," he wrote, quoting an early English workmen's compensation case, "to say that in the strictest sense and dealing with the region of physical nature there is no such thing as an accident."[71]

Scientists and philosophers have since called Cardozo's understanding into question: even physical nature, it seems, overflows with contingency. Human history does too, and there are few better examples of this in our legal history than the law of accidents. In our accident law, we experimented with a wide array of plausible alternatives in remaking American law for the modern world, each of which represented different paths that American lawmakers might have taken into the twentieth century. In turn, the paths ultimately taken were the contingent outcomes of encounters between these alternatives and the cultures, institutions, and individual men and women of American law. This book is the story of the alternatives and the encounters, and of why and how we took the paths we did.

1

Crippled Workingmen, Destitute Widows, and the Crisis of Free Labor

A certain number of lives are inevitably lost in the course of our modern industry—you cannot prevent it. . . . Now, . . . that being the case the proposition should be treated in a brutally frank manner, in the same way as it would be treated in the old days of slavery. If a slave was injured, it was so much injury to the owner of the slave. Of course, we are to-day free, but, practically speaking, there is always a certain danger attendant upon industrial employment.

—DR. ISAAC A. HOURWICH, TESTIMONY BEFORE THE
U.S. INDUSTRIAL COMMISSION (1900)

Industrializing economies in the mid to late nineteenth century experienced an explosion of accident rates alongside the rapid development of new industries and more powerful machinery. During the same period, virtually every industrializing Western nation developed new approaches for dealing with the accidents incident to industrialization. France, Germany, Great Britain, and the United States alike all developed new insurance mechanisms for workingmen and their families; experimented with changes in the law of employers' liability; and established systems of factory inspection and safety regulations. Yet there was much that was exceptional about the American experience. By virtually all accounts—contemporary accounts as well as those of historians writing a century later—the United States witnessed an industrial-accident crisis of world-historical proportions. Furthermore, the American accident problem was deeply bound up in a peculiar set of preoccupations borne of the American experience of slavery, civil war, and emancipation. "Free labor" had become the rallying cry for a diverse array of views about the proper organization of American economic, political, and social life, ranging from expectations of upward mobility and views about the wisdom of state regulation of the marketplace, to beliefs about the proper organization of the firm and the appropriate structure of the family. By the late nineteenth century, the industrial-accident problem seemed to present a paradox for free labor thinking, for a variety of practices loosely associated with free labor appeared to contribute to American industrial-accident rates. In turn, industrial accidents both called into question basic values in free labor thinking and gave rise to a spate of experimentation in adapting free labor to a new world of risk.

In some respects, it was the specter of modern warfare that pushed industrializing nations to develop new institutions and policies to deal with injury, disability, and death. In the United States in particular, the ghastly casualties of the Civil War highlighted the problems of disability and death in an era of new technologies for causing injury. Not counting deaths from disease and sickness (which pushed deaths to well over 600,000 soldiers from both sides combined) roughly 100,000 Union soldiers were killed in battle during the war, as were at least 50,000 Confederate soldiers. Members of the Union army alone suffered approximately 400,000 additional nonfatal wounds and injuries.[1] Such violence made a lasting impression on the men and women who witnessed it. Watching the fighting at the First Battle of Bull Run in 1861, one Union nurse wrote that the sight of the battlefield was "perfectly appalling." Men lay "bleeding, torn and mangled; legs, arms and bodies are crushed and broken as if smitten by thunderbolts."[2] Frederick Law Olmsted, working for the U.S. Sanitary Commission, witnessed waves of wounded men during the 1862 Peninsula Campaign. "They arrived," he wrote, "dead and alive together, in the same close box, many with awful wounds festering and alive with maggots." "The stench," Olmsted reported, "was such as to produce vomiting."[3] An eyewitness to the horrific violence at Antietam later that same year recorded "piles of dead men" lying in the "writhing agony in which they died," with "arms and legs torn from the body or the body itself torn asunder."[4] Walt Whitman wrote in the summer of 1864 of the wounded arriving in Washington, their wounds "all swelled and inflamed." Amputations, Whitman noted, often had "to be done over again" because of infection. Years later, he would still remember the "horribly mutilated" bodies of the "groaning and moaning" wounded.[5]

The onslaught of wartime casualties and the impressions they made on those who witnessed them generated a vigorous effort to organize effective delivery of medical care to wounded and sick soldiers on the battlefield. The Sanitary Commission for which Olmsted worked was formed as a semipublic body of volunteers who inspected medical facilities and performed battlefield ambulance and triage operations.[6] And though the Union army's medical corps was slow to develop the organizational capacity necessary to deal effectively with the unprecedented number of injuries, by the end of the war Union doctors were experimenting with new methods of sanitation, hygiene, and treatment.[7] The Civil War even gave rise to the nation's first major experiments in public policy for disability and injury in peacetime. In the wake of the war, the federal government developed institutions and programs designed to reintegrate injured Civil War veterans into postwar society. The National Home for Disabled Volunteer Soldiers sheltered veterans whose medical conditions and economic circumstances required inpatient care; by 1900, the National Home had housed a total of nearly 100,000 Union veterans.[8] Moreover, the system of Civil War pensions provided aid to tens of thousands of disabled veterans in the years after the war. By the last years of the nineteenth century, the veterans' pension program had devolved into a partisan spending program with little connection to disability policy.[9] Yet the Civil War veterans' programs presaged the emergence of attempts to deal with the growing problem of accidents in late-nineteenth-century American civilian life. Indeed, in the first decades of the twentieth century, the Civil War veterans' programs would lay important groundwork for accident-compensation policies aimed at the nation's beleaguered industrial army.

By the 1880s, the numbers of accidental deaths and injuries arising out of the processes of industrialization in Western economies seemed to many to overshadow the casualties of modern warfare. Indeed, Americans in particular had begun to observe that their peacetime industrial economy produced more deaths and injuries than the cataclysmic war that preceded it. President Benjamin Harrison's first message to Congress in 1889 announced that American railroad workers were subject "to a peril of life and limb as great as that of a soldier in time of war."[10] The New Jersey Bureau of Statistics of Labor and Industry went a step further, reporting in 1891 that "the destruction of human life is much greater in the peaceful pursuits of industry than in war, and if it were possible to enumerate them, it would be found far greater than during the four years of destruction in the late civil war."[11] Twenty years later, in 1911, work-accident reformers in Iowa would conclude still more gravely that the nation's annual casualty list in peaceful industries "equals the average yearly casualties of the American Civil War, plus all those of the Philippine War, plus all those of the Russo-Japanese War."[12] In the words of one reformer, the nation seemed to be developing an "army of cripples."[13] Moreover, the war analogy came quickly to have a political significance; from the 1880s onward, workingmen's organizations and labor reformers across the nation would reason that if disabled soldiers were pensioned, so too should the injured soldiers of the industrial army. "Is not the industrial soldier," asked the United Mine Workers, "of more real value to the nation than the soldier?" Where industry was a necessity, after all, war was a "relic of barbarism."[14]

There is, of course, little that is surprising about the observation that industrialization generated heightened accident rates. Leading accounts of legal change during the late nineteenth century take as their starting point the cascade of injuries from railroads, machines, mechanized workplaces, street-cars, and the many other dangerous incidents of modern economic life.[15] Yet it is worth exploring the relationship between industrialization and accidental injury in more detail because some historians have challenged the idea that industrialization and urbanization were accompanied by growth in accident rates. In particular, historians have used the mortality rates of workers in various occupations, as well as coroners' data on accidental death rates, to conclude that industrial manufacturing work was no more dangerous than non-industrial occupations and that, contrary to conventional wisdom, accident rates were generally constant over time in the late nineteenth and early twentieth centuries.[16]

The available statistics furnish good reason to doubt such conclusions. It is notoriously difficult to measure accidental injury and death rates during the nineteenth century. Statistics gathered in the middle part of the century by state railroad commissions, and subsequently by state bureaus of labor statistics, chronically underestimated accident rates because they relied almost entirely on employer self-reporting.[17] Apparent changes in accident rates in the early statistics often reflected little more than changes in the effectiveness of data gathering. Moreover, the great difficulty in measuring accident rates in the late nineteenth century is that while fatality rates provide the most reliable statistics, improvements in medical care during the period in question make mortality rates an unreliable measure of accident rates generally. The pressures that the Civil War placed on the American medical establishment helped prompt the development of modern organizational structures in hospitals and gave rise to the modern nursing profession.[18] More important still, the 1870s and 1880s witnessed the widespread introduction of germ theory and antiseptic surgery into American hospitals, fundamentally transforming the practice of medicine and dramatically improving the survival rates for surgeries such as amputations.[19] If more and more injuries that would have resulted in death in the 1860s were being treated successfully by 1900, then even relatively constant accidental-death rates over the course of the late nineteenth century would suggest sharply increased rates of serious accidental injury.[20]

From the available evidence, it appears that accident rates were growing sharply in the mid-nineteenth century in most Western nations. In England, the share of deaths caused by violence and injury rose by over 350 percent between 1700 and the mid-1800s, though deaths from homicide and execution fell sharply after the late 1700s. English students of accident statistics in the 1880s believed that the ratio of deaths from accidental injury to deaths from all causes had been increasing since the beginning of the century. In France, accidental deaths per 100,000 individuals almost doubled, from fifteen in the late 1820s to twenty-eight by 1860. Census takers continually added new categories to their listing of deaths by accident and injury. The chief of the French General Statistical Department concluded in 1865 that the number of accidental deaths was increasing throughout the Western world at a rate greater than the rate of population growth.[21]

Accident rates in the United States are more difficult to determine, but they too appear to have increased dramatically during the mid and late nineteenth century, especially in the Northeast and Midwest. Roger Lane's study of Philadelphia suggests that the accidental death rate in that city increased from 34.4 accidental deaths per 100,000 population between 1839 and 1845, to 58.6 accidental deaths per 100,000 population between 1895 and 1901.[22] At the national level, the 1850 census was the first to count deaths from accidents, measuring the number of accidental deaths from burns, drownings, scaldings, and other "accidents."[23] The 1860 census added new categories, including one for "accidents, railroad,"[24] and the 1870 census added "[m]ining accidents," "[i]njuries by machinery," and accidents from "[f]alling bodies."[25] By 1880, the share of deaths attributable to accident among men aged ten to fifty increased by over 70 percent, from 7 percent to 12 percent, since the census of 1850.[26] Growth in the share of deaths attributable to accidents was especially pronounced in the North.[27] And among particular classes of accidents, the increased share of deaths attributable to accidents was even greater. In 1860, railroad accidents accounted for only 0.6 percent of deaths among males aged ten to fifty; by 1890, that figure jumped to almost 3 percent, a fivefold increase.[28]

Despite trends common to the United States and other developing nations, accident rates in the late-nineteenth- and early-twentieth-century United States appear to have been exceptionally acute. The coal mining fatality rate, as measured per employee, ranged between two and three times as high in the United States as in Great Britain between 1880 and 1930. As measured by employee hour, railroad fatality rates were 50 percent higher in the United States than in Great Britain. Contemporary estimates of comparative accident rates were even more startling. Students of American industry estimated that the U.S. fatality rate in coal mines, as measured in deaths per worker, was four times as high as in Austria, three times as high as in Belgium and France, and more than twice as high as in Great Britain. Contemporaries placed U.S. accident rates among railroad employees, as measured in deaths per worker, at between three-and-a-half and four times as high as Great Britain for fatal injuries, and five times as high for nonfatal injuries. And by comparison to late-twentieth-century and early-twenty-first-century accident rates, late-nineteenth-century rates of accidental injury and death were staggering. In 1912, a leading study of deaths from accidental injury estimated

82,500 deaths per year; today, the population of the United States has tripled, but the number of accidental deaths has increased by less than a quarter.[29]

Workplace injuries were far and away the leading category of accidental injury and death in turn-of-the-century America, representing close to one-third of all accidental deaths and, by contemporary estimates, between one-half and two-thirds of all accidental injuries. Indeed, accidents were the leading cause of death among workers in hazardous industries as diverse as railroads, mining, metal work, rubber work, shipping and canals, quarries, telegraph and telephones, electric lighting, brick- and tile-making, and terracotta work. In 1890, railroad worker death rates were 314 per 100,000 workers per year. In that same year, coal miner fatality rates were comparable, ranging from 215 deaths per 100,000 workers per year in bituminous coal mines to 300 deaths per 100,000 workers per year in anthracite coal mines. Certain subsets of workers in these dangerous industries had even higher rates of accidental death. Trainmen, whose jobs required that they operate the coupling devices between cars, and brakemen, who operated the train's handbrakes, died in work-related accidents at rates of 900 and 1,141 deaths per 100,000 workers per year, respectively. Moreover, American wage earners were highly concentrated in some of the most dangerous trades; in 1890, railroad and mine workers alone represented more than one in twenty American wage earners. Even in industries not characterized by high fatal accident rates, such as textiles, increased mechanization caused high rates of disabling injury. In Massachusetts, for example, 63 percent of injuries in textile factories were caused by elevators or moving machinery. State officials found that harm to fingers, hands, and arms abounded in the state's textile mills. Women factory operatives were also subject to the risk of horrific injuries to their scalps by having their hair caught in power-operated shafts. In short, a significant portion of the nation's labor force was subject to extraordinarily high work-accident rates.[30]

High work-accident rates led many contemporaries to think about the relationship between industrialization and accidents. Nineteenth-century observers believed both that the number of accidental injuries was increasing rapidly and that the cause of the increase was the mechanization of production.[31] Muckraking journalists of the early twentieth century voiced this complaint quite vigorously. "The radical revolution in industrial methods," contended a typical article in the New York magazine the *Independent*, "has involved a vast increase of danger to the laborers."[32] Accidental death and injury, wrote another journalist, were "the inevitable concomitants of high-speed machine production."[33] Early statistical studies of accident rates in England in the 1850s had centered on the problem of railroad accidents, to which (the author noted) an "unusual degree of public attention" had "recently [been] directed."[34] Subsequent nineteenth-century and early-twentieth-century studies of accidents in England and the United States continued to focus on railroads, but also expanded to include factories and other mechanized workplaces.[35] "[T]he general feeling," explained a U.S. Department of Labor investigator, "is that the introduction of high power and complicated machinery has resulted in the increase in the number and severity of accidents."[36] American and English observers alike even posited an arithmetical ratio of injuries "to the quantity of mechanical force in use."[37] It comes as no surprise, then, that the first accident insurance company, though not aimed at employees—who, as we will see, often found it exceedingly difficult to purchase insurance—was founded in 1845 in London to insure passengers on that great symbol of industrialization: the railroad. In 1864, the Travelers' Insurance Company became the first company to take up the same line of business in the United States.[38]

Industrialization, in short, had devised myriad new and unfamiliar mechanisms for inflicting harm on the human body. If age-old sources of injury, illness, and premature death had been more or less integrated into the fabric of everyday life, new industrial causes of accident and death stood out in bold relief against the background of traditional and familiar sources of human suffering. As one accident insurance expert observed in 1891, "The various and continually multiplying uses of steam and of electricity are surrounding us with a thousand dangers which not only were unknown to our fathers, but which were strange to the boyhood and to the early manhood of those who have hardly reached middle age."[39] Charles Francis Adams, a railroad commissioner in Massachusetts and later critic of the Interstate Commerce Commission and head of the Union Pacific Railroad, remarked in 1879 that "there are few things of which either nature or man is, as a rule, more lavish than human life;—provided always that the methods used in extinguishing it are customary and not unduly obtrusive on the sight and nerves." By contrast, those features of industrial life that developed novel methods of human destruction were "anxiously investigated." Adams sensibly pointed out that given the extraordinary technological feat represented by the development of the railroad, the number of railroad accidents at the close of the 1870s—even if appalling by some standards—might be viewed as cause for celebration. Who would have thought merely a half century earlier that "a body weighing in the neighborhood of two hundred tons, moving over the face of the earth at a speed of sixty feet a second and held to its course only by two slender lines of iron rails" could ever have been made as safe as it was?[40]

But while familiar sources of tragedy appeared to be caused by some combination of natural forces, acts of God, and fate, railroad accidents seemed to bination of natural forces, acts of God, and fate, railroad accidents seemed to have human causes that were more immediate. As Carroll Wright of the Massachusetts Bureau of Labor Statistics observed in 1883, disability and death arising out of age-old sources could be chalked up to mere chance. In railroad accidents, by contrast, most Americans believed that "[n]o man dies without a cause, though the cause and the causer may remain alike unknown."[41]

What was it that made the American industrial-accident problem, as social insurance expert I. M. Rubinow described it in 1913, "vastly greater" in the United States "than in any European country"?[42] Contemporaries attributed the accident rate differential to any number of causes. Many observers pointed to the largely immigrant industrial workforce, made up of men who had been until recently peasants in the agricultural regions of southern and eastern Europe. Such workers were frequently said to lack the basic safety know-how of more highly skilled British and German workers. The presence of an array of non-English speakers in this immigrant workforce did not help matters, as the communication of safety warnings was often obstructed by linguistic barriers.[43] And indeed, the new immigrants who poured into the country in the late nineteenth and early twentieth centuries were especially hard hit by industrial accidents; as early as 1890, Hungarians, Bohemians, and Italians were three of the four nationalities with the highest accidental-death rates in the United States.[44]

Other factors cited included the long distances covered by U.S. railroads, which made effective safety inspections of the tracks difficult; the variety of firm-specific signaling systems; and the relatively greater significance in the United States of freight travel, which put less of a premium on safety than did the passenger-heavy British railroad system.[45] Unions often pointed to the relatively less powerful American trade union movement, whose weakness, they argued, had deleterious effects on occupational safety.[46] By the 1890s and the early twentieth century, many workingmen's organizations also blamed what they described as lax employers' liability laws. John Mitchell of the United Mine Workers of America, for example, argued that "[i]f as in Europe, it costs more to kill men here in America than to protect them, one half as many would be killed in the dangerous trades."[47] The Mine Workers' house organ concurred: "To us, it appears that lack of organization . . . together with no compensation law, or an efficient employers' liability law, are the prime factors in our high death rate in mills, mines, and factories."[48] State factory regulations and factory inspections were no more effective than the law of employers' liability in inducing employers to take steps to improve safety. Indeed, throughout the late nineteenth and early twentieth

centuries, many labor reformers and unions complained loudly of poor enforcement of safety regulations and of infrequent inspection schedules. Factory inspection offices were woefully understaffed with part-time, patronage-
appointment inspectors. At the turn of the twentieth century, there were only
117 such inspectors in all of the states combined, many of which had none at
all. Even a decade later, only twenty-eight states—slightly more than half—
had set up a government agency to enforce factory safety regulations.[49]

More broadly, the law of employers' liability and the poor enforcement of
state safety regulations contributed to what economic historian Mark Aldrich
has described as the "American system" of workplace safety in the late nineteenth and early twentieth centuries. American firms confronted scarcities in
capital and labor, and relative abundance in raw materials. Furthermore,
thanks to a law of employers' liability that made it difficult for employees to
sue their employers for work injuries, occupational hazards were relatively inexpensive. From the railroads to the mines to the factories, firms responded
to these conditions by minimizing their investments in expensive capital and
labor while maximizing their use of power-hungry, labor-saving devices, often at the expense of safety. Power and occupational hazards, after all, were
cheap.

On the rails, for example, American railroads used flimsy rolling stock, single track lines rather than the double track lines characteristic of British railroading, and heavier cars to maximize per-trip payloads over single track
lines. Heavier cars, in turn, required hand brakes operated by brakemen from
on top of the cars, and link-and-pin couplers operated from between the cars.
British railroaders, by contrast, could brake their much lighter trains with the
brakes on the engine and on a designated braking car, and could connect cars
without having to go between them.

In the mines, the "American system" meant developing any number of
risky labor-saving practices, ranging from relatively greater reliance on explosives to relatively speedy introduction of mechanization and electric power
into the mines in the early twentieth century. American mines also adopted
the "room-and-pillar" approach, rather than the English-style "longwall"
mining, partly because of the greater thickness of American coal seams, but
also because room-and-pillar mining involved less time-consuming, labor-in-
tensive excavation of waste from around the coal seam with which to build
roof supports. The labyrinthine mines generated by room-and-pillar methods, in turn, made inspection and monitoring exceedingly difficult, and made
mines susceptible to numerous small but deadly roof collapses.[50]

The deeper problem toward which American observers of the industrial
scene began to grope at the end of the century was that there seemed to be
an emerging tension between widely shared ideas about free labor and mar-

ket competition, on one hand, and the fallout from industrial accidents in core industries like railroading, mining, and metal work, on the other. The law of employers' liability, for example, seemed to many commentators to have developed a body of doctrines that minimized employers' responsibility for work accidents in the name of free labor. Under the law of slavery in the American South, slave owners had been able to recover for injuries to a slave caused by the negligence of those to whom the slave had been hired out to work. In contrast to the slave-law approach, explained journalist John Gitterman in 1910, "[t]he American principle" in employers' liability "is . . . briefly this": if the workingman objects to some dangerous task, "he has the privilege of throwing up his job. He is not a slave—he cannot be compelled to work under hazardous conditions." And so if he is injured—"if he scalds to death under his boiler, or has his head scraped off while attempting to couple cars"—he and his "widow and orphan children . . . must suffer the consequences." The ostensible virtues of free labor, it seemed, lay at the foundation of the law of employers' liability, where they contributed to the accident problem itself.[51]

Absent a law of employers' liability that imposed significant accident costs on employers, the free play of competition among firms seemed to drive employers to minimize their investments in expensive safety measures. By the close of the century, a new generation of American economists had concluded that competition tended, as Henry Carter Adams put it, "to force the moral sentiment pervading any trade down to the level of that which characterizes the worst man who can maintain himself in it." Competition, in other words, inexorably drove down working conditions. Nine out of ten employers might seek to uphold decent standards in industry. But if the tenth lacked such scruples (and some employer inevitably would lack such scruples) the industry would find itself caught in a race to the bottom until all remaining employers in the industry put their workers' lives at risk.[52] Manufacturers who experienced the competitive pressures of the market shared the progressive economists' belief about deteriorating workplace safety conditions and the dynamic of competition. Howell Cheney of Connecticut, for example, argued in 1910 that the "forces of competition" had "exaggerated the dangerous pressure and speed of industry," pushing industrial accident rates ever higher. A year earlier, the National Civic Federation—a body of some of the nation's leading businessmen—had cited the "pressure of business" and "ruinous business competition" as explanations for accident rates in coal mines and machine shops.[53]

Perhaps most of all, it seemed to many that the independence and discretionary authority insisted on by many American workingmen exacerbated accident risks. In 1906, H. T. Newcomb of the Delaware and Hudson Railroad

Company described the American workingman this way: "There is a difference in the character of the workman in this country and the European workman. The American workmen has a proper and laudable feeling of independence, but sometimes that feeling of independence makes him less willing to adhere to the letter of the law, and it is the letter of the law in these large operations—I mean the letter of the regulations of the road—which means perfect safety."[54] As a railroad executive, of course, Newcomb had self-interested reasons for emphasizing the contribution of employee independence and risk-taking to the industrial-accident problem. But many without such conflicts of interest agreed with Newcomb. Francis Bohlen of the University of Pennsylvania Law School, for example, a leading authority on American tort law, contended that the "American workman probably takes greater risks than any other."[55]

Indeed, workingmen themselves in fields ranging from machine shops to coal mines to the railroads often resisted the implementation of safety-oriented monitoring schemes or of safety mechanisms that required them to change their customary practices. In the mines, for example, miners and their unions fiercely defended dangerous (but seemingly profitable) practices such as overreliance on explosives to bring down large amounts of coal off the face of a seam. Miners also went on strike to protest the introduction of safety lamps (which they wrongly believed to be less safe than their customary open-flame lamps) and safer explosives, which tended to shatter the coal into less valuable coal dust. In these ways and in countless others, the strong independent streak among coal miners exacerbated safety hazards in the mines. A leading historian of mine safety has even gone so far as to suggest that with the exception of a short five-year period from 1905 to 1910, when mining disasters drew widespread attention, the demands of miners' unions were often "roadblocks for mining safety."[56]

In this respect, an important obstacle to workplace safety was the persistent and usually irrational optimism that workingmen seemed to bring to estimations of the risks they faced. As economist Henry Seager put it, "each individual thinks of himself as having a charmed life."[57] On the railroads, risk-taking by workingmen was often part of an ethic of manly bravado. The life of the "heroic engineer" was one of "skill and daring." In the yards, railroad switchmen "daily flirt with death," risking "life and limb to keep the business of the road moving steadily" and depending "for their safety on their quick brains, clear eyes, strong limbs and nimble hands and feet."[58] As the important Progressive Era work-accident law reformer Crystal Eastman described it, "extreme caution is as unprofessional among the men in dangerous trades as fear would be in a soldier."[59]

This is not to say that the lion's share of accidents was properly attributed to worker carelessness. The notion that accidents in the workplace were caused by the negligence of the employees was the favorite refuge of scoundrel employers, often even in cases in which the employer had—or could have had—a significant degree of managerial control over the relevant aspect of the work process. In many such cases, as labor reformers and union leaders never ceased to point out in outrage, employers' attributions of blame to the carelessness of their employees seem to have been little more than self-serving hypocrisy.[60]

But we should stop and look more closely at precisely what the outrage of labor leaders implied. Criticisms of employer accusations of employee carelessness themselves rested on ideas about the managerial authority that employers were exercising or could have exercised. To turn employers' discussions of employee carelessness back on the employer's failure to implement effective systems of safety, in other words, was to begin to appeal to the promise of rationally managed workplaces, systematically engineered from the top down. And therein lay a crisis for free labor thinking. Workers' relative autonomy and the legal standards that had been developed around it had become exacerbating factors in the American industrial-accident epidemic. Yet workers' relative autonomy was also one of the organizing principles in the mid- and late-nineteenth-century American body of thought that has come to be known as the ideology of free labor.

By the 1840s and 1850s, increasing numbers of Americans in the North viewed free labor as the centerpiece of economic and political freedoms. Indeed, slavery had come to seem an anachronistic institution throughout much of the Atlantic world, anathema to widely held ideals of human progress, moral and material.[61] To be sure, some American critics saw in wage labor what southern proslavery ideologue George Fitzhugh called "a more perfect compulsion" than slavery.[62] And not all such critics were southerners; a number of labor reformers in the antebellum North argued that labor markets reduced the wage worker to the dependent condition of "wage slavery."[63] Still, William Lloyd Garrison captured the increasingly dominant strain of thinking about free labor when he argued that even the wage laborer—though in many ways dependent on an employer—was a "free agent." The wage laborer, after all, "contract[ed] for his own wages" and "own[ed] himself." He was "the 'lord of his presence' . . . though he may be 'lord of no land beside.'"[64]

The outcome of the Civil War enshrined the ideal of free labor in American politics and law. The Thirteenth Amendment—ratified in 1865—provided that neither "slavery nor involuntary servitude, except as a punishment for crime," could exist within the United States. Many Americans, of course, flouted the commitment to free labor announced in the Thirteenth Amendment. In the South especially, peonage, sharecropping, vagrancy statutes, and convict labor recreated many of the conditions of slavery. Nonetheless, the free labor ideal stood as the central legacy of the war that ended slavery.[65]

This is not to say that Americans agreed on the meaning of free labor, that they agreed on its indicia, or that they agreed on the relative emphases appropriate for the array of values within free labor thinking, or even that they always agreed on the values for which the free labor ideal stood. There was in fact considerable disagreement on each of these points.[66] For some, the central value of free labor was its commitment to liberalism and individual autonomy. Leading liberals such as E. L. Godkin of the *Nation* and *Atlantic Monthly* editor William Dean Howells, for example, saw in the Union's triumph in the Civil War a vindication of the principles of classical liberalism. Free labor, in the liberal conception, meant the promotion of consensual relationships among autonomous private actors exercising what Howells called "moral self-control," rather than the coercive social relations that had characterized the slave South.[67]

Leaders in the American labor movement, by contrast, saw in free labor ideals a substantive commitment to independence rather than autonomy. Though similar in some respects to the liberal ideal of autonomy, independence stood for a different principle. Those who valued autonomy supported the maintenance of procedures for unconstrained freedom of choice, without regard to the substance of the choices that individuals made. Free markets in labor thus formed a critically important part of the liberal conception of free labor, for labor markets institutionalized the consensual formation of social relations. The labor movement, however, emphasized not procedures for the realization of autonomous choice, but substantive outcomes that established citizens' independence. In particular, the labor movement drew on the long tradition in modern political thought, harkening back to the American revolutionary period and beyond, that was concerned with the importance of an economically independent citizenry.[68]

A third way of thinking about free labor coalesced around the idea that it was the most efficient mechanism of production, superior in efficiency to various forms of unfree labor such as slavery and indentured servitudes. For centuries, Europeans had viewed slave labor and the slave trade as a means to riches and material progress.[69] In the mid and late eighteenth century, however, Enlightenment thinkers such as Benjamin Franklin and Adam Smith began to argue that slave production was more costly than free labor.[70] Drawing on Franklin and Smith, nineteenth-century American abolitionists contended (often against the weight of the evidence from slave emancipations in places such as Jamaica) that free labor was in fact more productive than unfree labor.

In slave labor, it was said, "fear is substituted for hope, as the stimulus to exertion. But fear is ill calculated to draw from a laborer all the industry of which he is capable."[71] In contrast, free labor's capacity to create powerful incentives for hard work could prod workers to new heights of exertion.[72] By the end of the Civil War the theory of the superior efficiency of labor markets was widely held, though cracks were already beginning to show in the form of inefficiencies and compulsions in Reconstruction plantation labor.[73]

A fourth conception of free labor—increasingly significant around the turn of the twentieth century among progressives and students of social insurance programs—focused on the structure of the family. Many mid-nineteenth-century advocates of free labor had argued that the critical distinction between free and unfree labor was not simply that the former promised independence or autonomy, nor that it was more efficient than unfree labor, but that it marked off the domestic sphere as a separate domain protected from the dangers of the marketplace.[74] By the turn of the twentieth century, married women acting in their capacity as consumers had begun to bridge the divide between home and market in what Marx called the "sphere of exchange." But in what Marx called the "sphere of production" (the paid labor market), progressives and social insurance experts sought to maintain the separation of market and home. In their view, the legitimacy of free labor rested on the sharp distinction it promised to preserve between markets in labor, on the one hand, and tranquility and virtue in the domestic sphere, on the other. Thus, as historians Amy Dru Stanley and Lawrence Glickman have explained in their accounts of the relationship between the free labor system and ideas about family structure, the family wage—that is, the free male laborer's support of dependent wife and children—became one of the central indicia of the success of the free labor system.[75]

To be sure, these different and sometimes competing conceptions of free labor were not mutually exclusive. They overlapped in important ways, and many Americans subscribed to more than one, and sometimes all of them. Moreover, so long as free labor ideology was able to define itself in opposition to slave labor, submerged variations in emphasis rarely surfaced. But by the late 1870s and 1880s, new challenges were beginning to separate out the competing strands that constituted free labor thinking, highlighting usually hidden differences in interpretation and emphasis.

Consider, for example, the spread of wage labor. Already in 1870, over two-thirds of all gainfully employed Americans were hirelings rather than independent proprietors or master craftsmen.[76] Subsequent years saw further increases in the proportion of workingmen who were wage earners. By 1873, the Massachusetts Bureau of Statistics of Labor announced that wage labor had become "a system more widely diffused than any form of religion, or of government, or indeed, of any language."[77] Indeed, the work of the newly created state departments of labor statistics came to focus virtually exclusively on the problems of wage earners. "It is characteristic of the condition of the free laborer today," wrote one student of social conditions at the turn of the century, "that he possesses no capital." Indeed, "his only means of livelihood is the sale of his labor power."[78] The Lincolnian dream of the wage laborer's upwardly mobile rise to economic independence, it seemed, was increasingly out of step with the social structure of a free labor economy in which wage-earning was not a temporary phase but a permanent condition. Moreover, wage labor also seemed to undermine free labor's capacity to preserve a separate domestic sphere sheltered from the marketplace. Low wages and cyclical unemployment, many Americans began to worry, forced more and more young people to avoid marriage altogether.[79] And in the final years of the nineteenth century, widespread public concern about child labor and prostitution indicated that the free labor system was failing in its aim of separating women and children from the exigencies of the marketplace.[80]

Even the efficiency claims of free labor seemed increasingly strained. By the 1890s, cyclical recessions suggested to many leaders of industry that free contracting in the marketplace—that is, competition—could be wasteful and inefficient. Men such as George Perkins of International Harvester, Marcus Hanna (the businessman who financed and planned William McKinley's 1896 presidential campaign), and August Belmont of the business-financed National Civic Federation came to believe that unconstrained competition among atomized economic units in the marketplace led inevitably to "recurrent depressions, strikes and lockouts, social distemper and political upheaval."[81] At the same time, the great merger movement of the 1890s consolidated the market relationships of many small enterprises into large, hierarchically organized firms. And in labor relations, sophisticated employers and efficiency engineers began to develop personnel management departments that sought to replace labor markets with hierarchically organized structures of employment. Frederick Winslow Taylor's scientific management movement, for example (to which we will have occasion to return), replaced markets with hierarchies, substituting managerial command-and-control regimes for incentive-based systems of labor management.[82]

Such concerns over the fate of free labor ideals in industrializing America coalesced in the industrial-accident crisis. This is not to say that industrial accidents accounted for the largest share of the social ills accompanying industrialization and wage labor. From the perspective of the needs of working-class Americans, accidents were only one among many forms of risk; sickness, old age, and unemployment were often greater scourges. I. M. Rubinow, for example, noted that accidents were "not . . . the most serious of the economic dangers confronting the wage earners," and observed that "historically various forms of sick-insurance and old age relief preceded accident insurance."[83] Similarly, Columbia University economist Henry Seager contended that illness was "[m]uch more serious than accidents in its effect on standards of living." Even the American Association for Labor Legislation, which by 1910 would be among the most important advocates of workmen's compensation laws, had initially developed an interest not so much in industrial injuries as in industrial disease and the attendant problems of hygiene and public health.[84]

Yet around the turn of the twentieth century, the industrial accident emerged in the United States as among the most visible of social ills. For one thing, work accidents seemed to pose an especially acute problem in some of the leading occupations of the new industrial economy. Workplace accidents were the leading cause of incapacity among working-age men in railroad work, mining, logging and timber work, and bricklaying and masonry; according to one 1890 study of the mining trade, deaths from work accidents accounted for 60 percent of all workingmen incapacitated from pursuing the trade.[85]

Industrial accidents also disproportionately affected wage-earning men supporting dependent wives and children. In 1890, accidents accounted for more than five times as many deaths among men aged fifteen to forty-five as among women of the same age; similarly, an 1899 study found that of almost 2,000 persons injured in New York work accidents, only eighty-five were women.[86] Families were thus thrown by the accidental injury of a male wage-earner into the ranks of the "dispossessed," "pawning their furniture," "using up what little savings bank account they have had," and "obliged to turn in humiliation and permanent injury to the charitable societies or to relatives and friends."[87]

Accidents stood out from other social ills as startling to bystanders, observers, and victims alike. As the important twentieth-century photographer Lewis Hine documented in one of his earliest photographic essays, a 1908 study of work accidents in Pittsburgh, the violence of encounters between flesh and machine was readily apparent in the form of missing limbs, in the scarred bodies of victims, and in the vacant stares of destitute family members.[88] In the years immediately following publication of Hine's photographs, such photographs of crippled workingmen and their families became a staple of reports on the work-accident problem. Moreover, if the imagery of accidents was startling to viewers, accidents often found their victims ill prepared as well. William Willoughby noted in 1898 that accidents seemed by their very nature to be difficult to anticipate or plan for. Even for those American workers who sought to make provisions for the possibility of accidental injury or death, Willoughby explained, the typical overoptimism of individuals frequently left injured workingmen and their families less than fully prepared. According to Willoughby, "measures of reform" in the industrial-accident area were "even more pressing" in the United States "than in Europe."[89]

The work accident also seemed to pose difficult questions about the relationship between the well-being of the laboring classes and the conditions of industrial production. Although many of the health problems of the late nineteenth and early twentieth centuries could be traced to unsanitary or toxic working conditions, the connections were often remote and attenuated. Work accidents, too, could present difficult causation questions. (As we will see in Chapter 2, the difficulty of tracing causation in work-accident cases created dilemmas for late-nineteenth-century torts jurists.) Yet as the simple act of tabulating accidents occurring in the workplace suggested, there seemed little doubt that going to work tended to raise the risk of injury to disturbing levels. Moreover, work accidents seemed to challenge Lincolnian optimism about hard work and upward mobility, for they often had disastrous consequences for precisely those wage earners who otherwise seemed to be hard-working and morally upstanding members of their communities. From the early 1870s, work-accident law reformers focused on the injured operative who had "always been able to pay [his] way," who had "never had any trouble before," and who had "heretofore been entirely independent and self-supporting."[90] And by the turn of the century, charitable organizations were reporting that they increasingly saw "people becoming chronic dependents and begging for charitable assistance, who never would have gotten in that position except for the accident to the wage earner."[91] Work accidents, it seemed, threw the ambiguous status of the industrial wage worker into bold relief, compelling victim and observer alike to ask hard questions about the relationships among capital, labor, and the public.

For all these reasons, many believed by the end of the first decade of the twentieth century that industrial accidents were one of the most important issues in American public life. United Mine Workers leader John Mitchell called compensation for industrial-accident victims "the most urgent practical measure" in the field of social reform.[92] Samuel Gompers of the American Federation of Labor asserted in 1910 that "compensation for the victims of injury" stood "above all" other issues in terms of its legislative significance; no other issue was "of half the importance."[93] And a year earlier the American Association for Labor Legislation had listed industrial accidents as the first and most important problem facing working-class families.[94]

Ultimately, the work-accident crisis seemed to call into question the narratives of progress that many Americans had come to associate with free labor ideals. If industrial accidents were epidemic, the modern wage labor economy hardly seemed consistent with triumphs for either individual autonomy or workingmen's independence. Free labor's efficiency was called into question by the enormous waste of labor power associated with employee injuries. And free labor's capacity to sustain the family wage—a central test of free labor's success—seemed in serious doubt. Moreover, as many Americans began to observe in the final decades of the nineteenth century, the United States appeared especially laggard in comparison to other Western nations in its law of industrial accidents. The New York Bureau of Labor Statistics expressed what would become the conventional understanding of virtually every interested group when it announced that "it would be difficult to think of another field of social or legal reform in which the United States is so far behind other nations."[95] Indeed, in labor reform circles it became a veritable refrain that the United States was "very backward" in the field of industrial-accident law, as one 1890 Colorado report put it, and lagged behind even those monarchical nations that were ostensibly anachronisms in an age of republican governance, as a mine worker journal remarked.[96] As president, Theodore Roosevelt picked up the same theme in 1907, remarking on the nation's "backwardness" as compared to the "rest of the industrial world."[97] Two years later, the U.S. commissioner of labor noted that there had been only scarce improvement on this score, concluding that the United States was still "behind the civilized world."[98]

Industrial accidents had brought out a cultural contradiction in free labor. To a considerable extent, free labor ideology was an author of its own crisis. Free labor values such as autonomy, manly independence, and competition had themselves exacerbated the accident problem. Free laborers seemed all too often to be victims of employers' failure to create effective systems of management, and of the consequent discretionary authority that fell to them. The damaged bodies of injured workers thus held conceptual dilemmas for the classical liberal and the labor leader alike, crises of confidence for the efficiency of free labor and for its family wage as well.

Indeed, the accident crisis pushed the categories of free labor thought to their limits. Beginning in the closing decades of the nineteenth century, many Americans struggled with only limited success to conceptualize the accident problem in the terms of free labor and slavery, to grapple with the problem of industrial risk using the conceptual tools available within free labor ideology. Gompers, for one, sought to redescribe occupational hazards as a kind of slavery. After the infamous Triangle Shirtwaist Fire of 1911—which killed 146 people, most of them young female factory workers—Gompers thundered at a mass meeting in the Great Hall of Cooper Union that "there comes a time when not to strike is but to rivet the chains of slavery upon our wrists."[99] And Eugene Debs of the Brotherhood of Locomotive Firemen (later founder of the American Railway Union, perennial presidential candidate, and perhaps the nation's best-known socialist) also saw industrial hazards in free labor terms, arguing that they sapped the independence of the "manly men" who did the work of the railroads.[100]

Others saw in the commodification of the injured worker's body a kind of latter-day slave auction, in which ostensibly free laborers sold their bodies and their lives for cash in the form of settlements and tort liability damages, to the extent such damages could be obtained. A typical crippled workingman, as one journalist described it, was "driven to sell . . . the arms with which he had supported his wife and child."[101] Muckraking journals announced that workingmen's lives now had "a value in dollars and cents that is calculable because the mortality figures set forth just how many men out of a large number will die every year."[102] As reported in the *New York Times*, scientific analysis of injury cases could "figure out just what a workman's economic value is at different ages."[103] Many who after 1900 would come to advocate workmen's compensation statutes took resistance to the commodification of workers' bodies as a core tenet. Although the wage laborer necessarily sold "himself together with his labor," workmen's compensation statutes would at least bar the sale of bodily security from the marketplace.[104]

Yet despite attempts to think of industrial accidents in free labor categories such as slavery and the sale of human bodies, industrial hazards seemed to resist description in the terms set by free labor thinking. Again and again, industrial risks seemed to turn free labor categories on their heads. As workingmen in Alabama's coal region pointed out, the real problem in the law of employers' liability was not commodification of ostensibly free laborers' bodies. The real problem was insufficient valuations. "[O]n a cabbage, on a codfish, and on a lobster," the Birmingham *Labor's Advocate* contended, "there is a market value." Under the law of employers' liability, however, "there was no fixed value placed on human life." "The labor market," the *Advocate* concluded, "is as permanent an institution as the slave block ever was, and the wage worker has become as worthless as the very dirt underneath his feet."[105] Lincoln appointee Henry C. Caldwell of Arkansas, U.S. circuit judge for the Eighth Circuit, agreed, arguing that the law of employers' liability in his circuit had made "human life . . . a cheaper commodity than lumber."[106] Lincoln himself had explained in December 1861 that free labor was "prior to and independent of capital" and therefore "the superior of capital," entitled to "much higher consideration." But from progressive lawyer Gilbert Roe's perspective, the "converse of that sentiment fairly state[d] the attitude of the courts" in employers' liability cases.[107]

By the turn of the century, some advocated abandoning free labor ideas in the law of work accidents altogether. Isaac Hourwich, counsel to several labor organizations in New York City, proposed to approach the question of employers' liability "in a brutally frank manner." Employers' responsibilities for the injuries of their employees, Hourwich argued to the U.S. Industrial Commission in 1900, should be treated "in the same way as it would be treated in the old days of slavery." When "a slave was injured, it was so much injury to the owner of the slave." "Of course," Hourwich continued, "we are to-day free." But "practically speaking," firms serving the needs of the industrializing nation were "consum[ing] . . . lives and limbs." As a consequence, Hourwich proposed reviving the slave law's allocation of accident costs in amendments to the law of employers' liability.[108] Sometimes it even seemed as if the memory of Civil War casualties might be overwhelmed by the sheer violence of peacetime industry. As if in ritual recitations, commentators noted again and again that although the "Rebellion" had caused unprecedented casualties, the numbers of casualties occurring every year in the nation's industries were "greater still."[109]

The great question was how the categories and preoccupations of free labor could be reshaped and adapted to deal with the accident problem. Liberals understood the accident crisis as posing a threat to autonomy in what appeared to be an increasingly interdependent world. Workingmen viewed the onslaught of work accidents as a manifestation of underlying injustices in competitive wage labor capitalism and of the dangers capitalism posed for independent workingmen. Efficiency-minded engineers and managers understood work accidents as a problem of wasteful and inefficient production. Progressives, charity officials, and social insurance experts saw the accident problem as a crisis for the family wage of male wage earners and dependent wives and children. These competing views of the accident crisis, in turn, produced competing prescriptions for resolving it.

In the decades straddling the turn of the twentieth century, Americans devised an eclectic array of legal and policy alternatives to address the problem of industrial accidents. Many of these alternatives were short-lived. As early as the 1840s, for example, the Pennsylvania mining trade press discussed accident-compensation funds financed by a tax on coal sales; several decades later, Maryland briefly experimented with a system of compulsory employer-financed relief funds.[110] Other approaches were simply never implemented. In certain progressive circles, reformers suggested that the federal government use its taxing authority and its spending power to tax employers and provide insurance benefits to injured workers.[111] Others argued that workers might be able to insure themselves if minimum wage laws raised their wages, or if new laws governing union organizing allowed them to raise their own wages.[112] That such policies and others were floated suggests the breadth of the experimentation in American accident law and institutions at the turn of the century.

By the late nineteenth century, four leading models for dealing with the fallout from the industrial-accident crisis had emerged, corresponding to the leading strands of free labor thought. Drawing on, adapting, and often transforming the free labor principles out of which they developed, each of these four models embodied a different conception of how best to solve the industrial-accident crisis, and by extension how best to address any number of similar emerging risks in the industrializing economy. The chapters that follow examine in turn the liberal model of common law personal injury litigation; the cooperative model of self-insurance through insurance societies; the managerial model of private employer relief funds; and the social insurance model of compulsory state compensation plans. The history of the interaction among these different approaches to industrial accidents is the story of how Americans sought to grapple with an exceptionally acute industrial-accident problem, and how they remade American law in the process.

2

The Dilemmas of Classical Tort Law

Where damage results from pure accident, and without fault on the part of the person to whom it is attributable, no action will lie, for though there is damage there is no concurring wrong.

—THOMAS COOLEY, *THE ELEMENTS OF TORTS* (1895)

[A] system of laws which permit[s] no recovery in so large a percentage of deaths and injuries occurring is unjust.

—OHIO STATE BAR ASSOCIATION, 1913

"The general principle of our law," Oliver Wendell Holmes explained in his 1881 masterpiece *The Common Law,* "is that loss from accident must lie where it falls." By "accident," Holmes meant injuries occurring "without fault."[1] To be sure, Holmes observed, there were some who advocated shifting liability in such instances of faultless harms. On this view it was said that "[e]very man" properly had "an absolute right to his person . . . free from detriment at the hands of his neighbors." Alternatively, the law could have opted to divide the damages between equally faultless (or equally at-fault) actors. Yet the law did "none of these things," explained Holmes, instead allowing injured plaintiffs to recover damages only when they could prove that the defendant's fault or negligence caused their injury and that they had not contributed to that injury by their own fault or negligence. Purely accidental harms lay where they fell.[2]

Holmes's words have become the classic expression of the late-nineteenth-century law of accidents. By the time he wrote them, tort law had emerged from its infancy of just a decade or so before to become one of the central fields in the American common law. In *The Common Law,* Holmes would become one of the field's great systematizers. Yet there was an important difference between Holmes's approach to the problem of accidental harm and the approach of most of the elite of the American bar. For Holmes, the principle that the law favored the active doers of the world over its passive victims seems to have been a part of his Darwinian perspective on human affairs. Those who fell by the wayside in the competitive struggle for life, in Holmes's view, were simply the losers in an ongoing evolutionary battle from which only the fittest would emerge. Law could do little to aid those who came out on the bottom of such natural and inevitable processes.[3]

For much of the elite of the American bar, however, the proposition that losses from faultless injuries properly lay where they fell represented something very different from Holmes's evolutionary sensibilities. The allocation of accident costs in cases of pure accident occupied a central place in late nineteenth-century tort law precisely because tort law as elaborated by the American legal elite represented an attempt to work out in practice the principles of classical liberal thought in an age of enterprise and accident. Lawyers, judges, and legal scholars constructed a grand doctrinal architecture for the law of accidents, centered first and foremost on defining the proper bounds within which individuals were free to act as they chose, unchargeable with liability for harms to others. In its boldest aspirations, the elaboration of liberal principles in the late-nineteenth-century law of torts sought to bring order to the increasingly messy world that lay outside the courtroom.

Yet even as classical tort doctrine reached its apogee in the last years of the century, the accumulated wisdom of the elite of the bar and bench was coming under sharp criticism for its inadequate grasp of the late-nineteenth-century accident problem. The abstract doctrinal structure of American tort law perched precariously atop a rising mountain of accidents from machinery, railroads, streetcars, and elevators. Personal injury lawyers and their runners, insurance company agents, industrial employers, and injured workers pushed and challenged the justifications offered for the law of torts. And in the end, the liberal project of organizing tort law around principles on which individuals could be free to act within a zone of uninfringed autonomy proved an impossible task. As critics of tort law would begin to point out by the turn of the century, late-nineteenth-century tort law had no good answer to precisely the problem that Holmes had identified in 1881 as the centerpiece of the classical law of torts: the nonnegligent victim of nonfaulty harm.

Holmes's notion that losses from accident must lie where they fall had its most significant early proponent in Chief Justice Lemuel Shaw of the Massachusetts Supreme Judicial Court. In 1842, Shaw wrote the leading early case in the law of employers' liability, *Farwell v. Boston and Worcester Rail Road*, holding that employees assumed the ordinary risks of their employment, including the risk of a fellow servant's negligence.[4] Eight years later, in *Brown v. Kendall*, he drew together the diverse mix of standards governing the common law of injuries to formulate a general standard of care for the emerging law of torts. In *Brown*, the defendant George K. Kendall had sought to use a stick to separate two fighting dogs. While raising the stick over his shoulder, he unintentionally struck the plaintiff, George Brown, in the eye, severely injuring him. The trial judge instructed the jury that the defendant was liable for the damages unless he had exercised "extraordinary care, so that the accident was inevitable." As Shaw described the legal authorities, the trial judge seemed to have accurately captured the rule: "if the injury was unavoidable, and the conduct of the defendant was free from blame, he will not be liable."[5] Shaw's bold move in *Brown* was to redefine what counted as an inevitable injury. The trial judge had understood inevitable injuries as those that could not have been avoided by even extraordinary care. In Shaw's new formulation, however, the inevitable injury for which a defendant could not be held liable was an injury that mere reasonable or ordinary care would not have prevented. A relatively rigid standard that inquired as to the possibility of prevention had been replaced by a looser standard concerned with the desirability of prevention. As Shaw would summarize his influential formulation a few years later in the case of *Shaw v. Boston and Worcester Railroad,* if the defendant was not "in fault" (as Shaw had put it in *Brown*) for failure to exercise "due precautions," it followed that an injury was "one of those cases of pure accident, to which all human beings are constantly exposed . . . and in which all losses and damages occasioned thereby *must lie where they first fall.*"[6]

Lemuel Shaw was not the first jurist to articulate the standard in nineteenth-century American tort law under which defendants were liable for only those damages caused by their fault or negligence. As early as the 1820s, decisions in jurisdictions such as New York and Pennsylvania had already begun to move toward the idea that defendants were liable for injury only where they failed to exercise reasonable care.[7] Even the maxim that absent fault, "damage lies where it falls" predated Shaw. The popular nineteenth-century folk wisdom that "as the tree falls so it must lie" was drawn from a passage in Ecclesiastes ("in the place where the tree falleth, there it shall be").[8] And as early as 1851, counsel for the defendant in a steamboat collision case had contended that where "neither vessel was in fault, the damage lies where it falls."[9] Nonetheless, led by Holmes, American lawyers by the late nineteenth century would attribute to Shaw the beginnings of the negligence standard in tort law. In particular, they would put his ideas to work in the project of elaborating tort law as a finely wrought set of doctrinal structures derived from classical eighteenth- and nineteenth-century liberalism. Shaw's notion (later Holmes's) that losses from pure accident lie where they fall played a critically important role in the attempt to work out what a meaningful system of liberalism would look like in practice. And yet this same notion created a powerful ambivalence that lurked just beneath the surface of late-nineteenth-century tort doctrine.

The central proposition of nineteenth-century political liberalism was the idea that individuals may act as they choose, consistent with the like rights of others. In John Stuart Mill's classic formulation, "the only purpose for which power can be rightfully exercised over any member of a civilised community against his will, is to prevent harm to others."[10] Similarly, for the German-born American political theorist Francis Lieber, as for American constitutional law commentators like Christopher Tiedeman, civil liberty consisted in the restraint of encroachments by one individual on the rights of another—in Tiedeman's words, the "right to do any thing that does not involve a trespass or injury to others."[11] The first American tort law scholars emphasized this same principle. Francis Hilliard's 1859 torts treatise—the first in the English language—announced that "the liability to make reparation" rested "upon an original moral duty, enjoined upon every person, so to conduct himself or exercise his own rights as not to injure another."[12] Similarly, Michigan law professor, judge, and nationally renowned tort jurist Thomas Cooley explained that civil liberty was properly established by "such limitations and restraints" on individual action "as are needed to prevent what would be injurious to other individuals."[13]

If tort law marked the bounds of individuals' liberty, it also separated the private sphere of individual action from the public sphere of state coercion. Self-help in the enforcement of legally defined boundaries between individuals was not an option; as Cooley explained, self-help "would be subversive of civil government" in all but a narrow, sharply limited class of cases.[14] Liberalism therefore required a state that would enforce interpersonal boundaries. Yet the creation of the state generated additional difficulties for the preservation of civil liberty, for liberalism entailed the protection of the individual not just against the encroachments of other individuals, but also against the state itself.[15] For one thing, agents of the state might commit tortious acts against individuals. More important for late-nineteenth-century torts jurists, reliance on the state to police the boundaries of individuals' spheres of free action raised the possibility that the state would be too aggressive, remedying losses that did not warrant the coercive reallocation of accident costs, and thus threatening the delicate balance among individuals in the private sphere. Tort law therefore needed to articulate a boundary between public and private, as well as the bounds of private rights as between persons. The law of torts, in short, stood as the keystone in the conceptual architecture that lawyers and historians have come to call classical legal thought.[16]

The burden of the law of torts in classical legal thought was no less than to elaborate a conceptual framework that allowed each person the free exercise of his rights consistent with the like free exercise of others' rights. But therein lay an apparently insuperable dilemma. On one hand, the free exercise of a person's rights could (and did) generate causal ripples outside the actor's own sphere of autonomous action. Often these causal effects caused injury to others, despite the exercise of reasonable prudence and care to avoid such injuries. If the harms thus caused were chargeable back to the actor, his own sphere of autonomous action would be compromised. On the other hand, a person freely exercising his rights could himself be the victim of injury caused by the reasonable and prudent exercise of the rights of others. If harms thus caused were not compensable, his sphere of autonomous action too would be cast into doubt. Accordingly, those who articulated classical tort law faced an ongoing problem in elaborating the principles of a liberal approach to accidents for cases of nonnegligent harms to faultless victims. A negligence standard that held individuals liable for damages only when they failed to exercise reasonable care would allow individuals to act freely within their rights, without compromising those rights by charging them with the costs of harms that they could not reasonably avoid. But such a negligence standard would also leave remediless the faultless victim of harm caused by someone else's free exercise of rights. A strict-liability standard that held individuals liable for damages they caused even when they exercised reasonable care, by contrast, would rectify such harms but would also impose charges on the free exercise of the nonnegligent injurer's rights.

In the case of the faultless victim of nonnegligent harm, it seemed, liberal principles were indeterminate. To put it in the terms of *Brown v. Kendall*, if George Kendall had exercised reasonable care in separating the two dogs, and if George Brown had not been careless in getting too close to Kendall and his stick, who could say which of them should bear the costs of Brown's eye injury? The rights claims of injurers like Kendall reasonably to pursue useful activities could be rearticulated as the rights claims of victims like Brown to rest reasonably and uninjured. A negligence standard for Kendall was a strict-liability standard for Brown because it allocated costs to him (even when he had acted reasonably) in the event he could not prove that Kendall had been negligent. A strict-liability standard for Kendall, in turn, would be a negligence standard for Brown, if it reallocated the costs of injuries to him when Kendall could prove Brown's contributory negligence.[17] Neither approach—negligence or strict liability—offered a conceptual basis for neatly carving out independent spheres of individual autonomy.

How, then, could Holmes announce so confidently that losses "by accident" (that is, without fault) properly lay where they fell? The key to tort lawyers' answer to this question was the adoption and explanation of the category of *damnum absque injuria*, or loss without a legal remedy. C. G. Addison, for example, began his 1870 torts treatise with the proposition that there were injuries that had no legal remedy, and he went on to set out the "many cases where persons have suffered serious injury from the acts and doings of others of which the law takes no cognizance."[18] Francis Hilliard, too, laid out numerous cases of interpersonal damages without a remedy at law,[19] as did Shearman and Redfield in their influential 1869 treatise on negligence cases.[20] The negligence standard itself generated the most important class of injuries without remedy. The first and primary category of "excusable trespasses" in James Barr Ames and Jeremiah Smith's casebook, which was in use at Harvard Law School from 1874 until the end of the century, consisted of injuries from mere "accident and mistake."[21]

Yet in the case of the faultless victim of nonnegligent harm, the law's creation of a class of *damnum absque injuria* seemed not so much a reason for Holmes's conclusion as a restatement of it. What principle could allow one person to cause injury to another without compensating the victim? Some, like Clarke Butler Whittier of Stanford Law School, simply saw shifting the cost of injuries from one undeserving person to another as a useless incurring of administrative costs.[22] Holmes, at once an architect of classical legal thought and its greatest critic, observed that the "prevailing view" in 1881 was that the "cumbrous and expensive machinery" of the state "ought not to be set in motion" merely to shift costs among equally undeserving individuals. Others saw in strict liability a standard that would threaten to bring all economic action to a halt: "We must have factories, machinery, dams, canals and railroads," explained New York judge Robert Earl in defense of the negligence standard.[23] Even Seymour Thompson, editor of the *American Law Review* and a progressive voice in the American legal profession, argued that the "law justly ascribes" the consequences of nonnegligent harms "to inevitable misfortune, or to the act of God, and leaves the harm resulting from them to be borne by him upon whom it falls."[24] Any contrary rule, Thompson contended, would "impose so great a restraint upon freedom of action as materially to check human enterprise."[25] Still others contended, often in ways that overlapped with the utilitarian arguments of Earl, Holmes, and Thompson, that the negligence standard rested on an imagined social contract: individuals gave up their "natural rights" to the inviolability of person and property in return for the like abandonment of rights by their neighbors.[26]

At the core of these defenses of the negligence standard in classical legal thought was the fear that a strict-liability standard threatened to collapse the distinction between public and private. The late-nineteenth-century bar believed that the threat to the private sphere represented by state intervention required the adoption of a negligence standard rather than a strict-liability approach. "The human mind, from its limitedness of vision," explained Francis Wharton, "is incapable of perfect diligence."[27] Minor mistakes were thus inevitable in the private lives of individuals. Similarly, Holmes suggested that the principle of strict liability for injuries would "make a defendant responsible for all damage, however remote, of which his act could be called the cause."[28] But if minor mistakes, chance injuries, and remote damages licensed the state to intervene in the private realm, there could be little or no room for individual action free from state control. If, as Holmes suggested, "[s]tate interference is an evil, where it cannot be shown to be a good," then state shifting of costs among equally faultless parties merely threatened to overextend the state into the private sphere. A cause-based strict-liability standard, in short, involved the state in pervasive and ongoing reallocation of resources in the private sphere.[29] By contrast, a negligence standard appeared to guarantee that individuals in the private sphere would be insulated from state interference in the exercise of their rights. So long as actors causing damages remained within the bounds of their legal rights, they were no more at fault than faultless victims. "No one is responsible for an injury caused purely by inevitable accident, while he is engaged in a lawful business," explained Thomas Shearman and Amasa Redfield.[30] So long as an injury was the result of a "lawful act, done in a lawful manner," wrote C. G. Addison, "there is no legal injury, and no tort giving rise to an action for damages."[31] In Minnesota lawyer Edwin Jaggard's formulation, "[t]he exercise of ordinary rights" was not actionable "even if it causes damages."[32] It was only when one went outside of one's own sphere of autonomy and thus inflicted a "legal injury" or an "invasion of some legal right," clarified Hilliard, that one incurred liability for damages.[33]

No one better captured the way in which the negligence standard and the rule of *damnum absque injuria* functioned to protect the distinction between public and private than Michigan jurist Thomas Cooley. Cooley grew up in the famous "Burned-Over District" of western New York, home to Martin Van Buren and the New York wing of Jacksonian Democratic politics. As a young man in the district, Cooley witnessed firsthand the raging evangelical movements sweeping through the Erie Canal area in the 1830s.[34] Historian Peter Walker has written that the "most extravagant religious revivalism, antimasonry, abolition, millennialism, prohibition, spiritualism, woman's rights, the Mormon church, the Millerites, either in their origins or their first significant manifestations converged in the Burned-Over District." These reform movements clustered around attempts to free the individual to make self-determining choices. In Walker's explanation, "the common lesson taught in the district" was that justice "depended upon the actions of autonomous man."[35] In the 1850s, after moving to Michigan and opening a law practice, Cooley joined the antislavery Free Soil Party, and later the fledgling Republican Party.

In Cooley's widely read treatise on constitutional limitations, it was his background in the politics of antebellum Jacksonian democracy that came through most strongly. He emphasized the dangers of legislation that extended special privileges to some and jeopardized the principle of equal rights for all.[36] Cooley's torts treatise, in turn, drew inspiration from the Burned-

Over District's reform ideal of moral autonomy. So long as an actor remained within the bounds of his legal rights and duties he was, in Cooley's conception, unchargeable by the state for harms falling on others. To be sure, Cooley conceded, common law principles held that there was no wrong without a remedy. But this notion was "a mere truism." The law provided remedies only for the infringement of rights, which (in turn) were defined as those interests harm to which could be remedied at law.[37] Under this tautological approach, no wrong was without a remedy, yet harms caused by the "lawful and proper exercise by one man of his rights" were generally not remediable because such harms were not legal wrongs. In Cooley's view, then, the faultless victims of purely "accidental" injuries were without legal recourse because there existed no "injuria"—no legal wrong—that the state could attach to another actor. To hold otherwise was to threaten state infringement of individual autonomy. As Cooley explained, "That which it is right and lawful for one man to do cannot furnish the foundation for an action in favor of another."[38]

Like lawyers before him who had seized on the maxim *damnum absque injuria*, Cooley had not really solved the problem of defining the bounds of individual liberty; he had merely reformulated it. Indeed, for Cooley and his peers, the faultless victim of nonnegligent harm remained a deeply destabilizing force in late-nineteenth-century tort law. Much of the doctrinal edifice of the law of torts during this period can thus be understood as a series of attempts to deal with the persistent problem of the faultless victim of nonnegligent harm. The doctrine of contributory negligence—probably the most important such doctrine in the late-nineteenth-century law of torts—highlighted wrongdoing on the part of victims. If the victims of injury acted outside of the bounds of their rights and duties, after all, the conceptual dilemma of the faultless victim and the nonnegligent injurer disappeared. In virtually every American jurisdiction a victim was unable to recover if the victim's own negligence—no matter how slight—had contributed to the injuries.[39] "Between two wrong-doers," or between a nonnegligent defendant and a negligent plaintiff, Cooley explained, "the law will leave the consequences to rest where they have chanced to fall."[40] In case after case, the deciding question was whether any negligence on the part of the plaintiff had contributed to the injuries from which she suffered; indeed, no less than 68 percent of the negligence decisions digested by the West Publishing Company between 1860 and 1880 raised questions of contributory negligence.[41]

In other cases of nonnegligent injuries, tort law justified the absence of a remedy by the consent of the victim to bear the risk of accident. The doctrine of assumption of risk attached predominantly to work accidents. Summed up in the maxim *volenti non fit injuria*—roughly translatable as "there is no legal injury to one who consents"—the doctrine held that "[n]o action can be maintained for damages resulting from conduct suffered by consent" of the victim.[42] Though employers owed employees a duty of due care in the provision of machinery, appliances, and competent fellow servants, the doctrine of assumption of risk meant that "an employer may relieve himself of all common law liability for accidents occurring to his servants, through defects in materials or in the character of fellow servants, by giving explicit warning of such defects, and notice that he does not intend to remedy them."[43] Similarly, when an employee learned of defects in machinery or incompetence in his fellows, either before or during the course of his service, the employee was "deemed to assume the risk of danger thus known."[44] In some instances courts even held that the rule applied to all defects within the constructive knowledge of an employee—that is, defects not actually known to an employee, but that should have become known to the employee through "the exercise of ordinary observation or reasonable skill and diligence."[45]

Tort law's resort to the implied consent of victims, however, was fraught with problems of its own. Conventional wisdom in late-nineteenth-century tort law held that for reasons of public policy persons could not contract out of liability for their own negligence. Certain entitlements were simply not alienable. Such waivers of liability were suspect for arising out of coercion. Moreover, such waivers appeared to give rise to the risk of harm to third parties who might be injured by carelessness that had been licensed by a person's belief that he would be held harmless against costs arising out of his negligence.[46] Nonetheless, together the contributory negligence rule and the assumption of risk doctrine seemed to relieve—at least for the moment—much of the pressure placed on tort law by the dilemmas of classical liberal political theory.

Even as the elite of the American bar worked out the elaborate doctrinal structure of classical tort law, a rising tide of personal injury litigation pressed harder and harder on weaknesses in the doctrine. Hilliard wrote his torts treatise in 1859 in response to the "very large and increasing proportion of actions of tort, which are continually arising in our courts of justice."[47] Twenty years later, after the publication of the third edition of Hilliard's treatise and the issuance of many additional works on the subject, Cooley decided that yet another torts treatise was warranted. The "new inventions and improvements" of the machine age, he explained, were having a "powerful tendency" to create "new occupations" and "more frequent controversies."[48]

What was most remarkable about tort litigation in these years, particularly personal injury tort litigation, was the unprecedented character of the wave of litigation itself. Of particular interest to treatise writers like Hilliard, for example, was the continual development of new theories for causes of action in torts cases. Time and again common law judges in the United States, as well as in England, were faced with new kinds of tort claims. The novelty of a particular claim or the "absence of any precedent for a particular action," Hilliard cautioned, was good but hardly conclusive evidence that a suit failed to state a cognizable claim.[49] Yet the avalanche of novel claims was overwhelming the delicate structures of the law of torts. For in the middle of the nineteenth century, personal injury law underwent a transformation that ushered in what would, by the turn of the century, become a crisis for the classical legal order.

This is not to say that the eighteenth-century common law had no body of personal injury law. Into the early nineteenth century, however, personal injury law pertained not so much to the rights of the immediate victim of bodily harm, but to the rights of those who possessed rights in the life and services of an immediate victim. Eighteenth-century American and English personal injury cases thus appear to have been concerned primarily with actions for loss of services—namely, damages to a master resulting from injury to members of the master's household. Tapping Reeve, the leading American authority on the law of domestic relations at the turn of the nineteenth century, explained that in the event of injury to a wife, "the husband may bring an action in his own name, to recover damages which he sustained, by reason of the battery." By the same token, a father was entitled to an action "when his minor child is beaten" and the father "has lost the services of that child, or has been put to expense by means thereof." Wives, children, and servants, by contrast, had no cause of action for injuries to their husbands, fathers, and masters.[50]

The action for loss of services had its roots in the early modern family-based structure of production and social organization. In a household economy, the roles of wife, servant, and child were closely intertwined and often overlapping. They were, in Blackstone's words, the "three great relations in private life."[51] Husbands expected wives and children to render service to the household, and acquired a familial authority over even those household servants not related by blood. The household economy remained the central mode of economic life in the United States into the early nineteenth century.[52] And in the South, of course, the household model of production persisted until the Civil War.[53] Indeed, southern masters brought actions to recover damages from third parties and independent contractors for injuries to their slaves up until the abolition of slavery.[54]

During the 1820s and 1830s, the shape of economic life in the North underwent a critical shift, and with it changed the structure of personal injury law. New mills and factories, especially in New England and New York, separated production from the sphere of domestic life.[55] Over precisely the same years, the slow trickle of personal injury cases became a steady stream.[56] Moreover, the emerging wage system and the new structure of domestic life lay at the heart of the new tort litigation. Whereas eighteenth- and early-nineteenth-century personal injury litigation generally took the form of an action for loss of services, mid-nineteenth-century personal injury litigation was centrally concerned with the support of dependent wives and children.[57]

The emerging structure of personal injury litigation in the mid-nineteenth century was especially evident in the law of wrongful death. In 1846, the British Parliament enacted a wrongful death statute known as Lord Campbell's Act, which reversed the English common law rule that tort actions expired with the death of the plaintiff. The act provided for wrongful death actions in cases of negligently or intentionally caused death, authorizing damages "for the benefit of the wife, husband, parent, and child of the person whose death shall have been so caused."[58] The very next year, New York enacted a similar wrongful death statute, copying the model of Lord Campbell's Act virtually word for word. But legislators in New York made one striking amendment to the English wrongful death statute. Lord Campbell's Act had provided for "such damages as [the jury] may think proportioned to the injury," payable, as we have seen, to the "wife, husband, parent, and child" of the deceased. The New York legislation, by contrast, dropped husbands from the list of potential beneficiaries. Damages were limited to the "*pecuniary injury* resulting from such death to *the wife and next of kin*" of the deceased person. Moreover, such damages were "for the exclusive benefit of *the widow and next of kin*."[59]

By 1869, twenty-nine of the thirty-seven states had enacted wrongful death statutes. (Northern states were far more likely than southern states to enact such statutes during these years: six of the eight states without wrongful death statutes in 1869 were southern or border states.) Moreover, the majority of the general wrongful death statutes followed New York's lead and excised the word "husband" from statutory provisions modeled on Lord Campbell's Act, thus limiting the payment of benefits in death actions to the widow and next of kin of the deceased. In all, by 1869 sixteen of the twenty-nine states with wrongful death legislation limited recovery to widows and next of kin. And in the next decade and a half, Arkansas, Montana, Nebraska, and Oklahoma followed suit.[60]

By restricting benefits to the "widow and next of kin," American wrongful death statutes barred actions by husbands to recover damages for the death of their wives. The term "next of kin" was (and is) a term of art in the law of intestate distributions. Husbands were not "next of kin" at common law; indeed, neither spouse was "next of kin" to the other for intestacy purposes.

Thus, as any number of courts held, widowers lacked standing under the statutes to sue for loss of services in the event of their wives' deaths.[61] In New Jersey, for example, the Supreme Court ruled that the state's wrongful death statute, unlike Lord Campbell's Act, gave a cause of action "in favor of the widow, but not in favor of the husband."[62] In Georgia, the Supreme Court concluded that "if the General Assembly had intended to have altered the common law so as to give to the husband a right of action to recover damages for the homicide of his wife, they would have so declared when providing for the particular class of persons specified in the [act]."[63] Likewise, the federal circuit court for the Eighth Circuit observed that "a widower is not one of the beneficiaries of the statute[s], and it is a fatal error to allow a recovery of damages for losses he sustains by the death of his wife."[64] Indeed, courts in some states held that fathers lacked standing under the statutes to bring actions for the death of a minor child. In Massachusetts, for example, courts held that no statutory remedy existed for deaths of persons leaving "neither widow nor children."[65] In sum, the wrongful death statutes inverted the household structure of eighteenth-century personal injury litigation, shifting it from husbands, fathers, and masters suing for loss of services, to wives, children, and dependents suing for loss of support.[66]

Transformations in personal injury litigation rarely occurred so neatly or quickly as they did in the wrongful death statutes. Personal injury litigation faced a host of obstacles during this period, obstacles rooted both in cultural institutions and in legal institutions. On the cultural side, persistent eighteenth-century patterns of authority and deference between master and servant slowed the growth of personal injury litigation. Nineteenth-century textile mills, for example, often modeled their labor management practices on the relations of authority, discipline, and deference in the household economies that they sought to replace. In Rhode Island and south-central Massachusetts, leading textile mill entrepreneur Samuel Slater sought in his mills to assert "traditional community values" through the use of a "family system" in which the mill took the place of the eighteenth-century household.[67] In the New England mills of the Boston Associates, the "boardinghouse system" took in countless young female mill hands and made them the core of the workforce.[68] Like Slater's "family system," the boardinghouse approach sought to "recreate . . . traditional communities . . . in which corporate hierarchy and deference, as well as neighborliness, were valued."[69] In Philadelphia's textile mills, by contrast, numerous small mill owners eschewed the family or boardinghouse approaches. But here, first-generation immigrant mill owners drew on traditions of guild obligation to create a very similar ethos of employer paternalism.[70]

Personal injury litigation by all accounts was exceedingly rare in the northern textile mills of the early to mid nineteenth century. To be sure, the mills did not present quite the same danger as the railroads and the mines. Yet as Herman Melville observed in his use of the textile factory steam engine as an extended metaphor for the dangers of the whaling boat in *Moby-Dick*, whirring bobbins and shuttles surely presented special dangers of their own.[71] Nonetheless, in isolated mill towns, suing an employer often meant antagonizing the most powerful men in the region and jeopardizing not only one's employment prospects, but also one's housing, church membership, and even access to town poor relief. As one turn-of-the-century labor union leader observed, "when a workman goes to law with his employer, he, as it were, declares war against the person on whom his future probably depends." The result was that workers only brought legal claims "when the injury [was] very great" and the worker was prepared to leave the employer's service.[72] In many textile mill company towns, workers would have been reluctant to bring suit even in these circumstances. The "family system" of mill hiring meant that very often multiple members of a single family worked under the roof of a single mill; litigating work accidents in such circumstances might have meant losing not one but several jobs.[73] In an industry in which mill owners often entered into agreements not to hire workers who had worked in another mill unless the worker had received an honorable discharge from the prior mill, injury litigation could be exceedingly costly.[74] In the words of one Manchester, New Hampshire resident and employee at the Amoskeag mills, "If you told the boss to go to hell, you might as well move out of the city. The boss had the power to blackball you for the rest of your days."[75] In such situations, injured workers usually appealed to their employers for assistance rather than risk suing them.[76] As one employment office clerk at Amoskeag during the first decade of the twentieth century remembered, injured employees brought lawsuits "every once in a while." In general, however, the company "worked out" a settlement with injured workers who were presumably loath to sue the city's most important establishment.[77] In the Pittsburgh steel industry, similar practices eventually produced a "social type": the crippled watchman, to whom steel mill managers gave low-exertion jobs.[78]

There was probably no better example of the twin forces of deference and local power than mining injuries. Mining and railroad work were the two most dangerous occupations in the mid and late nineteenth century. Yet in large part because of the isolation and local power of many mining companies, mining accidents never became as important as railroad accidents in the development of nineteenth-century tort law.[79] The local power of mining companies appears often to have been enough to deter the filing of lawsuits by accident victims and their families in mining communities around the country. In the intermountain West between the western slope of the Rockies and the Sierra Nevadas, coal mine operators controlled as much as a fifth of the total labor market and often collaborated among themselves on hiring practices.[80] In many frontier mining camps, the absence of government was the camps' most striking characteristic.[81] Mine operators backed by state troops and private police were virtually unchallengeable in company mining towns such as the fenced and guarded Thurber, Texas.[82] Company towns in the bituminous coal fields of western Pennsylvania, southern Appalachia, and northern Illinois were dominated by mining companies that owned the local real estate, housing stock, roads, and stores.[83] Even where no single mining company was dominant, as in the famed anthracite fields of northeastern Pennsylvania, personal injury litigation was often futile. In a region in which the average duration of any one mining enterprise was less than one year, employers were effectively judgment proof; most mines would have closed down long before the resolution of any legal action.[84]

If patterns of authority, deference, and power inhibited the growth of personal injury litigation, the law itself presented a number of doctrinal obstacles to bringing accident cases. Indeed, quite apart from substantive rules of tort liability, the law of evidence presented serious problems for would-be personal injury plaintiffs. During the first half of the nineteenth century, for example, an array of witness disqualification rules barred testimony from precisely those most likely to know what had happened: the parties, any real parties in interest, any interested witnesses, and the husbands and wives of the parties. Eighteenth-century English treatise writer Lord Chief Baron Jeffrey Gilbert had explained that certain classes of persons were "totally excluded from all Attestation . . . for want of Integrity and Discernment," including the parties to the suit or anyone with an interest in a litigation.[85] The disqualification rules laid down by Gilbert were readily adopted by American courts in the early nineteenth century.[86] The result, as legal historians John Langbein and William Nelson have each observed, was the effective exclusion from the common law courts of cases that would have relied on oral testimony.[87] Oral contracts made without a witness, for example, were exceedingly difficult to sue on, for neither the plaintiff nor the defendant could testify to the making of the contract.[88] By the same token, actions arising out of accidental injuries were required to go forward (if at all) without the testimony of the person who as often as not knew best what had happened.[89] One can only imagine how difficult it was to bring an action in railroad-crossing cases occurring on isolated stretches of track, with few or no witnesses. Similarly, in work-accident cases, a disabled worker unable to testify on his own behalf relied by necessity on the testimony of his fellow employees, all of whom would presumably be reluctant to testify against their employer if they wished to keep their jobs on good terms. As two early-twentieth-century observers noted, it was quite common for coworkers to "refuse to testify against their employer through fear of being dismissed from employment."[90]

By the 1840s, law reformers in the United States began to abolish the witness disqualification rules. Massachusetts courts had gradually narrowed the rules for several decades; the Supreme Judicial Court abolished the disqualification of atheists in 1818, and by the 1820s the agent of a party could testify to the contents of contracts made on behalf of his principal.[91] Moreover, in some states legislation abolished the disqualification rules for particular kinds of cases, including suits on gaming debts and actions to collect allegedly usurious loans.[92] The core of the disqualification rules remained intact, however, into the 1840s and 1850s. General statutory abolition of the disqualification rules began in Michigan, which abolished the disqualification rule for nonparty interested witnesses in 1846. Connecticut admitted party testimony in civil cases in 1848. New York abolished the disqualification of interested nonparty witnesses in the famous Field Code of that same year. The Code also allowed parties to call their opponents to testify, and in 1857 New York allowed parties to testify on their own behalf.[93] Massachusetts, following close behind, abolished its party disqualification rules in 1857 as well. And though southern states took longer than northern states to abolish the disqualification rules, the entire array of disqualification rules collapsed by the 1870s.[94]

Yet the mid-nineteenth-century law of evidence created new obstacles to personal injury litigation even as it struck down the old. In the very years in which the common law of evidence swept out the witness disqualification rules, the hearsay doctrine developed to exclude particular kinds of testimony—out-of-court statements by persons not testifying at trial—rather than particular classes of witnesses.[95] Of particular interest is the interaction of the hearsay rule and its exceptions with the corporate or organizational context of personal injury litigation. Today, the rule for agent admissions establishes that a statement is not hearsay if it is "a statement by the party's agent or servant concerning a matter within the scope of the agency or employment."[96] Such statements are the admissions of a party, and may be offered as evidence against her.[97] Courts interpret this rule expansively to encompass all statements "naturally made in the course of the agency," including post-accident statements by agents involved in the accident.[98] In contrast, the nineteenth-century party admission rule sharply limited the admission of agents' statements as evidence against a corporate principal. The nineteenth-century rule was closely linked to the now-antiquated evidence doctrine of the *res gestae*: statements "contemporaneous with" the event in question so that they were said to form "one transaction" with (or "spring out of") the event.[99] Thus, the nineteenth-century party admission rule allowed the admission of only statements that an agent made "at the time of, and in relation to, some act then being performed in the scope of the agent's duty"—in other words, statements "made at the same time, and constituting part of the *res gestae*."[100]

The *res gestae* rule had its origins in commercial contract cases in the early part of the century.[101] But by the last thirty years of the nineteenth century, accident cases formed the most important share of agent-admission cases; indeed, in the 1860s streetcar and railroad injury lawsuits became the paradigmatic *res gestae* cases.[102] In the 1866 edition of Simon Greenleaf's evidence treatise, for example, the editor's discussion of the doctrine centered on the case of a post-accident admission of negligence by a streetcar driver. Such an admission was not admissible against the streetcar company, the treatise explained, "being made after the injury was inflicted."[103] In subsequent decades, an outpouring of cases in the reporters testified to the power of the *res gestae* rule to exclude statements that plaintiffs sought to introduce in personal injury litigation. The pre-accident statements of a railroad company roadmaster as to the incompetence of an injured worker's fellow employee were excluded as not being part of the *res gestae*.[104] The declarations of a conductor as to the poor condition of a railroad track made a "moment before the accident" were "inadmissible" as not part of the *res gestae*.[105] Post-accident statements, though made "within an hour, describing the cause of the accident," were not competent against the principal,[106] nor were statements made ten to thirty minutes after an accident as to the excessive speed of the railroad car.[107] Even written post-accident reports by agents to their principals were held to be inadmissible against the principal as outside of the *res gestae* unless they "had been promulgated by the company as official documents adopted by and proceeding from it."[108]

The *res gestae* rule also operated to exclude a wide array of statements that plaintiffs sought to admit under other exceptions to the hearsay rule. In one particularly brutal case, the dying declaration of the plaintiff's husband was held inadmissible. While still lying on the tracks, after the wheels of a railroad car had been lifted off of his body, the deceased had managed to say that the "handhold" had let him down. But the Alabama Supreme Court explained that this statement "was no part of the main fact," as it had been "made after the car was removed from over the body."[109] Similarly, though midcentury courts permitted the introduction of "all declarations of pain, suffering, . . . [and] expressions of pain and distress at the time of such suffering," toward the end of the century courts increasingly applied the *res gestae* rule to exclude contemporaneous expressions of pain and suffering.[110]

Restrictive common law tort doctrines and inflexible evidentiary rules, however, could not stanch the outpouring of new tort litigation in the 1860s and 1870s. The number of accident cases shot up after 1870. Historian Randolph Bergstrom has found that between 1870 and 1890, the number of accident suits being litigated in New York City's state courts grew almost eightfold; by 1910 the number had grown again by more than a factor of five. Among contested cases, the rise in the number of personal injury suits was just as dramatic. Whereas in 1870 tort cases represented only 4.2 percent of the New York City trial court's contested caseload, by 1910 they made up 40.9 percent of that caseload, just under a tenfold increase.[111] Similarly, Robert Silverman has found that in Boston as late as 1880 there were no more than "a dozen or so suits . . . filed in superior court alleging damage caused by negligent operation of a horsecar." A mere twenty years later, however, there were over 800 personal injury cases involving streetcars in superior court, and 600 more in the municipal court.[112]

These developments in the law of personal injury hardly went unnoticed. E. Parmalee Prentice, writing in the *North American Review,* found an 800 percent increase in the number of personal injury suits pending in the Cook County, Illinois courts between 1875 and 1896. Eli Shelby Hammond complained in the *Yale Law Journal* that "slight wrongs or injuries that ordinarily were never noticed hitherto" were increasingly being "made the foundation for building up by perjury . . . claims for enormous damages." By 1907, Elon R. Brown of the New York State Bar Association explained that "[n]egligence cases are blocking our calendars with a mass of litigation so great as to impede administration in all other branches of law."[113]

At least part of the reason that accident litigation had been slow to come to mining and textile regions was the relative scarcity of lawyers in such isolated areas. In urban areas after 1860, however, there was no dearth of attorneys. From the end of the Civil War to the turn of the century, a boom in the number of lawyers—and especially in the number of first- and second-generation immigrant lawyers—occurred alongside the even more dramatic growth in the number of personal injury lawsuits (see Table 2.1). Census records provide a wide-angle view of the profession in the period from 1870 to 1900.[114] In the United States as a whole, the number of lawyers jumped by almost 150 percent between 1870 and 1900, and the ratio of lawyers to individuals in the paid workforce increased from 1 in 307 to 1 in 256. Breakdowns of these numbers by national origin are slightly more difficult as a result of changing census categories, but it appears that the main growth area in the legal profession in these years was among the children of immigrants. In the ten years between 1890 and 1900, the number of white native-born lawyers with parents of foreign or mixed birth in the United States grew by 80 percent, almost three times the overall rate of growth among lawyers.

Table 2.1 The growth of the legal profession: lawyers in the United States

	1870	1880	1890	1900	1910	1920	1930
Members of the workforce in all paid occupations	12,505,923	17,392,099	23,318,183	29,287,070	38,167,336	41,614,248	48,829,920
Lawyers	40,736	64,137	89,630	114,460	114,704	122,519	160,605
Pct. growth in the number of lawyers	—	57%	40%	28%	—	7%	—
Ratio of lawyers to members of the paid workforce	1:307	1:271	1:260	1:256	—	1:340	1:304
White native-born lawyers with foreign or mixed-birth parents	—	—	11,034	19,900	21,814	27,288	—
Pct. growth in the number of white native-born lawyers with foreign or mixed-birth parents	—	—	—	80%	—	25%	—
Ratio of white native-born lawyers with foreign or mixed-birth parents to similarly situated members of the paid workforce	—	—	1:321	1:266	—	1:306	—

Sources: Figures are compiled from Dep't of the Interior, Census Office, *The Statistics of the Population of the United States . . . Compiled from the Original Returns of the Ninth Census* (1870) (Washington, D.C., Gov't Printing Office, 1872); Dep't of the Interior, Census Office, *The Statistics of the Population of the United States at the Tenth Census* (1880) (Washington, D.C., Gov't Printing Office, 1880); Dep't of the Interior, Census Office, *The Statistics of the Population of the United States at the Eleventh Census* (1890) (Washington, D.C., Gov't Printing Office, 1890); Dep't of Commerce and Labor, Bureau of the Census, *Special Reports: Occupations of the Twelfth Census* (1904); Dep't of Commerce, Bureau of the Census, *Population 1910: Thirteenth Census of the United States Taken in the Year 1910, Volume IV: Occupation Statistics* (1914); Dep't of Commerce, Bureau of the Census, *Population 1920: Fourteenth Census of the United States Taken in the Year 1920, Volume IV: Occupations* (1923); U.S. Dep't of Commerce, Bureau of the Census, *Fifteenth Census of the United States: 1930 Population, Volume V: General Report on Occupations* (1933).

Note: A change in 1910 in the way the category of "lawyer" was defined (removing semiprofessionals such as notaries, abstractors, and justices of the peace) makes comparisons between pre- and post-1910 census information difficult.

If we look at New York State, it appears that similar patterns characterized the legal profession in many of the nation's important industrial cities. In Manhattan, the growth rate in lawyers as compared to the paid workforce considerably exceeded the state average; between 1870 and 1900, the number of persons in paid occupations for every one lawyer decreased by 36 percent, from 273 to 174. Once again, white children of immigrants represented the major growth category, with the number of lawyers in this class growing by 85 percent between 1890 and 1900, compared to a 49 percent overall growth rate in the number of lawyers in the city. Unlike Manhattan, Buffalo nearly matched the state average in the per capita growth in lawyers. In Buffalo, however, the growth in the number of lawyers who were the white children of immigrants was an astounding 170 percent from 1890 to 1900. Some cities lagged behind the state's average growth in the number of lawyers per capita. Albany, Syracuse, and Troy experienced smaller than average growth in the number of lawyers per person in paid occupations; Brooklyn and Rochester experienced small decreases in the number of lawyers per person. Even in these cities, however, the number of native-born white lawyers with parents of foreign or mixed birth grew disproportionately as compared to lawyers generally.[115]

Strong growth in second-generation immigrant lawyers may have created new cadres of lawyers with close connections to the kinds of working-class communities from which personal injury plaintiffs were disproportionately likely to come. Moreover, increased competition for business among lawyers appears to have pushed the newcomers at the bar—and particularly the children of immigrants, who generally lacked connections to steadier or more lucrative work—to generate new kinds of business. Young lawyers training to take on personal injury cases were instructed in no uncertain terms that although there were clear limits on soliciting business from accident victims, actively seeking cases was an indispensable part of the practitioner's livelihood. In Northwestern University Law School's course in "Legal Tactics," for example, Andrew Hirschl of the Chicago Bar advised students going into plaintiff-side personal injury law to distinguish between the "improper[ ]" solicitation of business and solicitation of business more generally. "Let me tell you frankly, gentlemen," he warned: "if you don't solicit them you won't get them. You might as well make up your minds to it. I have watched this thing for over thirty-three years, at the bar here and elsewhere. If you don't solicit those cases you won't get them. . . . [T]hey are being looked for by others, and if the others get them you won't get them. That is plain. . . . Now, those men are after these cases. And they will get them. If you are willing to sit in your office, then they will get the cases."[116]

Following Hirschl's advice, and indeed going considerably further, the plaintiffs' personal injury bar created intricate networks of "runners," including members of the police and railroad workforces, who received a percentage of the lawyer's take from each case.[117] Others among the plaintiffs' bar— though probably fewer than their opponents in the defense bar imagined— moved into the shady world of claims fraud, fabricating personal injury claims to bring suits against streetcar companies and other corporate defendants.[118] Moreover, at least some plaintiffs' lawyers engaged in questionable settlement practices. In one especially audacious example, upstate New York lawyer Arthur Clark sold out more than 300 clients' lawsuits against the Central New York Telephone and Telegraph Company, agreeing with the company that he would press his clients to settle for whatever the company offered in return for a $3,000 payment.[119]

The defense bar developed similarly dubious strategies. Sometimes this meant little more than ingenious exploitation of complex procedural rules or the overlapping jurisdictional rules of the federal and state court systems to stall cases on ancillary issues.[120] Often, however, it meant engaging in practices as unethical as those of the most unscrupulous plaintiffs' lawyers. Railroads paid off employees to make themselves unavailable to testify on an injured coworker's behalf.[121] Insurance agents and claims adjusters approached still-dazed victims seeking to execute releases for paltry sums.[122] Corporate defense lawyers struck corrupt bargains with plaintiffs' counsel in return for a steady flow of defense work.[123]

It is difficult to tell from any of this evidence whether growth in the number of injury claims resulted from the increase in the number of lawyers or vice versa. It may not matter, however, whether lawyers or claims came first in time. The two trends at once responded to, interacted with, and accelerated one another. Some suits were doubtless brought that would not have been but for the encouragement of lawyers seeking contingent fees.[124] Even when lawyers did not actively seek out cases, their increased presence in a particular city may well have heightened the probability that accident victims would approach them. And such increased demand for legal services, in turn, may have encouraged undecided fence-sitters to train for the profession.

In any event, from the perspective of the elite of the bar the boom in personal injury suits threatened the reputation of the profession—and even, some suggested, the rule of law itself.[125] It was the plaintiffs' bar that came in for the most criticism. "Barratrous speculations," the "communistic tendencies of the present time," and the lure of "enormous verdicts," it was said, had led to such practices as advertising and solicitation "at the expense of all manly and professional dignity."[126] Personal injury litigation was said to be "marked by a lower tone of professional ethics at the Bar and by a greater absence of abstract justice on the Bench than any other class of litigation."[127]

Irving Vann of the New York Court of Appeals argued in a widely reprinted commencement address at Albany Law School that personal injury lawyers on the plaintiffs' side were practicing massive fraud by encouraging perjurious testimony from so-called expert witnesses in order to reap substantial contingent fees, thereby "rob[bing] corporations of thousands of dollars every year."[128]

Jurists like Thomas Cooley agreed. The rising tide of accident litigation threatened to undo the abstract reason and cohesiveness of classical legal thought. The contingent fee disrupted the lawyer's professional obligations to court and client alike. It tempted lawyers to "deal deceitfully" with potential clients by exaggerating the difficulty of cases in order to extract higher fee percentages, and it placed the lawyer's selfish interest in the outcome of the case over his obligations to the "just administration of the law." Moreover, the contingent fee arrangement led plaintiffs' lawyers to file frivolous suits against corporate defendants in the hopes of exploiting the "effect of appeals to passion or prejudice" in the jury.[129] Cooley was right, of course. Little in the messy, murky underworld of personal injury litigation corresponded to the airy propositions of his torts treatise. Tort liability in the real world, it seemed, turned not on classical liberal principles, but on the questionable tactics of runners and insurance adjusters, the common law evidentiary system, and the persistence of employer power over injured employees.[130]

Another quickly developing trend was perhaps even more threatening to the doctrinal edifice of classical tort law. It was becoming apparent to many that an increasing number of the victims of personal injuries, especially victims of injuries suffered in the workplace, were themselves faultless. Injuries, it seemed, were the inevitable result of modern methods of industrial production. And if the avalanche of tort claims posed practical problems for classical tort jurists, the problem of inevitable injury raised once more conceptual dilemmas that tort doctrine had been unable to solve. Indeed, unavoidable accidents raised precisely the problem that lay at the core of classical tort law: the faultless (or "accidental," as Holmes would have it) victim of nonnegligent injury.

As late as the early 1880s, students of American industrial accidents believed that accidents were almost always the result of someone's fault. "Every death upon a railroad," explained Carroll Wright in 1883, "like every death by violence, is the result of somebody's negligence or wilfulness."[131] By the turn of the century, however, many accidents seemed increasingly difficult to trace to any human fault. The New York Bureau of Labor Statistics claimed that "in modern industry," with its "extremely complicated machinery," it was "impossible to locate the responsibility" in work-accident cases.[132] In

Maryland in 1902, the legislature announced that in "perilous occupations
. . . unavoidable or trade risk is responsible for at least ninety-five per cent" of
fatal accidents.[133] In Minnesota, the Bureau of Labor reported that most
work accidents were due not to employer or employee negligence, but to the
unavoidable "hazards of the industry."[134] Reports on the accident problem in
Iowa observed that the toll of work accidents was "in great part[] unavoidable" and that even "when all possible precautions have been taken, modern
industry will continue to exact a fearful toll of life and limb."[135] Crystal Eastman's widely influential study of work accidents in Pittsburgh made much
the same point: in a substantial number of work-accident fatalities, Eastman
contended, "no one is to be blamed."[136]

State bar associations, too, came to see industrial accidents not as resulting
from the fault of particular parties, but as the inevitable risks of enterprise.
"[I]n many, if not all, lines of employment," observed one Ohio Bar Association report, "there is an element of *inherent danger* which, in measuring employees' injuries, is quite as important as the element of negligence."[137] No
matter how careful the employee and employer were, explained another report to the Ohio Bar Association a year later, more than half of work accidents were "due to the natural hazards or dangers of the business."[138]

In a tort system that linked liability to fault, the rise of faultless injuries precipitated a compensation crisis. In recent years, legal historians have dis-
agreed strongly over the relative stinginess or generosity of common law
judges in nineteenth-century tort cases.[139] Outside of work-accident litigation, many plaintiffs—especially railroad passengers—fared quite well in appellate courts, even in states such as New York where courts were considered
relatively unfriendly to plaintiffs. But the appellate case reports provide a view
of only the top layer in a complicated multitiered process.[140] Looking below
the appellate level, tort law almost certainly served as a poor compensation
mechanism for accident victims. For one thing, work-accident cases, which
involved injuries to wage earners, tended to create urgent need for compensation. But despite having been the leading category of accidents in the second half of the nineteenth century, work accidents were sharply underrep-
resented among both appellate personal injury decisions and trial court
filings.[141] Most work injuries, for some of the reasons already reviewed, were
simply not brought into the tort system at all. And when we turn from the
trial court filings to the records of accident-causing enterprises themselves,
the inadequacy of tort law as a compensation mechanism becomes still
clearer. Thomas Russell's study of the claims department of the Oakland
Traction Company, a California street railway company, shows that between
1903 and 1905, only 581 of the 3,843 passengers injured while riding the
railway received any compensation from the company. The most common

amount paid on a claim was between $10 and $25. Moreover, in the thirty-five deaths involving Oakland Traction between 1896 and 1906, the company paid an average of $169 in each case—less than $6,000 total—to settle claims by victims' families and to cover medical costs and funeral arrangements. In twenty of the deaths, Russell finds no payment at all to the victim's family, and in no case did a family receive more than $300.[142]

The problems of faultless accidents and uncompensated injuries brought turn-of-the-century lawyers face to face with the central dilemmas of classical tort law. Nonnegligent accidents happened, it seemed, on an increasingly regular basis, inflicting uncompensated injury on faultless victims. Yet the rationales advanced by the classical lawyers for this category of *damnum absque injuria* were less and less persuasive in view of the mounting toll of accidents. "[A] system of laws which permit[s] no recovery in so large a percentage of deaths and injuries occurring is unjust," explained one bar association.[143] Indeed, the negligence standard—which courts had crafted as a guarantor of the boundaries of individual autonomy—had come to license the massive infliction of remediless injury on thousands of Americans each year.

Critiques of the negligence standard brought out recessive strains of strict or quasi-strict liability in the case law. In railroad crossing cases in New York, for example, the Court of Appeals solved the problem of *damnum absque injuria* by sharply limiting the category of faultless accidents. Whenever there was an accident without the victim's contributory negligence, there was sure to be railroad negligence;[144] and whenever there was an accident without railroad negligence, there was sure to be contributory negligence.[145] Negligence and contributory negligence swallowed the class of faultless injuries, and crossing cases were thus virtually always said to be due either to railroad negligence or to the contributory negligence of the victim.[146] Indeed, reading the railroad crossing cases one cannot help but sense that the courts were interested not in negligence and contributory negligence, but rather in determining which of the parties was better understood as the cause of the accident. As a result, the law of railroad crossings became effectively a strict-liability, cause-based standard in all cases in which victims had not been contributorily negligent.[147]

Rebuttable presumptions of negligence formed another quasi-strict-liability mechanism for redressing the problem of the faultless victim. Hilliard identified in 1859 a limited category of cases, including injuries to railroad passengers, in which "a loss, affirmatively proved, will be *presumed* to have resulted from the negligence of the defendant, throwing upon him the burden of disproving such negligence."[148] Soon thereafter, a series of English decisions held that when people were struck by objects falling from buildings and bridges, the circumstances of the injuries afforded "a presumption that [the

building or bridge owner] had not used reasonable care and diligence" in securing the building or bridge.[149] Absent rebuttal of the presumption, English
courts reasoned, the "thing spoke for itself"—*res ipsa loquitur.*[150] In the
United States, the English *res ipsa* decisions led to a wave of burden-shifting
cases. Landslides occurring in railroad cuts and causing train derailments; cinders and bolts falling from elevated railways; overhead telegraph wires falling
on the road below; falling bricks, buildings, scaffolds, or elevators; collapsing
gangway planks; exploding boilers; and suddenly starting machinery—all
came at one time or another under the rule shifting the burden of proof to
the defendant to disprove that it had been negligent.[151]

Other areas of tort law verged on strict liability as well. Courts held common carriers of passengers to "the utmost care and skill which prudent men
are accustomed to use under similar circumstances."[152] Dam owners were
strictly liable for the flooding of areas upstream of their dams.[153] Nuisances
interfering with another's enjoyment of his property were "violations of absolute legal rights" and thus "strict legal injuries."[154] Hilliard wrote that the
mere use of reasonable precautions did not vindicate a defendant in a blasting case.[155] According to Cooley, hunters trespassing on private lands were
strictly liable for any damages caused to the landowner.[156] Possessors of domestic animals were strictly liable for any ordinary damages to crops resulting
from their escape, and possessors of wild animals were strictly liable for any
damages caused by their escape.[157] By the same token, extrahazardous activities such as the storage of nitroglycerin[158] or petroleum,[159] excavations,[160] and
the production of noxious substances[161] could, in certain circumstances, lead
to strict liability for harm caused.[162]

Yet the move to strict-liability standards could not rescue the precarious intellectual project of classical tort doctrine. A cause-based approach to liability
might, to be sure, have gone a long way toward compensating nonnegligent
victims. But even under a strict-liability system, intractable problems of causation would have made it impossible to make bright-line distinctions among
the boundaries of the various parties' spheres of interest.[163] Both parties to a
bilateral accident, after all, were necessarily but-for causes of the accident.
And in cases involving extrahazardous activities or nuisances, for example,
the determination of which party—injurer or injured—had caused the accident often required a prior (and circular) inquiry into who had been entitled
to do what.[164] That inquiry, in turn, was likely to return to questions about
the parties' relative fault. A cause-based approach was therefore indeterminate in important classes of cases; even if classical tort law had adopted strict-
liability standards more widely, it still could not have clarified the boundary
lines between persons.

The development of strict-liability rules sharply undermined the intellectual clarity of tort doctrine. Even as recessive strains of strict liability emerged, they stood side by side with the still-dominant negligence standard. Treatises thus announced negligence as the general rule in accident cases while at the same time listing a growing number of strict- or quasi-strict-liability categories as ad hoc exceptions. In short, the carefully constructed architecture of the classical law of torts was losing its coherence and form. The law of torts devolved from conceptual order into messy doctrinal stalemate.

Moreover, even the doctrinal solutions with which torts jurists had experimented as solutions for the *damnum absque injuria* problem began to crumble under the accumulating weight of personal injury litigation. Beginning as early as 1856 with a Georgia statute relating to railroad accidents, some states had begun in the middle of the nineteenth century to enact employers' liability legislation limiting the effect of the rule that employees assumed the risk of injury by negligent fellow employees. Enactment of such statutes picked up speed near the turn of the century. By 1911 twenty-five states had enacted legislation variously abolishing the fellow servant rule, modifying the contributory negligence doctrine, and limiting the assumption of risk rule. Developments were perhaps most striking at the federal level on the railroads, where the Federal Employers' Liability Act of 1906 (reenacted in 1908) abolished the fellow servant rule for railroad workers in interstate commerce. The federal legislation went still further than many of the state statutes and abolished the doctrine of contributory negligence, providing that an injured employee could now recover damages from his employer notwithstanding the employee's own contributory negligence; damages would simply be reduced in proportion to the share of negligence attributable to the employee.[165]

Common law developments moved in similar directions. The rule of assumption of risk had offered a contract-based approach to bringing tort doctrine into line with classical liberal principles. But it was increasingly apparent that to allow parties to contract into their own liability rules would not settle the dilemmas of tort law. As early as the 1860s, courts began to confront a wave of attempts by railroad companies to adjust by contract their tort liability exposure for injuries to passengers and workers. Tickets issued to passengers or to stockmen accompanying cattle in shipment increasingly included printed waivers of liability for personal injury. Employment contracts released employers from liability for the personal injuries of their workers, sought to replace state statutes of limitations with restrictive thirty-day notice requirements, purported to waive state safety regulations, and attempted to condition the filing of personal injury suits on medical examinations by company physicians.[166]

Courts sharply curtailed the capacity of railroads and other firms to contract out of their common law liability for injuries to passengers and employees. Such contracts, in the conclusory phrase of the late-nineteenth-century courts, were void as "against public policy." Yet despite the unelaborated references to public policy, one can tease out of the cases at least three discrete rationales for holding contractual waivers of liability unenforceable. Each rationale, in its own way, pointed toward the impracticability of the elegant conceptual structure of classical tort law.

The first rationale was paternalist. Tort doctrine aimed to set the bounds of each individual's duties and rights in order to clarify the scope of freedom in civil society. But cases voiding consensual waivers of liability indicated, first, that the law placed substantive limits on what an individual could do even with respect to purely self-regarding activity. Just as the criminal prohibition on suicide restricted individual liberty in order to protect life, the right to sue for damages arising out of negligence was unwaivable because private tort actions served as the best "safeguard" against the destruction of life. "The state has an interest of the highest degree in the preservation of its citizens' lives," explained Shearman and Redfield, and the protection that the negligence regime afforded to each individual was thus "of such value to the state that it should not allow it to be waived."[167]

Second, many believed that such waivers of liability revealed the extent to which relations of inequality among persons undermined the classical framework. To uphold contractual waivers of liability between railroads and their passengers or employees, Seymour Thompson observed, was to "ignore the unequal situation of the laborer and his employer."[168] The appeal of the inequality argument diminished during the first decades of the twentieth century, largely because it was exceedingly difficult to distinguish authentic expressions of consumer or worker preferences from the effects of employer power. Nonetheless, this critique of contractual waivers remained strong into the early twentieth century.[169]

Third, and ultimately most devastating for the classical tort system, the cases suggested that the notion of individuals as self-contained rights bearers, whose boundaries could be definitively set out if only the law of torts were sufficiently clarified, was simply impossible. Agreements between parties as to their rights, duties, and remedies, it turned out, inevitably affected third parties. When a railroad contracted out of its liability to one passenger or employee, its incentives to take care of other passengers and employees would necessarily diminish. The U.S. Supreme Court noted precisely this consequence in 1873, when it observed that such private "individual contracts" supplanting the law of common carriers affected the "public interest."[170] Similarly, the Ohio Supreme Court ruled the waiver of liability in a stockman's rail pass unenforceable because of the ripple effects such waivers might have on third parties. "It cannot be denied," the court explained, "that pecuniary liability for negligence promotes care; and if public carriers in conducting their business can graduate their charges so as to discharge themselves from such liability, the direct effect will be to [reduce] the motives for diligence."[171] By the turn of the century, the problem of increased risk to third parties arising out of waivers of liability had become increasingly central to courts' refusals to enforce such waivers.[172]

As one New York court observed, whether one person could by contract exonerate another from liability for an injury inflicted by the latter's own negligence was "*quaestio vexata* in the jurisprudence of England and this country."[173] Indeed, the problem of express contractual assumption of risk was all the greater given that the doctrine of implied assumption of risk—a mainstay of tort law's doctrinal structure—was itself all about waiving the tort liability rules imposed by law and setting new rules between employer and employee. When an employer notified an employee of a particular defect in machinery, or when an employee knew of and consented to a particular failure in the employer's obligations of care, the employee was said to waive his right to sue for the employer's negligence.[174] The courts required consent but often deemed the mere failure to quit sufficient to constitute consent.[175] So, too, the fellow servant doctrine represented a contractual means by which employers transferred liability for work accidents to their workers. Thus, although it was fairly well settled that contractual waivers were unenforceable, a series of exceptional or dissenting cases emerged as courts sought to reconcile the apparent "public policy" problems of such waivers with the principles of the doctrinal framework. In New York, for example, one court held that the assumption of risk principle allowed a worker to waive the protections of safety regulations.[176] Elsewhere, courts enforced employment agreements waiving the right to sue for damages incurred while on employers' trains going to and from work.[177] Similarly, some courts enforced railroad company liability waivers by construing them to have been executed by the railroads in their capacity as so-called private carriers rather than in their capacity as common carriers.[178]

Ultimately, as in the law's oscillation between negligence and strict liability, conflict between the waiver cases and the assumption of risk rule produced doctrinal paralysis. Classical tort law proved unable to draw bright lines separating individuals from one another or separating individuals from the state. Private rights, it appeared, inevitably collided with one another as well as with public interests. By the third decade of the twentieth century, almost every American jurisdiction had replaced tort law with an administrative compensation system for work accidents, the most important category of personal injuries. Workmen's compensation statutes undid the resolution of *damnum absque injuria* constructed by Shaw, Cooley, and Holmes, replacing it with a scheme that aimed to shift to employers, at least in part, the costs of precisely those nonfaulty injuries which, in the formulation of Holmes and Shaw, were to lie where they fell. But to move to workmen's compensation is to jump to the end of the story, to tell it backward from its conclusion. More immediately, the shortcomings of classical tort law precipitated a scramble for alternatives to the law of torts among working-class families seeking protections against the mounting risks of injury and death.

3

The Cooperative Insurance Movement

If the national fraternal beneficiary societies can successfully combine, why cannot the labor organizations of the country absorb, manage, and direct the wealth they produce and keep it out of the pockets of the non-producers, the Goulds and Vanderbilts?

—NATHAN BOYNTON, *THE FRATERNAL MONITOR* (1894)

Legend has it that on October 27, 1868, John Jordan Upchurch of Meadville, Pennsylvania established the first American cooperative fraternal insurance association, the Ancient Order of United Workmen. As retold at countless cooperative insurance conventions and lodge gatherings during the late nineteenth century, Upchurch founded the United Workmen primarily as a labor organization. A Civil War veteran and master railroad mechanic, Upchurch hoped that the United Workmen would foster "ideas of right and justice between man and man," provide "one united body for the protection of [workers'] interest against all encroachments," and elevate "labor to that standard it is justly entitled to."[1] The United Workmen thus appeared to adopt a broad platform for the advancement of workers' interests, similar in many ways to the programs for workingmen's protection that labor groups such as the Knights of Labor adopted during the same years.[2] Within a year of its establishment, however, the United Workmen moved in a different, though not unrelated, direction. Railway workers such as Upchurch, for whom industrial hazards were especially acute, felt a strong need for some sort of insurance against death and disability. Accordingly, the United Workmen became primarily an association for the mutual insurance of its working- and middle-class membership. Indeed, the United Workmen very quickly became a leading early participant in the now little-known but remarkably important workingmen's cooperative insurance system of late-nineteenth-century America.[3]

The story of Upchurch's founding of the first cooperative workingmen's insurance association is likely little more than a useful, if apocryphal, myth of origin for the vast cooperative disability and life insurance movement that sprang up practically overnight in post–Civil War America. In 1860, cooperative insurance was a bit player in a tiny American life insurance industry. By the 1890s, cooperative insurance was the leading form of insurance in a life insurance market that had increased in size thirty times over.[4] The cooperatives had become more important in terms of number of policies and total insurance in force than the commercial life insurance industry, stock and mutual companies combined. And in the last two decades of the nineteenth century, nearly one in three American workingmen belonged to a cooperative insurance association of one sort or another.[5] In urban and industrial areas in the East and Midwest, the numbers were often even higher. In short, in the span of two decades cooperative insurance had developed into an institution of the first rank in American life.

Late-nineteenth-century cooperative self-insurance associations played a critical but now almost entirely ignored role in providing life insurance and disability benefits. Indeed, by the 1880s and 1890s, cooperative first-party insurance societies were probably the leading source of systematic compensation for accidental disability and death. In part, cooperative insurance's success in the field was due to its creative response to the endemic problems of adverse selection and moral hazard in disability insurance markets. Cooperative insurance associations adopted a set of premodern fraternal social rituals and symbols such as secret passwords, secret handshakes, and elaborate initiation rites. Though overwrought and sometimes even silly to our eyes, these rituals served the critical insurance functions of forging norms of solidarity among members that would discourage the self-interested departure of low-risk insureds from the insurance pool, as well as reduce the incidence of self-seeking claims on the pool.

The cooperative insurance system also represented one among a number of attempts by late-nineteenth-century American workingmen to adapt the Civil War ideal of masculine free labor citizenship to a newly industrializing republic. Like the post–Civil War workingmen's associations out of which the Ancient Order of United Workmen developed, insurance associations advanced a vision for the cooperative reconstruction not just of accident law, but of social conditions and the American economy more generally. In this sense, cooperative insurance advanced a critique (though as we shall see, a deeply ambiguous one) of the competitive system that generated the accident problem in the first place.

The cooperative associations' attempt to reconstruct American social life came to a head in the first decade of the twentieth century, when the leading cooperative insurance societies sought to stave off competing forms of social insurance by advocating state legislation that would allow them to form a quasi-public insurance system. In western European nations such as Germany and Great Britain, twentieth-century social insurance programs developed out of nineteenth-century workingmen's mutuals. And in the first decade of the twentieth century, American cooperative self-insurance societies sought to make a parallel move to establish themselves as a highly regulated oligopolistic disability insurance regime that would have shared many of the features of the British scheme. Ironically, it was in part the preoccupation of the American social reform imagination with the problem of accidents that blocked the European-style transformation of the American workingmen's insurance pools into compulsory state insurance programs.

Post–Civil War workingmen's insurance societies developed out of a long tradition of mutual insurance. English friendly societies, which became important institutions of working-class self-help in the eighteenth century, claimed to have their origins in antiquity. During the first half of the nineteenth century, mutual insurance pools sprang up across the United States and western Europe among a wide array of groups to protect against a variety of hazards such as fire and maritime losses.

Yet as late as the close of the Civil War, American workers had few sources of insurance. After the war, the spread of new industrial technologies (especially the railroad) and the restructuring of the family around the family wage model occasioned new experimentation with a variety of first-party insurance mechanisms to protect against the loss of wages and the medical care costs attendant on disability and death. Indeed, by the 1880s and 1890s commentators suggested that the Americans "lead the world in devising insurance schemes."[6] Life insurance, for example, existed only on a minor scale in the United States before 1840. Beginning in the 1840s, a boom in life insurance firms produced such future industry giants as New York Life and Mutual of New York. The number of companies operating in New York alone increased from fourteen in 1860 to sixty-nine in 1870; over the same decade, the number of life insurance policies in force in the United States grew from 50,000 to 650,000, and the value of those policies in force rose from $140 million to $1.8 billion.[7] Despite such strong growth, however, commercial life insurance firms did not develop an insurance product marketable to the class of Americans most subject to the vicissitudes of the new industrial economy. Life insurance policies for the workingman, explained an 1890 California report, were considered "'bad risks,' on account of the hygienic conditions under which he lives, and the accidents to which he is exposed at work."[8]

Commercial accident insurance represented another mechanism by which increasing numbers of mid-nineteenth-century Americans sought to insure against disability and death. The British Railway Passengers' Assurance Company of London had begun as early as 1849 to write insurance for passengers against losses from railway accidents, so-called accident ticket policies. And in the 1850s, a number of small accident insurance firms sprang up in Massachusetts to offer similar policies. Only in 1864, however, with the establishment of the Travelers' Insurance Company of Hartford, did American companies begin to write accident policies in significant numbers, and even as late as 1875, only three companies were engaged in the accident insurance business in New York State. Moreover, the largest share of personal accident insurance was sold not to the industrial workers who faced the greatest risk of accidents but rather to the business and professional classes to protect against accidents in travel.[9] Indeed, most firms refused to sell policies to individuals working in hazardous occupations such as mining, railroads, iron and steel works, lumber, and bridge building, as well as a host of less prominent but still dangerous trades (see Figure 3.1). Those accident insurance firms

Figure 3.1 Occupations excluded from commercial accident insurance

Acid works employee	Gang sawyer
Acrobatic performer	Glass work employee
Aeronaut	Glucose works employee
Army officer in field service	Gravity railroad employee
Artesian well borer	Hide and skin worker
Band sawyer	Horse railroad employee
Barb wire worker	Indian agent
Barge man	Iron and steel worker
Bark peeler	Lumberman
Baseball player, professional	Miner, coal, gold, silver,
Brass founder	quartz, or copper
Bridge builder, putting up	Moulding machine worker
Buzz planer or sawyer	Nail maker
Canal boatman	Oil man
Captain or mate of coasting	Percussion-cap maker
or seagoing vessel	Pulp mill employee
Cartridge maker	Quartz mill employee
Celluloid worker	Railroad employee
Chain maker	Roofer
Charcoal burner	Sailor
Cider-man or snapper	Scythe maker
Circular sawyer	Shingle maker
Circus rider	Slater
Coal heaver	Slate quarrier
Coke drawer or charger	Soap boiler
Cutlery forger, hot drop	Spindle maker
Cutlery grinder or polisher	Spindle grinder
Electric light employee	Stove maker or worker
Engineer or fireman of river,	Submarine driver
lake, sound, or tugboat	Tack maker
Engineer or fireman, seagoing vessel	Telegraph builder or repairer
Fibre manufacturer	Thresher, with machine
File maker	Varnish maker
Fireman	Vitriol maker
Firework maker	Well digger
Furniture factory employee	Wire maker

Source: Katharine Pearson Woods, "Accidents in Factories and Elsewhere," 4 *Publications Am. Stat. Ass'n* 1, 308–9 (1895).

that did write accident policies on railroad employees, such as the notorious Provident Life Insurance and Investment Company, soon found themselves swamped with claims.[10] The Provident quickly went out of business, but only after it tried to fend off railway workers' claims through what one observer called "litigation of the most pettifogging description."[11]

Accident insurance policies also typically disclaimed coverage for accidents caused by "voluntary exposure to unnecessary danger,"[12] "the influence of intoxicating drinks,"[13] the violation of any laws,[14] voluntary overexertion,[15] the failure to use "due diligence for . . . personal safety,"[16] and countless other specific hazards.[17] Companies required applicants to warrant that they were in good health and in possession of full use of their faculties and that their "habits of life [were] correct and temperate."[18] As a result of such policy exclusions, commercial accident policies covered only a small portion of the accidents that caused individuals to seek disability insurance in the first place. Moreover, their policy terms reproduced much of the doctrine of contributory negligence that seemed to be weighing down the still-developing common law of torts. Even then, accident insurance companies faced enormous problems of policing "fraudulent and fictitious claims."[19] Indeed, such problems led to a kind of macabre humor among insurance company executives. Samuel Clemens (better known as Mark Twain), who served as a director of the Hartford Accident Insurance Company in the 1870s, suggested darkly in one insurance convention after-dinner speech that an insurance company such as the Hartford was "an institution which is peculiarly to be depended on. . . . No man can take out a policy in it and not get crippled before the year is out." Sure enough, the Hartford failed later that year.[20]

Commercial insurance companies did develop at least one insurance product for working-class families. So-called industrial insurance consisted of small life insurance policies paid for by weekly premiums of as little as five cents, collected by insurance agents who went door to door on payday. Though the Prudential Assurance Company had offered industrial policies in England since 1854, the first company to offer them in the United States, the Prudential Insurance Company of America (then the Prudential Friendly Society), began writing policies only in 1875.[21] The Metropolitan Life Insurance Company and the John Hancock Mutual Life Insurance Company soon joined the field, and in the last decades of the nineteenth century industrial insurance grew at a rapid pace. In 1880 there was approximately $20 million of industrial insurance in force in the United States, representing 228,357 policies, or one policy for every 217 Americans. By 1900 there was almost $1.5 billion in force, representing approximately 11 million policies, or one policy for every seven Americans.[22]

Industrial insurance policies, however, were purchased by working families not so much to replace earnings or to sustain a family after the death of a wage earner as to pay for the costs of burial. The average industrial insurance policy provided families with no more than enough to pay for funeral costs, typically "about $100 for adults and $50 for children"[23]—an amount hardly sufficient to sustain the families of deceased wage-earners. As one early-twentieth-century student of urban working-class families observed, industrial insurance was "more properly described as burial-insurance than as life-insurance."[24] Families thus purchased policies not just for wage earners, but also for wives who worked in the home, as well as for children. Indeed, by the early twentieth century, women outnumbered men among industrial policyholders. Children under five, moreover, represented the single largest age cohort.[25] Industrial insurance, then, functioned only as an insurance policy against a narrow subset of the costs of deaths from accident, sickness, or old age.

Cooperative workingmen's insurance associations developed and flourished where other forms of insurance in the late nineteenth century struggled. This success was due, at least in part, to the remarkable methods that cooperatives developed to address the perennial moral hazard and adverse selection problems of disability insurance markets. Moral hazard describes the reduced incentives for prevention and for speedy recovery created for insureds by the fact of insurance that reduces the cost of insured events and disability. Adverse selection is the tendency for high-risk individuals to seek out insurance pools, and for low-risk individuals to flee insurance pools, at least when those pools are insufficiently subcategorized such that low-risk insureds pay more than their share of the total risk.[26] In disability and accident insurance, it is especially difficult to determine when an insurable event has occurred (thus exacerbating moral hazard problems) and to distinguish between low-risk and high-risk insureds (thus exacerbating adverse selection problems). Cooperatives were organized in ways that helped to minimize these difficulties. Local cooperative associations with face-to-face relations among their members were well situated to forge norms of solidarity and to monitor members' behavior.

Trade unions formed one important source of workingmen's cooperative insurance against death and disability. Unions had long engaged in relatively informal methods of mutual benefit, ranging from a simple passing of the hat in the event of the death or disability of a member, to the somewhat more formal "keg funds" among coal miners, financed through the sale of empty powder kegs. But when German economist August Sartorius von Waltershausen toured the United States in the mid-1880s, he observed that many American labor leaders had begun to use more systematic union benefit funds to bolster members' loyalty to the trade union system after the sharp decreases in membership that accompanied the recession of the 1870s.[27] Trade union funds were especially well positioned to provide disability insurance. Union locals fostered commitment and loyalty among their members, and the intimacy of members' face-to-face relationships allowed them to monitor one another's claims. Membership in such union funds was compulsory for all union members.[28] Moreover, the few union benefit plans that became widespread in the latter part of the century included benefit disclaimers for injuries arising out of immoral or unnecessarily dangerous activities. Union benefit plans also implemented formal visiting committees, whose role was both to reaffirm bonds of reciprocity and sympathy, and to monitor the condition of disabled members. Typically, a union appointed a committee of at least two members to visit a disabled fellow member; no two members of the committee were to visit at the same time, and each member was to report independently to the union on the disabled member's condition.[29]

As Waltershausen noted, however, trade union benefit funds in the United States on the whole had not had great success. In deciding whether to adopt insurance functions, trade unions faced a difficult dilemma. Relief funds could encourage loyalty to the union in tough times, but they also raised the cost of trade union membership.[30] Furthermore, effective administration of the trade union insurance funds required the expulsion of members who failed to pay their insurance dues. Unions' interest in broadening their organizational base thus inhibited the widespread development of accident relief funds in the late nineteenth century. By 1860, it became conventional wisdom among trade union leaders that unions should not attempt to develop insurance functions because of the attendant drag on union membership.[31] Thus, prior to the 1880s, only a few national trade unions outside the railway brotherhoods established insurance funds to replace lost wages in the event of disability or death.[32] The Knights of Labor, for example, included a mutual insurance program in their constitution but never implemented it. And labor leaders like Eugene Debs argued that unions "should be divorced from an insurance company, as thousands of men are expelled because they cannot maintain that branch of the order." Even by 1904, less than a quarter of American Federation of Labor trades unions offered such benefits.[33]

Railroad worker labor unions, by contrast, frequently made insurance against accidental death and disability central to their operation. Early railway brotherhoods were organized precisely to create accident insurance protections among men in high-risk railroad occupations. The Brotherhood of Locomotive Firemen, later led by Debs, formed in the early 1870s not as a collective bargaining organization, but as a fraternal mutual insurance society, as did the Order of Railway Conductors; indeed, Debs eventually quit the Locomotive Firemen because of their continued focus on insurance functions rather than organizing. Other railroad unions, such as the Brotherhood of Locomotive Engineers, began as collective bargaining organizations but shifted in the 1870s to become primarily mutual aid societies, offering accident, death benefit, and burial insurance.[34] As one leading student of the railway benefit funds observed, accident risk in railroad employment resulted from at least three sources: "the nature of the trade, the negligence of a fellow workman, or the negligence of the employers."[35] Under the common law of employers' liability, however, compensation was available at law only in the third class of accidents. The railway employee was therefore required to make provisions on his own against all other kinds of accidents, and railway brotherhoods became the leading mechanism for self-insurance against such accidents.[36]

The railway brotherhoods offered their members significant life insurance benefits, as well as sizeable permanent disability benefits. Typical railway brotherhood death benefits ranged from $1,000 to $3,000 and often reached as high as $4,500.[37] The brotherhoods paid permanent total disability benefits in similar amounts, usually in place of death benefits, and also provided significant permanent partial and temporary disability benefits.[38] The Brotherhood of Railroad Trainmen, for example, in the 1880s provided members injured while in the discharge of their duties with temporary disability payments of $1.07 per day for up to forty days.[39] In 1893 the railway brotherhoods even set up a Home for the Aged and Disabled Railroad Employees of America in Highland Park, Illinois, "to aid such who, by accident or from other causes, are permanently incapacitated for railroad work."[40]

Through the first decade of the twentieth century, brotherhood beneficiary departments were principally concerned with compensating victims of work accidents. In the Switchmen's Union of North America in 1901, for example, work-accident claims outnumbered all other claims by more than two to one. Over time, railroad brotherhood benefit associations would provide increasingly large shares of their benefits to members whose disability or death was not caused by a work accident; by 1914, the Switchmen's Union was granting benefits more frequently to sick members or to the families of members who died from natural causes than to members injured or killed in work accidents. But as the claims books of the brotherhoods testify, the late-nineteenth- and early-twentieth-century railroad brotherhood beneficiary departments witnessed an extraordinary onslaught of heartrending crushings, amputations, and deaths that far outpaced any other source of disability and death, especially among the men who worked on the tracks, between the cars, and in the yards (see Figure 3.2). Moreover, railway benefit associations quickly developed internal bureaucratic machinery to process the cascades of claims forwarded by their memberships. Local lodges of the Switchmen's Union, for example, forwarded claims by injured members to the central office in Buffalo, where a five-man beneficiary board determined

Figure 3.2 Switchmen's Union of North America, Claims Deptartment, 1901–1908, Claims 13–24

Wm. P. Lee	Run over by car	Sarah E., wife, Chgo, Ill.
Wm. H. Rogers	Run over by car	Floe, wife, Ft. Scott, Ks.
J. C. Galbraugh	Run over by train	E. E. Anderson, half-bro., Memphis, Tenn.
Joe E. Howell	Natural cause	Maggie, wife, Chgo, Ill.
Wm. Combs	Fractured skull	Sarah, wife, Hoboken, N.J.
James Taylor	Railroad accident	Mary, wife, Philadelphia
Wm. H. White	Run over by engine	Anna, wife, Louisville, Ky.
Henry Shenck	Amputation of leg	Clifford, son, Elmira, N.Y.
L. C. Hawk	Railroad accident	Jesse M., son, Colo. City, Colo.
J. P. Mullarky	Railroad accident	Hattie, wife, Conneaut, O.
Jno. H. Rimbey	Railroad accident	Angelina, wife, E. Mauch Chunk, Pa.
Mark Withers	Railroad accident	Margaret, wife, Topeka, Ks.

Source: Claims Department Record Books, Switchmen's Union of North America Papers, book 1, box 269, Kheel Center, Cornell University.

whether to grant or reject the claims. While resort to the common law courts could require a plaintiff to wait years to collect on a judgment, the brotherhoods typically were able to process a claim and make a payment within two to three months of the date of the injury.[41]

By the middle of the first decade of the twentieth century, the leading railway brotherhoods had a combined membership of more than a quarter million, representing as many as one in four railroad workers.[42] The seven great railway brotherhoods—the Brotherhood of Locomotive Firemen, the Grand Brotherhood of Locomotive Engineers, the Order of Railway Conductors of America, the Switchmen's Union of North America, the Brotherhood of Railway Trainmen, the Order of Railway Telegraphers, and the International Brotherhood of Maintenance-of-Way Employees[43]—distributed more than $4 million in death benefits each year to their memberships, as well as over one-half million dollars in permanent disability benefits.[44]

Outside the railroad brotherhoods, American workingmen needed a life and disability insurance mechanism that took advantage of the trade union's singular capacity to police for moral hazard and adverse selection but was institutionally distinct from trade unions so as not to create tensions between organizing and insuring. Cooperative insurance societies provided just such a system of insurance. Even though American cooperative insurance associations emerged only after the Civil War, in a short twenty years cooperative life and disability insurance rivaled commercial life insurance in size. By 1885 the almost $2 billion of insurance in force that cooperative associations reported to state insurance officials represented just under half of all life insurance in force in the United States (see Table 3.1).[45] Five years later, the quickly grow-

Table 3.1 Insurance in force in the United States, 1875–1910

Year	Cooperatives		Commercial life companies	
	Certificates	Amount (millions of nonindexed dollars)	Policies	Amount (millions of nonindexed dollars)
1875	—	—	774,625	$1,922
1880	—	—	608,681	1,476
1885	—	$1,969	814,691	2,024
1890	—	3,659	1,272,895	3,543
1895	—	6,589	1,877,808	4,818
1900	4,111,848	7,580	3,071,253	6,947
1905	6,118,938	10,412	5,306,101	10,554
1910	8,558,093	12,394	6,050,617	11,670

Source: J. Owen Stalson, *Marketing Life Insurance* 806 (1942). Stalson estimates that his figures underreport the total fraternal insurance in force by at least 20 percent. The chart above reflects Stalson's figures adjusted by his 20 percent estimate. Stalson divides cooperative insurance enterprises into "fraternal societies," which made up the overwhelming share of the cooperative insurance in force throughout the period, and "assessment societies," which represented roughly one-tenth of the cooperative life insurance market. For the assessment societies, Stalson's statistics begin only in 1899.

ing cooperative insurance movement had become the leading source of life insurance in the United States. By 1895 fraternal and other cooperative insurance associations reported $6.6 billion of life insurance in force, an amount substantially greater than the total life insurance in force through commercial companies—mutual and stock companies combined.[46] Throughout this period, moreover, the number of persons insured through cooperative insurance associations appears to have exceeded the number of persons insured by commercial life companies. By 1900, fraternal and cooperative societies reported over 4 million certificate holders, compared to just over 3 million policyholders in commercial companies.[47] Cooperative insurance data reported to state insurance commissioners indicated that one in fifteen Americans belonged to a cooperative insurance society,[48] and over the next ten years, the number of fraternal certificate holders doubled to well over 8 million.[49]

Yet the reported statistics likely underestimated the total number of Americans who participated in cooperative insurance associations. Reported statistics generally reflected the activities of the large, national insurance cooperatives. But many cooperatives were organized informally on a local basis. By the mid-1890s, it was common among insurance experts to estimate that the "immense" cooperative insurance system was as much as twice the size of its commercial competition.[50] Moreover, careful studies at the state level revealed that actual membership levels (including the smaller, local associations) were larger still. In Connecticut, for example, a study published in 1891 by the state Bureau of Labor Statistics found that more than one in six residents of the state belonged to a cooperative insurance society.[51] Given that the membership in these societies was virtually all male,[52] it seems fair to say that perhaps one-half of the adult men in Connecticut belonged to an insurance association.[53] Among the residents of towns and cities, the figures appear to have been even higher. In New Haven, one in four residents belonged to a cooperative insurance association; in Danbury, the famous hat-making town, and in Meriden, a small industrial city on the Connecticut River, cooperative insurance association membership was closer to one in three.[54]

Cooperative associations provided a wide range of benefit levels. Many of the small, local mutual insurance societies could offer only minimal life insurance benefits and little in the way of disability benefits. As we shall see, the inability of many associations—especially those of immigrant workers—to provide substantial insurance to their members contributed to the decline of the cooperative insurance movement in the first decade of the twentieth century. The more successful national cooperative associations, however, were able to offer their members disability and life insurance benefits that, although not exactly generous, provided meaningful income replacement in the event of the death or disability of a wage earner.

National associations were nominally divided into two kinds of organizations: sick and disability societies on the model of the English friendly societies, and life insurance associations. The former—whose ranks included such organizations as the Independent Order of Odd Fellows, the Knights of Pythias, and the Improved Order of Red Men—focused not on life insurance funds, but rather on cash sickness and disability benefits, which often ranged from $2 to $5 per week; the Odd Fellows, for example, provided temporary disability payments of at least $2 per week.[55] The latter, including such groups as Upchurch's United Workmen, the Royal Arcanum, and the Knights of Honor, concentrated at the national level on life insurance benefits, which typically ranged from $1,000 to $2,000, often along with lump-sum permanent disability benefits of one-half the life insurance benefit.[56] In an era when typical workingmen earned roughly $10 per week, such benefits represented somewhere between one-fifth and one-half of weekly wages for temporary disability benefits, and between two and four years of wages for life insurance benefits.[57]

Each type of insurance society, however, often offered both cash disability and death benefits. Disability associations adopted life insurance benefits, or contracted with third party insurers offering group policies.[58] Life insurance association members, by the same token, often organized temporary disability benefit systems at the local lodge level, frequently ranging from $2 to $5 per week.[59] Alternatively, life insurance associations allowed members to draw cash disability benefits against their insurance policies.[60] Thus state and federal surveys found that while some life insurance associations provided only death and funeral benefits, most offered disability benefits as well.[61] Indeed, the number of insurance associations offering disability benefits grew steadily through the 1870s and 1880s, significantly outpacing the growth in pure life insurance associations.[62]

Unlike the railroad brotherhoods, many workingmen's cooperative insurance associations were not organized specifically around the industrial-accident problem. Indeed, some elite cooperative insurers even sought to follow the lead of the commercial insurers and exclude workingmen in especially dangerous occupations.[63] Yet a number of cooperative insurance associations were formed precisely for accident-compensation purposes. Coal miners, for example, formed a bewildering array of fraternal organizations, often including dozens of different associations in even small mining towns, frequently organized along ethnic and religious lines, with different associations for Italians, Slovaks, Greeks, Russians, and blacks.[64] But such organizations were not limited to the coal mines. As the members of one New Haven association of bricklayers announced in 1868, workingmen founded cooperative insurance societies to protect members who became "disabled by reason of accident, at [their] own employment, not caused by [their own] immoral or disorderly conduct."[65]

Indeed, the problem of upholding the independence of the workingman in the face of the onslaught of industrial injuries led prominent labor union leaders to establish cooperative accident-insurance associations. George E. McNeill led the American eight-hour workday movement from the 1860s into the 1880s, first as secretary of the Grand Eight-Hour League and then as president of the Workingmen's Institute and the Boston Eight-Hour League.[66] In 1883 he joined the Knights of Labor, and throughout the 1890s he maintained close ties to the American Federation of Labor.[67] Into the first decade of the new century, McNeill remained an important participant at cooperative movement conventions.[68] In McNeill's view, the wage labor system usurped the independence of the free laborer and transformed him into "a man without the rights of manhood." Moreover, McNeill believed that the accident problem among wage laborers was the most glaring instance of the ill effects of wage labor. Accidents reduced the workingman to a "physically . . . deformed" creature, "ek[ing] out . . . [a] mere pittance" "at the risk of health and limb, and perhaps life." McNeill argued that ultimately only the consolidation of a "Grand Army of Labor" could "lift the laborer to a higher level of manhood."[69] In the meantime the problem of work accidents required the creation of collective worker institutions that could help maintain the independence of workingmen and their families during times of disability. Thus, in 1883 McNeill established the Massachusetts Mutual Accident Association, the primary function of which, as the high proportion of work accidents among the accidents listed in its records reveals, was to provide insurance for men injured at work.[70] Similarly, William E. Owen, a leader in the American Miners' Association and its successor, the Miners' National Association, was an officer in the Knights of Pythias, among several other fraternal orders, in the coal town of Belleville, Missouri in the late 1870s.[71]

Even in the large national cooperative life insurance associations that were not specifically designed around the accident problem, accident-victim compensation represented an important share of the associations' work. National associations, for example, were more likely to offer accident benefits at the national level than sick benefits.[72] And it was precisely those individuals most subject to industrial risks who made up the membership of the cooperative insurance associations. Working-class men in urban or industrial areas constituted the majority of the cooperative insurance societies' membership.[73] Contemporary observers frequently remarked on the working-class, urban, and industrial base of the cooperative benefit societies, whose memberships were composed of "the lower-paid workmen and the well-paid mechanics."[74] Indeed, one Connecticut study found that over 60 percent of mutual insurance society members were made up of lower-class workingmen and mechanics.[75]

Accordingly, cooperative insurance societies adopted disciplinary rules and regulations that were especially well suited to dealing with the moral hazard and adverse selection problems endemic to disability insurance. Cooperative insurance associations universally required medical examinations of prospective members, and virtually all the associations made "[t]horough investigations as to the character of applicants."[76] Members faced expulsion from the associations for making false statements of their age or lying during their medical examinations.[77] Association bylaws typically provided for the forfeiture of members' rights to relief when "disability [was] superinduced by drunkenness or fighting or other disgraceful practices."[78] Many associations also barred the recovery of death or disability benefits by members who had exposed themselves to "unusual danger." Once a member filed a claim, his fellow members were usually under an obligation to visit and monitor his progress. In many instances, no doubt, members undertook such visits in the spirit of fraternal good will. But it is apparent that visitation requirements also served to identify "suspicious cases." Members claiming benefits faced expulsion and denial of their claims for "evad[ing] supervision by the society," and visiting committees were obligated to report any irregularities promptly to their association's treasurer.[79] Delinquency in the payment of assessments or fines for violations of an order's code of behavior—including, in some societies, an injunction against working for less than specified rates in particular trades—could also result in forfeiture of benefits.[80]

Cooperative insurance societies designed their insurance pools to foster group loyalty and mutuality. National associations such as the Ancient Order of United Workmen were organized around local lodges that typically ranged from 50 to 150 members.[81] The national scale of the pool promoted actuarial stability for the life insurance side of the associations, while the local lodges (which often financed temporary disability benefits on their own) helped to establish norms of social solidarity among the members and maintained local supervision and monitoring over the more difficult to administer disability benefit side. Many of the most important cooperatives thus adopted the traditional rituals of such venerable fraternal organizations as the Masons and the Odd Fellows. Secret handshakes and gestures, unwritten passwords, and mysterious and arcane initiation ceremonies all found their place in the cooperative insurance societies.[82]

Two additional elements of the structure and operation of the cooperatives functioned to foster mutuality and commitment to the society. First, most cooperatives, especially before the mid-1890s, operated on an assessment plan.[83] Members were assessed a fixed amount—often $1—each time the society needed to raise funds in order to pay claims, usually between fifteen and twenty times per year.[84] By operating on an assessment basis, the associations argued, they could avoid the expensive and potentially corrupting practice of creating large reserve funds that characterized the old-line commercial companies.[85] Moreover, the assessment basis served to emphasize the fraternal and reciprocal nature of the beneficiary societies; assessments became not a regular and fixed cost of maintaining one's own insurance account, but rather an irregular obligation linked to fellow members' needs.

Second, members paid equal rates regardless of their age or risk profile.[86] As one fraternalist recalled, "There was no discrimination on account of age or physical condition or occupation. It was true equality and fraternity."[87] Like the assessment plan, the use of equal rates rather than risk-adjusted rates emphasized the collective spirit of the cooperative insurance project. To be sure, equal assessment rates effectively required young, low-risk members to subsidize high-risk (often older) members and thus created an adverse selection risk that low-risk members would stay out of the associations altogether. As we shall see, this adverse selection problem became acute after the turn of the century. But the use of equal rates also created a powerful incentive for members to stay in a given society for long periods. The assessments paid by a young member exceeded his personal cost of insurance; as an older member, however, that same individual would receive the benefit of having newer members share some of the cost of insuring him against the greater risks that accompanied age.

Given the importance of norms of mutuality and reciprocity in the cooperative insurance associations, perhaps it is not surprising that the fraternal ethic generally did not extend across racial or religious lines. Over 97 percent of the societies surveyed in the 1891 Connecticut study required that members be white.[88] Upchurch's United Workmen provided in its constitution that "only white male persons should be eligible to membership" and that "this provision should never be altered, amended, or expunged."[89] Numerous cooperative associations followed the United Workmen's lead and established formal rules of racial exclusion.[90] Black Americans, excluded from white cooperative insurance organizations, established their own cooperative insurance associations, such as the Colored Brotherhood and Sisterhood of Honor in Kentucky and the Colored Consolidated Brotherhood of Atlanta.[91] Although many of the black cooperatives paralleled existing white institutions in structure and even name,[92] black associations were distinct in a number of ways. Black women took a leading role in mutual insurance associations.[93] Moreover, among black Americans, the line between cooperative insurance and commercial insurance enterprises was blurred.[94] Black fraternal organizations such as the Grand United Order of True Reformers in Richmond, the Mutual Aid and Banking Company in New Bern, North Carolina, the Bank of Galilean Fishermen in Hampton, Virginia, and the Sons and Daughters of Peace in Newport News operated insurance programs that were described, in the case of the True Reformers, as the "Gibraltar of Negro Business."[95] In Florida the Afro-American Industrial Benefit Association evolved into the Afro-American Life Insurance Company.[96] The two largest black life insurance companies—the North Carolina Mutual Life Insurance Company and Atlanta Life Insurance—began as humble affairs, but by the first decade of the twentieth century, they had emerged as institutions of the first rank in southern black life.[97] Nor did black self-insurance societies appear exclusively in the South. Even before the great twentieth-century migration of blacks to northern cities, urban blacks in cities like Philadelphia established mutual beneficiary associations to provide for collective self-insurance.[98]

Catholics (barred by their own church from joining non-Catholic secret or fraternal associations) founded a number of separate insurance associations, including the Knights of Columbus, established in 1882 in New Haven, and the Catholic Order of Foresters, formed in Chicago in 1883.[99] The same period witnessed the formation of separate Jewish beneficiary societies in New York and elsewhere, as well as societies organized among Eastern Orthodox Christians.[100]

If combating the moral hazard and adverse selection problems in disability insurance markets were all that cooperative insurance was about, American disability insurance might have taken any number of different forms.

We might have seen a greater number of associations organized specifically around particular religious identities or beliefs, for example, rather than merely organizations with religious exclusions. Or perhaps we might have seen intensely nationalist associations. The cooperative insurance associations, however, adopted an approach to disability benefits that drew heavily on free labor ideology and its ideals of independence, fraternity, equality, and manliness. Indeed, in part the success of the cooperatives reflected their attempt to preserve and reestablish midcentury free labor ideals in a rapidly changing economy. And yet, the precise content of those ideals was hotly contested. Even within the cooperative insurance movement itself, two competing accounts of cooperation vied for the meaning of the movement. The first account—called here the "thin" theory of cooperation—bore a number of close similarities to the classical liberalism of the law of torts. On this view, cooperation was a process by which rational, self-interested individuals could assume new levels of self-control and responsibility. By contrast, according to a second account—the "thick" theory of cooperation—the cooperative insurance movement was not merely a process for the pursuit of individual interests, but rather one strand of the late-nineteenth-century movement that sought to transform the competitive wage labor system into a "cooperative commonwealth." From this second perspective, the industrial-accident problem was a stark exemplar of the crippling effects of wage labor on the nation's workingmen, effects that warranted a thorough reorganization of economic production in the industrial age.[101]

Elizur Wright, Massachusetts's first insurance commissioner, best captured the thin strand of the post–Civil War insurance movement. Born in 1804 into a Congregationalist family in Litchfield County, Connecticut, Wright grew up in the heady antebellum world of New England evangelical reform.[102] Like many pre–Civil War American reformers in the evangelical Protestant tradition, Wright believed deeply in human perfectibility, in the human capacity for "direct communion to God through conscience," and in the responsibility of each individual for his own moral choices. As Wright's correspondent and friend Theodore Weld put it, God had "committed to every moral agent the privilege, the right and the responsibility of personal ownership."[103] From such beliefs, Wright developed a strong opposition to alcohol and tobacco use. Moreover, in the 1830s he became a leading immediatist in the American abolitionist movement. A close associate of leading abolitionists such as Lewis Tappan and William Lloyd Garrison, Wright served as secretary of the American Anti-Slavery Society from 1833 to 1839.[104] Yet more so than some of his fellow abolitionists, Wright tempered his ideas about human perfectibility with concern for the persistence of tragedy in human life. "Men," Wright wrote to Garrison, "are not completely freed from sin by the grace of God."[105] And indeed, Wright was no stranger to tragedy. Five of Wright's children died in the 1830s, and in 1846 his house in Boston burned to the ground, almost taking his wife and remaining children with it. By 1839, Wright's hesitation to accept the strongest interpretations of human perfectibility led him to break with Garrison over the latter's increasingly radical platform of equality for women and the abolition of all forms of human government.[106]

Wright's less antinomian conception of human beings' capacity for self-responsibility led him in the 1840s and 1850s to become involved in the still-fledgling life insurance industry.[107] In 1858, Wright was named insurance commissioner for Massachusetts, a position he held until 1867.[108] During these years, as well as in his subsequent career as an independent insurance expert, Wright came increasingly to believe that life insurance offered the best means by which men could continue to assume responsibility for themselves, even in the face of the contingencies of modern life. Life insurance, he argued, solved "the great problem—how to secure independence by means of general dependence."[109] Many of Wright's contemporaries in the 1840s viewed life insurance as little more than a lottery; indeed, before 1800, life insurance had been seen as little more than a way of betting on lives.[110] But Wright saw that insurance on lives offered the opportunity to realize "fraternity without the destruction of independence and individuality."[111] Moreover, life insurance offered a way to adapt the ideal of moral responsibility for one's own actions to modern conditions without coercively disrupting the fabric of economic and social life. Life insurance and other mechanisms of prudence, thrift, and individual responsibility, Wright believed, could make trade unions entirely unnecessary.[112] Indeed, until his death in 1885, Wright argued that if American workingmen would insure against contingency and follow the teachings of the antebellum temperance advocates, they would be able to rise above the poverty of urban and industrial life.[113]

The thin theory of life insurance as a mechanism for the achievement of personal moral responsibility was held widely among officials in state bureaus of labor statistics, who argued that cooperative insurance societies taught citizens the virtues of self-reliance—"the wisdom of thrift, the independence of self-help, and the pride of self-government."[114] Similarly, many cooperative association members viewed insurance as a voluntarist mechanism for accommodating the individual to the dilemmas of industrial life. From this perspective, insurance allowed individuals to solve the social problems that otherwise might cause an unwarranted expansion of the functions of the state. "We are not of the opinion that insurance forms any of the functions of government any more than the sale of groceries and dry goods," announced the *Fraternal Monitor* in 1891. "Governmental insurance, whether voluntary or compulsory, can never be made a success even under monarchical forms of government."[115]

The thick theory of cooperative insurance, by contrast, offered very different ideas about the meaning of cooperation and very different lessons for the meaning of the accident crisis. Wage labor—as organizations and individuals as diverse as the Knights of Labor, the agrarian farmers' alliances, and reformers such as Edward Bellamy and Henry George contended—increasingly threatened to undermine the independence of the American workingman. Cooperation, by contrast, offered a model of production that might preserve the dignity of the workingman and restore to him a fair return on his productive capacities. An outpouring of radical labor pamphlets decried the "degrading" and "monarchial"[116] social economy by which capitalist wage labor "rob[bed]"[117] the producing classes of what was rightly theirs. In contrast, the promise of what labor radicals variously called an "American co-operative labor social economy,"[118] an "[e]conomy of [c]ooperation,"[119] or "universal co-operation"[120] was that it might ensure the workingman an equitable share of the wealth he created.[121]

For these cooperationists, the law of employers' liability for industrial accidents exemplified the inequitable distribution of the profits of enterprise. If labor was the source of value in the production process, the competitive capitalist economy stripped the workingman of his rightful share of the returns on production yet left him to bear the increasingly grave risks of personal injury and death. It was a "scandal," labor leader George E. McNeill argued, that "a man is pensioned for wounds" received in warfare, "but must be pauperized when receiving injuries in the peaceful pursuits of life."[122] In industrial workplaces, McNeill observed, "[t]he slaughter continues" without the fanfare given to lives destroyed on the battlefield.[123]

And yet organized protest against the law of employers' liability appears to have been relatively rare among American workingmen into the late 1860s.[124] In 1868, the National Labor Union added a call for liability reform to its political platform.[125] By the 1880s, employers' liability law reform appeared regularly as a legislative goal of workers' organizations, alongside maximum hours laws, land reform, and repeal of the law of labor conspiracies.[126] Similar liability reforms became important in the legislative agenda of the railway brotherhoods.[127] Even then, however, labor unions in the late nineteenth century rarely made workplace safety or employer compensation of injured workers central issues in collective bargaining with employers.[128]

At least in part, the strange silence in certain quarters of the labor movement stemmed from the ambiguous position in which nineteenth-century workingmen's organizations found themselves with respect to the issue of employers' liability. A core mission of the workingmen's organizations was to defend workers' discretion and independence in the processes of production. In many cases, labor organizations experienced considerable success in maintaining workers' discretion and independence from managerial domination. Well into the late nineteenth century, American firms were characterized by a rich diversity of organizational styles, including specialized manufacturing; so-called inside contracting, under which a small group of employees contracted with the firm owner to provide finished goods, and then directed the work processes themselves; and foreman-dominated driving systems, which often were so clumsy as effectively to allow significant de facto worker control over production. By the end of the nineteenth century, however, sophisticated employers were reorganizing production—workingmen's efforts to the contrary notwithstanding—around more systematic mechanisms of managerial control.[129]

The difficulty with employers' liability reform was that it seemed to require that workers become complicit in employers' attempts to strip them of discretion and autonomy in the production process. Arguments for expanded liability rules paradoxically required that workingmen's organizations challenge the assumption articulated in the common law of employer's liability (often an erroneous assumption, to be sure) that workers controlled the details of the production process. It was this claim, after all, that underlay the notions that workers were better positioned than employers to avoid work accidents, and that workers should therefore bear the risk of accidents themselves. Employers' liability reform, then, oddly seemed to require that workers redescribe the workplace not as worker-controlled but as manager-controlled. Yet of course this was precisely what late-nineteenth-century workingmen's organizations (embroiled in a battle over the control of the workplace) did not want to say. To do so was to accept employers' terms in a hotly contested debate over who properly exercised power over the conditions and processes of production, and thereby (in ways that Italian theorist of ideology Antonio Gramsci would have recognized) tacitly to legitimate employers' increasingly sweeping claims of managerial prerogative in the firm.[130]

Protest against the political economy of the law of employers' liability, then, emerged not just in organized political lobbying for liability rule reform or in collective bargaining over safety conditions, but also in the interplay between the cooperative insurance societies and the cooperative commonwealth movement more generally. Labor leaders such as George McNeill and William E. Owen took up important places in workingmen's cooperative insurance funds.[131] And for men such as McNeill and Owen, as for many of the supporters of a cooperative political economy, cooperative insurance associations represented one wing—in fact, the most successful and widespread wing—of a broader movement for cooperative economic institutions.[132] The insurance certificate would replace proprietorship (at least temporarily) as the embodiment of free labor independence. Where once the self-owning wage laborer had been able to rise to the level of master craftsman or independent proprietor with at least a small real property holding, now the insurance policy against death and disability would allow the self-owning workingman to invest in the value of his self-ownership to protect against the consequences of injury. The workers' body itself would form the new property on which independence could be established. As some cooperationists believed, the insurance societies would serve as an entry wedge for the cooperative movement more generally; in the fraternal insurance associations, cooperative members would learn the habits of cooperation and its benefits.[133] For others, cooperative insurance societies represented a way-station that would provide benefits to the "casualties" of industrial capitalism during the interval before the cooperative economy established itself.[134]

In at least a few instances, workingmen's insurance cooperatives were supported by a sophisticated theoretical foundation. As the editors of the German-language labor newspaper *New-Yorker Gewerkschafts-Zeitung* observed, Marx contended that wages equaled the subsistence cost of reproducing the workforce. Such subsistence costs, however, were socially constructed, and thus wages "depend[ed] on the needs, habits, and expectations of a country's workers."[135] Over time, the editors argued, payments into a mutual benefit fund would heighten workers' expectations, which in turn (on Marx's theory) would result in higher wages. At the very least (and here the *Gewerkschafts-Zeitung* found widespread agreement among workingmen's organizations), the increased solidarity among workingmen that might be fostered by such cooperative funds would increase the union's bargaining power and thus increase wages.[136] Workingmen's organizations, in other words, could effectively contract around the law of torts by requiring their employers to compensate them in wages for the risks they took on the job. "So it is already in our power," the editors concluded (too optimistically, no doubt), "to make the employers financially liable for the care of their victims."[137]

The collectivist structure of the cooperative self-insurance societies even gave voice to calls for a thoroughgoing cooperative reconstruction of American society as a "cooperative commonwealth." In 1894, Nathan S. Boynton, president of the National Fraternal Conference, envisioned reconstructing the American economy as a producers' commonwealth. "If the national fraternal beneficiary societies can successfully combine," Boynton asked, "why cannot the labor organizations of the country absorb, manage, and direct the wealth they produce and keep it out of the pockets of the non-producers, the

Goulds and Vanderbilts?" Indeed, through "co-operation," Boynton contended, America's producing classes would soon be able

> to own, control, and manage the railroads, the mines, the printing offices, and all of our manufacturing enterprises, without any strike, contention or paralysis of business just as the great fraternal beneficiary system has secured control of a vast business, representing four billions of dollars, and is successfully controlling and managing it without any conflict with capital, and without a single strike, boycott, or lockout.
>
> In no other way, in my opinion, will the contention between labor and capital ever be settled. . . . It is only a matter of time in my opinion when it will be successfully carried out.[138]

Like Boynton, Abb Landis (a cooperative insurance advocate from Nashville) argued that the success of the cooperative insurance movement was a harbinger of the cooperative economy to come. "No thoughtful observer can regard our present industrial régime as final," he wrote just after the turn of the century. According to Landis, the "remittent warfare between capital and labor" showed that the existing economic system was "obviously a temporary condition." Cooperative insurance societies, however, demonstrated that the "capitalist and labor may be combined in the same person, and that great industries may be competently managed by officers elected by the whole body of the workers." "Why is it not possible," Landis asked, "to extend this principle of mutual cooperation and entirely eliminate the capitalist and forever be rid of his exploitation of labor with its attendants of friction and ferment?"[139] In the place of trusts, bankers, and dividends to stockholders, Landis, like Boynton, envisioned an economic structure that rewarded labor in proportion to its equitable share of inputs in the productive process.

Ideological conflict in cooperative workingmen's insurance resulted in part from the need to adapt the cooperatives' ideological commitments to the realities of running a going concern. As one cooperative organ observed, cooperatives needed always to attend to the "two sides" of cooperation, "the business side, and . . . the social and educational side."[140] The business side of the insurance associations, however, required that they make difficult decisions that limited their ability to provide for the neediest members of the community.

From the beginning, cooperative insurance societies had excluded many of the most vulnerable segments of the community. Physicians conducting medical screenings asked prospective members about their families' medical histories, as well as their own; a parent's death from consumption might be enough to exclude a would-be member.[141] The standard medical examination form of the Royal Arcanum required prospective applicants to list all physicians with knowledge of their physical condition and required the applicants to waive any doctor–patient privilege that might attach to medical information about the applicant or render a physician incompetent to testify against the applicant in court.[142] Although such medical screenings made good actuarial and business sense, in practice they limited to the healthiest members of the community the scope of the associations' benevolence and fraternity.

The exclusion of high-risk members from cooperative self-insurance societies highlighted the cooperatives' need to maintain a steady influx of young, low-risk members. Most commercial life insurance mechanisms in the late nineteenth century employed a system of building reserves while policyholders were young, charging higher premiums as policyholders aged, or reducing benefit levels for aging policyholders.[143] But in the name of fraternal ties among members, the American cooperative societies adopted an assessment system of equal rates and equal benefits for members of all ages. As a result, young (typically low-risk) members effectively subsidized the insurance of older (typically high-risk) members. Such a system could work, as insurance experts at the turn of century observed, but it required that each society have a stream of new young members able to pay for the insurance of aging members.[144] In the caustic words of one insurance expert, for the cooperative insurers to succeed without robbing the final generation of new members of their assessment payments, they would need to "continu[e] business to the end of the world, always increasing in numbers."[145]

Cooperative insurance societies also worried about the flight of low-risk members once they joined.[146] A younger member could significantly reduce the cost of his insurance by leaving a society burdened with a relatively large number of older, high-risk members. Indeed, when the cooperative associations began to mature in the late 1870s and early 1880s, the number of new cooperative insurance associations grew sharply as low-risk members of existing societies splintered off into new, lower-cost associations. One student of insurance associations estimated that by 1888 there were as many as 1,200 American insurance societies.[147] The creation of new cooperatives accelerated in the 1890s. As one turn-of-the-century study found, of 568 societies whose founding dates could be ascertained, only 78 had been founded before 1880; far and away the largest cohort—some 230 societies—had been founded in the five years after 1895.[148] While new societies sprang up, older societies died off in high numbers. Between 1881 and 1885, 73 cooperative insurance associations failed in New York state alone. A year later, 19 additional cooperative insurance societies went out of business. With each succeeding year more failures arrived: 17 in 1887; 10 in 1888; 16 in 1889. By 1905 several hundred associations either had ceased reporting to the state superintendent of insurance or had been officially placed in receivership.[149] The cooperative insurance movement, in short, was unraveling, as low-risk members fled in repeated cycles of risk cascades from one risk pool to the next.

Moreover, by the early twentieth century, developments in the law of insurance contracts made it increasingly difficult for cooperative insurance societies to police moral hazard and adverse selection problems. By the 1880s and 1890s, commercial life insurance companies had become extremely sophisticated in drafting life insurance policies.[150] Courts responded by interpreting insurance contracts *contra proferentem* (against the drafter) in all cases of ambiguity.[151] The ensuing dialectic between courts' interpretive decisions and insurance company lawyers' responses to those decisions placed a premium on sophisticated policy-drafting.[152] Cooperatives rarely had access to the kind of sophisticated counsel that commercial companies used to draft policies. Yet as in cases involving commercial companies, courts applied the doctrine of *contra proferentem* to cooperative policies.[153] Cooperative insurance enterprises thus found themselves caught in the dialectic process of insurance contract writing and judicial interpretation without the legal acumen of the commercial insurers.[154] Cooperatives' policies relied on broad and often vague standards to govern the conduct of associations and their members. Under the doctrine of *contra proferentem,* however, courts effectively insisted on a rule-bound construction of all insurance contracts, interpreting ambiguities against the insurer.[155] Courts also placed restrictions and procedural limitations on the ability of cooperative associations to amend their insurance provisions retroactively against existing members[156] and to expel their members.[157] By the first decade of the twentieth century, courts had thus severely hampered the effectiveness of the cooperatives' capacity to police for moral hazard and adverse selection.

Criticism of the fraternals' financial structure mounted in the 1890s as low-risk members continued to flee and as new associations arose to lure such members away from older societies.[158] The cooperatives responded to such criticism by pointing to lapse rates as the means by which societies could remain solvent while maintaining equal assessment rates and equal benefits for members without regard to age or risk profile. When members left a cooperative insurance association (or "lapsed"), they forfeited the value of their paid-in assessments. The resulting surplus, argued the fraternalists, allowed the cooperative insurance associations to maintain their fiscal solvency over time.[159]

The lapse argument, however, was startlingly unfraternal in its implications. Existing members essentially funded their own benefits by expropriating the paid-in assessments of lapsed and often less fortunate members. Moreover, the lapse imperative opened the floodgates in the 1880s and 1890s for a series of Ponzi-scheme operations in the guise of fraternal insurance associations.[160] These newly dubbed "endowment societies" observed that, because of high lapse rates and the consequent forfeiture of benefits by other members, death benefit insurance associations paid out to certain members significantly more than those members had paid in. For members who stayed in and reaped the benefits of lapsed members' contributions, such associations offered an extraordinary investment opportunity. The difficulty with the standard death benefit of the life and disability insurance associations, however, was that "you ha[d] to die to win." What, reasoned the endowment associations, prevented an association from moving up the payment date? In fact, what prevented an association from accelerating the assessment schedule and accomplishing for live members in five years a result that took the death benefit societies thirty years to accomplish for dead members?[161]

At the outset, endowment benefit organizations such as the Iron Hall promised $1,000 certificates maturing in seven years, at a rate of $2.50 per assessment. Not to be outdone, the Sexennial League promised $1,000 after six years; the Anti-Poverty Association of the Age advertised its ability to reduce the period before maturity on the same $1,000 to five years while guaranteeing sickness, accident, and funeral benefits in the meantime. At the height of the phenomenon, there were fifty-six registered endowment orders in Massachusetts alone, with $12.5 million in contributions from 364,000 members.[162]

Many of these associations were wholly fraudulent Ponzi schemes; others appear to have been the product of misplaced optimism and ignorant management. Usually it was difficult to tell which was which, and in any event the result was always the same. Those who got in early received stupendous returns, and those who came later seldom saw their money again. In 1882 the New York superintendent of insurance warned of "downright frauds" and "wild and delusive schemes." "The pretenses and promises of some of the managers would be grotesque if they were not put forth in a serious way," wrote another insurance superintendent.[163]

The flood of fraudulent and utopian schemes slowed by the mid-1890s as the first wave of five- to seven-year policies came due on which payments could not be made. The Iron Hall went into receivership in New York State in 1892, and two years later Massachusetts banned endowment insurance contracts altogether. Many cooperative insurance associations resisted the lure of the endowment order schemes. But the episode had a permanent impact on the public perception of even the honest cooperative insurance associations. As late as 1911, the New York State department of labor continued to monitor closely local fraternal organizations in immigrant communities to "weed[ ] out" fraud and to protect the "bona fide fraternal societies."[164]

*   *   *

Given that the cooperative insurance associations faced mounting difficulties in the first decade of the twentieth century, how is it that they nevertheless represented a viable path not taken in the development of American accident law? It is, after all, exceedingly difficult to imagine the lodges and fraternal rituals of the cooperatives surviving on a widespread basis through the twentieth century.

The key to understanding the long-term possibilities of the cooperatives is that in other Western nations, mutual insurance associations of one kind or another (as well as a whole host of other private institutions, including employers, unions, and trade associations) played critical roles in the construction of twentieth-century social insurance programs. To this day, such programs have had a profound influence on the structure of accident-compensation law throughout western Europe, Australia, and New Zealand. As a leading comparative study of accident law puts it, "resort to the litigation process" in developed nations outside the United States is "both less necessary and less lucrative than it is in the United States"; American accident law in the twentieth and twenty-first centuries is thus characterized by a relatively high dependence on tort litigation as compared to other developed western nations.[165]

The kinds of social insurance programs that have shaped the accident-law systems of other developed nations were not simply etched on a blank slate. Social insurance systems require an infrastructure, and the need to develop and implement a state bureaucratic apparatus was—and continues to be—a considerable obstacle in the development of novel state systems of insurance. It was here that nineteenth-century mutual associations played their critical role; such institutions as workingmen's insurance organizations provided a ready-made foundation on which state-based social insurance systems could be built.

The best example for comparison to the United States is the case of the English friendly societies. Friendlies shared many of the traits of the American fraternals; like the American cooperative self-insurance system, the friendly societies offered working-class members benefits in the event of accident, sickness, or death, though unlike the American cooperatives, death benefits were usually little more than funeral benefits.[166] And in the English case, the friendly societies transitioned from the nineteenth century into the twentieth century as crucial building blocks for British social insurance programs. The British state had long fostered friendly societies as institutions for the provision of sickness, disability, and old-age benefits. Indeed, late-nineteenth- and early-twentieth-century British social provision policy was centrally concerned with minimizing the role of bureaucratic state apparatus and developing partnerships between voluntary and government institutions.[167] Accordingly, during 1909 and 1910 the friendly societies were transformed into the "approved societies" that formed the foundation of Britain's national health insurance system, enacted in the 1911 National Insurance Act. The act provided cash sickness, disability, and maternity benefits, as well as medical care benefits, to wage-earners belonging to an "approved society," which was to be a not-for-profit association governed by its membership.[168] Employers and employees made mandatory contributions, which were supplemented by a government contribution and paid over to the approved society. The society, in turn, provided cash disability, sickness, and maternity payments to its members.[169] Commercial insurance companies, it should be noted, quickly established nominally separate nonprofit societies (the better to promote their burial insurance policies) that captured a significant share of approved society membership. Nonetheless, the British health insurance system provided the friendlies with a significant institutional role well into the twentieth century. By the late 1930s, friendlies still enrolled 43 percent of insured British wage earners, and it was only after World War II that the reorganization of the British welfare state eliminated the friendly societies' role in administering benefits.[170]

Britain was hardly alone in the use of preexisting mechanisms of workingmen's insurance as a tool in the invention of modern social insurance institutions. In Germany, systems of social insurance emerged out of a welter of workingmen's and employers' insurance institutions. German compulsory accident insurance, for example, which was proposed by Bismarck as the first of his 1880s social insurance programs, was under Bismarck's plan to be administered through a centralized bureaucracy; as ultimately enacted in 1884, however, German compulsory accident insurance operated through groups of employers' associations.[171] Other nations on the Continent developed an array of public–private partnerships to provide social insurance benefits for working-class populations; Denmark, France, Belgium, and Switzerland each subsidized the provision of health insurance to wage-earning families through local insurance societies and mutual aid organizations.[172]

Why, then, didn't the U.S. cooperatives go the way of their English and Continental counterparts? Why didn't American insurance societies become building blocks in the construction of an American system of social provision? Such a system would have fundamentally redirected the way in which the United States deals with the problems of disability compensation; as noted above, the existence of state disability benefits has had a strong influence on limiting the extent to which western European accident-law systems rely on tort litigation. In addition, such a system would have provided a continuing legacy for the cooperative commonwealth impulse of the nineteenth-century insurance movement—not in the sense of cooperative ownership over the means of production, to be sure, but in the perhaps less radical sense of organizing the collectivity to provide social insurance protections for those unable to participate in the wage-earning structure of industrial society. Moreover, some contemporaries believed that the American cooperatives might follow the lead of European cooperative insurance systems. As late as 1908, students of workingmen's insurance in the United States thought that "co-operative insurance" had "laid a foundation for future state universal insurance," and that the cooperative insurance societies might be integrated "into a great and powerful system covering the land."[173]

In fact, American cooperative insurance societies had sought to form a quasi-public, collectivized system of workingmen's insurance like the one established through the English friendly societies in 1911. Beginning in 1886, a number of the most important and well-established cooperative insurance associations—including the Ancient Order of United Workmen, the Knights of Honor, the Order of United American Mechanics, and the Royal Templars of Temperance—joined together to establish the National Fraternal Congress (NFC).[174] From the start, the NFC's missions were to limit the entry of new fraternal associations into the field and to limit competition among existing associations for one another's younger and healthier members.[175] The creation and enforcement of a standardized premium structure for all fraternal associations was a critical part of these projects. Throughout the 1890s, the NFC encouraged member societies to revise their premium structures by moving away from the equal assessment basis and toward a premium rate that varied with the age of the member.[176]

As a private body, however, the NFC lacked the enforcement power necessary to prevent new societies from entering the market and offering lower rates to young members; the NFC was thus unable to control the unraveling tendencies of the cooperative insurance societies. Beginning in 1900, the NFC sought uniform state legislation that would bar entry into the field by new societies offering premiums below the NFC's standard rates.[177] By barring the entry of low-rate competitors, the NFC hoped to bring all new cooperative insurance association members into one of the existing societies. The influx of new members into the existing societies would keep rates low for older members. Moreover, the establishment of a fixed set of associations embracing all those seeking life and disability insurance through cooperative associations would stem the disintegration of the associations through the continual sorting and resorting of the membership into separate risk pools. Indeed, the uniform legislation movement sought to create nothing less than "one national organization" for the "welfare of the body politic" and "the welfare of each individual" therein.[178] Groups within the cooperative movement even advocated the creation of a federal regulatory agency as the best way to reorganize the relationship between the cooperatives and the government.[179] By 1908 seven states had adopted the uniform state legislation. In 1910 and 1912, the NFC drafted new uniform legislation, again adopting minimum rate tables and now adding reserve requirements. By 1911, the NFC was able to report that thirteen state legislatures had enacted its proposed uniform legislation,[180] and by 1919 fully forty states had enacted the legislation.[181]

To be sure, a persistent strand of voluntarism among many cooperationists divided the cooperative insurance movement over the questions of uniform legislation and barriers to entry. Even as the NFC sought new regulations to stabilize the industry, many associations actively opposed new state regulation of cooperative insurance associations.[182] Such opposition partly reflected the self-interest of upstart societies' leaders, whose leadership positions were threatened by limitations on the growth of new societies.[183] But opposition to regulation also reflected those voluntarist traditions of the thin theory of insurance movement that sought in insurance an antidote to increased state intervention in social and economic life. The NFC thus experienced repeated difficulties controlling splinter coalitions opposed to its attempts to use uniform legislation to form a quasi-public body of cooperative insurance associations.[184]

Yet voluntarism among U.S. cooperatives cannot alone explain the divergent paths of U.S. and English workingmen's cooperatives. Strong voluntarist ideologies also characterized the English friendly societies into the beginning of the twentieth century. Indeed, friendly society opposition to social insurance programs along German lines is a storied part of the history of the development of the British welfare state. The obstacles posed by the friendlies to the development of social insurance were overcome only with the leadership of strong charismatic political advocates of social insurance such as David Lloyd George and Winston Churchill, the intervention of German models that broke the British policy logjam, and the careful construction of social insurance schemes that would incorporate the friendlies into the social insurance state.[185]

The critical distinction between the western European experience and the American experience is that in Europe, leading social insurance advocates, thinkers, and politicians turned to the cooperatives as a way of grappling with a wide range of problems in the politics and structure of social provision. Local associations of workingmen, as we have seen, offered a number of attractive institutional capabilities in the administration of benefit programs such as health insurance, not the least of which were face-to-face interactions and the attendant norms of solidarity and fraternity.

In the United States, by contrast, political and intellectual leaders in social insurance reform in the years leading up to 1910 were singularly preoccupied with the industrial-accident problem. For political leaders such as Theodore Roosevelt, the social problem that required state intervention was the work-accident problem, not the more diffuse array of social insurance concerns ranging from old-age pensions to unemployment insurance to state health insurance.[186] As a 1909 report of the U.S. commissioner of labor observed, in the United States it was the study of "methods of compensating workmen for disability incurred in the course of their employment" that drew attention to state-guaranteed workmen's insurance systems.[187]

The significance of work accidents as the vehicle by which American leaders came to social insurance debates is that while the work-accident problem animated American social insurance dialogue, it also limited the appeal of the cooperative insurance associations as useful building blocks. For at just the time that social insurance discourse was coming onto the scene in the United States, two developments—exceptionally forceful in America—deeply undermined the institutional capacity of cooperative insurance associations to grapple with the problem of industrial accidents.

For one thing, the massive influx of over a million new immigrants each year around the turn of the century radically changed the landscape of workingmen's insurance in the United States.[188] New immigrants from southern and eastern Europe developed collective mutual protection societies of their own.[189] Many such societies in immigrant communities, however, were never able to provide substantial benefits to workingmen or their families.

Indeed, it appears that as the influx of eastern and southern European immigrants accelerated, increasing numbers of American workingmen participated in small, local fraternal organizations in which death benefits provided families with only enough to pay for funeral expenses. The elite of the cooperative insurance associations, such as those that reported annually to state insurance commissioners, traditionally paid a death benefit of $1,000 or $2,000.[190] Many mutual benefit associations, however, offered far less. Fifty-four percent of the families in the Wainwright Commission's study of work accidents in New York State received some form of insurance benefit after the accidental death of a male wage-earner, but 60 percent of those receiving insurance benefits received less than $500.[191] In Chicago, a state commission found in 1918 that although four of five working-class families had insured the life of at least one family member, most families' insurance policies were small: the average insurance policy in the Chicago study was for $419.[192] In Pittsburgh in 1908 and 1909, only one in four working-class families possessed more than $500 of insurance against death from industrial accident.[193] Such policies ensured sufficient funds to pay for funeral costs, but they provided little more protection than that. In the grim words of one Polish mother in Chicago, the reasoning of those who purchased insurance in the new immigrant communities was "[w]ork, work and earn for your grave."[194] The cooperative self-insurance approach to accident compensation thus seemed increasingly insufficient in many of the most compelling cases.

Moreover, a dramatic reconceptualization and reorganization of work in America in the decade after 1900 made cooperative, first-party approaches to work-accident policy and law seem increasingly out of step with industrial conditions. As a mechanism for compensating accident victims in the workplace, the cooperative insurance system had many virtues; it provided members and their families with prompt and reliable compensation at a minimum administrative cost. As a mechanism for encouraging safety and deterring accidents in the first place, however, the utility of the insurance associations rested on the validity of two assumptions. First, the success of cooperative self-insurance depended at least in part on the idea that workers themselves acted as effective agents in the administration of an accident-law regime. Indeed, the nineteenth-century law of employers' liability rested on the claim— often inaccurate—that workers themselves were largely in control of the operations of the industrial workplace and therefore were the most effective preventers of work accidents.[195] Moreover, as noted already, sophisticated working-class advocates of first-party insurance argued that self-insurance among workingmen held the promise of allowing workers to impose the costs of work accidents on employers. Workingmen who banded together to create mutual insurance programs, the argument went, would come to expect higher wages and would acquire the collective power to exact those higher wages from employers.

Second, cooperative workingmen's insurance associations could also effectively address safety concerns and deter accidents if accompanied by a command-and-control regulatory system that effectively enforced safety measures in workplaces.[196] By the first decade of the twentieth century, however, state factory inspection regimes in the United States were increasingly seen as failures.[197] Factory inspection and safety legislation were hindered by inadequate penalties, understaffed enforcement offices, and party patronage positions in the offices. Even Wisconsin, with its strong tradition of labor legislation, experienced similar difficulties enforcing its factory safety regulations.[198] As a result, by 1909, when the attention of reformers turned to the nation's industrial-accident problem, few believed that the factory inspectors could effectively regulate industrial safety.[199] State commissions described factory inspection systems as "absurd"; progressives bemoaned that the few good inspectors were "removed at will in the interests of powerful employers"; and even manufacturers acknowledged that poorly equipped inspectors had "not succeeded in preventing accidents to any great extent."[200]

If regulatory approaches to making the workplace safer were impracticable, the ability of workers themselves to act as effective agents of accident prevention became critical to the continued centrality of first-party cooperative insurance in American accident law. But in the first decades of the twentieth century, the new prominence in the industrial safety debate of expanded employers' liability rules and workmen's compensation at once signaled and reproduced dramatic changes in the organization of the American workplace. Led by Frederick Winslow Taylor and his gospel of "scientific management," managerial experts in the organization of production processes assumed central roles in the American economy. Meanwhile, students of American industry—at once describing the transformations wrought by new managerial strategies and tacitly participating in them—began increasingly to doubt the capacity of workingmen themselves to gauge the risk of accidents and to insure themselves accordingly. "[E]very man," it was said, "depreciates the risk of his peculiar calling. The car-coupler, the laborer on a construction train, or the electric-light lineman, is perfectly sure that there is no occupation safer than the one in which he is engaged."[201] As a result, contemporaries began to focus not so much on the incentives of the common law rules for workers, but rather on the poor incentives that those rules created for employers to ensure workplace safety.[202] Indeed, by 1910, even many cooperatives had come to see the work-accident problem as one with which they were peculiarly unprepared to deal. As one cooperative trade publication article put it in 1911, accident insurance was "outside the sphere of fraternal protection" because industrial accidents resulted from the hazards of particular industries "and therefore should be borne by" those industries. And because placing the costs of accidents on the industry itself produced incentives to minimize those costs, employers were best positioned to "provide our workmen with an insurance at a minimized price."[203]

By 1908 and 1909, the momentum in workingmen's insurance against accidents had shifted decisively away from the cooperative insurance associations. And in the years after 1910, the cooperationists' chances of creating "one national organization" for the collective self-insurance of its members collapsed. Total cooperative life and disability insurance in force as a percentage of commercial life insurance in force fell from 137 percent in 1895 to 109 percent in 1900 to 99 percent in 1905.[204] Cooperative life and disability insurance in force as a percentage of commercial life insurance in force fell sharply to 41 percent by 1916 and then to 23 percent by 1920.[205] Cooperative life insurance in force per capita in the United States fell from an all-time high of $105 in 1910 to just $37 in 1920 after adjusting for wartime inflation (see Table 3.2).

More dramatically still, the relative financial significance of cooperative insurance to the average family enrolled in an insurance society decreased

Table 3.2 Life insurance in force per capita in the United States, constant 1890 dollars

Year	Cooperative	Commercial
1885	39.32	42.41
1890	58.10	54.09
1900	93.83	86.00
1910	104.99	98.85
1920	37.09	93.76
1925	45.72	173.92

Sources: 72 *Ann. Rep. Superintendent of the Ins. Dep't of the State of N.Y.*, pt. II, at xxiii (1931); Stalson, *Marketing Life Insurance,* 806, appendix 18. For a description of the math, see John Fabian Witt, "Toward New History of American Accident Law: Classical Tort Law and the Cooperative First-Party Insurance Movement," 114 *Harv. L. Rev.* 690, 838 n. 822 (2001).

sharply after 1900, and especially after 1910. Measured in constant 1890s dollars, the average value of a cooperative life insurance policy fell from $1,362 in 1900 to $873 in 1910 to a mere $368 in 1920.[206]

The failure of the American cooperative insurance system to go the way of the English friendly societies helped shape the basic institutional features of American accident law in the twentieth century, cutting off one pathway for the development of American accident law. Yet in 1909 and 1910, the significance of the decline of the cooperatives was obscured by the successes of two very different models for dealing with the accident problem, each of which promised new departures in the allocation of work-accident risk and offered further alternatives to tort. On one hand, accident-compensation schemes were being adopted by increasing numbers of sophisticated private employers. On the other hand, leading jurisdictions were beginning to study more seriously the possibility of enacting state compensation schemes for work accidents. As we shall see, the rise of these new models for dealing with the accident crisis was closely related to the difficulties confronting the ill-fated cooperatives.

4

From Markets to Managers

As the apostles of scientific management have shown us we Americans
have wasted foolishly in the individual processes of our industry. In the
whole body of our industry we have often wasted, not only foolishly,
but cruelly, and nowhere more cruelly than in the matter of provision
for the wreckage of industry, the killed and wounded in our industrial
warfare.

> —WILL IRWIN, "THE AWAKENING OF THE AMERICAN
> BUSINESS MAN" (1911)

Little more than a decade after the founding of the first post–Civil War cooperative life insurance societies, a very different approach to the problem of
work accidents developed in some of the nation's leading firms. Employers
had long provided informal, ad hoc relief to injured employees. Beginning in
the 1880s, however, a generation of managerial engineers, of whom Frederick Winslow Taylor would become the most famous, established systematic
accident-benefit schemes for their employees. In the same decade appeared
the first glimmerings of a movement among the managers of employees to
bring systemic rationality to work safety. By such efforts to design new institutions for dealing with the sharp rise in accidents that accompanied industrialization, managers sought to reform work safety and the treatment of accidental injury in the name of efficiency. In the process, they substantially
transformed ideas about what kinds of institutions were conducive to efficiency. Moreover, they developed a set of managerial technologies that
would largely undo important strands in the free labor organization of economic production.

The political economy of Jacksonian America had replaced entrenched monopoly with markets as the leading mechanism for economic development;
equal rights for all market actors rather than special incentives for a few became the dominant approach to political economy.[1] In the North, this shift
was especially pronounced in the field of labor, where the incentives of a system of contracting came to be thought of by many as superior in efficiency
terms to coercion. Markets in free labor put the "silent compulsion of economic relations," to use Marx's phrase, to work in the extraction of labor
power from the worker.[2] In Marx's critical account, the market mechanism
for labor control "surpasse[d] all earlier systems of production, which were

103

based on directly compulsory labor, in its energy and its quality of un-
bounded and ruthless activity."[3] And indeed, many early advocates of free labor were remarkably frank about their reliance on the motive force of hunger
and poverty to spur on a labor force.[4] But in more affirmative accounts,
which began to emerge as early as the last decades of the eighteenth century,
and which eventually predominated in the northern United States by the
time of the Civil War, free labor was the key to the progressive development
of human societies away from the anachronistic regimes of feudal authority,
status hierarchies, and slavery. From Adam Smith to Benjamin Franklin to
William Lloyd Garrison, leading thinkers in the Anglo-American tradition
viewed the incentives provided by free labor as vastly more efficient than the
compulsions and coercions of unfree labor alternatives.[5]

By the 1880s, however, close observers of the American economy had begun to question the efficiency of competitive markets in the spheres of both
exchange and production. Competition among firms seemed to be causing
harmful price-cutting and overproduction. Railroads found themselves with
hundreds, even thousands of miles of duplicative track. Shippers in St. Louis
and Atlanta, for example, as Gabriel Kolko pointed out in his controversial
1965 book on railroad regulation, "had the option of twenty competitive
routes between the two cities."[6] Charles Francis Adams, president of the
Union Pacific Railroad and former chairman of the Massachusetts Board of
Railroad Commissioners, argued that "unhealthy railroad competition" and
the "present competitive chaos" needed to give way to "some healthy control" or an "orderly, confederated whole."[7] Similarly, in steel and iron production and in the Pennsylvania anthracite coal fields, wasteful overproduction by newly mechanized firms with unprecedented production capacities
forced industrywide price-cutting and appeared to be driving firms to the
brink of bankruptcy.[8] "As prices fall and profits shrink," observed economist David Ames Wells in 1889, competitors engage in ever-downward cycles
of further price slashing in order to retain markets and customers "until
gradually the industrial system becomes depressed and demoralized, and the
weaker succumb (fail), with a greater or less destruction of capital and waste
of product."[9]

Many began to rethink the value of free labor in the employment relation,
as well. It bears noting here that the "freedom" of the free labor employment
relation had always been ambiguous. Mid-nineteenth-century approaches to
labor management, for example, presented a curious mix of market mechanisms and unrationalized employer–employee hierarchy. Business historians
have labeled mid-nineteenth-century workshops and factories the "foreman's
empire." Although there was considerable variation among industries, foremen—usually skilled workers with little formal training who had risen

through the ranks—generally utilized the "driving" method of labor management, a method that combined "authoritarian rule and physical compulsion." Foremen "pushe[d] the gang" of workers using an array of gestures and profanity known as "Rolling-mill English" to get the work done.[10] Moreover, the emerging law of employment contracts adopted a set of default terms for the employment relation that made employees' subjection to their employers' control the core feature of employment.[11]

Yet in important respects, market mechanisms reached deep into mid-nineteenth-century firms, many of which adopted management practices that relied on the preservation of a skilled workforce.[12] Such firms did not engage in the deskilling and hierarchical rulemaking that characterized industrial work in places such as the New England textile mills. At the Baldwin Locomotive Works in Philadelphia, for example, management espoused a producerist ethic that linked managers and workers together in a roughly, though of course not wholly, egalitarian partnership in the skilled work of producing custom-built railroad locomotives.[13] Nearby textile mills in Philadelphia adopted a similar strategy of reliance on skilled operatives in whom the mills vested significant discretion.[14] Moreover, even as some employers sought to impose new forms of discipline in the industrial workplace, workers actively resisted their attempts and often were able to retain considerable discretion in the direction of their own labor. Practices such as the inside-contract system, under which manufacturers contracted with skilled workers inside the firm on a task basis, permitted skilled workers to take charge of particular production projects.[15] In iron rolling mills, workers collectively contracted with their employer on only a tonnage rate and controlled among themselves the division of labor and the allocation of pay.[16] For other skilled craftsmen such as coal miners, steel workers, and machinists, specialized skills and knowledge made it possible to remain relatively self-directing in the details of industrial work processes.[17] Thus, late into the nineteenth century, skilled workers were able to make and implement union work rules to maintain a measure of autonomy in the production process.[18] Even among unskilled workers, piece-work payment systems (though often exploitative in their own way) had the similar effect of contracting particular labor arrangements out of the hierarchical master–servant relation.

In those firms that sought to replace worker discretion with command-and-control hierarchies, employer control of the production process was often crude and imprecise by twentieth-century standards. Foremen dominated the shop floor, with little accountability and few standards of conduct to guide the exercise of their authority. Ineffective cost-accounting mechanisms obscured the relative costs and merits of various approaches to employee management. And while the often-arbitrary power of the foreman system was in theory antithetical to the culture of skilled industrial craftsmen, the foreman system of labor management operated on a nonrationalized basis and was often ineffective and sloppy.[19] As a matter of practice, then, workers frequently retained considerable discretion over work processes.

The crisis of confidence in markets of the 1880s, however, called into question this mix of internal markets and often haphazard employer control. There had, to be sure, been earlier challenges to the idea that free labor was efficient labor. The experience of emancipation in Jamaica after 1838, for example, seemed to many English and American capitalists to call into question whether former slaves would work for wages as productively as they had worked under the compulsion of slavery.[20] Reconstruction in the United States seemed to hold a similar lesson for many northern whites who sought to take over southern plantations after the Civil War.[21] But with the great railroad strikes of 1877, the nationwide strikes inspired by the Knights of Labor in 1886, and the Homestead strike of 1892 (which featured the famous pitched battle between steel workers and Pinkerton detectives hired by Henry Clay Frick) employment relations came to appear especially susceptible to the waste and friction that many had begun to identify in competitive markets more generally.[22] Relations between labor and management, on this view, presented another example of the ways in which the American market economy led to inefficient and wasteful systems of production. The "foreman's empire," it seemed, lacked the systematic precision that modern conditions appeared to require.

Influential leaders in American business responded to the late-nineteenth-century crises of overcompetition and labor conflict by moving to replace markets with hierarchies. Some of the nation's leading firms sought to establish a new corporatist political economy that would eliminate ruinous competition and reduce labor–management conflict by removing both of these aspects of economic life from the market. Firms in industries such as steel sought repeatedly, but with little success, to form "gentlemen's agreements and pools . . . in an effort to control production." When enforcement problems caused most such initiatives to collapse, American industrialists turned to the business trust and the corporate merger to police against competitive pressures.[23] Large-scale enterprise, argued industrialists such as S. C. T. Dodd of Standard Oil, James Hill of the Great Northern Railway, and Charles Schwab of U.S. Steel, offered the benefit of substantial economies of scale. Moreover, men such as Charles Francis Adams of the Union Pacific Railroad argued in the 1880s that the advancement of civilization led inevitably toward big business. "[T]he principle of consolidation . . . is a necessity—a natural law of growth," Adams argued. "You may not like it: you will have to reconcile yourselves to it." In the "modern world" business necessarily "does its work through vast aggregations of men and capital. . . . This is a sort of latter day manifest destiny."[24]

A second strand of the hierarchical reorganization of economic production focused not on cooperation and consolidation among firms, but rather on the reorganization of production within the firm. American labor management practices in the mid-nineteenth century had given little indication of the strength of the managerial movement that was to come. Into the middle of the nineteenth century, American enterprise exhibited little systematic organization of the production process. So long as the scale of production remained relatively small, Alfred Chandler has argued, there was little call for systemic attention to the rational organization of the workplace itself. And yet by the turn of the twentieth century, American firms laid claim to the prerogative of managerial control of the production process with a vigor unmatched in Western economies. In Chandler's magisterial interpretation, the coming of the railroad brought with it new opportunities for rational managerial approaches to running business enterprises. Railroads themselves posed significant challenges of organization, management, and coordination. Time zones had to be standardized so as to establish consistent and reliable scheduling, track gauges had to be standardized and integrated, bridges and overpasses had to be built according to industry standards for car sizes and weights, large and widely dispersed workforces had to be managed, and goods in transit had to be coordinated with schedules and railroad cars. Moreover, the railroads created for the first time the possibility of taking advantage of economies in large-scale production. Before the railroad, raw material could not be amassed in sufficient quantities nor finished goods shipped quickly enough to support mass expansion of the production process. But with railroad shipping bringing new speed and capacity to the movement of materials and goods, firms were suddenly able to expand production dramatically. And with expansion came a new need for, as well as new economies of scale to facilitate, the rationalization of the production process to coordinate materials, labor, and distribution.[25]

In the early 1880s, a new generation of managerial engineers began to rationalize labor management theory, advocating administered, hierarchical, and rationalized modes of labor management. Railroad managers established professional and semiprofessional associations such as the American Society for Railroad Superintendents and the Society of Railroad Comptrollers. Mechanical engineers formed the American Society of Mechanical Engineers in 1880, which was followed quickly by the establishment of the American Institute of Electrical Engineers in 1884.[26] New journals and magazines designed for engineers and railroad officials such as *Engineer and Surveyor* (1874), *Engineering News* (1875), *Engineering Magazine* (1890), and

Cassier's Magazine (1891) facilitated the dissemination and rationalization of professional knowledge.

By the turn of the century, leading management engineers in the steel industry argued that under modern production methods the "human machinery" was the "most important part" of the firm, and indeed accounted for a substantial portion of most firms' variable costs.[27] The foreman system and the crude approach to production with which it was associated, however, were wholly unable to cope with the complex new demands of labor management in the age of large-scale mechanization. A rational and "scientific" approach to labor management, on the other hand, promised to provide new ways to legitimate managerial incursions on traditionally worker-controlled aspects of the production process.[28] Organizations of engineers such as the American Society of Mechanical Engineers thus began to emphasize labor management questions rather than mechanical or purely engineering matters.[29] The new problem in the organization of production, it seemed, was the adoption of "new shop methods" as "a corollary of modern machinery." As engineer John Patterson put it in 1900, "the problems of to-day in factory management are not so much problems of machinery as of men; not so much of organization as of personal relations."[30]

Frederick Winslow Taylor stood at the forefront of the movement to rationalize the American workplace. Born in 1856 to a wealthy Philadelphia Quaker family, Taylor became a journeyman machinist after a mysterious (and apparently stress-related) eye ailment ended his preparations for the Harvard College entrance exam. Within a few short years he had become a foreman at the important Philadelphia steel company Midvale Steel, and a close advisor to its owner. In 1885, he joined the American Society of Mechanical Engineers.[31]

Quakers like those among Taylor's forebears had played an important role in developing and popularizing the ideas underlying the ideal of free labor. The "Quaker ethic," as David Brion Davis has called it, held that God resides in the soul of every individual. It followed for Quakers that the compulsion and forcible hierarchies of southern slavery were anathema, and in the years around Taylor's birth, antebellum Quakers helped to galvanize the antislavery movement.[32] Taylor, however, had little use for Quaker notions of human perfectibility or for the consensual approach to social relations that followed from such notions.[33] In his view, the free labor system of the postwar years, which relied on "initiative and incentive" to induce labor, had led to systematic shirking—"soldiering," he called it—by obstructionist workers.[34] Thus, while one variation on the post–Civil War free labor ideal viewed free labor contracts as a more perfect compulsion to labor, Taylor saw nineteenth-century free labor contracts as allowing and even facilitating the persistence of worker laziness.[35]

In Taylor's view, labor markets that relied on initiative and incentive were hopelessly wasteful. In combination with clumsy, ill-trained foremen, incentive-based systems of labor management necessarily meant that "each workman shall be left with the final responsibility for doing his job practically as he thinks best, with comparatively little help and advice from the management." As a result, instead of a standard practice for a given step in the production process, there were "fifty or a hundred different ways of doing each element of the work," ways that had been "handed down from man to man by word of mouth." "[T]here was," however, "but a remote chance" in such a system "that [any one worker] should hit upon the one best method of doing each piece of work out of the hundreds of possible methods which lay before him." Theodore Roosevelt and Gifford Pinchot had begun to teach the nation to recognize waste in the exploitation of natural resources such as forests, water, topsoil, and minerals. But Americans remained blind to the waste of labor power caused by the prevalence of market methods of labor management. "Our larger wastes of human effort," Taylor complained, "which go on every day through such of our acts as are blundering, ill-directed, or inefficient . . . are less visible, less tangible, and are but vaguely appreciated."[36]

The answer was to reengineer work and to put into place precisely calibrated methods for even the most routine tasks in the production process. Scientific reorganization of the processes of work would allow management to "substitut[e] . . . science for the individual judgment of the workman."[37] Through time and motion study, managers could determine by ostensibly scientific methods the "one best way" to carry out even the simplest of tasks, and then require minute compliance with prescribed methods by workers. Indeed, in light of the presumptive incapacity of the worker to comprehend adequately the processes of production, Taylor and the management specialists he inspired set out to eliminate entirely the discretion of the individual worker. Scientific management's first principle was the "deliberate gathering in on the part of those on the management's side of all the great mass of traditional knowledge, which in the past has been in the heads of the workmen, and in the physical skill and knack of the workmen."[38] Hence, Taylor developed a series of new managerial techniques, ranging from standardized and minutely controlled processes of production and maintenance to the famous stopwatch time studies, all of which were designed to replace workers' informal know-how with ostensibly scientific rationality.[39] Full implementation of specific techniques advocated by Taylor in American workplaces was relatively limited. Nonetheless, Taylorism and its accompanying varieties of management engineering worked a thorough transformation in the ways in which Americans conceived of work.[40]

Most important for our purposes is an often overlooked facet of Taylor's project. In advocating the importance of managerial control, Taylor also announced a new principle of managerial responsibility. Firms could be and, indeed, properly ought to be responsible for managing wide swaths of American social life. "In its essence," Taylor explained to a congressional committee investigating scientific management in 1912, "scientific management involves a complete mental revolution." To be sure, workers needed to rethink "their duties toward their work, toward their fellow men, and toward their employers." But scientific management also involved an "equally complete mental revolution on the part of those on the management side—the foreman, the superintendent, the owner of the business, the board of directors—a complete mental revolution on their part as to their duties toward their fellow workers in the management, toward their workmen, and toward all of their daily problems."[41] Worker discipline and managerial responsibility, in Taylor's view, went hand-in-hand.

In the case of work accidents, for example, Taylor favored employer-provided accident insurance benefits, financed in part by fines paid by the workers for disciplinary infractions. By 1900, Taylor's Midvale Steel had set up precisely such an accident insurance plan. Employees contributed five cents per week to the insurance fund in return for injury and death benefits.[42] And therein lay the seeds of a transformation in the ways in which American firms handled industrial injuries.

Early-twenty-first-century economists generally define efficiency as the allocation of resources to their highest-value users. Markets, for example, are efficient on this view when they facilitate the transfer of some good from a willing seller to a willing buyer. A market transaction improves allocative efficiency because the buyer values the good more highly than the seller. No sale would have taken place otherwise.

Engineers at the turn of the twentieth century had an altogether different conception of efficiency as an economy of inputs to outputs. They understood as efficient those processes that conserved resources, measured not in dollars but rather in terms of the sheer amount of natural resources, raw materials, and muscle power required.[43] Conversely, engineers viewed processes that exhausted excess resources as inefficient and wasteful. As one engineer put it in 1901, "the most conspicuous tendency of human activity is to get a maximum result by a minimum of expenditure. Minimum cost of fuel, of transportation, of brain and muscle, must hereafter be considered in the mighty competition that characterizes the commerce of the world."[44]

The inputs to outputs conception of efficiency was quite common at the close of the nineteenth century and into the first decade of the twentieth. As historians since Frederick Jackson Turner have recognized, the closing of the frontier generated a new sense of scarcity among many Americans, a new sense that American resources—like those of Old World nations—might be bounded. This sense of limited resources, in turn, gave rise to the new natural resources conservationism to which Taylor had compared his scientific management efforts. In 1908, President Roosevelt created the National Conservation Commission, which issued a report in 1909 on the condition of the nation's forests, waterways, lands, and mineral resources. A year later, Gifford Pinchot—who served as Roosevelt's chief of the U.S. Bureau of Forestry and later as governor of Pennsylvania—published his influential book, *The Fight for Conservation*, in which he asked in Malthusian tones whether the current generation of Americans would, like its predecessors, be able to conserve its "marvelous resources" and "transmit them, still unexhausted, to our descendants."[45]

Engineers turned to the problem of waste in railroad and industrial accidents with the same spirit of conservation that Roosevelt and Pinchot brought to natural resources. Only a few years earlier, observed one electrical engineer, the United States had been a "young nation with vast natural resources." "[B]ut suddenly we find that our resources have been squandered and are approaching exhaustion."[46] In his view, the greatest waste was not in natural resources but rather in human resources. Inefficiency was responsible for the "terrible . . . harvest of death, disaster, and misery" embodied in the nation's disgraceful accident record.[47] In the words of another engineer, the problem of "conserving the nation's resources" was deeply bound up in "the prevention of accidents."[48] Indeed, even those who focused on such natural resources as water, forests, minerals, and lands saw in the accident problem a pressing problem of conservation. "[I]f the conservation of natural resources is for man, it is an obvious suggestion that man himself should be conserved," observed Wisconsin conservationist Charles Richard Van Hise. By Van Hise's lights, "losses of life by accidents are appalling in this country," and "by proper precautionary measures . . . the accidents may be reduced by one tenth their present number."[49]

As early as the 1880s, American engineers began to focus on the prevention of accidents in industry as central to their project of rationalizing labor management, and by 1890 engineering trade journals devoted substantial coverage to railroad and other industrial accidents.[50] "[T]he life and health of every skilled workman," argued the efficiency-minded engineers, "represent an asset that a factory cannot afford to ignore."[51] The "appalling mortality" evidenced by railroad and manufacturing accident statistics, however, threatened to undermine and even destroy the efficiency of the American railroad system.[52] Much to the dismay of the engineering professionals, the United States, as one engineer put it, "stand[s] first among all countries in the number of lives lost through accidents. In railroading, in mining, in manufacturing, and in general building operations, the number of accidents in the United States is annually greater in proportion to population than in any of the civilized countries of the globe."[53] Others called the deaths in the United States from railway accidents and fire, among other causes, "a national disgrace,"[54] and bemoaned the "waste of life in American coal mining."[55] Indeed, the casualties among American railroad workers during 1898 and 1899, reported the editors of *Cassier's Magazine,* were equivalent to "two and a half times the reported total of killed and wounded in the British Army in South Africa [in the ongoing Boer War]."[56]

In management engineers' view, wasteful competition among firms sustained the nation's comparatively high industrial-accident rates. Most late-nineteenth-century economists (and apparently many managers as well) did not believe that, as Lemuel Shaw had suggested in 1842 in *Farwell v. Boston and Worcester Rail Road,* workers charged a premium for dangerous workplaces in the form of higher wages.[57] Moreover, many engineers believed that employee injuries were exceedingly inexpensive under the common law of employers' liability.[58] Inattention to costly work-safety measures thus offered firms in competitive industries the opportunity for substantial savings. Competition among machine shops, for example, had driven many shop owners to limit their investment in expensive safety provisions.[59] Similarly, "ruinous competition" among coal mine operators had led them to adopt inefficient mining techniques and to neglect critical safety measures such as the proper ventilation of the mines.[60] The result was an "increasing waste of resources and the still more unpardonable increasing waste of human life—the yearly loss of 250,000,000 tons of coal and the killing or injuring yearly of 8,000 to 10,000 men."[61]

The annual slaughter in the coal mines was also, according to American management engineers, evidence of the ways in which primitive labor management practices produced wastefully high accident rates. Fatality rates in American bituminous coal mines soared between 1880 and 1910, rising from two workers killed in every thousand per year to four workers in every thousand.[62] At first blush, mine accidents often appeared to be the fault of the miners themselves. Roof falls were often caused by a miner's careless placing of supporting timbers. Cave-ins usually resulted from leaving insufficient coal in supporting coal pillars. Blasting mishaps usually occurred after a miner carelessly checked on an apparently failed fuse, only to have the charge explode unexpectedly. Moreover, roof collapses, small cave-ins, and blasting mishaps were much more common than catastrophic mining disasters, accounting for at least three-quarters of all coal mining fatalities. But as the most sophisticated mining engineers observed, extraordinarily high accident rates were largely the result of the basic structure of labor management in the mines. Mine operators paid workers according to tonnage rates that rewarded miners who ignored safety measures in return for increased yields. Tonnage payments that did not penalize miners for producing undesirably fine coal (known as "slack") encouraged miners to employ dangerously large amounts of explosive without first undercutting the coal face. "Shooting off the solid," as it was called, was exceedingly dangerous.[63]

The basic design of the mines also helped make American mining more dangerous than European mining. In England, for example, "longwall" mines placed miners along a few long coal faces, under roofs supported by pillars made up of excavated waste from along the coal seam. Longwall mining made supervising workers relatively easy and minimized the danger of roof falls. In the United States, by contrast, the "room-and-pillar" method used a sprawling complex of small rooms propped up by coal and timber pillars. Miners worked in isolation in a labyrinth of tunnels and cut-outs in the coal seam. Supervision was virtually impossible, and the problem of roof collapses was exacerbated by the multiplicity of small rooms and often by carelessly installed timber supports.[64]

In setting tonnage rates and adopting dangerous room-and-pillar mining practices, management engineers argued, mine owners had implemented poorly thought out approaches to designing and managing work in American mines. Careless miners might also have been necessary antecedents to many mining accidents. But miners would always be careless. Management systems, on the other hand, could be made more or less effective, and in the mining case, ineffective systems had produced wasteful accident rates.

Management engineers' first answer to the industrial-accident crisis was to experiment with the kinds of firm-specific employee accident-compensation funds, or "establishment funds" as they were known, that Taylor implemented at Midvale Steel.

As the Chandler thesis would predict, employee accident-relief funds first emerged as an important accident compensation mechanism on the railroads. The Philadelphia and Reading Railroad endowed a $20,000 accident fund for its coal mine workers after an 1875 strike in the Pennsylvania anthracite fields, and created an accident plan for its engineers in 1877.[65] In the latter year—a year of massive railroad strikes—the Chicago, Burlington, and Quincy Railroad considered and rejected the adoption of welfare benefits for the elite of its locomotive engineers.[66] And a year later, the Lehigh Valley Railroad of eastern Pennsylvania adopted an assessment-based fund for accident relief, financed by the joint contributions of employees and the railroad corporation itself.[67]

Beginning in 1880, the nation's largest railroad companies began adopting systematic establishment funds. The Baltimore and Ohio Railroad established an accident-relief fund in 1880; the Pennsylvania Railroad Company formed a relief department in 1886; the Philadelphia and Reading did so in 1888; and the Chicago, Burlington, and Quincy followed suit in 1889, as did the Pennsylvania lines west of Pittsburgh.[68] By 1889, an Interstate Commerce Commission survey found that twelve of eighty-five railroad companies surveyed had organized establishment funds.[69] And by the second half of the 1890s, more than one in every five railroad employees in the country was covered by a railroad accident-relief association benefit program; indeed, fully one-fifth of American railroad workers were enrolled in one of the six largest relief associations: the Baltimore and Ohio, the Pennsylvania, the Pennsylvania Lines West, the Philadelphia and Reading, the Chicago, Burlington, and Quincy, and the Plant System.[70]

Outside the railroads, accident-relief funds were less common. The Cambria Iron Works, an early large-scale steel producing firm based in Johnstown in western Pennsylvania, established an accident fund financed through employee fines shortly after the Civil War. In the brewing industry, brewers and their employees in New York and Cincinnati—mostly of German extraction—established jointly financed accident relief funds. And in mining, the Calumet and Hecla mines in Michigan and the Philadelphia and Reading Coal and Iron Company in Pennsylvania established mutual aid societies for their injured employees in 1877.[71] The prominent organ and piano manufacturing firm Alfred Dolge and Son in upstate New York adopted a mutual aid society for its employees in 1881, which by 1890 had expanded into a system of disability, death, and pension benefits.[72] Similarly, the Buffalo Smelting Works, Steinway and Sons, and Bausch and Lomb Optical Company all established benefit associations before the turn of the century.[73] Nonetheless, few manufacturing firms appear to have established significant, lasting accident-relief funds before 1881: of 461 establishment accident funds surveyed in 1908 by the U.S. Department of Labor, a mere five had been established before 1871, and only twenty-one between 1871 and 1880.[74]

Outside the railroad industry the creation and systematization of accident funds began to accelerate significantly in the first decade of the twentieth century. Between 1900 and 1910, leading firms such as United Traction and Electric Company (1901), General Electric (1902), Westinghouse Air Brake (1903), New York Edison (1905), and Swift and Company (1907) created systematic injury-compensation programs for their employees.[75] At New York Edison, the company's management announced that "[t]ry as we may, some one will blunder" and accidents would ensue. Company officials claimed that under the common law system, "discontent, class feeling, and an impression of injustice" had inevitably followed employee injuries. The firm therefore undertook to use the funds it had earmarked for liability insurance premiums to create an accident-compensation fund. The fund would compensate injured employees without regard to the firm's common law defenses. Moreover, the accident fund, Edison's management hoped, would encourage the implementation of safety measures and establish "good relations between the company and its employees."[76] At the Allis-Chalmers Company of Wisconsin in 1907 the firm replaced the informal circulation among the employees of "subscription rolls" in the event of a fellow employee's disability or death with a mutual aid society financed through employee contributions of twenty-five cents a month.[77]

Manufacturing enterprises and mining companies established close to three times as many accident-relief funds between 1891 and 1908 as they had during the preceding twenty years.[78] By 1908, close to 10 percent of all wage earners in the country fell under the auspices of one sort of industrial welfare policy or another.[79] And in many of the most heavily industrialized regions, membership in an establishment fund was considerably more common. Crystal Eastman found that in Pittsburgh, for example, 23 percent of all injured workers were enrolled in employer establishment funds.[80]

Establishment funds generally paid one-half or two-thirds of an employee's weekly wages for durations ranging from thirty-nine weeks to two years during the course of a work-related disability. At large firms, death benefits generally ranged from $100 to $500, and sometimes even higher, depending on the firm and the wages of the deceased employee. Railroad accident funds tended to provide somewhat larger benefits, averaging $588 in death cases in 1908. At smaller firms, however, death benefits tended to be considerably lower. One study of forty-two New Jersey firms in 1904 found that an establishment fund at the sizeable Gibson Iron Works provided death benefits of between $1,000 and $2,000; at the forty-one remaining firms, however, death benefits ranged from $25 at Newark's Johnson and Murphy Shoe Company, to $150 at Camden's Farr and Bailey Manufacturing Company.[81] Virtually all establishment funds required that members sign waivers of the right to sue as a condition of enrollment in the accident-compensation plan; where such waivers were unenforceable, funds required injured members to elect between collecting fund benefits and bringing a risky tort claim.[82]

Most establishment funds also implemented monitoring mechanisms to minimize adverse selection and moral hazard problems. Thus, in some firms such as the Baltimore and Ohio Railroad, membership in an accident-relief fund was a condition of employment, which prevented the adverse selection dynamic under which only high-risk employees opt into an insurance pool.[83] More frequently, however, firms adopted the approach taken by the Pennsylvania Railroad Company, which left membership in the relief fund optional but implemented maximum age rules and required physical examinations for all employees seeking to join.[84] In addition, relief funds (like the working-men's cooperatives) employed "visiting committees" that combined the functions of wishing disabled employees a speedy return to health, on the one hand, and checking for possible malingering, on the other.[85]

At the end of the first decade of the twentieth century, two major firms controlled by J. P. Morgan and his associates implemented accident-relief plans. In 1908, International Harvester adopted a voluntary accident-benefit insurance plan that 75 percent of its employees joined.[86] And in 1910, U.S. Steel announced the establishment of its "Voluntary Accident Relief Plan" for employees of all U.S. Steel-affiliated firms.[87] Many of the subsidiaries of U.S. Steel had less systematic relief policies in place before the announcement of the 1910 plan. In 1901, for example, Andrew Carnegie had donated $4 million to endow an accident-relief fund for the employees of the Carnegie Steel Company. Carnegie's endowment created a fund that covered 85,000 employees in 1908, paying $500 to the widows of employees killed by work accidents, plus $100 additional for every child, or between seventy-five cents and a dollar a day in disability benefits for disability arising out of injuries suffered while on duty.[88] The great volume of claims, however, soon forced the Carnegie fund to suspend all aid in cases of temporary disability lasting less than one year.[89]

Although the 1910 U.S. Steel initiative merely collected together and systematized these existing programs, it was nonetheless a signal moment in the history of American welfare capitalism. For one thing, the sheer size of the U.S. Steel program was unprecedented. Accident-relief payments amounted to $2 million per year,[90] constituting over one-third of U.S. Steel's total employee welfare expenditures between 1912 and 1920.[91] And unlike prior employee accident-relief policies, the U.S. Steel plan was financed entirely through employer contributions.[92] The central principle of the U.S. Steel relief fund was the idea that (as one paper given at the 1910 conference of the American Iron and Steel Institute put it) "compensation to injured workmen is a legitimate charge against the cost of manufacture and that the victim of an industrial accident or his dependents should receive compensation not as an act of grace on the part of his employer but as a right."[93] In the words of the president of the National Tube Company of Pittsburgh (one of the constituent corporations of the U.S. Steel corporate family), it was not "right or fair to say that a man enters our employ knowing that the work is hazardous, and that therefore the risk is his. I think the industry should bear that burden."[94] The U.S. Steel accident-compensation plan thus endorsed Frederick Taylor's principle of managerial responsibility, going one step further than Taylor had by shifting from employee-financed funds to employer-financed funds.

The engineering profession argued that accident benefits such as those implemented at U.S. Steel would have the effect of legitimating new claims of managerial prerogative in the operation and control of the enterprise itself.[95] The Baltimore and Ohio Railroad's Relief Department, for example, drew praise in the 1890s from management engineers interested in the rationalization of labor management as "an intelligent and well directed effort in the true line of industrial progress." Indeed, the expansion and systematization of such relief policies as the B&O's "would do much to bring about a reconciliation [between capital and labor], to say nothing of the relief to the injured from the point of view of humanity."[96] As a series of articles that appeared in *Engineering Magazine* in 1906 suggested, a "square deal" for employees would reconcile the modern factory operative to the status of "merely a more or less mechanical attachment" to the machine tool.[97] If the new engineering problem in the production process was the management of men rather than the development of new and better mechanization, employer relief policies offered employers and managers the opportunity to foster employee loyalty in the increasingly depersonalized world of the large manufacturing enterprise.

In some cases, especially in the 1880s and 1890s and on the railroads, establishing new levels of managerial control of the workplace meant combating the threat posed to managerial domination of the firm by labor organizations. Nationwide railroad strikes in 1877, 1886, and again in 1894 emphasized the disruptive potential of labor organizations among railroad workers. Undermining worker allegiance to the brotherhoods therefore became a central goal of railroad management, and railroad relief funds were frequently employed toward this end.[98] After the especially bitter 1886 strikes on many of the nation's railroads led by the Knights of Labor, for example, the Philadelphia and Reading Railroad Company's statistician suggested to the railroad's president that an accident-relief fund would be "the most expedient way by which an alienation of the men from orders such as the 'Knights of Labor' may be made effective, thereby establishing a closer relationship between the road and its workers."[99]

Furthermore, in the eyes of management engineers, employer-financed accident benefits would lead to substantial reductions in waste. By internalizing accident costs to the enterprise, they suggested, accident funds would rationalize the relationship between inputs and outputs in the production process. Slason Thompson of the Western Railway Club, for example, noted that "[i]t should hardly be necessary to observe that the real responsibility [for railroad accidents] is a matter which lies higher up than with the train crew." According to Thompson, "a part of the duty of officials in charge of the conduct of transportation is the enforcement of the operation of signaling systems as well as of their installation." After all, "no military officer" would endeavor "to shift the responsibility of matters entrusted to his command to the shoulders of his inferiors." Nor, then, should railroad management allow the responsibility for work accidents to fall on the shoulders of employees. Yet at common law, the engineers argued, employers were able to ignore accidents because they were generally not liable for the costs of injuries to workers. Thus, the common law created perverse incentives to waste human labor power. Employer-financed relief funds and expanded employers' liability, on the other hand, would encourage firms to reduce accident costs. As Thompson put it, it seemed that "the proper way to prevent accidents on railroads was to lash a director of the company to the front of each locomotive."[100]

What did it mean for managerial engineers to identify the firm as the entity to which accident costs were properly internalized? The mid-nineteenth-century law of work accidents had taken it for granted that employees were in the best position to prevent and avoid accidents. In the famous case of *Farwell v. Boston and Worcester Rail Road,* for example, Chief Justice Lemuel Shaw of the Massachusetts Supreme Judicial Court ruled that employers were not liable for employee injuries suffered because of the negligence of a fellow employee on the ground that "these are perils which the servant is likely to know, and against which he can as effectively guard, as the master."[101] In work accidents, he asserted, the safety of employees depended not so much on the care of the employer as on "the care and skill" of the employees themselves.[102] If Shaw had spoken about internalizing the costs of accidents, he presumably would have said they should be internalized to the worker, not to the firm.

The engineering literature of the late nineteenth century described a different kind of workplace, one that reflected both changes in the structure of work and management engineers' aspirations to substitute managerial power for worker control. To be sure, the engineers argued that accidents at work were almost always the result of employee carelessness, ignorance, and inattention. Boiler operators grew accustomed to—and complacent about—startlingly dangerous steam conditions;[103] miners held foolish folk ideas about the varying degrees of danger associated with different concentrations of coaldamp in mines; blasting workers resisted the implementation of scientifically tested safety devices; railroad engineers invariably grew accustomed to small but potentially disastrous deviations from prescribed safety procedures; and workers in fields such as electricity could not be trusted to understand the basic principles fundamental to safe working environments. In these respects, the engineers shared Shaw's view of the conditions under which work accidents occurred: they were the result of worker actions and worker negligence, not employer negligence. But engineers differed from Shaw on the implications of employee carelessness. According to the engineers, if employee carelessness was inevitable and unpreventable, and if occasional negligence, forgetfulness, and ignorance were endemic to the human condition (and particularly so among uneducated and lazy or careless workers), it stood to reason that accident prevention and the efficient rationalization of economic processes necessarily depended on the implementation of newly scientific approaches to the management of production and labor, not on the workers themselves.[104]

What the engineering literature added up to was a new theory of causation and responsibility in workplace accidents.[105] Causation in accident cases was bilateral at the very least. Both the injured worker and the firm were necessarily "but for" causes of any workplace accident, and many accidents inevitably involved any number of additional parties. Yet the engineers talked about causation in terms of which party had been best positioned to prevent the accident.[106] And almost inevitably their answer was that sophisticated firms, not incorrigibly careless workers, were best situated to create engineering solutions to work-accident problems. With the engineering know-how of modern managers, firms had the ability to bring scientific rationality to the issue of work accidents. This was why accident costs were properly internalized to firms rather than to employees. Employees were inevitably careless and powerless. Employers, on the other hand, could bring systemic planning to bear on work safety.

This new theory of enterprise responsibility and causation, in turn, gave rise to engineers' second answer to the industrial-accident crisis: the beginning of a movement for industrial safety. Two examples—boiler explosions and railroad collisions—provide a sense of the new causal theory and its relationship to developments in industrial safety.

Improvements in boiler safety present one of the few success stories in the otherwise dismal story of late-nineteenth-century workplace hazards. The first boiler explosions accompanied the early development and introduction of steam power into American industry in the 1830s.[107] A growing number of establishments turned to steam power, and as boilers became more powerful, boiler explosions wreaked havoc in early American manufacturing. Fatal boiler explosions were reported as early as 1838, and in the 1850s and 1860s disastrous boiler catastrophes repeatedly made headlines. In New York City, for example, the Hague Street Disaster of 1850 claimed the lives of sixty-seven workers, and in Philadelphia an 1867 explosion killed another twenty-eight people. All in all, boiler insurance firms estimated that over seven thousand people were killed in boiler explosions in the United States between 1883 and 1907.[108]

During the last three decades of the 1800s, engineers warned frequently of the dangers and accompanying costs associated with nonrationalized boiler use in steam-powered manufacturing enterprises and steam-powered locomotives and vessels.[109] "Among the dangers which menace boiler explosions," explained one engineer in 1891, "are explosion, corrosion, leakage, burning, and leaky or dilapidated front or setting." And while some of these problems merely meant the waste of fuel or diminished power capacity, others "herald[ed] danger to life and limb as well as wreckage of property."[110] Indeed, J. M. Allen of the Hartford Steam Boiler Inspection and Insurance Company estimated that roughly 1,000 boiler explosions occurred in the United States between 1880 and 1886, causing $3 million in damages in destruction of property and delays associated with rebuilding repairs, as well as some 1,500 deaths and many more injuries.[111]

According to many engineers, boiler explosions might virtually be eradicated through scientific boiler construction, operation, and inspection. Engineers developed and advocated the use of automated devices that allowed operators to open and shut steam valves from a safe distance, for example, and developed new and stronger designs for boiler construction.[112] Most of all, engineers pointed to the extraordinary success of expert inspection of boilers as evidenced by the record of boiler insurance companies. Defective boilers, it was estimated, accounted for as many as 75 percent of all boiler explosions. And it was "the special province of boiler inspection to discover" such defects. Boiler insurance firms such as the Hartford Steam Boiler Inspection and Insurance Company, founded in 1867, collected comprehensive statistics on boiler accidents, making it possible for the first time to carry out scientific investigations into the relative merits of alternate boiler design. And by all accounts, boiler insurance and the accompanying inspections by trained engineers sharply reduced the incidence of boiler explosions.[113] Indeed, although the engineering profession conceded that "such accidents can never be wholly got rid of," engineers believed that expert inspection had made "a long step . . . in that direction."[114] Boilers stood as a shining example of what rational engineering could do for safety.

Railroad collisions were a second great preoccupation of accident-prevention engineers in the 1890s, but here the results were ambiguous. Train collisions, in the words of one engineer, represented the "most disgraceful, because entirely avoidable, class of accidents."[115] In the 1880s and early 1890s, engineers had focused on improvements in the physical infrastructure of the railroad industry as the most productive way to reduce the accident rate, developing and implementing improvements in bridge construction, track gauges, roadway and car design, automatic couplers, and air brakes.[116] But by the late 1890s and the first decade of the twentieth century, management engineers on the railroads had come to believe that employee negligence was far and away the greatest cause of railroad collisions.[117] Nearly 70 percent of accidents on the railroads, according to one engineering estimate, were "due entirely to the mental or physical state of the human agent."[118] "[A]dmirable rules for the government of employees," observed another railway engineer, "are habitually disregarded."[119] At grade crossings, junctions, drawbridges, and passing tracks, locomotive engineers persistently and inevitably violated state and company rules requiring them to stop, either out of concern to meet scheduling deadlines or out of becoming accustomed to risk-taking.[120] As a result, it was futile to leave safety to the workers themselves.[121] Indeed, in the management engineers' view, it was inevitable that "men will be careless." Railroad companies, they argued, "should provide for this trait in human nature" by implementing automated safety devices that took the discretion and human agency out of railroad safety.[122]

In particular, engineers advocated the automated block system as an alternative to the signaling system used by most American railroads in the 1890s. Under the prevailing signal system, railroad employees whose duty it was to give signals stood at critical junctures in the railroad line and used flags to give signals to oncoming traffic indicating the presence of trains ahead. The drawback to this approach, as the engineering press was quick to point out after railroad disasters, was that it left "a single employee to judge" whether to observe safety rules designed to "protect the lives of half a hundred passengers."[123] Poor judgment or carelessness by a signal man, or the decision of a locomotive engineer to override the signal, could lead to catastrophe. The automated block system, by contrast, employed electric-powered signals. Automatic train stops, in turn, employed automatic braking devices to preclude the entry of a train into a particular section (or "block") of track so long as another train remained in that block.[124]

Engineers experienced little success in introducing automated block systems or train stops for the reduction of railroad collisions. Both remained exceedingly rare on American railroads. A larger, but still relatively small, portion of American railroads implemented manual block signals. The manual block signal system divided the track into sections; trains were prohibited from entering a block of track unless it was empty. The manual system, however, still relied on individual railroad workers to track the progress of trains through the blocks and to set signals accordingly. Moreover, only 22 percent of American railroad mileage was in the manual block system by 1906. And between 1897 and 1907, passenger and employee fatalities from railroad collisions skyrocketed, increasing by almost 400 percent. Only between 1922 and 1928 did the Interstate Commerce Commission briefly adopt new automated train stop rules. By then the combination of more effective manual block systems and declining traffic density on the nation's railroads had already led to sharp declines in the collision rate.[125]

Despite their differing levels of success, the common feature of the boiler and railroad collision experiences was the idea that the best way to prevent accidents and catastrophes in the modern industrial workplace was to remove discretionary authority from the hands of the worker. "[H]uman nature is fallible," observed the editors of *Cassier's Magazine* in 1905. It was therefore "incumbent upon transportation experts to adopt every possible method and device to secure safety."[126] "[I]f there is blame anywhere," noted another engineering journal with reference to an 1892 train disaster, "it rests with the company rather than with the operator, for the simple reason that human nature is not equal to the strain" of the constant vigilance required in railroading.[127] Signaling systems and safety measures, observed still another engineer, were "a part of the duty of officials in charge of the conduct of transportation."[128] Likewise, in boiler operations, rampant employee carelessness required expert inspection. Moreover, engineers applied their scientific approach to rationalizing any number of other dangerous conditions in industrial life. Bursting flywheels and engine room explosions, blasting, work under compressed air, mining, and railroad and electrical work all presented similar problems of hazardous production processes in which proper engineering could effectively reduce the risk of accidents.[129] In all of these areas, managers might reduce the "unnecessary slaughter and maiming" incident to modern industry to "a theoretical minimum."[130]

As with accident-compensation benefits, a generation of engineering ideas about industrial safety came together at U.S. Steel, where in 1906 and 1907 managers consolidated the company's decentralized, plant-by-plant safety departments into a single Central Committee on Safety.[131] As the historian of the corporation's labor relations has observed, the safety movement at U.S. Steel was the "real center" of the corporation's subsequent labor relations policy, "the source from which practically everything else has sprung."[132] The committee inspected safety conditions in all U.S. Steel subsidiary plants and acted as a company-wide clearing house for safety information. It developed and tested safety devices; disseminated among employees "full details, photographs, diagrams, and complete information of all matters dealing with safety";[133] and implemented such basic safety provisions as railings along high walkways, tunnels allowing for safe travel across railyards, enclosed gears, safer crane hooks, and belt and shaft guards, to name only a few.[134]

There were obvious connections between accident-insurance benefit programs and new ideas about work safety. Firms that took on extra accident costs through accident-benefit plans had increased reason to make their workplaces safe. The Dodge Manufacturing Company of Indiana, for example, implemented a set of accident-relief benefits through the Dodge Mutual Relief Association,[135] while at the same time its management adopted the engineering view of work safety, attributing "the blame for 75 percent of factory accidents to the . . . indifferent attitude of the employer toward employe."[136] Midvale Steel adopted a system of employer-sponsored accident benefits just as Taylor had begun to reengineer its employment practices. And leading firms such as U.S. Steel set up both safety programs and accident-benefits plans.

Notwithstanding prominent cases such as U.S. Steel, however, implementation of new engineering ideas about work safety and accident relief in actual workplaces was a slow process. As Slason Thompson's mock proposal to lash railroad company directors to the front of locomotives had suggested, managerial engineers and those who ultimately controlled firms often failed to see eye to eye.[137] Rationalizing inputs to outputs, as the engineering conception of efficiency aimed to do, was not the same as profit maximization. Indeed, with the exception of catastrophes such as boiler explosions and railroad collisions that threatened to inflict considerable property damage or to generate considerable bad publicity, the leaders of many late-nineteenth-century firms exhibited relatively little interest in adopting many of the safety measures and accident programs advocated by their management engineering experts.

In the employee accident-benefit area in particular, there were at least two great regulatory obstacles to engineers' industrial-accident initiatives. First, courts regularly refused to enforce employment contract provisions barring injured employees from suing their employers in tort. A few early decisions flirted with enforcing employee waivers, but the strong trend in virtually all American jurisdictions soon moved decisively in favor of unenforceability, and a number of legislatures confirmed the trend by enacting legislation expressly barring the enforcement of such employment contract waivers.[138] Many employers responded by adjusting their accident-benefit systems so as to condition receipt of benefits after an accident on waiver of the right to sue. In such schemes, the acceptance of benefits operated as the kind of post-injury settlement of the tort action that courts enforced as a matter of course. Yet even here, employers experienced difficulty preventing employees from bringing tort actions after receipt of their benefits; though many courts enforced such election-of-remedy schemes, others refused to do so.[139] And in a number of states, legislatures enacted statutes barring the use of an employee's acceptance of accident-compensation benefits as a bar to tort suits.[140] At the federal level, the Erdman Act of 1898 did the same for employees of interstate railroads.[141]

The second great obstacle to such schemes—exacerbated by the first—was the competitive disadvantage placed on firms adopting accident-benefits schemes. The American Manufacturing Company of New York City estimated that its private accident-relief fund increased its accident costs fivefold over the common law liability rules.[142] U.S. Steel estimated that its private accident programs cost substantially more than it had paid under the law of employers' liability.[143] Moreover, just as few Americans (whether progressive economists or managers or labor leaders) believed, on the logic of Lemuel Shaw some sixty years earlier in *Farwell v. Boston and Worcester Rail Road,* that wages adjusted to compensate employees for the risks of dangerous work, so too did few Americans believe that employee compensation would adjust downward to reflect the value of accident-benefit plans.[144] Contemporaries were hardly surprised, then, that such accident programs were initiated most frequently in firms that had "very little fear of competition," either because of dominant market positions as in the case of U.S. Steel and International Harvester, or because of a combination of natural monopoly and cost-plus rate regulation as on the railroads.[145] Outside such industries, it was the rare firm that could say with Edward O'Toole of the U.S. Coal and Coke Co. that it would "gladly pay" the additional costs "necessary to permit business to be conducted in a more safe and humane manner."[146] Even railroads, in the early years of railroad employee-accident benefits, had sought to promulgate such schemes through trade associations rather than on a firm-by-firm basis.[147] And by the early twentieth century, one of the most publicized employee-accident benefit schemes was established not by any particular firm, but by the brewing industry as a whole in an industrywide collective bargaining agreement.[148]

Even putting aside questions about the legality of such industrywide agreements under the antitrust laws, the difficulty with these sorts of accident-benefit plans was that they inevitably proved difficult to police. Because of the predominantly German nationality of brewery owners and their employees, and because of the industry's guild-like features, the brewing industry may have possessed solidarity norms and monitoring abilities sufficient to hold together an industrywide agreement to pay expensive accident-insurance benefits. But in other industries, the ability of any one firm to cut back on such benefits in order to gain competitive advantage would have made it exceedingly difficult for any other firm to put an expensive accident-insurance plan into place. This is what economist Henry Carter Adams meant when he argued that competition would "force the moral sentiment pervading any trade down to the level of that which characterizes the worst man who can maintain himself in it." "Even a vast majority of manufacturers in a given industry," explained another observer of employer practices in the area of work accidents, would be "unable to bring about reforms" absent "the aid of uniform legal regulations to force the recalcitrant minority into line."[149] The play of competitive forces thus seemed to obstruct the achievement of efficiency through rationalized employer accident and safety policies. What was needed, suggested economist John R. Commons, was a regulatory solution that would "equalize competition" and "prevent the worst employers from dragging down the others."[150]

The solution that would burst on the scene beginning in 1909 and 1910 was workmen's compensation. Management engineers had cautiously supported broader employer liability and workmen's compensation for work accidents since the early 1890s.[151] Workmen's compensation statutes, which effectively substituted insurance benefits for tort actions against employers, promised to solve both of the regulatory difficulties faced by those who sought to reengineer safety and accident compensation in the workplace. By replacing tort actions with compensation claims, the statutes themselves would ensure that employers would no longer need courts to enforce employment contract provisions waiving employees' rights to sue. Moreover, the statutes would impose the costs of accident relief across entire industries, eliminating the competitive disadvantage of firms with expensive accident-benefit schemes, and even rewarding safe workplaces through reduced compensation costs. At the end of the first decade of the twentieth century, many of the nation's most sophisticated firms joined in a complex coalition of progressive reformers and labor unions to support workmen's compensation legislation.

5

Widows, Actuaries, and the Logics of Social Insurance

> Every year the stream of industrial accidents flows on, and every year it sweeps hundreds and thousands of families away from their little perilous stations of self-respecting independence down the irresistible current first to poverty and then to charity.
>
> —WILLIAM HARD, "THE LAW OF THE KILLED AND WOUNDED" (1908)

In the fall of 1907, a young lawyer named Crystal Eastman arrived in Pittsburgh to study industrial accidents in the great steel mills, coal mines, and railroad yards of western Pennsylvania. Eastman's study was part of the famous Pittsburgh Survey, an investigation of social conditions in what was by many measures the nation's most important industrial city. The Pittsburgh Survey produced widely discussed reports on topics ranging from the life of the steel worker to the cost of living in an industrial city. Nonetheless, the book Eastman produced—*Work-Accidents and the Law,* published in 1910—became perhaps the Survey's most influential work.[1]

In clear and powerful prose, Eastman described the failings of the institutions that had developed since the Civil War to deal with the risk of industrial accidents. She showed that tort law's incessant search for fault was increasingly "oblivious" to the "actual facts" of modern, hierarchically organized firms and of costly, time-consuming tort litigation.[2] Insurance societies, she explained, rarely provided adequate insurance for workmen in dangerous trades; among the Slavic immigrants Eastman studied, three out of four married men had less than $500 in life insurance and savings combined. And only the "largest and most prosperous employers" had adopted accident-relief policies; the "stress of competition" had sharply limited the growth and generosity of employer accident plans.[3]

Eastman's proposed solution was to enact laws, like those already in place across western Europe, requiring that employers compensate all employees injured in the course of their work. The fault of the employer, the employee, or some fellow employee would be irrelevant, except where an employee injured himself by his own intentional wrongful act. Injured employees would have to establish merely that their injuries "arose out of and in the course of" their work. Compensation amounts would be determined as a proportion—

126

one-half or two-thirds—of the injured employees' weekly wages; ideally, employers would also pay injured employees' medical expenses. Common law courts might even be replaced by administrative boards convened to resolve injury claims. In any event, wasteful litigation, crowded court dockets, and costly lawyers would be eliminated.

The solution, in short, was workmen's compensation. In the months after the publication of Eastman's study, commentators described the progress of workmen's compensation with phrases like "prairie fire" and "whirlwind." Eastman herself was appointed to the influential Wainwright Commission of New York State that drafted the nation's first compensation statute, enacted in June 1910 and effective that September. Over the next decade, forty-two of the forty-eight states followed suit. As one Wisconsin study described it, compensation statutes had arrived with a kind of "magical rapidity."[4] Only the South lagged behind; the five states still without compensation programs in 1925 were all in the Deep South.

What was not clear in 1910 was what the politics of workmen's compensation statutes would be. Some features of the legislation were drawn from the same body of free labor principles that had animated earlier experiments in dealing with industrial accidents. Eastman, for example, described workmen's compensation statutes as critical to sustaining the free labor ideal of the family wage: the husband who supported a dependent wife and children. Indeed, it was one of Eastman's great contributions to place the problem of the "destitute widow and children" at the center of the workmen's compensation movement.[5] Yet in other respects, Eastman's aim of protecting the family wage departed radically from what had gone before. With her help, workmen's compensation ushered into American accident law the still-new science of statistics, aggregating the individualized inquiries of classical tort law into actuarial categories. Moreover, the statutes took as a starting premise the kinds of manager-dominated firms that had already begun to develop internal work-injury compensation schemes; these firms, in turn, provided strong political support for the statutes, alongside a coalition of state federations of labor and progressive social insurance advocates. Many in this coalition even believed that workmen's compensation statutes would be the first in a series of new social insurance programs, ranging from health insurance to old-age pensions to unemployment insurance.

Compensation statutes sought to save the family wage by reworking the values of individual autonomy, independence, and self-ownership on which classical tort law and workingmen's cooperative insurance societies had been founded. In the process, workmen's compensation subtly shifted the work-accident debate from the ideology of free labor, with its questions about the meaning of self-ownership in a wage labor economy, toward actuarial categories and aggregated risks. The story of workmen's compensation is the working out of the consequences of this halting and partial paradigm shift.

Historical accounts have long oscillated between radically incompatible competing interpretations of workmen's compensation. On some accounts, the statutes appear as a sharp break from what had gone before. This view was typical of the social justice theory of workmen's compensation statutes articulated by the first generation of compensation historians. For these early historians, workmen's compensation was an unambiguous advance from a stingy nineteenth-century law of employers' liability to a regime organized around serving the needs of injured workers.[6] By the late 1960s, historians had reversed the political significance of the statutes. Historians in the then-ascendant corporate-liberal school explained the enactment of compensation statutes as a novel gambit by employers to reduce and standardize the mounting costs of jury awards under the common law of employers' liability, a gambit that presaged the capture of the emerging regulatory state by the very industries it purported to regulate. Yet like the advocates of the social justice theory before them, corporate-liberal historians saw workmen's compensation as sharply discontinuous with the past. In their view, compensation under the new statutes modernized accident law for the twentieth century. It took cases away from increasingly generous juries, cut out expensive middlemen like insurance companies and personal injury lawyers, ameliorated an increasingly difficult area of employer–employee conflict, and allowed firms to standardize their accident costs by eliminating unpredictable jury awards.[7]

Other accounts describe workmen's compensation as more continuous with what preceded it. The prior regulation theory, for example, holds that workmen's compensation statutes were enacted largely because they did not require the development of a new field of regulation. Unlike such social insurance programs as unemployment insurance and old-age pensions that were not enacted until the New Deal, workmen's compensation required no new state intervention in the economy, but merely amended the regulatory regime of an area already governed by courts applying the common law of employers' liability.[8]

Perhaps the leading account in the literature on workmen's compensation legislation is what we might call the "bargain theory." Under this interpretation, which also adopts the continuity view, workmen's compensation was simply a variation on the employer-accident plans in which employees waived their right to sue for work accidents in return for limited but certain compensation. The difficulty was that courts refused to enforce employment contract terms waiving the right to sue. As the theory goes, employers and employees turned to state legislatures to create a public regime mimicking the benefits of the private accident plans that they would have entered into in the labor market, but for the courts' refusal to enforce the contractual waivers.[9]

Serious difficulties confront all of these historical accounts.[10] The social justice theory has never had an especially good explanation of why many sophisticated firms supported workmen's compensation but opposed other social insurance reforms designed to serve the needs of poor workers. The prior regulation theory cannot explain why many railroad accidents—the most heavily regulated field of work accidents in the nineteenth century—have not, to this day, been placed under an administrative compensation scheme. The corporate-liberal theory fails to account for the substantial majority of employers opposing the statutes, and the sharp, widely expected increases in employers' liability insurance premiums in many states, ranging from 20 and 50 percent in New York and Ohio to 300 percent in California.[11] And neither the corporate-liberal theory nor the bargain theory can explain the fact that the nation's first major workmen's compensation statute created a post-injury option for injured employees, who were allowed either to take limited damages in the compensation system or to roll the dice for higher awards in the tort system. The New York statute that kicked off the compensation movement thus failed to provide the employer advantages attributed to workmen's compensation by the corporate-liberal and bargain theories.[12]

This is not to say that these accounts ought to be disregarded. No single interpretation need explain everything about workmen's compensation, and the one offered here surely will not. The point is that notwithstanding generations of writing on the subject, there is still much that is unexplained about the compensation statutes. As if to compensate for the difficulty of accounting for the significance of the most important work-accident legislation in American history, interpretations have swung wildly between descriptions of the statutes as pro-employee and then pro-employer, as backward-looking and then forward-looking. Yet in these oscillations lies a clue to the meaning and significance of the workmen's compensation statutes. For workmen's compensation was all of these things at once. With Crystal Eastman's help, the statutes worked an equivocal transformation in the organizing principles of American accident law, one that (like historians' interpretations in the decades since) looked both forward and back.

Eastman provides our starting place in grappling with the halfway transformation that was workmen's compensation. Looking back from the 1930s, one commentator described Eastman's *Work-Accidents and the Law* as "perhaps the strongest single force in attracting public opinion" to the problem of industrial hazards.[13] The book has long been remembered for its critique of those who attributed responsibility for accidents to negligent employees rather than to the firms and industries in which they worked.[14] Eastman's less recognized contribution was to organize work-accident debates around the image of the wounded family.

In the late nineteenth century, the capacity of the family wage to shelter dependent women and children from the labor market became, in historian Amy Dru Stanley's phrase, a "testing ground" of the wage labor system.[15] Wage labor seemed increasingly to require workingmen to enter into a lifetime of back-to-back labor contracts without the chance for economic independence or independent proprietorship. Life-long employees under the control of their employers uncomfortably recalled slavery's life-long economic subordination. By setting women and children outside the labor market, however, the wage labor system distinguished itself from regimes of coerced labor. Under slavery, women and children had worked alongside men, and families had been subject to forced separations. As economic independence receded as a realistic aspiration for American workingmen, sustaining the family wage became increasingly important to the moral legitimacy of wage labor. Yet one of Eastman's central insights as a social critic was to see the contradictions inhering in the family wage between male freedom and the support of dependent women. As Eastman had seen from remarkably early in her own life, the autonomy of male free laborers was often at odds with the preservation of separate sphere domesticity. Dependent wives essentially had nondiversified investments in their husbands' wages. "[N]o woman," as she wrote in 1896 as a fifteen-year-old, "who allows husband and children to absorb her whole time and interest is safe against disaster."[16]

By 1907 and 1908, industrial hazards became a primary manifestation of the "disasters" for the family wage about which Eastman had hinted in her 1896 paper. A workingman free to be injured at work was a workingman at risk of not being able to support his wife and children. Industrial accidents thus undid free labor's distinction between home and work. Like slavery, injuries to male wage earners threw women and children into the labor market and broke up previously intact families. In Eastman's view, workmen's compensation statutes would provide insurance for the family wage against this great disaster to which turn-of-the-century families were exposed.

Eastman, to be sure, was an unlikely proponent of ameliorative social reform to secure women's dependence on their husbands' wages. In an era with few women professionals, she was a New York University–trained lawyer with a graduate degree in political economy from Columbia. Along with her brother Max, editor of the radical avant-garde journal *The Masses,* Eastman gained prominence in the 1910s as an iconoclastic feminist, socialist, and peace activist. In later years, her early ideas about happiness and women's economic status would lead her to endorse wages for housework in the form of "motherhood endowments": state subsidies of housework to provide women with "real economic independence."[17] Nonetheless, Eastman's work on behalf of workmen's compensation was less about transforming the family wage than about shoring up its increasingly unstable structure.

In *Work-Accidents and the Law*, Eastman approached the problem of work accidents "from the 'home' side." The "most appalling feature" of the work-accident crisis she studied in and around Pittsburgh, Eastman contended, was "that it fell exclusively upon workers, bread-winners." Virtually all the workplace fatalities she studied had killed men (only 3 out of 526 killed women). Sixty-three percent of the fatalities "meant the sudden cutting-off of the sole or chief support of a family." "The people who perished," Eastman concluded, "were those upon whom the world leans." Studying the "home side" of the accidents therefore meant telling stories about widows, children, and families. With the help of highly sentimentalized photographs by a young photographer named Lewis Hine (later to become famous for his photographs of industrial America), and with the use of captions written for their shock value ("One Arm and Four Children"; "One of the Mothers"; "One of Six"; "A Breadwinner of Three Generations Taken"), Eastman recounted the fate of dozens of Pittsburgh families in the wake of work accidents. A widow with two children had been forced from her home into back rooms at a parent's house. Another widow and her five children moved from their home and took in "washing and mending for the laborers who live nearby." A third widow and her four young children saw their income reduced from $20 per week to $3—"a pinching economy." For these families and many more like them, Eastman described work accidents as devastating household events.[18]

In the spirit of Eastman's report, the state and federal commissions created to study work accidents also made dependent wives and children central objects of concern. The U.S. Department of Labor published studies of the "effect of workmen's compensation laws in diminishing the necessity of industrial employment of women and children."[19] In Minnesota, a study commissioned by the state told story after story of families driven into poverty by work accidents: the pregnant widow of a dead sawyer; the sewer digger's family left "in destitute circumstances"; the dependent widow and two children of a deceased telephone lineman. Across the state line in Wisconsin, commissioners even drew up elaborate charts mapping the impact of work accidents on dependents.[20] In New York, charity leader Edward Devine argued to the Wainwright Commission that the work accident was perhaps the most dangerous destroyer of homes in the industrial wage-earning economy:

We see people dispossessed for the first time in their lives because of this accident, and going into the ranks of people who expect to be dispossessed whenever they move. We see people pawning their furniture; we see people using up what little savings bank account they have had; we see people obliged to turn in humiliation and with permanent injury to the charitable societies or to relatives and friends, and other people who have heretofore been entirely self-supporting and independent.

The implication for work-accident cases was clear: "I came practically to the conclusion long ago," Devine testified, that "the Charitable Society had no business to be dealing with them." "[T]he State," he finished, "ought to be dealing with them on an entirely different basis."[21]

Upholding the family wage was of course not a novel goal in American personal injury law. From its beginnings in the 1840s and 1850s, the American law of accidents—and especially the wrongful death statutes—had promoted a specific conception of men's and women's relationships to economic production. The organization of manufacturing industries and labor markets had removed men's work from the household and marked women's work as distinct from male labor and as peculiarly domestic in its scope. The wrongful death statutes enacted in the 1840s and 1850s had taken part in this reorganization of work and the family by providing widows—but not widowers—a new cause of action for loss of support.[22]

State and federal workmen's compensation commissions carried on the gendered structure of the wrongful death statutes, even writing the model of the family wage into the new statutes. By 1900, many states (including New York) had eliminated the provisions that limited wrongful death actions to widows. But like the wrongful death legislation of the 1840s and 1850s, New York's path-breaking 1910 workmen's compensation statute provided that in the event of a fatal work accident, compensation for lost wages was to be provided only if the workman left a dependent "widow or next of kin."[23] As litigation under the wrongful death statutes had established, widowers were neither next of kin nor widows.[24] They therefore had no claim under the compensation statute for damages arising out of the deaths of their wives. Moreover, this gender asymmetry in the compensation statute (like the earlier asymmetry in the wrongful death statutes) was a peculiarly American phenomenon. In most significant respects, the compensation statute had closely tracked its 1897 English predecessor. Yet the Wainwright Commission borrowed the gender asymmetry not from the English statute but from New York's own original wrongful death statute.[25] In its workmen's compensation statute of 1910, then, New York replicated its earlier departure from English accident law's symmetrical benefit structure and returned to the asymmetrical gender structure of New York's mid-nineteenth-century law of wrongful death.

New York was hardly alone in the reinscription of the family wage into the nation's accident law. Of twenty-six compensation statutes enacted in U.S. jurisdictions before 1914, fourteen adopted asymmetrical death-benefit schemes. Six of these—including the statutes governing the important industrial states of Illinois and New York—precluded payment of compensation to widowers. Other states—including California, New Jersey, and Ohio—created presumptions of dependency for widows while requiring widowers to prove dependency in order to make out a claim for compensation arising out of the death of a spouse. Still others enacted asymmetrical invalidity requirements under which widowers could recover death benefits only if disabled or otherwise incapable of self-support.[26] At the federal level, the first Federal Employers' Liability Act provided for liability in railroad employee death cases "for the benefit of his [the dead employee's] widow and children."[27] The federal government employees' accident-compensation scheme enacted in 1908 paid death benefits only in cases in which the employee left a "widow, or a child or children under sixteen years of age, or a dependent parent."[28] Important bills passed by both the House and the Senate in 1912 and 1913, but not enacted into law, would have created a workmen's compensation scheme for railroad employees in interstate commerce; death benefits would have been payable to widows, or to dependent parents, siblings, grandparents, or grandchildren, but under no circumstances to widowers.[29] And the Longshoremen and Harborworkers' Compensation Act enacted in 1927 created a conclusive presumption of dependency for widows while requiring widowers to prove dependency in fact.[30]

The gender asymmetries of the workmen's compensation statutes were not merely instances of the feminine term "widow" posing as a generic. In the only reported case raising the question, the New Hampshire Supreme Court rejected a widower's claim for workmen's compensation benefits under a gender-specific death-benefits scheme.[31] Workmen's compensation was just that: work*men's*, not yet work*ers'* compensation. The husbands of deceased working women would not be heard to bring claims under the statutes. Significantly, there appears to have been much less litigation over the question of widower eligibility under the workmen's compensation statutes than there had been under the wrongful death statutes; husbands dependent on their wives no longer challenged the gender categories that workmen's compensation sought to sustain. Perhaps such husbands could not find lawyers to challenge the statutes given the unavailability of significant contingency fee awards under workmen's compensation's limited damages schedules. But perhaps, too, the gendered categories that had still been in formation when the wrongful death statutes were enacted had solidified over time. At the very least, the precedents set in wrongful death cases meant that family wage categories had hardened as a matter of law. Asymmetrical benefit schemes in workmen's compensation statutes would endure virtually unchallenged through the 1970s; the U.S. Supreme Court struck them down as unconstitutional sex discrimination in 1980.[32]

In the family wage, workmen's compensation supporters found a part of the free labor tradition that offered support for their legislative movement. Other aspects of the free labor worldview, however, seemed less consonant with workmen's compensation. The Reconstruction amendments to the federal constitution—the Thirteenth, Fourteenth, and Fifteenth Amendments—had written into American constitutional law legal and political commitments arising out of the Civil War. The Due Process Clause of the Fourteenth Amendment guaranteed all persons "due process of law"; the amendment's Equal Protection Clause purported to ensure "the equal protection of the laws." In the generation thereafter, federal and state courts developed a body of case law in which these two clauses of the Fourteenth Amendment—promulgated to guarantee the civil rights of former slaves in the postslavery South—became limitations on the power of government to regulate contracts, especially between employers and employees. Courts struck down laws that prohibited manufacturing industries in tenement houses, that limited the hours of bakery workers, and even laws that regulated the hours of women workers.[33] To be sure, courts also upheld many statutes regulating contractual relationships. Indeed, courts upheld far more statutes than they struck down.[34] Still, the threat of judicial review—what Henry Farnham of the American Association for Labor Legislation called the "bugaboo of constitutionality"—gave pause to many would-be reformers, especially in the field of male wage earners' employment.[35]

The critical question in 1909 and 1910 was whether workmen's compensation (which rested on compulsory participation in an insurance scheme for employers and employees) was consistent with these constitutional limitations. Courts articulated the boundaries of permissible legislative regulation by reference to a principle drawn from classical tort law: *sic utere tuo ut alienum non laedas,* or "use your own property so as not to injure others."[36] At the core of the *sic utere* principle lay a basic requirement of the law of torts: causation between the activity to be regulated and some injury to others. The state's authority to regulate *A,* either by commanding restraint of a particular property right's exercise or by requiring that *A* compensate *B* for *B*'s injury, turned on whether *A caused* injury to *B.* Absent such causation, requiring *A* to compensate *B* constituted impermissible redistribution of *A*'s property to *B* without due process and in violation of the law's ostensible commitment to the equal treatment of persons.[37]

Courts elaborated the constitutional causation requirement in cases raising now little-remembered challenges to two kinds of nineteenth-century railroad legislation: spark fire statutes and cattle injury statutes. Beginning in the 1840s and stretching over the next several decades, legislatures across the country enacted legislation making railroads strictly liable, regardless of negligence, for any injury done to buildings or other property of others by fire communicated from railroad engines.[38] Railroads claimed that this spark legislation constituted a taking without compensation. Damages awards to property owners in such cases, they contended, were illegitimate redistributive transfers from *A* to *B*.

Courts, however, unanimously rejected the railroads' arguments.[39] Legislation making a railroad strictly liable for spark fires simply made a choice as between two available and equally permissible applications of the *sic utere* principle. To be sure, the common law rule held that as between a nonnegligent injuring railroad and a faultless victim property owner, the loss lay where it fell: on the property owner. As Justice Horace Gray summarized the reasoning behind the rule for the U.S. Supreme Court in 1897, the state had "authorized" railroads to propel railroad cars by steam and fire, and because they were thereby "pursuing a lawful business, they are only liable for negligence in its operation." This was the rule of *damnum absque injuria,* or injury without a remedy. But as Justice Gray observed, similar arguments were available to the other side: "To this the citizen answers: 'I also own my land lawfully. I have the right to grow my crops and erect buildings on it, at any place I choose. I did not set in motion any dangerous machinery.'" In fact, Gray continued, the plaintiff landowner had as powerful a takings argument as the railroad: "the state, which owes me protection to my property from others, has chartered an agency which, be it ever so careful and cautious and prudent, inevitably destroys my property, and yet denies me all redress. The state has no right to take or damage my property without just compensation." To allow the state to impose the costs of such fires on the landowner, Gray concluded, would be to allow the state to do "indirectly through the charters granted to railroads" "what the state cannot do directly." It was therefore "perfectly competent for the state to require the company" that caused the fire to pay the ensuing damages.[40]

The spark statute cases did not mean that legislatures were free to allocate accident losses to whomever they pleased. In the case of *Ohio and Mississippi Railway Company v. Lackey* (1875), the Illinois Supreme Court struck down a statute making railroad companies liable for the expenses of coroners' inquests and burials for "all persons who may die on the cars, or who may be killed by collision, or other accident occurring to such cars or otherwise." The statute attempted, the court explained, to reallocate costs "no matter how caused," "even if by the [decedent's] own hand." *Lackey* thus stood for the proposition that reallocating accident costs was impermissible absent the kind of ostensibly clear causal connection that existed in the spark cases. The statute impermissibly transferred resources from railroads to those groups who otherwise would have borne such costs: railroad passengers and the public.[41]

Lackey quickly became a prominent citation in a line of cases decided by courts around the country striking down statutes that made railroad corporations liable for injuries to cattle and other domestic animals run over by engines or cars. The difficulty with these "stock" statutes, and the key distinction between them and the spark statutes, was that the stock legislation sought to charge railroads with liability in cases in which courts perceived questions of causation as considerably more difficult. The stock statutes, courts reasoned, created an unrebuttable presumption that the railroads had caused the injuries to the animals. But such a conclusive presumption was unwarranted. It would charge a railroad with liability even where the animals' owner had been guilty of gross negligence or "wanton and intentional acts in subjecting his animals to injury or destruction."[42] The stock statutes, in other words, proposed to make railroads liable even where owners were responsible for their animals' injuries. State courts therefore uniformly held these laws unconstitutional on the theory that they allocated accident costs without regard to responsibility for those costs.[43] As a result, the stock statutes violated the rule that "private property cannot be taken for strictly private purposes at all, nor for public purposes without compensation." The statutes, in other words, were instances of what late-nineteenth-century American lawyers called "class legislation," requiring one class of persons to pay another, even where the beneficiaries of the statute might be the authors of the misfortune for which they were to be compensated.[44]

Together, the spark statute and stock statute cases sketched a theory of due process as a constitutional baseline of entitlements as between *A* and *B*, reallocation of which was permissible only by the consent of the parties, or to remedy an injury to one caused by the other. Workmen's compensation statutes seemed perilously close to the line separating permissible and impermissible accident-cost allocations. The new statutes adopted the strict-liability standard that had been implemented in both the spark and the stock statutes. And workmen's compensation statutes such as those enacted in other western nations, and such as the one first enacted in New York in 1910, were compulsory. They applied to employers and employees regardless of consent, without providing either the opportunity to opt out. Moreover, workmen's compensation statutes raised a host of ancillary constitutional questions in addition to those raised by the Fourteenth Amendment and its state constitution analogues. Could legislatures shift accident cases to administrative tribunals, or would constitutional guarantees require judges and juries even in workmen's compensation cases? Could states provide for limited compensation awards in work-fatality cases, or would late-nineteenth-century state constitutional prohibitions on limiting the damages available in death cases require that damages be unlimited and determined on a case-by-case basis?

The early record of compulsory accident compensation in the courts was, as a Minnesota report put it, a "discouraging . . . history of defeats."[45] Maryland in 1902 had enacted a poorly drafted insurance scheme abolishing the fellow servant rule for employee injuries on railroads and streetcars and in mines and quarries, but providing employers the opportunity to opt into a compensation program that would award deceased workers' families automatic but limited compensation. A 1904 Maryland court, however, had held the statute unconstitutional for vesting judicial powers in the state insurance commissioner, for taking away from employees the right to sue in negligence for unlimited damages, and for denying them the right to have their cases heard before a jury.[46] Four years later, the U.S. Supreme Court had struck down as unconstitutional the first Federal Employers' Liability Act on the ground that it was beyond Congress's power under the Commerce Clause to amend the law of employers' liability for all interstate railroad employees, rather than merely for those who were themselves engaged in interstate commerce.[47]

Questions abounded about whether a new round of work-accident reform legislation would fare any better. Social insurance expert I. M. Rubinow remembered constitutional law as "the most carefully discussed problem at the Atlantic City Conference" of state workmen's compensation commissioners in 1909.[48] Everyone agreed that early state commissions placed "great stress" on the constitutional issues.[49] Commission counsel in Wisconsin and Connecticut concluded that compulsory compensation statutes would be "clearly unconstitutional"; on the same question, their counterparts in Illinois, Massachusetts, and Minnesota expressed grave doubts.[50] Henry Seager of New York's Wainwright Commission would later recall "how much anxious thought we gave to trying to draft an act that the Court of Appeals would uphold."[51] Prominent commentators even predicted that constitutional amendments would ultimately be necessary at both the state and federal levels.[52]

The commissions' response was to try to draft compensation statutes designed to skirt the constitutional difficulties. Joseph Cotton of the Wainwright Commission, very likely the primary drafter of the New York legislation, spoke for all the commissions when he said, "This Commission does not want an unconstitutional law."[53] And so the typical early workmen's compensation statute was, in Henry Seager's words, "maimed and twisted so that it might commend itself to the judges."[54] In Illinois and Wisconsin, commission counsel recommended elective compensation statutes that gave employers and employees the right to opt out of the new compensation system.[55] Elsewhere, state commissions limited their legislation to dangerous industries such as railroading and blasting. The common law of tort had carved out a special zone of strict liability for extrahazardous activities. Late-nineteenth-century courts' due process jurisprudence was similarly more lenient with state labor regulations where dangerous industries were concerned. Dangerous industries were by definition those most likely to cause harm. Courts had thus allowed legislatures to create a kind of presumption that the *sic utere* maxim authorized regulation in dangerous industries.[56] Accordingly, the Wainwright Commission (among others) drafted New York's statute to apply only to "employments . . . determined to be especially dangerous," specifically construction and demolition, electrical work, blasting, railroad work, tunnel construction, and "work carried on under compressed air."[57]

So limited, workmen's compensation statutes seemed to many to satisfy the constitutional requirements of due process. In dangerous industries, the statutes' supporters reasoned, employers surely were as responsible for industrial accidents as railroads were for spark fires. Injuries and fires were simply the inevitable consequences of industrial activity. It followed that to make industrial firms bear the costs of such injuries or such fires was merely to implement the *sic utere* principle under which firms would have to pay for the injuries they caused. What's more, because employees were sometimes responsible for their own injuries, compensation statutes would require employers to pay for only one-half or two-thirds of an employee's lost wages. The result would be a rough justice, consistent with constitutional requirements of due process, but without the costly, time-consuming litigation of the common law of torts. In these claims, however, lay the germ of a radically new way of thinking about industrial accidents, and indeed about law and social policy more generally.

In March 1905, four years before Crystal Eastman would arrive in New York City to organize the work of the Wainwright Commission and to complete her Pittsburgh study, a bizarre work accident took place in the city's East River. While digging a subway tunnel under the East River, a laborer (or "sandhog," as tunnel diggers were called) named Richard Creedon noticed a tiny leak in the roof of the pressurized air chamber in which he was working. Air pressurized at thirteen pounds per square inch began quickly to enlarge the hole in the shield separating the chamber from the silt of the river bed. Creedon sought to plug the hole with bags of clay and mud kept on hand for just that purpose. Suddenly, however, the air pressure overcame the silt and water above. Creedon was blown up through a hole four feet in diameter, through seventeen feet of river bottom and ten feet of thirty-five-degree water. Witnesses variously estimated that Creedon was carried some ten to fifty feet further up into the air before falling back into the river.[58]

Edward Devine, who would later testify in favor of workmen's compensation legislation before the Wainwright Commission, described the incident as follows:

[Creedon] tried to stop it, but the hole grew rapidly larger, not because water was coming in, but because [pressurized] air was escaping. Into the hole made in this way in the roof of the tunnel the man himself was finally driven by the force of the compressed air and up through the mud and sand of the bed of the river and through the river itself into the air above, very much to the astonishment of the crew of a tug-boat who had the honor of rescuing a man thrown into the river from an altogether different direction from what is customary.[59]

In most respects, the fantastic tunnel incident stood out as radically unlike the kinds of work accidents about which Eastman and others were writing. The *New York Times* described it as "unparalleled in the records of submarine engineering accidents." Moreover, unlike most of Eastman's subjects—and unlike two other sandhogs feared dead in another tunnel blow-out under the East River that same day—Creedon was miraculously uninjured. As he told the story, once through the river bed and out of the water, he had opened his eyes and enjoyed a "fine view of the city."[60]

And yet in one respect, the blow-out in the East River subway tunnel captured what the work-accident crisis had wrought. For the tug crew that came to Creedon's rescue, the world seemed turned upside down; here was a man—in Devine's words—"thrown into the river from an altogether different direction from what is customary." In just this way, workmen's compensation acts seemed to supporters and opponents alike somehow to upend the customary principles of American law. Dozens of commission reports, hundreds of legislative hearings, and the vast literature that grew up around compensation proposals labeled workmen's compensation "revolutionary," "radical," and "collectivist." Workmen's compensation was "a step in the dark," it was "unjust, radical, and socialistic," it was even "freak legislation," to quote one Washington State merchant.[61]

The novelty of the statutes lay in their statistical approach to thinking about accidents, an approach that had already begun to reshape the law of a number of western European nations. Statistical thinking is a remarkably recent development in Western thought. The word "statistics" itself, which derives from the word "state" and describes the science of gathering facts bearing on the condition of the state, did not appear in English until the late eighteenth century.[62] Only in the nineteenth century did the statistical study of the state come of age in what philosopher of science Ian Hacking has called the "avalanche of printed numbers" generated by nineteenth-century nation-states. There were precursors, of course. As early as the 1650s, for example, mathematicians such as Pascal had calculated regularities in games of chance. Eighteenth-century astronomers had discovered a "law of error" in observations of the position of stellar objects. The new move in the nineteenth century, however, was to develop data on social rather than mathematical or natural phenomena, and to draw from that data new "laws" of social life. From relatively insignificant phenomena like the predictable yearly accumulation of so-called dead letters in the Paris post office, to more weighty concerns such as the yearly numbers of births, marriages, and deaths, these "statistical laws," as Belgian astronomer Adolphe Quetelet called them, seemed to govern human events by the hand of an inexorable logic, generating predictable, law-like regularities in the basic features and practices of social life.[63]

To think in terms of probabilities was to make possible new approaches to the problem of risk. Probabilistic mathematics, for example, made possible the modern actuarial calculations that underwrote the development of insurance systems. And so it was in the beginnings of the European social insurance state that the new technologies of social probability and actuarial thinking emerged onto the center stage of social policy.[64] As François Ewald observes of France, the key underlying observation of social insurance advocates was that such things as industrial accidents "repeat themselves with overwhelming regularity." An 1889 study of accident statistics in the French mining industry, for example, revealed that "taking a large number of workers in the same occupation, one finds a constant level of accidents year by year. It follows from this that accidents, just when they may seem to be due to pure chance, are governed by a mysterious law."[65] In the face of such statistical regularity, risk-spreading programs suddenly seemed exceedingly important. Individuals could not be blamed for such events, as it was inevitable that they would occur. Social insurance, however, could provide individuals guaranteed protections against the inexorable risks of industrial life. Moreover, social insurance could spread across an entire society the costs of accidents that were bound to happen to an unlucky few.

Statistical thinking about social risks was slower to develop in the United States. As a leading historian of American numeracy has written, "all of the major developments in the mathematical theory of statistics in the nineteenth century originated in Europe."[66] There were important trends in the middle of the century toward the use of actuarial principles in the law of marine and fire insurance. Yet not until debates over work accidents at the turn of the twentieth century did the statistical laws of nineteenth-century Europe come into common parlance in the politics and law of the United States. Oliver Wendell Holmes Jr.'s 1897 "Path of the Law" address at the dedication of the Boston University School of Law, given eight months before Great Britain would enact its workmen's compensation law, noted that tort law was increasingly concerned with those "injuries to person or property" that were the incidents of "well known businesses" such as "railroads, factories, and the like." Twenty years earlier in *The Common Law*, Holmes had focused on "isolated, ungeneralized wrongs" between persons. His new frame of analysis was statistical. Injury cases no longer presented questions of justice as between individuals. The new question was "how far it is desirable that the public should insure the safety of those whose work it uses." This was distinctly a question of aggregates. Under the common law of tort, "the chance of a jury finding" for one party or the other was just that: "merely a chance," and it was "therefore better done away with" in favor of averages and aggregates. "The man of the future" in the law, Holmes announced in what is among his most famous aphorisms, "is the man of statistics and the master of economics."[67]

Holmes likely picked up probabilistic thinking from such men as Charles Sanders Pierce, with whom Holmes associated as a fellow member of the famed Metaphysical Club in the 1870s.[68] But in the arenas of everyday American law, it was state labor department officials tabulating industrial accident tolls, and work-accident reformers who saw in those yearly tolls the same regularities that had been observed a few decades earlier in France, who introduced Quetelet's notion of "statistical laws." As one journalist noted, industrial accidents seemed to be "the inevitable concomitants of high-speed machine production."[69] "The Moloch of industrial activity," concluded an Illinois commission, "demands a sacrifice of life and limb, constant, as the actuaries tables show, and inevitable so long as human contrivances and human understanding are fallible."[70] In New York, the Wainwright Commission concluded "beyond peradventure that the hazardous employments of the State annually exact their toll of life and limb of the workers, with astounding certainty"; the toll was "as remorseless and as certain as the death rate on which the tables for life insurance are based."[71] Statistical calculations of the kind Quetelet had made so influential in Europe provided a way to get a handle on the astonishing regularity of workplace injuries. "There is a definite ratio of industrial accidents to exposure to accident," explained Joseph Cotton of the Wainwright Commission. "The average machine stamp will once in so many thousand times crush and mangle a finger"; "each revolving belting will in so many thousand revolutions tear away a worker's arm." Indeed, statistical laws made such injuries inevitable: "although you can reduce that ratio by care and preventative devices . . . an appalling ratio of maims and cripples still accompanies and must always accompany the use of machinery."[72] As prominent muckraking journalist William Hard told his readers, the "stream of industrial accidents" was an "irresistible current," sweeping away thousands of families each year.[73]

I. M. Rubinow summed up this strand of thinking when he announced that in the statistical view, "an industrial accident is not an accident at all."[74] Workmen's compensation acts had moved analysis of work accidents from the close specificity of individualized inquiries into particular accident cases to a higher plane of statistical generality. From this abstracted perspective, the failings of individual employees—their carelessness, their inattentiveness, their occasional recklessness—seemed to have no significance for the regular toll of industrial accidents. The Moloch of industry would have its yearly sacrifice notwithstanding the individual actions of particular workingmen. And at the heightened level of generality at which the statistician thought about social phenomena, the core category of nineteenth-century American tort law—the pure accident of nonnegligent victims and nonfaulty causes, which tort had treated as *damnum absque injuria*—seemed virtually to cover the field. "Certain dangers, including negligence of the workman and of his fellow-servants," explained Eugene Wambaugh in the *Harvard Law Review*, "are inevitable as a business proposition. A man who plans a suspension bridge, or a tunnel, for example, knows that experience tables tell in advance almost as well as after the fact how many lives must be lost."[75] Workmen's compensation expert E. H. Downey of the University of Wisconsin tied the work-accident experience directly to early statisticians' studies of dead letters in the Paris post office:

> Of a million letters posted in a given community a certain number will be wrongly addressed and a certain number left unstamped. Of a thousand men who mount dizzying heights in erecting steel structures a certain number will fall to death; and of a thousand girls who feed metal stripes into presses a certain number will have their fingers crushed. The proportions vary little from year to year: given sufficiently large numbers under stable conditions, they can be calculated with an approximation to mathematical accuracy.

Accidents from human error, Downey concluded, were "as inevitable as" accidents from "any other" cause.[76]

The architects of tort law had sought to collapse the destabilizing *damnum absque* category, to reduce to nil the number of cases falling into it. But from the perspective of the statistician, the regular toll of accidents could be attributed neither to the fault of victims nor to the negligence of injurers. Injuries that arose in the course of employment were nobody's fault in the personal sense. They were instead attributable to the inherent hazards of industry. Actuarial categories and statistical laws thus seemed to undercut moral responsibility, autonomy, and independence as meaningful categories in analyzing the problem of industrial accidents. The result was a demoralization of the work accident. Since accidents were "a necessary hazard of the work," in the words of a Washington State commission, "the moral fault of the workman" had been "eliminated."[77]

Crystal Eastman's genius was to marry the symbolism of the family wage to the emergence of this new actuarial mode of social thought. As a graduate student at Columbia in 1903 and 1904, Eastman had studied sociology and statistics under Franklin Henry Giddings, one of the greats of early American sociology.[78] Among Giddings's major contributions to American sociology was the introduction of statistical methods to the study of society. As one retrospective on his career described it, Giddings accounted for relations of cause and effect "in terms of chance and probability."[79] In turn, Eastman's study of industrial accidents for the Pittsburgh Survey put Giddings's statistical ideas to use in rescuing the family wage from the onslaught of industrial accidents.

The statistical notion of the "yearly loss" formed the starting point of Eastman's report on work fatalities in Pittsburgh. The 526 fatalities she counted in one year, she wrote, surely would recur in a regular annual toll. "Each year has turned them out as surely as the mills ran full and the railroads prospered," Eastman wrote. "In five years there would be 2,500. Ten years would make 5,000."[80] In Eastman's view, if it was inevitable that industrial accidents would take their regular annual toll of workingmen, workmen's compensation could at least ensure that dependent women and children were not thrown into the labor market for failures of support that were beyond their control. Indeed, by turning the spotlight on the inexorable accumulation of faultless dependents, Eastman's study illuminated the shortcomings of a tort system in which cases turned on questions of employee and employer fault.

Yet if the statistical view offered new support for the family wage, it also posed a crisis for other elements of the complex of views that made up the free labor paradigm. What good were individual autonomy and independence, for example, if individual efforts seemed to have no effect on the yearly accumulation of industrial catastrophes? The work-accident problem at the turn of the twentieth century thus generated an American analogue to the intellectual crisis of statistical determinism that had come to preoccupy European statisticians from early in the nineteenth century. Nineteenth-century social statistics had seemed to imply a new kind of determinism in which the free will of individual human beings appeared to have been crushed under the iron laws of social life. French statistician Pierre Simon Laplace proclaimed in the 1810s that social phenomena of all kinds followed ineluctably "from the great laws of the universe"—indeed "follow from them just as necessarily as the revolutions of the sun." Across the channel, Henry Thomas Buckle wrote his *History of Civilization in England* based on the theory that statistics proved human history to be "governed by laws as fixed and regular as those which rule the physical world." Small wonder, then, that many in Europe noted that from the statistical perspective "it seems as if free will exists only in theory." Social life appeared to be shaped not by human beings but by laws of society that could be detected only under the bright lights of the statistical method.[81]

Eastman's study of work accidents performed a similar statistical annulment of individual agency. Popular myth, she observed, held that "95 percent of our accidents are due to the carelessness of the man who gets hurt." But in Eastman's careful analysis of coroners' inquest reports, the "personal factor in industrial accidents," as she called it, seemed almost to disappear. In point of fact, she contended, responsibility for only one in four workplace fatalities could be attributed solely to "those killed or their fellow workmen." On the whole, the problem of accidents was best understood not at the level of each "distinct and separate incident," but at a higher level of generality that encompassed modern industry as a whole and thereby allowed for "generalizing or drawing conclusions." Yet at this level of generality, individuals no longer seemed to have control over their own fate. Industrial accidents seemed instead to be governed by a law of social life outside of the efforts of individual actors. And in the face of such statistical regularities, classical tort law's attempt to assign fault and responsibility through individualized inquiry into each work-accident case seemed beside the point. Following Quetelet, who had substituted *l'homme moyen*—"the average man"—for the individual as the appropriate unit of social analysis, Eastman argued that "[a]ll that can be hoped for is a rule that is fair in the *average case*." The aim of workmen's compensation statutes was therefore not to provide what Eastman called "merely justice between individuals" but rather to establish "a distribution of the loss which shall be to the best interests of all concerned."[82]

It would be wrong, however, to suggest that the new perspective of statistical regularity generated a wholesale fatalism. From the perspective of aggregates, individual efforts might wash out in the run of cases. But the structures and institutional environs—the *systems*—in which individuals acted might redirect the sum of the outcomes of such individualized efforts. English statistician William Farr had explained to the International Statistical Congress in 1860 that statistical laws were not grounds for a "system of fatalism." "Introduce a system of ventilation into unventilated mines," for example, "and you substitute one law of accidents for another." Reengineered systems and effectively managed institutions, in other words, had the power to change the expected yearly toll of accidents. As Farr concluded, "These events are under control."[83] Yet the control to which Farr and his American followers in the workmen's compensation movement referred was not the control of workingmen and their fellow servants. It was the control of "system." Five decades later, American journalist George W. Alger would explain in his influential book *Moral Overstrain* that the cause of the American industrial-accident problem was not carelessness among individual employees. It was "lack of system" among employers.[84]

The American workmen's compensation movement thus coalesced with the claims of the first generations of managerial engineers. Scientific managers would be best able to create systems designed to minimize the yearly toll of industrial accidents.[85] As Eastman emphasized, an "employer intelligently determined to reduce the number of industrial accidents" could establish systems of "yard management" and "discipline among employees."[86] The "effective force in creating and managing the employment," contended another commentator, "is the employer." Employers and managerial engineers created and controlled the systems of the workplace; "the employer provides the place of work, assembles the machinery, materials, apparatus, selects the personnel, determines the processes and directs the operations." Making employers (those in the position to scientifically manage their firms) responsible was therefore "the key to the prevention of industrial injuries."[87] Indeed, the prevention-inducing effects of making employers bear at least a substantial share of the costs of accidents resounded through the compensation movement. If the workman in "modern machine industries . . . is a part of the service of machines which do not belong to him, and which he has not chosen, . . . he ought not be held responsible" for the accidents resulting from them. Workmen's compensation, as Theodore Roosevelt had said in his great Georgia Day speech of 1907, would mean "that with the increased responsibility of the employer would come increased care."[88]

In this sense, workmen's compensation endorsed the claims of responsibility and control that many engineers had already sought to advance through private work-accident funds. Workmen's compensation supporters described "scientific accident prevention" as closely linked to workmen's compensation. Accident prevention efforts, they agreed with the managerial engineers, could not be "left to the haphazard initiative of a number of individuals," but rather "must be thoroughly organized and systematized if they are to attain efficiency."[89] Moreover, workmen's compensation programs provided those firms that had already adopted their own accident-benefit programs the opportunity to solve the competition problem that had constrained the growth of such schemes. Voluntary compensation programs were expensive relative to the costs imposed on firms by the law of employers' liability.[90] Compulsory workmen's compensation would force all the firms in an industry to take on the increased costs associated with the private work-accident funds. Accordingly, many of the large, sophisticated firms that sought to establish accident-benefit schemes provided important support for compensation statutes.[91] Under workmen's compensation "*all employers* would have to stand such cost," even the "reactionary" employer.[92] Compensation statutes would thus "equalize competition" and "prevent the worst employers from dragging down the others."[93]

University of Chicago sociologist Charles Richmond Henderson thought that this standardization of costs across industries represented "the logic of social insurance."[94] In a broader sense, however, Henderson's "logic of social insurance" might have described the entire set of actuarial and managerial innovations accompanying workmen's compensation. In its mix of managerial and actuarial thinking, workmen's compensation precipitated a halfway transformation from free labor to risk. Where classical tort law dealt in individualized inquiries into the boundaries of individuals' freedom of action, workmen's compensation statutes aggregated accident cases and averaged the outcomes. And where cooperative insurance societies embodied the persistent ideal of manly workingmen's independence, in compensation schemes the state assumed general responsibility for the support of dependent widows and children.

In the process, the focus on risk deflected old questions about the meaning of free labor and self-ownership. To be sure, the ideas of risk and compensation for injury necessarily presupposed *some* background set of entitlements, some background state of the world; addressing the risks of employment, in other words, presumed a status quo ante from which there was a risk of departure. But to focus on departures from the baseline status quo was subtly to shift one's sights away from the question what that baseline should be. Workmen's compensation thus quietly legitimated the rise of the wage labor system and of scientifically managed firms. From the perspective of the scientific manager, the great triumph of workmen's compensation was the way it advanced a particular and contested conception of the structure of work while deflecting public debate away from that conception.[95]

Perhaps this legitimation of wage earning and scientific managerial control explains the reluctance of some of the nation's most prominent labor leaders to come out strongly in favor of workmen's compensation statutes. Indeed, it may seem more than a little odd that we should not have dwelled much in this chapter on labor unions' positions regarding compensation statutes. It is not that unions opposed workmen's compensation. At the federal level, for example, compensation legislation was first introduced into Congress at the behest of the railroad brotherhoods.[96] And in New York, 77 of 113 labor union representatives testified in favor of compensation legislation during hearings held in 1909 (138 of 207 employers testified against it).[97] Labor union leaders thus generally tended to support workmen's compensation statutes, though at first they did so on the condition that the statutes supplement employees' tort actions (as under the British system) rather than replace them.[98] Yet the unions were hardly out in front of the movement to enact compensation statutes. Arthur Evans of the Brotherhood of Railway Trainmen said in 1909 that no appreciable number of workingmen had even "given the matter [of workmen's compensation statutes] consideration."[99] Joseph Cotton of the Wainwright Commission found that the union representatives with whom he met typically had "no very helpful suggestions to make."[100]

State federations of labor and national labor leaders alike generally supported workmen's compensation legislation, but often in ways that hinted at a deep ambivalence. In November 1910, Samuel Gompers described the enactment of workmen's compensation legislation less as a desirable end than as a foregone conclusion, suggesting that "unless labor takes an active part in this movement its interests . . . will not be properly safeguarded."[101] When railroad brotherhoods divided over a federal workmen's compensation law, for example, Gompers even found himself struck uncharacteristically silent as to his views on compensation for work accidents, declining to "advocate strongly" a measure as to which some railroad workers felt "a sort of indifference or hostility."[102] And when Gompers spoke out in favor of compensation legislation, as he typically did in 1909 and 1910, he did so in ways that bore a striking resemblance to the managerial engineers' description of the model modern workplace. The opportunity for the workingman to "demonstrate his individuality and capacity and intelligence," Gompers observed in 1909 testimony in favor of compensation legislation, "is passing fast." He explained that "labor is becoming so divided and sub-divided and specialized that the workman has simply . . . become part of the machine," and it was Gompers's view that this minute division of labor in modern enterprise provided strong support for the enactment of compensation statutes.[103] Gompers may have been right in this. Nonetheless, in defending workmen's compensation's new approach to risk allocation by reference to the structures of the modern firm, he inevitably reproduced the emerging model of the reengineered firm. Workmen's compensation (and labor's support for it) made just that much more likely the triumph of the managerial engineers' view of employees as factors in the production process on par with the machinery.

*   *   *

We return to the question that began this chapter: What were the politics of workmen's compensation? The statutes enacted around the country beginning in 1910 promised to save the free labor family wage for the twentieth century. Moreover, the free labor values enshrined in the post-Reconstruction constitutional law shaped the statutes and limited the extent to which they departed from the existing legal framework, prompting some states to consider elective statutes, and impelling a number of states to limit compensation programs to dangerous industries. Yet the statistical and managerial categories that the statutes ushered in were radically forward-looking, breaking sharply from the autonomy and independence strands of free labor ideology.

In the actuarial categories of workmen's compensation lay still further layers of ambiguity. The logic of the actuary fit neatly with the engineering of the scientific manager. But actuarial categories were themselves open to a number of different lines of political development; there were in fact many logics of social insurance. Risk, after all, is a free-floating idea. It attaches to virtually any theory of the good life as the haunting possibility of failure, collapse, disaster, and death. What workmen's compensation statutes had introduced was therefore a new set of actuarial tools adaptable to many political ends. Even as the compensation movement was getting underway, a heated contest began over the politics of the new theory of risk that the movement embodied.[104]

From its very beginnings, work-accident reform had been understood by many progressive social insurance reform advocates as something other than a solution for the troubled political economy of engineers' private accident-compensation schemes. It was that, too, of course. But social insurance experts saw workmen's compensation as the beginnings of what progressive constitutional lawyer Ernst Freund called "social solidarity" in American law.[105] Progressive social policy experts thus understood workmen's compensation statutes as a kind of entering wedge in the establishment of a whole panoply of social insurance schemes, schemes that by the middle of the twentieth century would become the modern welfare state.

The legislative triumphs of workmen's compensation spread the appeal of what an Ohio commission called "the Social Remedy of Insurance" well beyond its core progressive supporters.[106] State commissions from Ohio to New York to Tennessee linked workmen's compensation to problems of "unemployment, sickness, . . . old age and death."[107] Secretary of the Treasury William McAdoo called for the application of insurance principles to "the whole field of social problems."[108] State federations of labor from states as diverse as Minnesota, Pennsylvania, Utah, Ohio, and Massachusetts endorsed health insurance in resolutions highlighting its close relation to workmen's compensation.[109] Theodore Roosevelt's Progressive Party platform of 1912 called for compulsory health insurance, and by 1916 the leadership of the American Medical Association—later a steadfast opponent—was endorsing compulsory health insurance as the "next step" in social insurance policy.[110] Others, such as journalist William Hard and New York's Wainwright Commission, turned to unemployment insurance as the next logical extension of workmen's compensation.[111] The secretary of the U.S. Department of Commerce and Labor similarly urged unemployment insurance legislation, contending that after the passage of compensation statutes, "the old idea of individualism no longer obtains."[112] Still others saw "pensions for old age" as the starting point for social insurance after workmen's compensation.[113] Tort lawyers such as Harvard's Jeremiah Smith believed that compensation for work accidents would transform other areas of personal injury law in its image.[114] A few farsighted observers in 1911 even linked workmen's compensation to the need to develop new systems for dealing with automobile safety and motor vehicle accidents.[115] Whatever the particular program, there was widespread agreement that workmen's compensation had "brought in its train new conceptions of social responsibility," what one medical journal called "a new social and economic condition in this country."[116]

For those attracted to such notions of social responsibility, soldiers' pensions became a leading metaphor for workingmen's insurance. Viewed from the perspective of yearly death tolls, the industrial-accident problem seemed like a kind of "perpetual campaign," producing a yearly "army of human cripples." "Soldiers suffer because they are professional destroyers," observed Secretary of the Interstate Commerce Commission Edward A. Moseley in 1908, "but members of th[e] great industrial army are struck down every year in this country because they are producers." And if soldiers received pensions, then surely so too ought the injured "industrial soldier," as journalist William Hard called him, receive what mine workers' leader John Mitchell described as "a pension . . . for injuries which were just as inevitable."[117]

The military metaphor coexisted uneasily alongside free labor ideals of autonomous and independent workingmen. To be sure, the military efforts of the Civil War had ensured a postwar era of free labor. And men such as Secretary Moseley defended workmen's compensation expressly by reference to the post–Civil War soldiers' pensions. But for many who valued independence and self-sufficiency, Civil War pensions seemed to encourage mass dependency on the government and raised disturbing images of widespread subordination to a hierarchically organized command structure.[118]

Yet the solidarity of the military metaphor did carry forward the gendered division of labor in the free labor family. The industrial soldier might not be independent or autonomous. He continued, however, to fill the role of masculine provider for dependent women and children. The military metaphor thus embraced at once a hierarchical organization of employment and a thoroughgoing state commitment to the welfare and well-being of the work-ingman and his family. For some like August Belmont of the National Civic Federation, the analogy between soldiers and employees suggested that the employer "bears a similarly responsible relation to"—and had a similar com-mand over—"the welfare of the wage earners who fill the rank and file of the voluntary armies of industry." For others, the military metaphor suggested the extent to which workmen's compensation statutes had "opened the way to the favorable consideration of other forms of social insurance."[119]

In its broadest formulations, the new conception of social responsibility as-pired to a breathtakingly radical democratic collectivism. It aimed not just to spread the risks of injury, but also to take on more fundamental risks such as poverty. If collective social insurance were to insure workingmen's safety, health, employment, and old age, perhaps it could also insure their material subsistence. As Joseph Cotton explained in a memorandum written for the Wainwright Commission, workmen's compensation would "establish the so-cial policy that the industry must keep its workers from poverty."[120] Poverty, too, could be counted, aggregated, and assembled into statistical data. Per-haps it could also be managed and subjected to the control of newly engi-neered institutional systems.

Indeed, supporters of workmen's compensation such as Louis Brandeis be-lieved that risk-spreading mechanisms like workmen's compensation could also be made democratically accountable. Brandeis, who was among the last great champions of the self-owning, independent proprietor, seems to have seen workmen's compensation both as a potential threat to the measure of independence wage earners retained in the 1910s, and as an opportunity to build new democratic institutions into the modern firm. According to Brandeis, accident prevention and compensation were properly the joint activities of workers and employers, participating on a basis of equality. Brandeis thus sought "to secure the fullest cooperation of employer and em-ployee" in a system of "Cooperative Accident Insurance Law" that would combine the principles of workmen's compensation with the organization of the workingmen's cooperatives. Under Brandeis's proposals, "juries of work-men" would convene to inquire into work accidents, calling witnesses and hearing evidence. Workmen's compensation systems would thus operate un-der a twofold democratic system, controlled from above by democratically accountable state policymakers and applied from case to case by a democrati-cally constituted factfinding body. Workmen's compensation, in other words, would itself be subjected to a democratizing discipline. The politics of risk and actuarial categories might be radically new indeed.[121]

"I suppose we are all in favor of workmen's compensation," announced one lawyer at a 1911 bar association meeting.[122] Yet widespread agreement in favor of workmen's compensation masked sharp disagreements over what the statutes stood for. Workmen's compensation represented at once the triumph of new actuarial technologies and the revival of old family wage categories, victory for scientific managers and the promise of a new collective solidarity. The statutes were thus rich in diverse possibilities for subsequent developments in accident law and in social policy more generally. Compensation represented a halfway revolution in American law, one that in 1910 was poised to go in several very different directions.

Today, of course, we have the decided advantage of hindsight. We know that the United States did not enact further social insurance programs until the New Deal. We know that it was not until the 1970s that the nation would witness significant expansions of the workmen's compensation idea into other fields of accident law, and that even then administrative substitutes for tort law would generally only supplement (not replace) tort in discrete fields such as automobile accidents. And we know that almost a century after 1910 the United States would stand virtually alone among western nations in not having enacted compulsory state health insurance during the twentieth century. Why was it that the solidarity principle of social insurance had such an uneven and halting career outside of the work-accident case?

One answer lies in the authority of American courts to arbitrate among the competing values that workmen's compensation statutes sought to embrace. The actuarial categories of workmen's compensation deemphasized important values in free labor culture—autonomy, independence, personal responsibility—in the name of another free labor value, the family wage. But as the supporters of compensation were painfully aware, all of these free labor values had been written into the nation's constitutional law. As a result, progressive constitutional lawyer Ernst Freund warned at the beginning of 1911 that "the constitutional status of workmen's compensation was one of uncertainty." By the end of the year, Freund would be forced to downgrade compensation statutes to a status of constitutional "confusion."[123]

6

The Passion of William Werner

The shades of Mr. Ives and his lost case for workmen's compensation
still haunt the periphera of this field.

—SAMUEL HOROVITZ AND JOSEPHINE KLEIN, "THE
CONSTITUTIONALITY OF COMPULSORY WORKMEN'S
COMPENSATION ACTS" (1938)

Half a century of experimentation in allocating the risks of industrial accidents culminated in March 1911 in the case of *Ives v. South Buffalo Railway.*
In *Ives,* decided less than nine months after New York State enacted the nation's first major workmen's compensation statute, the state's highest court
struck down the statute as an unconstitutional taking of employers' property.[1] *Ives* was greeted with a storm of disapproval. J. Mayhew Wainwright of
New York's Wainwright Commission called the case "a crushing blow to
workmen's compensation." *Ives* quickly became a centerpiece—alongside the
U.S. Supreme Court's infamous decision in *Lochner v. New York,* striking
down a maximum hours law—in the greatest court controversy since *Dred
Scott.* Indeed, Theodore Roosevelt made *Ives* a focus of his famously controversial proposals for the recall of judicial decisions. Yet in a few short years
(due in no small part to Roosevelt's efforts) *Ives* became part of the *ancien
régime* of American law. By the end of 1913, it had been overruled by constitutional amendment in New York. Less than four years after that, it was decisively rejected by the U.S. Supreme Court. Today *Ives* is largely forgotten except as a curious outlier in a now-abandoned body of constitutional law.[2]

If the *Ives* decision seems strange to lawyers today, it is because the case
now lies on the other side of a watershed in American law. The case and the
controversy that erupted around it captured a contest of paradigms in American law between the categories and preoccupations of free labor, antislavery,
and contract, on one hand, and the organizing principles of risk, insurance,
and actuarial statistics, on the other.

In particular, *Ives* featured a clash between deeply divergent ways of thinking and talking about causal relationships in an industrial society, ways of
thinking and talking that in turn reflected very different underlying views of
the organization of American social and economic life. Causal reasoning then
as now rested not so much on abstract logic as on what H. L. A. Hart and
Tony Honoré call the "common-sense notions" that attach to the purpose

and context of a particular causal attribution. In our everyday reasoning, we construct stories and theories about cause and effect on the basis of conventions rooted in some set of values and aimed at more or less specific ends. When lawyers at the turn of the twentieth century attributed causal significance to some particular agent or set of agents, they too were engaged in a deeply convention-bound activity. For it is conventions—shared "habits of mind" about recurring situations, to draw on Howard Margolis's formulation—that allow us to single out specific causal factors from the infinite web of necessary antecedents to any one consequence.[3]

Consider a problem of the kind made famous by Ronald Coase's economic theory of social costs: a paper mill that "causes" damage to the quality of its downstream neighbor's fly fishing along an otherwise bucolic river. What does it mean to identify the paper mill as the cause of the injury? We might also have said that the cause of the injury is the direction of the river's flow (upstream fly fishing, after all, remains unharmed), or the relatively small size of the river such that it cannot absorb the pollutants, or perhaps the downstream neighbor's choice to pursue trout rather than some other, hardier fish. We could even say that the cause of the injury was the neighbor's decision to locate her fishing downriver of the property on which the mill has been built, or her failure to secure an agreement from upstream riparian property owners not to build a mill. Or maybe her decision to engage in fishing at all rather than some other activity is the source of the injury to the quality of her rest and relaxation. In the right circumstances, we might appropriately say any one or more of these things. When we single out one causal factor rather than another, our attribution of causal significance generally reflects the purposes for which we make the attribution, as well as the values we bring to it. Singling out the paper mill as the cause of damage to the downstream fly fishing, for instance, asserts the relative priority of fly fishing over industrial uses of the river. Our conventional intuitions, in this instance, tacitly allocate an entitlement to the fly fisherwoman; only then can we pick out the paper mill as the agent of change and assign causal responsibility to it. But in doing so we should not fool ourselves into thinking that the paper mill is somehow the One True Cause of the entitlement conflict in question. If the mill owner were entitled to discharge the offending pollutants into the river, it would be just as plausible to identify as the cause of the neighbor's misery her own foolish decision to fly fish downstream of property entitled to emit such pollutants. (No doubt this would be precisely the reaction many would have to attempts to fly fish in the Bronx River.) The conflict between the two activities is inescapably a joint product of the two activities. Our common-sense attributions of responsibility to the mill rather than to the neighbor therefore rest on a set of shared understandings about the appropriate uses of the river, which in turn translate into a set of conventions about what is a cause of what.[4]

"Common-sense" intuitions, of course, change over time and space; one era's conventions are another's outrage. *Ives* marks a rupture in the contours of legal common sense and the emergence of a new set of conventions for making sense of the world. In *Ives*, a court, a legal system, and a judge—William E. Werner, the author of the opinion and the rising star of the New York Court of Appeals—all found themselves in the midst of not one but two interrelated reconfigurations of the basic conventions by which lawyers and policymakers understood and described the social relations and institutions around them. The world of Judge Werner and his colleagues was one still described and understood in terms organized around the principles of free labor. Values such as independence and autonomy had been established in the controversies between slavery and freedom. Classical tort law aimed to preserve these values in the courts. Moreover, the constitutional causation requirement had emerged in the late nineteenth century to guard these values against legislative redistributions. Workmen's compensation statutes, however, entailed a new set of common-sense practices in the attribution of cause in work accidents, a set of practices closely connected with the consolidation of the scientific management theory of the firm. Compensation statutes adopted a theory of causation that took managerial power and responsibility as a core premise. At the same time, workmen's compensation involved the rise of a distinctly actuarial approach to causation, cutting across the particularity of individual cases in favor of statistical tendencies and the regularities of large numbers.

Werner was exactly right—his critics notwithstanding—to identify workmen's compensation statutes as a radical innovation in American law. Once the move had been made from individualized common-sense causation to actuarial causal tendencies, the modern administrative state was equipped to socialize any number of risks such as old age, sickness, and unemployment on the basis of their causal link to employment. Yet in this sense, the *Ives* decision became a powerful force in the emerging social politics of risk and insurance. Even as the abandonment of *Ives* signaled the triumph of workmen's compensation (and, as we shall see, the eventual demise of William Werner), *Ives* and its fallout set patterns for the development of insurance systems in the United States in the century to come.

The great puzzle of *Ives v. South Buffalo Railway*, observed constitutional scholar Thomas Reed Powell several years after the decision, was not merely that its logic seemed so misguided. *Ives* was "puzzling" because its reasoning seemed strained even as its author purported to find its result an unfortunate (but legally required) conclusion. What kind of jurist, wondered Powell, would adopt such seemingly faulty legal analysis to achieve a self-defeating outcome?[5]

The judge whom Powell thought so enigmatic was in many respects exemplary of the late-nineteenth- and early-twentieth-century bench, a kind of Weberian ideal type of the *Lochner*-era judiciary. William E. Werner brought together in a single figure the many strands of late-nineteenth-century American free labor culture. His heroes were Lincoln and the fiery abolitionist senator Charles Sumner. He grew up in the same region of upstate New York in which leading classical torts jurist Thomas Cooley had been raised a generation earlier, when it had been called the Burned-Over District and had been home to the evangelical revivals of the Second Great Awakening. As a young man, Werner worked as an industrial wage earner in several of western New York's most dangerous industries, and later he would be a member of several different fraternal societies (organizations like those whose cooperative insurance programs produced any number of insurance disputes in Werner's own courtroom).[6] As a judge, Werner vigorously participated in Cooley's classical tort law project of trying to carve out zones of autonomy with clearly demarcated boundaries; Werner also became intimately familiar with the messy realities of personal injury litigation, ranging from questionable settlement practices by tort defendants to exorbitant fee arrangements by plaintiffs' lawyers. In his professional life, Werner developed ties and friendships with the leaders of the great industries of western New York and was a close observer of the problem of "destructive competition" on the railroads in the 1890s.[7] In his personal life, Werner carefully sheltered his private family relations in a domestic sphere untouched by the cares and worries of his professional life.[8]

The singular feature of Werner's life in the eyes of those who described him was its "stranger than fiction" rags-to-riches story. He was, in the words of the upstate New York press, "a self-made man," a "court of appeals judge who rose from errand boy" "by personal application," "overcoming unusual difficulties" and winning great "struggles with adversity." Werner was born in 1855 in upstate New York to German Protestant immigrants who died when he was fourteen. As an orphan teenager, Werner became an iron molder's apprentice in Buffalo, a job that he left when he decided that the work was too strenuous for his slight frame. In his early twenties Werner worked in a tin stamping factory to finance his studies in bookkeeping and commercial law in a local business college's night division.[9]

After studying law in the office of a locally prominent lawyer, Werner was admitted to the New York bar in 1880, where he developed considerable local renown over the next decade as a trial lawyer in commercial cases arising out of such routine matters as negotiable instruments, mechanics' liens, life insurance, bailments, and mortgages. Werner was appointed special county judge in 1884 and was elected county judge in 1888, positions that allowed him to keep his law practice. In 1889, he married Lillie Boller, daughter of the prominent owner of a Buffalo lumber mill, despite her father's initial concerns about a union with the as-yet-undistinguished Werner. In 1894 he was elected to the state's Supreme Court, then as now New York's trial court of general jurisdiction. In 1900, Werner was designated by then-Governor Theodore Roosevelt to sit on the Court of Appeals, New York's highest court. And in 1904 Werner was elected to a full term of fourteen years on that court. His "meteoric rise" from orphan wage earner to Court of Appeals judge, one upstate newspaper explained, was an illustration of the "almost limitless possibilities of American manhood."[10]

Werner cut a positively Lincolnesque figure in upstate New York politics. He was, local journalists said, "a harmonious blending of the human and the intellectual . . . a combination of strength, moderation, learning, and industry," whose "early struggles against poverty have been to him a finer inheritance than wealth."[11] The "kind of man" who "would stop to shake hands with a working man," he had risen through "native ability and hard, well-directed effort." This was precisely the kind of man Lincoln described as typifying the American wage earner: rising from humble beginnings to a position of substance in the community. His move from rural hardscrabble obscurity to prominence as a lawyer and politician resembled that of Lincoln himself; as one upstate publication put it, Werner was "one of the products of American democracy of which American democracy has a right to be proud."[12]

Werner joined the Republican Party, which he described as the party of Lincoln. "The Republican Party," he explained in a speech given around the turn of the century, "began its career through a fusion of various elements opposed to the extension of slavery."[13] The Civil War was, in Werner's view, "the great central fact" of American history, with "far reaching practical and incidental results." Indeed, "the history of the Civil War is the history of our country," he explained in a speech titled "Lincoln the Liberator." In an era in which many public speakers—in the North and South alike—downplayed the severity of the sectional conflict and the significance of the divide over the question of slavery, Werner's account of the Civil War featured abolitionists as the heroes of the conflict. The liberation of the slaves had been the "destiny" of the nation.[14] This was the end for which the Republican Party had been formed, and for which Lincoln had been martyred. In Werner's view, the task of latter-day followers of Lincoln was to defend the triumphs of the Civil War generation, and to "stand upon the defensive as the party of conservatism" in the face of the "industrial agitation" of more recent years.[15]

As a leading upstate Republican and "one of Rochester's most influential citizens," Werner developed close ties to the elite of Rochester area industry, including executives of the New York Central Railroad and the Rochester Chamber of Commerce.[16] And yet in contrast to the conventional image of a turn-of-the-twentieth-century judiciary in league with the plutocrats of industry, Werner was turned off by excesses of wealth, or what he called "[t]he mad rush for money, the insanity for dress and display, the restless ambition to attain." In letters to his wife Lillie, Werner complained of the "stale utterances" of the wealthy elite of New York City; "the Lord must have been short of good raw material," he noted, "when he made such men rich and famous."[17] It was the "workmen," not the "money kings," Werner explained in a paper delivered in 1901 to the Rochester Credit Men's Association, who were the "real producers." Some years later, Werner would even go so far as to denounce in a bitter dissent "the pharisees of commerce" who "wax fat at the expense of their innocent competitors and of the poor and helpless consumers."[18]

Werner was instead by all accounts a man of "democratic tastes,"[19] a "man of the people" whose law practice had been built "without wealthy relationship or patronage."[20] His (small-d) democratic tastes made him an exceedingly promising politician in the New York Republican Party. New York judgeships at the county and state levels were elected positions, and in the 1880s and 1890s the politics surrounding them could be quite fierce. As county judge, Werner worked a never-ending series of partisan speaking engagements at upstate political clubs. He performed naturalizations that, although not strictly part of his duties, were provided for "the accommodation of our constituents." He held counsel regularly with a group of upstate Republican Party politicians and loyalists whom he called "the boys." And by the 1890s, he was "prominent in the State and national leagues of Republican clubs" and enjoyed an "especial popularity with the German-American element" of the state.[21]

The depth and strength of Werner's local political connections became clear in the hotly contested Republican Party canvass for the party nomination to the state Supreme Court in 1894. Werner loyalists used brute force to push their candidate through. Just as the voting began, a "gang of rowdies" "made a dash for the ballot box," which caused a "free for all scuffle." The police, "using their clubs freely," "cleared the room" in such a way that all the supporters of Werner's opponent "were driven from the room." Of the normal Republican vote in the ward of 650 votes, only 402 votes were counted after the melee, 387 of which were counted for Werner. The *Rochester Union and Advertiser* called the events a "disgraceful scene," noting that the "Werner men" were rumored to have been in the control of the police, and that in any event Werner's supporters had wrested control of the agenda without giving his opponent's representatives time to object.[22] As the *New York Times* would note a few months later, "The popular impression is that questionable methods were used in aiding Werner's canvass." Werner's "reputation as a politician," the *Times* contended, was "higher than his standing as a lawyer," and there were "many Republicans in the district who are not pleased with the result."[23]

Werner continued to keep a hand in politics after being designated by Roosevelt in 1900 to serve on the Court of Appeals pending reduction of the court's backlog of cases. In 1902 he accepted a rare Republican nomination to challenge an incumbent Court of Appeals judge, a challenge that was denounced by many as unseemly political ambition in a judge. His eventual election to a full term on the court in 1904 was part of a partisan deal to allocate seats on the Court of Appeals between Republicans and Democrats.[24]

By 1909, Werner was angling for a nomination to the U.S. Supreme Court. "There is to-day no place in the arena of the world's activities," Werner explained, "where there is greater need for patriotism and courage, and larger opportunities for constructive statesmanship than upon the Bench of the United States Supreme Court." And Werner was well-positioned for such an appointment. He and his wife had been "on terms of close friendship with President Roosevelt and his family," and President Taft continued his predecessor's practice of inviting Werner to annual White House receptions each January.[25] Upon the death of Justice Rufus Peckham, also from upstate New York, Werner worked behind the scenes with his friend Louis Wiley, business manager of the *New York Times* and closely connected to a number of upstate newspapers, to promote himself as a candidate for Peckham's slot on the Court. A "favorable article or two in the press," he wrote to Wiley, "could certainly do no harm and might possibly do some good; if not now at least for a future day," and in the next month a number of upstate New York papers touted Werner as the best replacement for Peckham. If indeed there had been a slot on the Court for a New Yorker, it went in the spring of 1910 to Governor Charles Evans Hughes, who remained governor just long enough to sign the Wainwright Commission's workmen's compensation statute into law. But Werner felt assured that the attention he had received "will at least call attention to the fact that I am still alive" and would "do no harm if it does no good."[26]

The difficulty was that Werner's judicial posts offered only a shadow of the excitement and the drama of party politics with "the boys." In his view, "the best judge for the people" was the judge who remained out of the public eye, the judge who "imperceptibly maintains the people in their rights such that they barely think of him at all."[27] Werner, however, found this kind of social invisibility tedious. Judging made for a "dull" life full of "onerous duties in-

terspersed with cares and vexations." Werner frequently found himself inex-
plicably "depressed, sad, moody and almost helpless." The run of the mine
cases were, in his words, "utterly prosaic." The boredom of judging was such
that from the late 1880s through the 1890s Werner wrote dozens, perhaps
even hundreds, of love letters from the bench to his wife Lillie. "I am in the
middle of a tedious criminal trial," he would note; or perhaps there would be
"a lot of unimportant testimony," "much of which is wholly irrelevant."
Werner would then "lapse into a condition of semi-consciousness" as to the
goings on in his courtroom and turn his attentions to his letters, "without
danger" (he assured Lillie) "to the interests of the parties." In the eyes of the
litigants he was "supposed to be the incarnation of solemn dignity," he noted
in one amused missive. But the litigants had no idea that their judge was in
fact elsewhere, "little dreaming," as Werner noted in another letter, "that as I
look solemn and assiduously write, I am writing to you." If during a "moment of temporary aberration of mind," a question was addressed to which
Werner was required to respond, Werner confided to Lillie that he would
simply "look wise" and ask "the stenographer to read the last lines of testimony" back to him.[28]

What is most striking about Werner's approach to judging is that in the
face of the tedium of processing cases, and in sharp contrast to his partisan activities, he began to develop a powerful set of ideas about what it meant to be
a judge. One might describe these ideas collectively as the theory of the heroic guardian judge. Werner's notion of the heroic judge emerged around
the turn of the century in the richly narrated stories he began to tell in bar association speeches and after-dinner talks. These stories little resembled either
Werner's background in the political machinations of the state Republican
Party, or the confessions of boredom that he shared with Lillie. Quite the opposite, Werner developed a kind of adventure narrative for the rule of law,
dramatizing the gravity of its role as guardian of the nation's most fundamental values. He began to reconceive the judge not as dispute manager but as
heroic defender of the law's basic commitments against the encroachments of
modern politics. In times of public crisis, it turned out, the judge might be
required to step out from the obscurity of deciding everyday disputes in order to defend the nation's most enduring values. A "life of judicial service,"
Werner announced in a typical speech, may seem "barren of incidents which
arrest immediate attention."[29] But judging was in fact a glorious vocation for
those with the perseverance, the "special training," and "stern discipline"
that "fit them for the arduous task." Judging, Werner explained, was concerned with "the romance of perseverance, of pluck, of back bone." These
romantic virtues, in turn, formed the "most fascinating subject of human history." The stories of the men "who have had this genius of persistence,"

Werner elaborated in one especially fantastic flight of fancy, "read like the tale of the Arabian Nights." Judges were Werner's manly guardians of society, charged with a duty that he described in the words of Edmund Burke: "[t]he nerve that never relaxes; the eye that never blenches; the thought that never wanders; the purpose that never falters." These, Werner declared, "are the masters of victory."[30]

In Werner's account, the role of the judge as hero-guardian had never been more important than in the first decade of the new century. The triumphs of the Civil War generation of Lincoln and Sumner had never been more endangered. "Co-operation on gigantic lines is rapidly supplanting individual effort." The emergence of great trusts suggested the "massive unification that is going on in the field of trade." At the same time, organized labor "numbers its members by the millions." "The spirit of combination" was in the air, and "the age of system" threatened to render obsolete the values of self-responsibility. "Never before in our history" had the basic commitment to "a government of laws" been "put to severer tests than in this period of paternal and class legislation, when all the supposed ills of the body politic are sought to be cured by remedial statutes." Yet in this "swelter of modern existence," with "its false conceptions of the value of wealth and so-called luxury," and its "haste in the pursuit of passing phantoms," the judiciary marched as "Spartan comrades, shoulder to shoulder," quietly following "the path of duty."[31] It was the judiciary—warriors against the encroachments of combination, class legislation, and paternalism—that would rescue the principles on which the republic rested. "I venture to say," Werner intoned, "that the judicial work of this country today . . . will compare favorably with that of any previous age or generation."[32]

Judicial review of paternalistic and class legislation formed the ultimate test for the heroic guardian judge. In this sense, Werner inverted the judicial philosophy that would become the great legacy of Justice Oliver Wendell Holmes. It gave Holmes "great pleasure to sustain the Constitutionality of laws that I believe to be as bad as possible."[33] Werner, on the other hand, took his greatest pride in striking down legislation that he thought well designed "to correct a great public evil" when it nonetheless violated fundamental constitutional principles. It was precisely the public importance of such legislation that made striking it down a measure of Werner's and the nation's commitment to the constitutional framework. Thus, for example, Werner wrote a 1905 decision in the case of *Wright v. Hart,* striking down New York's so-called bulk transfer legislation, which limited merchant debtors' sales of their entire inventory absent notice to their creditors. The social problem addressed by the statute, Werner conceded, "was one of substantial reality." "But that does not meet the argument against the constitutionality of the statute."[34] Law, in Werner's view, stood as a bastion of "conservatism" against changes wrought by fleeting majorities. So conceived, law might sometimes conflict with "modern ideas of right and justice." But absent the law's conservatism, "we should soon have chaos."[35] "Upon the courts," Werner concluded in a 1908 bar association speech at the Waldorf-Astoria, "lies the burden of annihilating these laws, be they ever so much desired by one class or another, when they are found to be repugnant to the Constitution."[36] And so in February 1911, only one month before issuing the *Ives* opinion, Werner urged his fellow hero-guardian judges to summon the "force" that had "held the wavering line at Shiloh, climbed the flame-swept hill at Chattanooga, and stormed the defenses of Lookout Mountain," the force that had "marched with Sherman to the sea; rode with Sheridan into the shadows of the Shenandoah Valley" and had "stood silent witness with Grant and Lee at Appomattox."[37] By a like force of law, Werner's heroic judiciary would hold back the "radical changes" proposed by modern legislation.[38]

This hero-guardian narrative animated Werner's tort decisions as well. Werner, it is worth remembering, knew intimately the dangers of late-nineteenth-century industrial wage earning. Though he had originally planned to become an iron molder, he had found that "the work taxed his strength" and that "his constitution could not stand this laborious occupation."[39] Later, as an employee in a tin-stamping factory, Werner found himself in a notoriously dangerous industry. Yet in his tort decisions, Werner adopted an approach typical to late-nineteenth-century classical tort law, one that was concerned first and foremost with the articulation and defense of the boundaries of freedom of action.

Consider an 1889 case, decided while Werner was still a county judge, involving injuries to a plaintiff's clothing caused by sparks falling from defendant's engine at a railroad overpass. The case was a minor one; the plaintiff sought damages in the amount of $15 for holes burned in the two coats he had been wearing. But Werner's reversal of the judgment for the plaintiff that had been entered by a justice of the peace warrants attention, for it typified Werner's approach to accident cases. Werner's goal here, as in later cases, was to determine the boundaries of the parties' respective spheres of liberty. "The defendant's engine," Werner explained, "was moving along its track under the sanction of the law," and "there can be no recovery for damages sustained by such accidents as are necessarily incident to the character of the business involved." Again, Werner repeated, "here the running of a locomotive was lawful."[40] It followed for Werner that there could be no recovery; because the defendant had acted within the sphere of its lawful freedom of action, the injury to the plaintiff was *damnum absque injuria:* injury without a remedy.

Whether it was the lawfulness of a locomotive's operation along its track, the rights of a bicyclist within "a sphere of [his] own" in a later case, or any number of situations in the accident cases he decided over the course of his career, Werner's preoccupation in tort cases (and here he followed closely in the footsteps of Thomas Cooley) fixed on defining the legitimate spheres of action of the respective parties.[41] In nuisance cases arising out of property damage caused by industrial activities, for example, Werner became widely known for his insistence that courts vigorously and uncompromisingly enforce existing property lines. During the 1880s and 1890s, the Court of Appeals had pioneered a solution to the problem of important industrial activities that produced relatively slight injuries to neighboring property owners. The key doctrinal development here was a device now known as the "conditional injunction." Under the conditional injunction, courts recognized ongoing injuries to property rights while at the same time allowing the injurer to continue its activity on the condition that it pay a fixed sum to the victim. The conditional injunction thus prevented grasping victims of relatively minor injuries from extorting all but the entirety of the injurers' profits in return for permitting the activity to continue, and prevented stubborn victims from shutting down the offending activity altogether. In elevated railroad cases in New York City, for example, the Court of Appeals issued orders prohibiting the building of elevated railroads that infringed neighboring property rights, but allowed the railroads, in turn, to buy out the property owners by paying damages. No single property owner could hold out to extort blackmail sums from the railroad and thereby obstruct valuable development.[42]

In the first years of the twentieth century, it looked very much as if the Court of Appeals would extend the conditional injunction beyond elevated railroad cases to mediate between the interests of small property holders and industrial development more generally.[43] The conditional injunction, however, clashed with classical tort law's aim of establishing clear demarcations among individuals' respective spheres of free action. Conditional injunctions effectively compelled sale by the injured party of the entitlement in question at a price established by the court, even when the injured party was unwilling to sell. By contrast, once the guardian judge in a tort case had established the rightful bounds of an actor's liberty, his role was to defend those boundaries against nonconsensual infringement. Accordingly, in *Whalen v. Union Bag and Paper Co.*, Werner (writing for a unanimous court) reversed a conditional injunction granted by the court below. *Whalen* involved a paper mill operated by the Union Bag and Paper Company that was polluting the river to the detriment of Whalen, its downstream neighbor. A lower state court had ordered Union Bag and Paper to cease operation of the mill or pay the neighbor a sum of $100 monthly: a classical conditional injunction. Werner, however, reasoned that "[f]ollowed to its logical conclusion," the forced sale effected by the conditional injunction "would deprive the poor litigant of his little property by giving it to those already rich." To be sure, the damages remedy that was the condition of lifting the injunction might compensate the property owner at the market rate. But the fact that the property owner had not already parted with his property right in reasonably clear water at its market price suggested that the owner might value the right above its market rate. Indeed, the fact that the industrial user would be willing to pay the damages in order to evade the injunction suggested that the industrial user also valued the property right at a greater than market rate. The consequence of a conditional injunction, as Werner rightly pointed out, might thus be to redistribute property from the injured property owner to the industrial activity. But redistribution was precisely what Werner believed heroic judges were meant to block. He therefore issued an unconditional injunction barring the mill from polluting the river absent the consent of the plaintiff.[44]

Apart from *Ives*, *Whalen v. Union Bag and Paper* represents perhaps the best known of Werner's tort decisions. But *Whalen* was not nearly as easy a case as Werner thought it was. As the paper mill and fly fishing scenario at the beginning of this chapter suggests, it was not at all clear whether the paper company caused injury to the downstream property owner (as Werner confidently assumed) or whether the downstream property owner caused injury to the upstream paper company by denying it a particular industrial use of its riparian property. Like most assignments of causal responsibility, Werner's theory of causation in *Whalen* turned on a deeply ingrained but barely articulated set of background common-sense notions about entitlements in riparian settings and about the relative priority of natural and industrial land uses. In the *Whalen* context, Werner's common-sense notions of cause and effect were relatively uncontroversial at the time the case was decided. Today, these same causal intuitions remain relatively well settled, though many courts have gone on to embrace conditional injunctions in such cases. In the work-accident context, by contrast, the common-sense causal intuitions of Werner and his colleagues proved to be out of step with the animating premises of the quickly growing workmen's compensation movement.

The New York workmen's compensation statute had been in effect for only one day when Earl Ives was injured while working for the South Buffalo Railway Company on September 2, 1910. The South Buffalo Railway owned and operated eight miles of track running north and south, from Buffalo in the north to the Lackawanna Steel Company in Lackawanna, N.Y. in the south. As it still does almost a century later, the railway carried coke from Buffalo (then the nation's second leading railroad center behind Chicago) to the steel plant, bringing back iron and steel bars to be shipped through the Great Lakes, along the Erie Canal, or by rail.[45]

Earl Ives had worked along the eight miles of track for more than a year as a switchman earning $27 per week, a wage significantly above most Buffalo labor union members, whose wages ranged from $26 per week for bricklayers at the high end to under $12 for blacksmiths' helpers and barely $8 for press-feeders. At 11:30 in the morning on September 2, Ives stood on the thirty-second car of a thirty-five car train loaded with coke. Ives, by the account set forth in his complaint and agreed to by the railway, "gave a signal to the engineer of the locomotive attached to said train to take up the slack in the train." But "upon the engineer so doing, the jar in taking up the slack" caused Ives "to fall to the ground," where "he sprained his left ankle and was otherwise bruised and injured."[46]

Ives himself had given the signal, and upon the occurrence of the apparently expected subsequent movement of the train (Ives's own complaint does not allege it to have been otherwise), the admittedly experienced and well-paid switchman fell to the ground, injuring his ankle in such a way as would (he claimed) disable him from working for a total period of seven weeks. Ives's case was thus hardly the kind of accident that had galvanized the compensation movement. His injury was relatively slight and only incidentally arose out of the kinds of heavy industries that seemed to exact a regular and inevitable toll of crippling injuries. Indeed, taken on its own, Ives's particular injury hardly looked like one of the inevitable by-products of industry about which the compensation movement talked so often. If Ives himself had only exercised greater care, the injury likely would have been entirely preventable. In an action at common law, Ives would therefore very likely have been contributorily negligent, perhaps so clearly as to justify a judge in taking the case from the jury and entering judgment for the defendant. Moreover, Ives's injury was precisely the kind of injury for which the railroad brotherhood cooperative insurance programs had long and successfully provided meaningful benefits. Nor was there evidence in the record of a dependent wife or children; Earl Ives's case thus did not appear to present the kinds of difficulties for American families that had motivated workmen's compensation supporters.

Ives's own apparent negligence may explain why he and his lawyer, a local Buffalo lawyer of no special reputation about whom there is little information, elected to file under the new compensation remedy rather than bring a common law action for damages. In 1910 and 1911, however, there was much speculation that Ives's compensation claim was based not on his lawyer's estimate of the strengths of his legal claim, but rather on a collusive agreement between Earl Ives and the railway. Everett P. Wheeler, experienced litigator, founder of the Association of the Bar of the City of New York, and member of the Council of the American Bar Association, privately disclosed to the National Civic Federation (on whose behalf he filed a brief in the case) that he was "very anxious about the *Ives* case" because he "feared . . . collusion." The Court of Appeals itself sought assurance at oral argument "that the cause was not trumped-up." And it was later reported that while Earl Ives "was in the hospital an agent of the railroad visited him and put him on the payroll in return for his consent to let the railroad sue itself in his name." The railroad, the Philadelphia *North American* contended, had hired "the attorneys on both sides" of the case.[47]

It is impossible to determine conclusively whether *Ives* was a collusive suit. At a minimum, it is clear that the South Buffalo Railway seized on Earl Ives's relatively insignificant injury as the ideal test case for the statute. There is also reason to suspect significant communication between Ives's lawyer and counsel for the railway prior to the filing of the complaint. Ives's complaint and the railway's answer, which stipulated to the truth of Ives's story and defended the railway solely on the basis of the statute's supposed unconstitutionality, were filed on the same day in late September. A number of additional considerations support the further possibility of collusion, though the evidence is again inconclusive. Ives's claim for damages, for example, barely seems significant enough to have warranted his lawyer's taking the case. The damages sought amounted to the paltry total of $50: the ten-dollar maximum weekly disability benefit available under the statute for the seven weeks of Ives's anticipated inability to work, minus the statutory two-week waiting period. The court costs added to the judgment on behalf of Ives ultimately amounted to three times the value of the underlying award. These court costs did not include attorneys' fees, on which the statute placed new limits. The value of the award thus hardly seems sufficient to have justified Ives's lawyer's work at the trial court and in two subsequent appeals.[48]

Perhaps Ives's counsel took on the case for the notoriety it might receive, though it was hardly predictable that the case would become as important as it did. But it is significant that the complaint he filed was remarkably tame. Complaints are generally more than mere outlines of the barest minimum legal requirements; they set the agenda and the tone for the proceedings to come. Complaints are thus often used as settlement tools or as attempts to frame the narrative in the terms most sympathetic to the plaintiff. Ives's lawyer failed, however, to allege anything more than the bare requirements of the statute: that Ives had suffered an injury "[a]rising out of and in the course of his employment as aforesaid, and that such injury . . . was not caused in whole, or in part, by any serious or willful misconduct of plaintiff."[49] Moreover, in the not-improbable event that the untested statute would be held unconstitutional (as it eventually was), or in the event of some other unforeseen difficulty with Ives's novel compensation claim, Ives's lawyer might have been well advised to have added a claim of negligence against the railroad. At the very least, he might have sought under New York's liberal amendment of pleadings rules to add such a claim after the railroad moved to dismiss the action as unconstitutional.[50] Yet counsel did none of these things. Ives was left with a bare bones complaint that served mainly to abstract the case from the pressing social problems that had produced the statute in the first place; it was a document that seems aimed to isolate as cleanly as possible the question of constitutionality that would be posed by the railroad's answer.

By the time the *Ives* case arrived in the Court of Appeals, it was being hailed as "a test case of supreme importance."[51] The statute had been upheld in the state trial court and the state intermediate appellate court in quick succession, where it had been watched from far and wide by advocates and opponents of new social insurance programs. Louis Marshall, a nationally prominent corporate and civil liberties lawyer with close ties to the National Association for the Advancement of Colored People, joined the railway's defense team. Newspapers from the *Labor Advocate* in Birmingham, Alabama to the *St. Paul Dispatch* in Minnesota, along with numerous others, followed the *Ives* case's progress.[52] And in New York State, Edgar M. Atkin of the New York Edison Company reported that "not a single claim" had been brought under the compensation act since the filing of the *Ives* case; employees were choosing instead to wait "until its constitutionality was determined in the decision in the *Ives* case."[53]

So when the Court of Appeals struck down the compensation statute, reversing the decisions of the two lower courts, the consequences seemed vast. The statute, Werner wrote for a unanimous court, was "plainly revolutionary." Its "radical character" represented a sharp "departure from our long-established law and usage." To be sure, the statute was supported by "a most voluminous array of statistical tables," as well as "extracts from the works of philosophical writers" and a series of "attractive and desirable" "economic, philosophical, and moral theories." In fact, Werner himself professed—both in the opinion and in private correspondence—to view the statute as an improvement in social, economic, and philosophical terms over the common law. "No word of praise could overstate the industry and intelligence" with which the Wainwright Commission had gone about its "far-reaching" work. Its arguments, Werner conceded, were "cogent," "plausible," even "sound." But in law, such theories were "subordinate to . . . our written Constitutions." Judicial review of the compensation acts represented "the purely legal phases" of the compensation movement. In law, rights turned "not upon philosophical or scientific speculations," but upon their "foundation in the fundamental law." If "economic and sociological arguments" were allowed to "subvert the fundamental idea of property," Werner concluded, "there is no private right entirely safe." The heroic guardians of the bench would thus not be "permitted to forget that the law is the only chart by which the ship of state is to be guided."[54]

Measured against the requirements of the law, Werner announced, the compensation statute was an impermissible redistributive reallocation of property from employers to employees.

> If the argument in support of this statute is sound we do not see why it cannot logically be carried much further. Poverty and misfortune from every cause are detrimental to the state. It would probably conduce to the welfare of all concerned if there could be a more equal distribution of wealth. . . . If the legislature can say to an employer, "you must compensate your employee for an injury not caused by you or by your fault," why can it not go further and say to the man of wealth, "you have more property than you need and your neighbor is so poor that he can barely subsist; in the interest of natural justice you must divide with your neighbor so that he and his dependents shall not become a charge upon the State?"

If compensation statutes were constitutional, added Chief Judge Cullen in a concurring opinion, so too were laws "requiring a man to pay his neighbor's debts." Werner concluded that "[i]n its final and simple analysis," requiring employers to compensate their employees for injuries arising out of and in the course of the employment "is taking the property of *A* and giving it to *B*, and that cannot be done under our Constitutions."[55]

The act was most closely analogous, Werner explained, to the statute that had been struck down thirty-five years before in Illinois in *Ohio and Mississippi Railway Co. v. Lackey,* a statute that had made railroads liable for coroner and burial costs in any death occurring on the cars of the railroad. The Illinois statute had imposed liability for deaths "no matter how caused, even if by the party's own hand."[56] To the same effect, Werner wrote, were the stock statutes imposing liability on railroads for running over horses and cattle, statutes that had repeatedly been held unconstitutional from the 1870s into the 1890s. From these cases, Werner drew his conclusion: "When our Constitutions were adopted it was the law of the land that no man who was without fault or negligence could be held liable in damages for injuries sustained by another"; such liability therefore "plainly constitutes a deprivation of liberty and property under the Federal and State Constitutions."[57]

Werner's opinion brings us back to Thomas Reed Powell's puzzle. Why was the Court of Appeals convinced—as it appears to have been—that the statute was both desirable as a matter of policy and unconstitutional as a matter of law? As commentators have pointed out since soon after the decision was handed down, it was hardly so radical or novel to allocate liability without regard to fault. Legislatures had made railroads strictly liable for fire damage caused by sparks from the train; employers were liable at common law for the torts of their employees regardless of their own fault; ship owners were liable under the law of admiralty regardless of fault for the care and maintenance of seamen.[58] Werner himself had even favored no-fault, strict-liability standards in criminal misdemeanor cases involving the violation of food and drug regulations.[59] The imagined role of the judge as hero-guardian may well have disposed Werner and his colleagues to strike down overreaching legislation, but what was it that made them think that the compensation statute overreached?

A clue to solving the puzzle of *Ives* lies in Werner's claim that making employers liable for the employees' injuries regardless of fault was tantamount to redistribution. At first blush, it is a strange contention. Didn't the railroad spark statutes and the stock cases stand for the proposition that the law might allocate responsibility for damages to a party so long as that party had caused the damages? Contemporaries of Werner immediately picked up on this point. Redistribution was "easily distinguishable from" compensation statutes, explained the *Harvard Law Review* commentary on the case, "in that the former would be taking property for no event with which its owner has a responsible connection." The employer, in contrast, was surely a cause of— was responsible for—the injury in question. Jeremiah Smith of Harvard Law School, though himself sympathetic with Werner's conclusions, saw it this way too. The principle of workmen's compensation legislation, Smith explained, was "that he who causes harm . . . is, as its author, bound to make it good."[60]

Smith, however, had Werner's reasoning backward. For at the core of Werner's opinion lay the contention that workmen's compensation allocated liability not so much without regard to fault as without regard to causation. In Werner's view, as a few commentators pointed out at the time, liability without fault implied liability without the requisite causation.[61] A person acting properly within the boundaries of his own liberty could not be said to be the legal cause of an injury to third parties. If an industry or calling was "per se lawful and open to all," Werner explained, an employer in that industry could not be "compelled to assume a risk which is inseparable from the work of the employee." Such a risk "may exist in spite of a degree of care by the employer far greater than may be exacted by the most drastic law." And in such cases of injury despite extraordinary employer care, it would be absurd to assign causal responsibility to the employer.[62]

Causation in Werner's common-sense approach was thus closely linked to fault. This link should hardly be surprising. We see it routinely in the law of torts today. In tort, an antecedent act is a legal or proximate cause of some consequence if the consequence was reasonably foreseeable. Yet foreseeability is also a measure of the fault or negligence of the actor.[63] The features of an antecedent act that lead us to single it out from among the infinite network of antecedents as causally responsible are often the very features that make that act unreasonable or negligent. Consider railroad-crossing accidents, for example. The train's movement, the railroad's failure to block entrance onto the tracks, the injured crosser's movement across the tracks, her speed or lack thereof—all of these things are causes, in the sense of being necessary antecedents, of a railroad-crossing accident. We determine whether the railroad, its employees, or the injured crosser acted negligently in the situation by reference to a baseline of customarily expected behavior. And we often follow the same inquiry in assigning causal responsibility among the array of antecedents. As Hart and Honoré observe, that "which interferes with or intervenes in the course of events which normally would take place"—that which seems abnormal or, alternatively, faulty—stands out as the relevant cause. All else—the direction of the tracks, the available light at the crossing, and so on—fades into the background not as cause but as mere condition.[64]

That problems about causation lay at the core of the *Ives* controversy makes sense in light of the constitutional law of liability legislation at the turn of the twentieth century. Causation—as Louis Marshall's defense of the railway company pointed out—had been the critical factor in constitutional cases involving tort statutes for several decades. Causation had provided, for example, the crucial distinction between permissible statutes providing for strict liability for railroad spark fires, on one hand, and impermissible statutes seeking to provide for strict railroad liability for lost cattle, on the other. If stock statutes had threatened to make railroads liable for injuries to cattle that were properly understood as the consequence of the cattle owners' actions, or perhaps the consequence of the actions of the cattle, workmen's compensation just as surely made employers liable for some injuries in which common-sense reasoning would generally assign causal responsibility to the employee. There would of course be many cases in which employers could be said to be causally responsible for employee injuries. But so too would there be cases in which employees (and not employers) were causally responsible. Yet the statute made employers liable for these injuries as well. It applied, as Werner explained, "for every accident in the course of employment," even where "the employee is at fault." It applied, he continued, to injuries suffered because of "an accident which no human being can foresee or prevent, or which if preventable at all, can only be prevented by the reasonable care of the employee himself."[65]

The existence of the employment itself, of course, and thus the existence of the employer, were necessary antecedents to any work injury. The employer was therefore a "but for" cause of the injury in the sense that absent the employer, the employee would not have been injured. Yet the chain of necessary antecedents absent which the injury would not have taken place stretched infinitely back in time. That chain could plausibly be said to include a whole host of people to whom we would not ordinarily assign causal responsibility, such as the trolley car driver who brought the employee to work that morning, or the maker of the tools or machinery involved in the injury. Likewise, in railroad cattle injury cases, such a causal chain of necessary antecedents would include the railroad cars that struck the cattle. Yet mere inclusion in the list of necessary antecedents was insufficient to establish the kind of causal connection required to sustain a legal assignment of responsibility. This was the lesson of the stock cases. But this elision of the distinction between necessary antecedent and legal cause was precisely what the compensation statute purported to do. It sought to make employers liable even in those cases in which conventional ways of thinking about causation in law would have assigned causal responsibility elsewhere.

Indeed, as far as we can tell—and in all likelihood as far as the court knew—Earl Ives's injury presented precisely such a case. Ives had initiated the train of events out of which his injury arose. He had signaled for the engineman to pick up the slack in the train, and he had done so as an experienced switchman presumably well equipped to grasp the consequences of his actions. And in this sense, Werner proved prophetic. Ives's case presaged a whole host of workers' compensation cases in the century since in which few conventional causation stories would assign causal responsibility to the employer: a newspaper deliveryman assaulted by hitchhikers he had picked up, for example, or an employee spraining his ankle during a game in the company softball league.[66] Yet under the regime of workers' compensation, we assign liability to the employer in such cases with remarkably little controversy. Workers' compensation acts skirt the causation question in individual work-accident cases by substituting a less exacting requirement that the injury be one "arising out of and in the course of" employment. This requirement ensures that the employer will be in some remote sense causally connected to the injury; at the very least, it usually requires that the employment increased the risk of the employee's injury.[67] But other than in the probabilistic sense of raising the chances of the injury, workers' compensation fails to ensure that the connection between employer and injury will be closer than the causal relationship between the railroad and the burial costs associated with a death on one of the railroad's cars.

In this light, the Court of Appeals's concern for the implications of the compensation statute begins to make sense. Conservative torts lawyers had recognized for several decades that novel theories of causation might cause the law to veer dangerously close to redistribution. The conservative lawyer Francis Wharton, as Morton Horwitz has pointed out, warned as early as 1874 against theories of causation that assigned causal significance to the sum of all necessary antecedents to a particular consequence. John Stuart Mill had proposed such a theory of causation. But although Wharton conceded that such notions of causation might be sound in the natural sciences, in law, he argued, they led inevitably to a "practical communism." The state would simply be able to select out "a capitalist" from among the array of available antecedents. "The capitalist, therefore, becomes liable for all disasters of which he is in any sense the condition."[68]

This seemed to be precisely the logic of the compensation statutes. Morris Tyler of Yale Law School had complained in 1899, shortly after the introduction of workmen's compensation in Great Britain, that compensation stood for the principle that "he who has should give to him who has not, simply because he has."[69] Werner agreed. If compensation acts could make an employer liable even when he was not the legal cause of an injury, "it is equally competent, to visit upon him a special tax for the support of hospitals and other charitable institutions, upon the theory that they are devoted largely to the alleviation of ills primarily due to his business."[70] To tinker with the causation requirement in tort would be to make rights in property subject to politics and to potential reallocation by legislators and partisan interests. The "boys" from Werner's upstate political clubs would come to have virtually plenary power over the boundaries of legal rights.

The great difficulty for Werner was that compensation acts embodied at least two distinctly novel theories of causation, each of which represented a substantial departure from the causal conventions that shaped his and his colleagues' thinking. For one thing, Werner had not come around to the managerial theory of causation. It was his intuition that the worker, not the employer, was still the party in the best position to avoid accidents, and thus the party best described as the cause of that accident. In this respect, Werner's underlying understandings of labor and of the implications of the compensation statutes were deeply rooted in the free labor values of the Civil War experience. As Walter S. Nichols explained in defense of Werner's *Ives* opinion, workmen's compensation dealt with free laborers as "subject, like medieval serfs, to . . . task-masters." Morris Tyler had described the implications of compensation statutes as reversing the process of the "movement from status to contract," determining "a man's right and duties . . . more by what closely resembles status than by his own free choice." In good free labor fashion, however, opponents of compensation insisted that "the employee is not a mere piece of mechanism." The United States had "exchanged slavery" for a "lesser servitude to society." Wage laborers, as a brief filed on behalf of the railway observed, jointly and voluntarily participated with their employers in the firm's production of goods and injuries alike. And in such a system of free wage labor, it was, in Nichols's words, "the right and ability of a freeman to assume the risk of his employment."[71]

It was thus simple common sense for Werner, as it had been for Chief Justice Lemuel Shaw in the 1840s, that wage earners were free agents.[72] At the very least, the details of the work process were the joint products of employer and employee; more likely, many of those details were effectively controlled by the employees themselves. This intuition about the nature of the workplace led Louis Marshall's brief for the railway to suggest that the "tendency" of compensation legislation would be "to increase accidents, to multiply injuries, to militate against the safety of the workman, and to jeopardize life and limb."[73] If employees exercised meaningful control in their work, the reasoning went, and if they had relatively less reason to fear injury because they would recoup a share of the costs, accident rates might well go up rather than down. On this understanding Werner was led to conclude that the compensation act "does nothing to conserve the health, safety or morals of the employees." Werner had not yet grasped the power of managers in the age of Frederick Winslow Taylor to reshape the environment of the firm. According to Werner and his colleagues, risks were allocated primarily by nature, not by human reengineering. It was "the law of nature," he wrote, that in human activities "the risks which are inherent and unavoidable must fall upon those who are exposed to them." "Human law," argued Chief Judge Cullen's concurrence, "cannot change" the "physical law of nature . . . that imposes upon one meeting with an injury, the suffering occasioned thereby."[74]

The second causal theory embedded within the compensation acts was the theory of the actuary, whose categories the compensation statutes were ushering into new prominence in American law and public life. In *Ives*, Werner sought to deflect this theory, too. By 1911, Werner had been aware of the growing power of probabilistic thinking for some time. As early as a 1901 address in Rochester, he had conceded that the great changes in modern industry seemed to be controlled by the kinds of social laws of statistical regularity that nineteenth-century astronomers, physicians, and social scientists had begun to develop. The "universal tendency towards consolidation" in business firms, he said, was a "natural and necessary condition." For in everything "from the sublime circling of the celestial orbs to the movement of unseen microbes," Werner continued, "the universe is governed by inexorable laws." The actuarial laws of nineteenth-century statistical science, however, were not to be succumbed to but rather resisted and channeled. The "duty" of the heroic guardian judge was "to so direct and control" the course of such change as "to secure the most permanent and widely beneficial results."[75]

As a classical torts jurist, Werner's inquiry in torts cases asked whether the parties in question had acted consistently with the boundaries of their liberty. Workmen's compensation statutes, in contrast, came at work accidents in gross, taking employers and employees in the aggregate. Industrial enterprises caused regular injury tolls that seemed to be independent of the vagaries of individual cases. The inquiry under the compensation statutes was thus not who in any individual work-accident case had caused the injury in question, but rather who—employers or employees—was best described as responsible for the aggregate toll of casualties in a given industry. The managerial theory of compensation statutes led to a kind of presumption of employer responsibility, moderated by a damages rule that capped employers' damages at one-half or two-thirds of employees' lost wages. The additional step of the actuary was to convert the presumption of the scientific manager into an unrebuttable presumption: a statistically derived general rule to be applied prophylactically to virtually all cases. Causation would, in a sense, be determined by legislative fiat for compensation cases as a whole on the theory that employers were best described as the cause of the injury in the majority of the cases; the individualized causation inquiry of tort law would be replaced by an inquiry into the status of the parties accompanied by an unrebuttable presumption of employer causation based on statistical tendencies.

The workmen's compensation statutes, to be sure, were not the first time probabilistic thinking had been brought into the law of torts. The very idea of the "reasonable man" by which fault was to be measured in classical tort law sometimes verged on a kind of statistical average, approximating *l'homme moyen* of nineteenth-century Belgian statistician Adolphe Quatelet. And as long before as the early 1870s, the tragically short-lived but brilliantly inspired Boston lawyer Nicholas St. John Green had analogized causal thinking in tort law to the kind of aggregate causation that he called the causation of the "underwriters." St. John Green thus anticipated by more than two decades Holmes's suggestion in his "The Path of the Law" address that the "economic value" of personal injuries could be estimated in gross and averaged to calculate recoveries in the accident cases that were incident to businesses such as railroads and factories.[76]

Nonetheless, workmen's compensation represented a striking new introduction of actuarial categories and probabilistic principles to American law. The "reasonable man" was not exactly coterminous with the "average man"; even customary acts engaged in by every member of a community could (in theory) be faulty or negligent in a particular tort case.[77] And before the enactment of compensation statutes, the ruminations of St. John Green remained little more than the academic exercises of one of the profession's most accomplished thinkers. Holmes's extension of St. John Green's ideas, on the other hand, was organized around precisely the kinds of problems that characterized the work-accident crisis; indeed, Holmes's "Path of the Law" address had come just months before Britain enacted its workmen's compensation statute. More than any other feature of American accident law, workmen's compensation statutes brought a systemic commitment to aggregation.

According to Werner, however, aggregating the causation inquiry impermissibly violated the property rights of individual employers. As he explained in 1912, a year after the *Ives* decision, the problem with the compensation statute was that it had imposed "upon the employer the burden of responding in damages" even in those cases in which the "employer might be wholly free from fault, and the injury due entirely to the carelessness of the employee." It was not sufficient under the Constitution to lump such injuries in with the run of cases. Employers had to be dealt with as "individual citizens," in the words of Chief Judge Cullen, and could not be "compelled to contribute to the indemnity of other citizens" except "by the power of taxation imposed on all . . . for the maintenance of public charity." The compensation acts, Walter Nichols insisted, sacrificed "the independent manhood and political equality of the individual citizen." Morris Tyler explained that such legislation "ignores, abrogates and treats as worn out, that fundamental notion of personal responsibility." Employers would be held liable even when not responsible, and employees compensated even when to blame. In either case, the principle "which lies at the bottom of so much of our law"—that individuals must be held to account "for the consequences of [their] own acts"— would be violated.[78]

In both its managerial and its actuarial registers, the causal theory of the compensation acts had introduced a new set of conventions for describing social relations such as those between employees and employers. Where Werner and his colleagues understood the employment relation as one between individual free actors in which employees were effective agents in the work process, compensation acts took managers as the agents responsible for the firm and took employees in the aggregate. The result was a deep shift in commonsense notions of what was a cause of what, a shift of which the compensation acts were at once an index and an accelerator.

The unanimous Court of Appeals was not alone in seeing workmen's compensation as the harbinger of radically new and perhaps dangerous principles for American law. What place could there be in the worlds of the manager and the actuary for the independence, self-responsibility, and autonomy strands of the free labor worldview? Louis Marshall described the *Ives* decision as "a substantial dike against the tide of socialism." "[Y]our manly position in standing by your guns in respect to the opinion rendered by you in the *Ives* case," he wrote privately to Werner, "has met with the approval of thinking men."[79]

Most lawyers and scholars, however, viewed the Court of Appeals's decision differently. As Columbia University economist Henry Seager observed, *Ives* was "criticized by able lawyers and teachers of law from the Atlantic to the Pacific," and outspoken critics included such luminaries of constitutional law as Ernst Freund, Frank Goodnow, and Roscoe Pound. Influential New York City corporate lawyer and former commissioner of labor in New York State P. Tecumseh Sherman said flatly that the decision was "wrong"; a lawyer on the west side of the Hudson thought it was "doubtful if the decision . . . can be sustained." I. M. Rubinow later reflected that *Ives* "was severely criticized, as, perhaps, no decision of a higher court has ever been criticized before," even by the "most conservative lawyers and writers." Almost immediately, some leading legal commentators began to suggest that *Ives* would likely not be the final word on the subject.[80]

Despite suggestions that *Ives* might not find support in other jurisdictions, the decision seemed "a very serious blow to the hopes of those favoring the system of compensation."[81] And among those of a more radical temperament, it set off a "storm of protest" and an "outcry of surprise and indignation."[82] It did not help matters much that the day after the *Ives* decision was handed down, the Triangle Shirtwaist Company in New York City went up in a deadly and famous conflagration. The Triangle Fire killed 146 people, an overwhelming majority of them young women from the city's immigrant communities. Fueled by accumulated scraps of fabric on the floors, the fire raced through the eighth, ninth, and tenth floors of the Asch Building just off Washington Square, trapping employees behind fire exit doors locked to prevent employee theft and causing many to jump to their deaths from the windows to escape the blaze. "We've got to smash the constitution," cried protesters after the Triangle Fire; Florence Kelley took the occasion to say that she regarded "that decision as infamous and Judge Werner as a terrible enemy of the working class."[83] As far away as Alabama, the labor press demanded that the Due Process Clause on which the decision purported to rest be "swept out of the constitution and out of the judicial mind." "[T]he results" of the decision, predicted socialist lawyer Morris Hillquit, "will be of greater consequence than anyone suspects."[84]

Theodore Roosevelt, who as governor had put Werner on the Court of Appeals in 1900, quickly emerged as the most prominent critic of *Ives*. Roosevelt had been highly critical of the courts' treatment of work-accident re-form legislation since the U.S. Supreme Court had struck down the first Federal Employers Liability Act in 1908 for exceeding Congress's power under the Commerce Clause.[85] In October 1910 he had lashed out at Simeon E. Baldwin, then running for governor in Connecticut, for a 1909 opinion Baldwin had written while on the Connecticut Supreme Court denying that state courts were constitutionally obligated to apply the second, reenacted Federal Employers' Liability Act.[86] After March 1911, *Ives* became for Roosevelt the state law twin of *Lochner v. New York*. Indeed, Roosevelt analogized *Ives* to *Dred Scott*, suggesting that "*Dred Scott* was worse in degree, but not in kind" than the decision of the Court of Appeals. *Ives*, he argued, was "a most flagrant and wanton abuse of a great power." Judges such as those who decided *Ives*, Roosevelt announced, had "no right to sit on the bench." Privately, Roosevelt even vowed to "try to take every man off the bench who made that decision." Not surprisingly, Roosevelt quickly made *Ives* a centerpiece in his campaign for the recall of judicial decisions.[87]

Roosevelt's recall movement fizzled under withering criticism from defenders of the courts. His heightened post-*Ives* criticism of the judiciary helped to precipitate his break from the Republican Party and his formation of the Progressive Party in 1912. Intemperate comments about the judiciary in the months after *Ives* may even have cost him reelection to the presidency in 1912 by alienating leading Republican supporters.[88]

If the movement for recall of judicial decisions failed, however, the *Ives* decision itself was effectively recalled several times over. Within just one or two years, *Ives* seemed to have been laid to rest by popular consensus. *Ives* was "out of harmony with the spirit of the times," explained one lawyer. It represented, in Harvard law professor Roscoe Pound's phrase, an "artificial type of reasoning" that was "fast disappearing from the books."[89] By 1913, Rubinow believed that it was virtually "impossible to put one's finger upon any organized body of men who would at present, in the open, dare to take a stand against compensation." And in November of that year, New York voters approved by an overwhelming margin a constitutional amendment authorizing the state legislature to enact a workmen's compensation law.[90] By the time the Court of Appeals heard a second workmen's compensation case in 1915 under a reenacted statute and under the new constitutional amendment, only three of the judges who had been on the bench in March 1911 remained there. Werner, though still on the court, did not even participate in the case.

The Court of Appeals's 1915 decision in *Jensen v. Southern Pacific Co.* unanimously upheld the statute under the new state constitutional amendment. In an opinion joined by future Supreme Court justice Benjamin Cardozo, and written by newcomer Judge Nathan L. Miller (a future Republican governor of New York), the Court of Appeals embraced precisely those premises of the compensation statutes that Werner had rejected as unacceptable departures from the traditions of American tort law. The *Ives* decision had indicated that the compensation statute violated both the state and the federal constitutions, though whether its ruling in fact reached the latter was ambiguous. The New York constitutional amendment necessarily reached only the state constitutional question, and in this sense the *Jensen* decision went further than the amendment in overruling *Ives* by reaching the federal constitutional question. The *Jensen* court no longer focused on the individual case; the idiosyncracies of Earl Ives's exceptional case would no longer control the constitutionality of the statutory scheme. "Any plan devised by the wit of man may," the court conceded, "in exceptional cases, work unjustly." But the statute was to be judged, the court explained, "by its general plan and scope and the general good to be promoted by it."[91]

The *Jensen* court's categories of analysis were those of the actuary and the statistician. As Thomas Reed Powell later observed, the *Jensen* decision "regards the employees as a class and looks at the benefit which the class as a whole will derive from the statute rather than at the possible disadvantages which will accrue to the few. . . . Judge Miller regards the statute from the standpoint of its general operation and effect, rather than from that of the most grievous deprivation it may occasion in a few isolated instances." In Powell's words, *Jensen* represented nothing less than the "transition to a changed viewpoint." Here were the very same "economic and sociological arguments which the *Ives* opinion" had praised "but dismissed as immaterial" to the legal analysis. The Court of Appeals "looked with new glasses" on the compensation problem. And seen through this new lens of aggregates and averages, of mass social analysis, compensation statutes seemed entirely salutary. *Ives*, announced the editors of the *California Law Review* later in the year, was now a "discredited decision."[92]

Werner's nonparticipation in the *Jensen* case was most likely a result of his declining fortunes and deteriorating health after *Ives*. In the same November 1913 election that enacted the state constitutional amendment overturning *Ives*, Werner was defeated in his bid to become chief judge of the Court of Appeals. The election was widely considered a referendum on his *Ives* decision. Roosevelt's Progressive Party had even offered to nominate Werner on the condition that he publicly back away from the *Ives* decision.[93] Roosevelt and Werner, after all, had been close since the turn of the century, and Werner flirted with distancing himself from *Ives*. At public events, he began to emphasize the Court of Appeals's recent decision to overturn an 1896 assumption-of-risk case that Roosevelt had often singled out for special condemnation. And in a dinner given for Werner with a group of influential New

York City residents, Werner signaled that he had shifted his position on workmen's compensation. Workmen's compensation, he said, "has come to stay"; the question was "not whether we shall have it" but only whether a scheme could be worked out that was "not unjust to the employer." Compensation, Werner concluded, was "a movement in which it is worth our while to lend a helping hand."[94]

Newspaper reports indicated further that in September 1913, Werner privately told an upstate New York partisan of Roosevelt that "if he had the *Ives* decision to give over again he would give a different decision." Roosevelt claimed to have confirmed the statement in a later conversation with Werner, who (Roosevelt later contended) had "admitted that the decision . . . was in error." Werner subsequently suggested weakly that the reports were untrue. But to private correspondents that same September he had conceded that "the court may have been wrong in its conclusions on the constitutionality of the Wainwright Act." He had narrowed his defense of the decision to the claim that *Ives* presented a question "upon which there is, to say the least, room for differing views."[95]

Werner appears not to have been willing to make public his private confessions of error in *Ives*. Absent a public statement, the Progressive Party would not extend him its nomination for chief judge, and by the end of September the flirtation between Werner and Roosevelt was over. "We cannot afford," Roosevelt declared, "to indorse such a travesty of justice as the decision . . . in the *Ives* case."[96] The Progressive Party instead nominated Learned Hand, a federal district court judge from the Southern District of New York who in 1909 had testified in favor of the compensation act before the Wainwright Commission. Hand, who was at the very beginning of what would become one of the legendary judicial careers in American history, refused to campaign for the position. But the Progressive Party—which with Hand as its candidate was more likely to pull away Republican votes than Democratic votes— mounted strong attacks on Werner's record as author of the *Ives* opinion.

Even so, initial vote counts indicated a narrow victory for Werner. "Werner Wins," announced the *New York Tribune* the day after the election; the *Times* agreed. Nicholas Murray Butler, president of Columbia University, congratulated Werner that "the principle for which you stood has been vindicated." Werner's closest supporters even sought to revive his now-improbable hopes for a Supreme Court nomination. But after ten days of back and forth in the vote counts, Werner's Democratic opponent Willard Bartlett was named the winner by a tiny margin. Hand's 195,000 votes—the democratic expression of the legacy of *Ives*—had secured Werner's loss.[97]

Werner's life fortunes quickly declined after his electoral defeat. Awaiting the contested and shifting election returns, he wrote to his daughter, had been a "nerve racking process." And within days of the announcement of the election results, Werner's wife Lillie became seriously ill.[98] Lillie recovered, yet by the spring of 1914 it was as if the stranger-than-fiction narrative of Werner's life had suddenly been jolted into the realm of fact. The "bubble was pricked," Werner wrote to one correspondent. In these "trying times," he wrote, "a man may be most faithful, painstaking and conscientious in the discharge of his public duty and yet reap the disfavor of public opinion because, forsooth, he dares to do his duty in the face of public clamor." Stripped of his glorious narrative of the hero-guardian judiciary, his political ambitions deflated, Werner was left once again with the "never ceasing grind" of processing cases that he had once sought to dispel by writing love letters from the bench. "I wonder," he mused, "why any man can wish to spend his time grinding out decisions over other people's troubles." In December 1914, Werner was diagnosed with anemia. "My strength has been failing for some time," he wrote. The *Times* reported that same month that Werner would take time off from the bench. An attack of dysentery slowed him again in 1915. On March 1, 1916, Werner died.[99]

Just a few months after Werner's death, Benjamin Cardozo wrote an opinion overturning Werner's 1905 decision in *Wright v. Hart*, the case in which Werner had ruled New York's bulk sales statute unconstitutional. At the time of Werner's *Wright v. Hart* opinion, Cardozo explained, "such laws were new and strange. They were thought in the prevailing opinion to represent the fitful prejudices of the hour." "The fact is," Cardozo concluded, "they have come to stay."[100]

Cardozo might as well have been writing the epitaph to Werner's workmen's compensation opinion. In 1917, almost a year to the day after Werner's death, a trio of decisions by the U.S. Supreme Court upheld workmen's compensation statutes under the federal constitution. A Court that included Willis Van Devanter and James McReynolds, justices who twenty years later would famously resist the legislative reforms of the New Deal, unanimously upheld the reenacted New York statute that the New York Court of Appeals had already upheld in *Jensen*. The Court even upheld the provision of a Washington compensation statute mandating that employers insure against accidents through a state insurance fund, though here the Court split 5-4. Justice Mahlon Pitney wrote all three decisions. Already a well-known opponent of organized labor and author of a number of the Court's most infamous antilabor decisions, including *Coppage v. Kansas* (1915) (striking down a statute making illegal so-called yellow-dog employment contracts by which employees agreed not to join a union), Pitney would go on in *Hitchman Coal and Coke Co. v. Mitchell* (1917) to enjoin the

United Mine Workers from organizing workers at a firm that prohibited its employees from joining a union, and in *Duplex Printing Press Co. v. Deering* (1921) to make a dead letter of the anti-injunction provisions that unions had long sought and had finally obtained in the 1914 Clayton Act. With Pitney's three 1917 workmen's compensation opinions, the basic premises of the workmen's compensation statutes had come to be accepted across virtually the entire political spectrum of American legal culture, from Crystal Eastman and John Mitchell on the left to Pitney, Van Devanter, and McReynolds on the right. By the end of the 1910s one hardly needed to be a progressive, let alone a radical, to support workmen's compensation statutes.[101]

Yet Werner's efforts were not without consequence. To be sure, Werner seems not to have seen it this way. It turned out that he had not envisioned that the Spartan judge-heroes he described in speeches as "shoulder to shoulder" in "the path of duty" would confront the kind of adversity he faced after *Ives*. In point of fact, Werner and his fellow judges were more often shoulder to shoulder at the Waldorf-Astoria for bar association dinners, and Werner seems to have experienced his attempt at judicial independence in *Ives* as profoundly disappointing.[102] Nonetheless, *Ives* ultimately proved momentous for the trajectory and development of the emerging paradigm of risk and insurance.

Within weeks of the decision, workmen's compensation advocates began to formulate responses that would allow the movement to continue despite the adverse decision. One route to evading the consequences of *Ives*, of course, was by state constitutional amendments authorizing workmen's compensation statutes. This was the preferred response of the American Association for Labor Legislation, whose leading members sought to make the best of *Ives* by pushing through broad constitutional amendments that would authorize not only workmen's compensation but "other enlightened legislation" such as "insurance against . . . sickness, invalidity and old age, and [legislation] for the good and welfare of the state." The AALL ultimately proved unable to enact such omnibus amendments, but New York voters approved an amendment specifically authorizing workmen's compensation statutes, as did voters in California, Ohio, Vermont, and Wyoming.[103]

Very quickly, however, there developed a perceptible change of emphasis in the compensation movement. After *Ives*, leadership in the movement shifted from social insurance advocates like Crystal Eastman and the AALL to constitutional lawyers such as Ernst Freund and Wainwright Commission counsel Joseph Cotton. The Federal Employers' Liability and Workmen's Compensation Commission, which convened soon after the *Ives* decision was issued, devoted its early meetings to the constitutional questions, which in the wake of *Ives* were "deemed of primary importance."[104] Lawyers specializing in fed-

eral appellate practice moved to redress a peculiarity of Supreme Court jurisdiction that precluded Supreme Court review of state court rulings (such as
Ives) that upheld a claim of federal right. And in state compensation commissions across the nation, lawyers with expertise on the now unavoidable constitutional questions came to the forefront of the debates.[105]

In each of these areas, lawyers aimed to avoid the cumbersome process of
amending constitutions, and rather to adjust the compensation statutes to
meet the constitutional objections. Their first move was to begin, like good
lawyers, to narrow the holding in *Ives* by explaining it as the correct response
to a particularly flawed statute. The goal was to provide an account of the law
of compensation that would supply a basis for the result in *Ives* but that could
be distinguished from future compensation statute cases.

The first such account focused on the provision of the 1910 New York statute allowing injured employees to elect after their injury either compensation, with its strict-liability standard and limited damages awards, or a tort
suit, with its negligence standard and unlimited damages. Louis Marshall had
argued on behalf of the railway in *Ives* that this provision was a chief problem
with the New York statute. Later in the same year in which *Ives* was decided,
the Montana Supreme Court struck down a Montana compensation statute
limited to the coal industry on precisely this same ground: the Montana statute, too, had allowed injured employees to choose their remedy.[106]

Notwithstanding that this feature of the New York statute had not been so
much as mentioned in the *Ives* decision, constitutional lawyers seized on it as
having been the statute's fatal flaw. As Raynal C. Bolling, a lawyer for U.S.
Steel, explained, "[t]he vice" of the New York act "lay in the fact that it allowed a choice of remedy after the accident."[107] Commissions at the state and
federal level took the hint. The Federal Employers' Liability and Workmen's
Compensation Commission concluded that the Court of Appeals "might
well have been justified" in *Ives* given that the statute at issue there had created "a double liability." And when the New York Court of Appeals came
around to disavowing *Ives* in *Jensen* in 1915, the formal rationale it adopted
for distinguishing *Ives* as a matter of federal constitutional law was that the reenacted New York statute made compensation the exclusive remedy for injured employees, eliminating the injured employee's choice between compensation and tort. The two statutes were "therefore so plainly dissimilar that
the decision in the *Ives* case is not controlling."[108]

In truth, post-accident employee election of remedies had hardly been peculiar or unique to the New York statute. It was a feature of the English statute on which many American compensation schemes were modeled and remains a feature of the English law of work accidents into the early twenty-first
century. Moreover, in addition to being incorporated in the United States's

earliest compensation acts in New York and Montana, provisions allowing injured employees to choose their remedy had also been part of early bills in Congress to establish a federal workmen's compensation scheme for railroad employee injuries.[109]

After *Ives,* however, the American compensation movement shifted decisively to a quid pro quo theory of the compensation statutes. Compensation statutes were not impermissible takings of employer property without due process, this theory held, if they gave something to employers as well as employees. "There must be a benefit flowing to the person taxed," explained an article on compensation in the *Yale Law Journal.* "Justice requires equal rights on both sides," explained another law review commentary. Absent a benefit to employers in the form of immunity from suit in tort, compensation acts impermissibly redistributed entitlements from employers to employees. This was "a discrimination inconsistent with . . . our constitutions," a "naked burden" "without compensating circumstance." The whole point of compensation statutes, constitutional lawyers now argued, was (as Thomas Reed Powell explained in 1917) that "each gains something for his losses and loses something for his gains." In the words of the U.S. Supreme Court, "the exemption from further liability is an essential part of the scheme."[110]

To be sure, the Court two years later in 1919 ruled in a sharply divided 5–4 decision that the quid pro quo approach was not required as a matter of federal constitutional law; as far as the federal constitution was concerned, states could establish compensation programs absent employer tort immunity.[111] But by then the politics and momentum of the compensation movement had changed. And as the *Jensen* decision in the New York Court of Appeals suggested, state constitutions remained significant obstacles.[112] After *Ives,* only Arizona, New Hampshire, and Nevada had ex post employee election in their compensation systems, Nevada having enacted its statute the very day *Ives* was decided. Two years later, Nevada made compensation the employee's exclusive remedy; Arizona followed suit in 1925, though New Hampshire did not do so until 1947.[113]

Ives thus had the consequence of building into the risk-spreading mechanism of the compensation statutes the baseline entitlements of the nineteenth-century common law. This baseline was constituted by precisely the rights of property and liberty whose boundaries classical tort law had sought to articulate. New risk-spreading legislation could not systematically reallocate entitlements from one class to another without some corresponding benefit for the disadvantaged class. *Ives,* in other words, ensured that the principles of nineteenth-century classical liberalism would still obtain in the era of social insurance, even if only in the rough approximation of an exchange of expanded liability standards for immunity from unlimited damage awards.[114]

The second set of lawyers' responses to *Ives* involved the move from mandatory or compulsory compensation statutes to elective compensation statutes. There had been some support before *Ives* for the notion that compensation statutes would be constitutional only under an "elective plan" that combined presumptions in favor of election, on one hand, with abolitions of employers' common law defenses for nonparticipating employers, on the other. Wisconsin commissioners, for example, planned in 1910 to use what they called "constitutional coercion" by abolishing the common law defenses of employers refusing to come into the compensation program. Early supporters of compensation such as the members of the New York commission, however, had rejected elective statutes out of concern that elective programs would attract few firms. But *Ives* decisively moved compensation programs toward the elective approach, having what one commentator called a "profound effect on all subsequent legislation." New Jersey led the way, adopting less than two weeks after *Ives* an elective statute that was designed expressly to evade the threat of a similar decision by the New Jersey courts. By 1913, twenty-one of twenty-five states enacting compensation statutes had adopted statutes that employed "the New Jersey method of beating the courts."[115]

The move to elective statutes, like the move to the quid pro quo theory of compensation, had important consequences for the evolution of compensation programs. Quid pro quo implied that the enactment of social insurance legislation was conditioned on its provision of some kind of tangible benefit in the form of a set-off to employers. The elective system, in turn, placed inexorable downward pressure on compensation levels. As early as 1913, commentators observed that the "elective system of compensation has had a very serious and detrimental influence upon the quality of the compensation legislation." In order for an elective system to induce employer participation, "compensation must be made cheaper than liability." E. H. Downey wrote some years later that elective statutes had thus "operated as a deterrent to an adequate scale of benefits." Downey concluded that "the discredited opinion of a single reactionary court" had "influenced the whole subsequent course of legislation."[116]

Remarkably, virtually all the legal adjustments of the compensation statutes accepted the actuarial and managerial theories of causation that Werner had seen as inconsistent with the law's basic principles. The lawyers who rewrote the compensation statutes to meet the challenges posed by *Ives* found themselves on the opposite side from Werner of the paradigm shift that had haunted the *Ives* controversy. Pitney's opinions upholding the constitutionality of workmen's compensation statutes endorsed the new managerial theory of the firm. Employees were to "contribute [their] personal services"; employers were "to control and manage the operation." This duty to manage the firm, in turn, meant that the regular toll of industrial injuries was "an expense of the operation, as truly as the cost of repairing broken machinery."[117] To be sure, there might be instances in which convention would assign causal responsibility to the employee, the employer's duty and power to control and manage notwithstanding. But in the "highly organized and hazardous industries of the present day, the causes of accident are often so obscure and complex that in a material proportion of cases it is impossible by any method to correctly ascertain the facts necessary to form an accurate judgment."[118] And so Pitney adopted the actuarial mode of the compensation statutes as well: "As all parties know, from time to time some of the workmen will be killed or injured," though "nobody knows or can know in advance which particular men" will be the victims.[119]

Judicial acceptance of the compensation statutes meant the acceptance of their strikingly new theory of legal causation. "In excluding the question of fault as a cause of the injury," Pitney wrote, "the act in effect disregards the proximate cause and looks to one more remote, the primary cause, as it may be deemed,—and that is, the employment itself."[120] This move from proximate causes to more remote causes, of course, was precisely the theory of causation that an older generation of lawyers, from Francis Wharton to William Werner, had rejected as leading straight to the redistribution of property in a kind of "practical communism." Under the theory of causation embraced by the compensation statutes, it no longer mattered, as the Court of Appeals explained in *Jensen*, whether there were individual cases in which the employer was held liable for damages despite not having caused injury to the employee in any legal sense. So long as there was a reciprocal benefit flowing to the employer in the form of tort immunity, "the theoretical taking no doubt disappears in practical experience." The constitutional concerns raised in particular instances were simply washed out in the run of cases, which amounted in Ernst Freund's words to "a practical approximation toward justice in preference to a theoretically perfect justice to each individual case."[121]

Looking back from 1938, two leading students of workmen's compensation would note that "[t]he shades of Mr. Ives and his lost case for compensation still haunt the periphera of this field." Even if the legal response to *Ives* had abandoned the basic premises and conventions of Werner and his colleagues, the implementation of those premises in *Ives* had done tremendous work to shape the trajectory of the social insurance movement of which compensation statutes were the leading edge. Workmen's compensation programs had "grown up in mushroom form," in a kind of wild, unplanned pattern, a few adopting compulsory form, but most designed as elective.[122] Moreover, neither the elective structure that compensation statutes adopted after *Ives*, nor the quid pro quo theory that supported those statutes, furnished useful models for the other social insurance programs desired by compensation advocates such as the AALL. There were no easily matched changes in liability that could serve as an inducement for employers to elect into, for example, a health insurance scheme or an unemployment insurance scheme. Nor was there a readily available immunity that could be provided to employers to create a reciprocal employer benefit in, for example, an old-age pensions scheme. As the head of the New York Chamber of Commerce warned the day after the Supreme Court's trilogy upholding compensation statutes, the opinions in favor of compensation provided no basis for the view that they might furnish precedents for further social insurance programs; there was, he stated flatly, "no right to assume that [the] general statement[s]" made in the Supreme Court's cases "would include health insurance laws."[123] The common law baseline in the law of employers' liability had provided just enough of a hook to sustain the elective structure and the quid pro quo theory of the post-*Ives* compensation statutes. But that baseline seemed to provide little assistance for further forms of social insurance.

Perhaps it should not be surprising that members of the Court of Appeals in 1911 were caught on the trailing edge of the momentous paradigm shift in the law of work accidents from the categories of free labor to the organizing principles of risk and insurance. Werner's idols were the Union heroes of abolition and the Civil War. Judge John Clinton Gray was sixty-eight years old and had been appointed to the court in 1888, more than twenty years before the *Ives* decision. Judge Willard Bartlett was sixty-five. Chief Judge Cullen had even fought in the Civil War. As Theodore Roosevelt described them, the judges on the court were "six . . . elderly men."[124] In *Ives,* these elderly hero-guardians of the judiciary sought simply to defend the deeply rooted common-sense categories with which they had grown up.

By the time the U.S. Supreme Court upheld workmen's compensation, the experience of the Civil War was losing its grip on American legal thought. On the eve of the United States's entry into World War I, the industrial wage earner had become the new soldier. Compensation for injured wage earners was, in Justice Pitney's words, like "the grant of pensions to disabled soldiers." The employee, Pitney wrote (quoting the Washington Supreme Court before him), was the "'soldier of organized industry, accepting a kind of pension in exchange for absolute insurance on his master's premises.'"[125] In Pitney's formulation, however, the social solidarity of the military analogy had been defanged of the risk-spreading possibilities it had possessed in the hands of John Mitchell, Crystal Eastman, and the AALL. Indeed, workmen's compensation had become a kind of hybrid, sharing features drawn from earlier experiments in dealing with the accident problem. The pensions of the industrial army would be formulated along actuarial and managerial lines yet they would still be bound by a rough approximation of the baselines of classical nineteenth-century liberalism.

Ives had played no small part in the orientation of work-accident reform. In the words of Princeton University political scientist Edward S. Corwin, *Ives* had been "overcome in a measure" by such devices as the elective statute—"but only in a measure."[126] We have failed adequately to appreciate the *Ives* case because, with the lawyers who sought to rescue compensation from the *Ives* decision, we stand on the other side of the rupture in common-sense paradigms of which the case itself is a marker. We take for granted with hardly a second thought that risks are expertly managed by technically trained engineers. It is second nature that the state often deals in aggregate tendencies rather than individualized detail. Virtual unanimity on questions such as these coalesced with remarkable speed after 1911. In work accidents, the categories and organizing principles of free labor had haltingly made room for the paradigm of risk and insurance.

7

The Accidental Republic

We can never insure one hundred percent of the population against one hundred percent of the hazards and vicissitudes of life, but we have tried to frame a law which will give some measure of protection to the average citizen and to his family against the loss of a job and against poverty-ridden old age.

> —FRANKLIN DELANO ROOSEVELT, REMARKS ON SIGNING THE
> SOCIAL SECURITY ACT, AUGUST 14, 1935

The human tragedy indicated by the dry statistics of the *Columbia Study* . . . escapes the popular mind. No political pressure group is interested in playing it up; and there are many vested interests in the *status quo.*

> —FLEMING JAMES, "THE COLUMBIA STUDY OF COMPENSATION
> FOR AUTOMOBILE ACCIDENTS: AN UNANSWERED
> CHALLENGE" (1959)

Industrial-accident rates in the United States began to decline soon after the enactment of workmen's compensation statutes. Economic historians disagree as to whether employers' costs under the new statutes caused the declines. Nonetheless, whether because of changed employer accident costs or because of the widespread public attention that work-accident law reform brought to the crisis of industrial accidents, workmen's compensation brought in its wake the first widespread safety movement in the American workplace. From 1907 to 1920, work-fatality rates per manhour in American industry dropped by two-thirds; nonfatal work-injury rates and lost workdays per manhour (both much more difficult to measure than fatalities) appear to have declined by half. At U.S. Steel, accident rates fell from about one full-time worker in four injured per year in 1907 to fewer than one full-time worker in three hundred in 1939. On the railroads, where work-accident liability was split between the Federal Employers' Liability Act for employees in interstate commerce and state workmen's compensation acts for all other employees, accident rates fell from a post-1900 high of 2.8 fatalities for every thousand employees in 1904, to 1.2 fatalities for every thousand employees in 1920. Among the dangerous industries of the turn-of-the-century economy, only the mining industry—in which increased monitoring of safety conditions was exceedingly expensive—failed to experience such declines in fatal work accidents. Significant reductions in fatal accident rates in the nation's coal mines would not occur until World War II.[1]

There was a great irony in the reduced injury rates accompanying workmen's compensation statutes, an irony toward which the monitoring difficulties of the coal mining industry pointed. Reductions in industrial-accident rates seemed to require a trade-off in diminished worker discretion and independence. The relative autonomy of the worker in late-nineteenth-century industry had helped create the industrial-accident crisis. Increased work safety in the decades after 1910, in turn, was driven by the expansion and consolidation of managerial bureaucracies. The abatement of the work-accident crisis thus witnessed the eclipse of many of the informal mechanisms of worker control that had characterized nineteenth-century free labor. Building on management systems that had emerged in the workplace safety movement and in employer accident-benefit programs during the late nineteenth century, employers founded safety departments run by engineers, hired industrial hygiene experts, and established new offices of human resources. Indeed, workmen's compensation popularized the term "human resources" in American journalistic and legal parlance, promising to apply to employees the conservation principles that had already been applied to natural resources.[2] Making workers free from risk thus seemed to require making them less free in their day-to-day employment; free labor, to put it another way, seemed to give way to *risk*-free labor, or at least risk-reduced labor.

If work-accident law reform helped remake the firm and rationalize the employment relation, compensation statutes also substantially reworked many of the nation's legal and political institutions. Consider, for example, the critically important (though often taken for granted) phenomenon of judging. In the early twenty-first century, judging in the federal system is performed more often than not by administrative law judges in federal agencies such as the Social Security Administration, the Immigration and Naturalization Service, and the Securities and Exchange Commission, rather than by life-tenured judges appointed under Article III of the U.S. Constitution.[3] Administrative judges (what one commentator has called "the hidden judiciary") abound in state governments as well, making "judicial" determinations in cases ranging from unemployment insurance claims, health department complaints, and traffic violations to state and local taxation questions, zoning board variances, and public utility regulations.[4] In short, the twentieth century witnessed an explosion of administrative-bureaucratic adjudication outside of traditional courtrooms. The first mass systems of administrative adjudication in the United States arose out of workmen's compensation programs, which replaced judges and juries with specialist administrators. Moreover, it was in early workmen's compensation cases that American lawyers carved out space for administrative law judges in relation to state and federal jury trial rights, in relation to common law judges in the states, and in relation to the federal judges created as an independent branch of government under Article III of the U.S. Constitution.[5]

Consider also the scope of federal power under the Commerce Clause. Beginning in 1937, federal courts allowed Congress to exercise dramatically expanded authority under the Commerce Clause, largely abandoning the attempt to draw boundaries between interstate and intrastate in the field of economic regulation. It was precisely this distinction that had produced the *First Employers' Liability Cases,* which struck down the first Federal Employers' Liability Act (FELA) as beyond Congress's Commerce Clause power. The FELA purported to modify the law of employers' liability for all injured employees of interstate common carriers, regardless of whether the injured employee was himself employed in interstate commerce. Within months, Congress reenacted the FELA, now limited to those railroad employees suffering injury while themselves employed "in commerce between any of the several States."[6] The result was that each and every FELA case for the next three decades raised the excruciatingly difficult, and ultimately hopeless, question whether a boundary could be drawn between interstate and intrastate commerce.

Even in 1906, when the first FELA was debated in Congress, opponents had predicted that the "law will cause inextricable confusion as to where the State and national law should govern." "How is the question as to whether or not an employee is engaged in interstate commerce or in intrastate commerce to be determined?" wondered one railroad lawyer.[7] Over the next three decades, the quixotic nature of the project in federal and state courts, including the Supreme Court, became abundantly clear. The Supreme Court alone decided forty-three cases between 1908 and 1934 in which it was required to decide whether an injured employee had been engaged in interstate commerce.[8] The Court's ad hoc decisions created a morass of incoherent rules. A railroad employee operating an engine that pumped water for use on interstate trains was engaged in interstate commerce—but not a railroad employee mining coal for use on an interstate train.[9] A railroad employee unloading goods from out of state was engaged in interstate commerce (and thus covered under the FELA)—but not if the goods had arrived too long before the unloading.[10] A railroad watchman guarding interstate trains was engaged in interstate commerce—but not if he was merely looking for a hiding place from which to guard an interstate train, and not if he was pursuing bandits who had taken goods from an interstate train.[11]

Ultimately, the practical muddle of FELA cases made clear that distinguishing between interstate and intrastate commerce for either statutory or constitutional purposes was a futile task. In the words of two Harvard Law School graduates writing under the tutelage of Felix Frankfurter, the "elusive concept" of interstate commerce was in fact "an unworkable concept."[12] When in the late 1930s and early 1940s federal judges finally gave up on the project of policing the boundary between interstate and intrastate economic activity, they did so with thirty years' experience in hundreds of FELA cases to suggest just how quixotic a project it was. As the Supreme Court commented drily in 1943, the "over-refinement of factual situations" in railroad cases had "hampered the application" of the FELA's jurisdictional provisions.[13] The Court would note in 1938 (with reference to experience under both the FELA and the Interstate Commerce Act) that there was simply "no point in . . . drawing . . . a mathematical line" between interstate and intrastate commerce.[14]

The development of administrative adjudication and the expansion of the Commerce Clause were both foundational developments in the establishment of the twentieth-century administrative state. Indeed, in fields ranging from administrative adjudication and federal Commerce Clause powers, to the decline of Fourteenth Amendment contract freedoms and the emergence of a patchwork of overlapping accident-law systems, to the gendered family wage of work-accident law and the emergence of new forms of entitlement-claiming on the state, workmen's compensation laid down patterns for central developments in the law over the next century.

Yet if the work-accident experiments of the late nineteenth and early twentieth centuries laid groundwork for the American administrative and social insurance state, enactment of the compensation statutes also marked an end to the early eclecticism of the American law of accidents. Employers, insurers, plaintiffs' lawyers, and unions began to organize around workmen's compensation, forming powerful interest groups to lobby state and federal governments on issues ranging from accident law to the array of social insurance programs that so many had thought might follow on the heels of changes in the law of work accidents. By the 1920s and 1930s, work-accident law thus came to represent both the beginnings of the administrative state and its limits.

Workmen's compensation seemed to have a bright future. By 1917, compensation programs covered 13.5 million American wage earners, who constituted 69 percent of the paid workforce. In New York alone, workers and their families filed an extraordinary 40,855 claims in 1914, the first year of operation for the state's reenacted compensation statute. That number rose to 50,861 in the second year, and 58,562 in the third, a number of claimants that represented almost 3 percent of the state's paid labor force. By 1930, just under 200,000 new workmen's compensation claims were filed in the state each year. In the nation as a whole, the numbers were vast. As early as 1917, workmen's compensation systems around the country received in excess of 350,000 claims per year.[15] The prediction of Harvard Law School's Jeremiah Smith—that workmen's compensation principles would one day govern throughout the law of personal injury—seemed well on its way to being borne out.[16]

Among the most significant developments in expanding the scope of workmen's compensation statutes was a critically important, yet rarely noted, shift in constitutional law. Just as courts had carved out special rules in tort law for extrahazardous activities such as blasting, they had allowed legislatures to use an industry's dangerousness as a kind of proxy for a finding that the industry caused harm to some third party and could therefore be regulated. Accordingly, early workmen's compensation statutes had been drafted to apply only to specifically enumerated dangerous industries. State compensation commissions had hoped in this way to persuade courts to uphold the constitutionality of the new statutes. By early 1917, the commissions' strategy appeared to have worked. The U.S. Supreme Court upheld compulsory workmen's compensation programs as constitutional. Yet these holdings applied only to hazardous employments, and the Court even suggested that it might bar the application of the programs to industries "proved by experience" not to be hazardous.[17]

After 1922, the dangerous industry category would no longer be a hindrance to the expansion of workmen's compensation programs. New York again led the way. The state legislature in 1916 and 1917 increased the number of employments deemed hazardous under the compensation statute, extending the statute to any employee in the service of an employer whose principal business was hazardous, whether or not the injured employee was engaged in that business. In 1918, rather than continue a pattern of piecemeal expansions of the statute, the legislature deemed hazardous all employments with four or more workmen regularly engaged in the same business, excluding domestic servants and farm laborers.[18] The theory of the 1918 amendment was that any employment in which an accident took place was, ipso facto, a dangerous employment and thus subject to regulation under compulsory workmen's compensation programs. This theory had been floated in 1910 at a national conference of workmen's compensation commissions, and it found an early supporter in Theodore Roosevelt, who had articulated it in his annual address to the Congress in 1908.[19] Together with the 1916 and 1917 amendments, the 1918 amendment worked a breathtaking expansion of the dangerous-industry category. To come under the statute it was necessary only to work for an employer who in some part of its business employed four or more workmen. The dangerous-industry category, in short, had expanded to cover virtually all wage earners.

Four years later, in *Ward and Gow v. Krinsky,* which involved an injured newsstand employee, this expansion of the compensation statute was upheld by the U.S. Supreme Court. In yet another workmen's compensation decision by the conservative Justice Mahlon Pitney, a clear majority of seven justices (McReyonolds and McKenna dissenting) adopted the ipso facto theory in its entirety: "That there was inherent hazard in Krinsky's occupation," Pitney reasoned, "is conclusively shown by the fact that in the course of it he received a serious and disabling personal injury arising out of it." At the high level of probabilistic abstraction adopted by the workmen's compensation statutes, injuries even in less obviously dangerous occupations might now be "foreseen," and indeed here the "Legislature actually foresaw it and made provision for it, long before it occurred."[20]

With *Krinsky,* the Court freed the technologies of the actuary from the constraints of the dangerous-industry category, allowing legislatures to act on the basis of the statistical inevitability of injuries in even relatively safe employments. Moreover, by opening up the dangerous-industry category in constitutional law, the Court had gone a long way toward abandoning interpretations of the Reconstruction constitutional amendments as guaranteeing the right to freedom of contract in the employment relation. By the first decade of the twentieth century, much of the controversy in constitutional law as applied to labor regulations centered on the question whether courts would defer to legislative findings of a hazard to be regulated. In hazardous industries such as mining, the Supreme Court sustained legislative findings of dangerousness, and upheld legislative determinations of a reasonable relationship between the employment contract regulation at issue and the danger.[21] In industries such as baking, the Court did not, reasoning that to do so would inevitably mean that there would be "no length to which legislation of this nature might not go."[22]The question of dangerousness was of such importance that Josephine Goldmark and Louis Brandeis even sought to remake constitutional litigation around persuading the justices to defer to legislative findings of dangerousness.[23]

The significance of *Krinsky,* therefore, was that the Court had abandoned the project of policing legislative determinations of dangerousness, surrendering to legislatures the question whether a particular employment was hazardous and, accordingly, regulable. To be sure, the workmen's compensation statutes looked like a relatively uncontroversial place to allow such legislative discretion. As Pitney pointed out, employers would incur few costs under the statute unless their employees suffered work injuries.[24] And once a determination of dangerousness was made, the reasonableness of the relationship between a compensation statute and the danger posed was not difficult to establish. Yet the implications were far-reaching. As Justice McReynolds noted in a typically dyspeptic dissent from the *Krinsky* majority, "[m]any have suffered fatal accidents while eating, but eating could hardly be called hazardous." In McReynolds's view, "hazard" must be "something more than the mere possibility of injury." Anything was "possible," of course, and at the level of aggregates possibilities became statistical certainties. In a probabilistic sense, McReynolds complained, a hazard "is always present." To allow the regulation of hazardous activities under such a definition would be to allow legislatures a broad new latitude in the regulation of the employment contract.[25]

Yet if *Krinsky* suggested that workmen's compensation principles would face fewer obstacles in the Reconstruction amendments, other kinds of legal obstacles ensured that compensation statutes would not sweep across the American law of work accidents. Indeed, it soon became apparent that there would be no single system of work-accident law, only a proliferation of many systems.[26]

As early as the fall of 1911, leading figures in the workmen's compensation movement sought to harmonize the various federal and state work-accident regimes so as to make their respective jurisdictions "clearly defined."[27] But from the mid-1910s onward, jurisdictional lines in American law helped to break up work-accident reform into a patchwork of different legal regimes, sitting cheek-by-jowl in close, complex, and often seemingly overlapping relation to one another.

Within three months of upholding the constitutionality of workmen's compensation statutes in 1917, the U.S. Supreme Court (over a vigorous dissent from Justice Holmes) barred the application of state workmen's compensation systems to longshoremen and stevedores injured while engaged in maritime work. Indeed, it did so in an appeal of the very decision—*Jensen v. Southern Pacific Co.*—in which the New York Court of Appeals had unanimously overturned *Ives*.[28] The Supreme Court ruled in *Jensen II* that states lacked the authority to interfere with the uniformity and characteristic features of the federal admiralty and maritime jurisdiction. Over the next ten years the Court would twice strike down as unconstitutional attempts by Congress to overturn the *Jensen II* decision by delegating to the states the power to make maritime work-accident rules.[29]

The Court also held in *New York Central Railroad v. Winfield* (over a vigorous dissent by Justice Brandeis) that the Federal Employers' Liability Act impliedly preempted state workmen's compensation acts in cases involving injuries to railroad workers in interstate commerce.[30] In one sense, *Winfield* (decided the same day as *Jensen II*) was an application of the quid pro quo theory of workmen's compensation to the injured interstate railroad worker; he could not have recourse, as Brandeis would have had it, to both a tort suit and a compensation claim. In the sense that is of greater interest here, *Winfield* was further evidence of the way in which jurisdictional lines would divide work-accident law into a multitude of different programs. By the end of the 1920s, U.S. work-accident law was made up of forty-nine geographically bound workmen's compensation statutes, one for each of the forty-four states as well as the District of Columbia, Hawaii, Alaska, Puerto Rico, and the Philippines;[31] federal workmen's compensation regimes for particular kinds of employees, such as longshoremen and harbor workers, and federal employees;[32] a federal employers' liability scheme for interstate railroad employees, operating on the basis of nineteenth-century negligence principles before courts and juries; and a very similar federal employers' liability scheme for seamen.[33]

Even as jurisdictional fault-lines hardened, interest group lobbies quickly solidified. The compensation statutes had been enacted with the support of a broad mix of different groups, ranging from progressive reformers and labor unions to large manufacturing firms and managerial engineers. Notably, railroads represented a field of work-accident law that had already given rise to entrenched, organized interest groups that were heavily invested in the existing law of employers' liability. On the defendants' side, railroad lawyers organized in the Railroad Attorneys' Conference bitterly opposed early reforms such as the FELA and also came out against proposals for a federal workmen's compensation statute for interstate railroad employees.[34] On the plaintiffs' side, the personal injury bar worked hard—and sometimes successfully—to create opposition to workmen's compensation reform among selected railroad brotherhood locals.[35] In the case of injuries to interstate railroad employees, the clash of well-organized interest groups hindered enactment of a workmen's compensation regime even as compensation statutes swept the field virtually everywhere else. Indeed, such railroad employee injuries to this day remain outside of a workers' compensation regime. This pattern of policy obstruction by entrenched interests would repeat itself again and again over the next century throughout the law of personal injury.

Perhaps the greatest early example of the mounting power of interest groups in accident-law reform came in the area of automobile accidents. As early as 1911, a few visionaries had understood that motor vehicle injuries would present the next great challenge for American accident law after the industrial-accident crisis of the turn of the century. By the late 1920s, motor vehicles had emerged as, by some measures, the new leading cause of accidental deaths in the nation, involved in close to one-third of all accidental deaths. Indeed, automobile injuries seemed to be recreating many of the

same problems of wasteful litigation and court congestion that work accidents had caused for the legal system several decades earlier. Thirty percent of
all new suits filed in certain urban areas, for example, involved motor vehicle
accidents.[36]

Within a decade of the enactment of the first workmen's compensation
statutes, a movement for automobile accident compensation systems began
to develop. Scholars discussed such automobile compensation plans as early
as the late 1910s.[37] States appointed commissions to study the issue. And
during the 1920s and into the early 1930s, bills were introduced into state
legislatures in nine states that would have replaced tort litigation in automobile injury cases with a no-fault compensation scheme like workmen's compensation.

The motor-vehicle-accident compensation movement of the 1920s culminated in the well-known Columbia Plan of 1932, which was prepared under
the auspices of the Columbia University Council for Research in the Social
Sciences. Drawn up by a committee of distinguished lawyers and scholars, including Dean Charles Clark of Yale Law School and a team made up of faculty at Columbia and Yale, the Columbia Plan proposed that states build on
the "close analogy between the industrial situation where workmen's compensation has been developed and the motor vehicle situation." Compensation systems would accordingly replace tort law with programs that imposed
limited, scheduled liability on the owners of motor vehicles for injuries
caused by the operation of their motor vehicles.[38]

But motor-vehicle-accident compensation programs ran headlong into a
wall of opposition from the organized interests that had coalesced around
personal injury litigation. Personal injury plaintiffs' lawyers, insurance defense lawyers, the bar associations to which they belonged, and insurance
companies all joined together to "most vociferously oppose[ ]" the Columbia
Plan. In the face of such opposition from what the great midcentury tort
lawyer Fleming James called the "many vested interests in the status quo,"
the failure of the plan was (in the words of a more recent commentator)
"overdetermined."[39]

In combination with *Ives v. South Buffalo Railway,* the arrival of organized
interests brought an end to the period of relative openness and contingency
that had characterized the early decades of industrial-accident policy experimentation. Between the Civil War and the 1910s, Americans had experimented with a wide array of alternative accident-law institutions, a number of
which formed possible foundations for future developments in accident law.
Already by the end of the 1910s, however, the rise of powerful lobbies had
begun to close off the relatively open policy frontier that had presented itself
to lawyers, labor organizations, employers, and social reformers in 1900. In

California, for example, as Philippe Nonet has recounted, employers' trade associations such as the Chamber of Commerce joined with insurance companies to bring adversarial lobbying tactics and litigation techniques to the law of work accidents as early as the late 1910s and 1920s. The state's organized labor unions, in turn, actively involved themselves in their members' compensation claims beginning in the late 1930s. By then, the workmen's compensation system had come, in Nonet's words, to rest upon "a special kind of adversary system—the permanent confrontation of organized interest groups."[40]

Indeed, the need to counter employers' and insurers' lobbies in ongoing legislative wrangling over amendments to compensation statutes caused plaintiffs' personal injury lawyers to organize and to act collectively in ways they rarely had before. In 1946, plaintiffs' workmen's compensation lawyers from around the nation would form the National Association of Claimants' Compensation Attorneys. A quarter century later, the NACCA reconstituted itself as the American Trial Lawyers' Association, or ATLA. And over the next three decades, ATLA would become one of the most influential lobbies in American politics. The workmen's compensation bar had given rise to organized advocacy by the world's most powerful organization of trial lawyers.[41]

The history of accident-law reform in the mid-twentieth-century United States is thus a story of incremental reform at the margins of the law of accidents—"confined," in the famous words of Justice Holmes's dissent in *Jensen II*, "from molar to molecular motions."[42] In the decades following enactment of the original workmen's compensation statutes, the programs were extended fitfully (and often at employer-defendants' behest) into the area of industrial disease. In the mid twentieth century, Congress enacted various no-fault compensation schemes for nuclear accident victims, black lung disease among coal miners, and childhood vaccine injuries.[43] No-fault automobile accident schemes were ultimately enacted during the 1970s in over two dozen states, but even here the various no-fault plans were supplements to the tort system, not substitutes for it, typically creating a no-fault system for minor accidents while leaving more significant injuries to the tort system.[44]

By the 1980s, organized lobbies among repeat-play defendants such as product manufacturers and medical care providers managed to ram through state legislatures various "tort reform" measures such as caps on noneconomic damages awards and amendments to joint-and-several liability rules that traditionally have made joint tortfeasors individually liable for entire damages awards. Such measures, however, added up not so much to genuine restructuring of the law of torts as to what Robert Rabin has called "victim take-away programs," using the lobbying power of organized interests to expropriate entitlements from the relatively diffuse, less organized body of consumers.[45]

To be sure, workmen's compensation ideas continued to have considerable influence in the law of accidents. But as torts scholar Wex Malone wrote in the 1950s, the "contagious principle of workmen's compensation" found room not in new compensation systems but rather within the relatively autonomous body of evolving common law tort doctrine.[46] If compensation notions failed to gain the political traction required to effect broad institutional reform, they gradually worked their way into the law of torts in the case-by-case decisions of common law judges. In products liability cases, for example, midcentury tort law witnessed a dramatic widening of so-called enterprise liability for the costs of injuries to consumers, as well as workers. The consumer, like the laborer, was now viewed in the law of torts as dependent on what Karl Llewellyn called "an industry with which . . . he cannot cope."[47] In products liability, however, workmen's compensation liability standards had been decoupled from limited workmen's compensation damages awards. The result was what has come to be called a "legal revolution" in the law of civil liability. Defendants' exposure to tort judgments has expanded significantly, and liability insurance rates have increased markedly.[48] Ironically, the phrase "enterprise liability" itself appears to have been coined in 1911 by the managerial engineers who helped to manufacture new ideas about firms' control over and responsibility for their operations. Originally crafted to legitimate new managerial authority in the early-twentieth-century firm, enterprise liability has become a kind of Frankenstein's monster haunting the managers who invented it. Their dismay at the development of enterprise liability thus represents one of the great examples in American tort law of the phenomenon of unanticipated consequences.[49]

Within just a few decades of the outpouring of relatively plastic work-accident law alternatives, American accident law had become a hardened patchwork of compensation systems and tort law. The patchwork has much to be said for it—and much to be said against it. But technical arguments on the merits and demerits of the United States's many-systemed accident regime are not our subject. The important point here is that virtually no one in the early years of American accident law anticipated or advocated this patchwork of regimes. Our hodge podge of systems in the law of accidents is an artifact—an accidental product—of a half-century of eclectic experimentation in alternative systems, experimentation that was ultimately shaped and constrained by decisions like *Ives* and the rise of organized interests.[50]

The outcomes of accident-law experimentation were all the more important because they set patterns for the development of important features in the modern American state. For one thing, many of the same forces that shaped the trajectory of the workmen's compensation statutes exerted similar constraints on social provision policy more generally. The threat of judicial review by courts interpreting the Due Process and Equal Protection Clauses profoundly influenced the development of New Deal social insurance legislation, pushing lawmakers away from approaches to social insurance that would have created nationwide risk pools for such contingencies as unemployment.[51] The jurisdictional boundaries of American federalism helped push social provision policies for unemployment and poverty onto a state-by-state, rather than federal, basis, where they were shaped by competitive races among the states to reduce the tax burden on local employers.[52] And as in the case of accident law, organized interest groups formed to stymie change in controversial fields such as health insurance.[53]

Significantly, the social insurance programs put into place in the New Deal gathered together a coalition of interest groups remarkably like the one that had first coalesced around workmen's compensation legislation. Sophisticated employers and welfare capitalists, once again seeking to use the state to force all firms to bear some of the costs of expensive benefit programs, joined together with progressive economists and social insurance reformers in support of Roosevelt's 1935 Social Security Act.[54] The crisis of the Great Depression also exerted renewed pressure on American labor unions, bringing to the fore a new generation of unions that built on the labor movement's earlier support for workmen's compensation to reorient the American labor movement toward the state. Even the national leadership of the American Federation of Labor, which in 1910 had come around only reluctantly to workmen's compensation legislation—and had resisted any further social insurance legislation—came out in 1932 in favor of unemployment insurance.[55]

At the same time, many of those most heavily involved in drafting the Social Security Act had early experience in workmen's compensation. As a young legislator in New York State in 1911, Franklin Delano Roosevelt had experienced firsthand the legislative tumult surrounding the *Ives* case and the Triangle Shirtwaist Fire. New Deal Secretary of Labor Frances Perkins, who called the Triangle Shirtwaist Fire the "first day of the New Deal," had administered compensation claims from 1919 to 1928, first as a member of the New York State Industrial Board, and then as its chair. From 1929 until 1932, she oversaw the state's compensation program as state Industrial Commissioner under then-governor Franklin Roosevelt.[56] Edwin Witte served on the Wisconsin Industrial Commission in the 1910s and 1920s, overseeing the state's workmen's compensation program, before becoming executive director of the committee that drafted the Social Security Act of 1935.[57] William Leiserson of the committee's board of technical advisors had been closely involved in the Pittsburgh Survey that produced Crystal Eastman's book on work accidents, and had served on New York's Wainwright Commission, drafting a report on unemployment and unemployment insurance

that became an addendum to the commission's work on industrial accidents.[58] Both Witte and Leiserson had been strongly influenced in their
thinking about social insurance by their teacher, the influential University of
Wisconsin professor John Commons, whose own views on social insurance
had been shaped by his experience on the Pittsburgh Survey and as an admin-
istrator of Wisconsin's workmen's compensation statute.[59]

Not surprisingly, ideas drawn from accident-law reform powerfully influenced New Deal policymaking. Through the influence of his many students,
Commons inspired an important group of social reformers to advocate social
insurance programs organized around workmen's compensation principles.
By charging employers with the costs of their employees' unemployment, for
example, Commons argued that government could create financial inducements for employers to prevent unemployment, just as workmen's compensation created financial inducements for employers to prevent work accidents. Indeed, Wisconsin in 1932 had enacted just such an unemployment
program, in which individual employers created firm-specific reserve accounts out of which unemployment benefits were paid. A firm's unemployment costs would thus closely track its layoff practices.[60]

Ultimately, the Social Security Act did not go quite as far as the Wisconsin
school might have liked; the House version of the act even barred states from
adopting reserve account statutes such as Wisconsin's. Nonetheless, the act's
unemployment insurance provisions encouraged states to adopt insurance
schemes that would link employer contributions to the employer's own layoff
practices, thus providing strong financial incentives to prevent unemployment in the first place. Linking employment stabilization to reduced employment costs (as workmen's compensation had linked safety to accident costs)
formed what subsequent commentators have described as "the distinctive
American contribution" to unemployment policy.[61]

Traces of the workmen's compensation model underlay the views of Roosevelt himself. When, in the late spring and summer of 1934, Roosevelt created the Committee on Economic Security to craft what would become the
Social Security Act of 1935, he drew on the basic lessons of workmen's compensation. The aim of new federal social security legislation, he instructed
the committee, was to safeguard individual wage earners and their families
against those "misfortunes which cannot be wholly eliminated in this man-
made world of ours." Securing the wage earner and his family against the
"hazards and vicissitudes" of modern wage earning became one of the central
themes of Roosevelt's presidency, and a core metaphor in his campaign was
the work accident and the experience of workmen's compensation.[62]

By the spring of 1935, the analogy between industrial accidents, on one
hand, and such problems as unemployment and superannuation, on the

other, had become commonplace. Chief Justice Charles Evans Hughes, who as governor of New York State had helped to start the workmen's compensation movement in 1909 by calling for the creation of the Wainwright Commission, wrote in 1935 that the "fundamental consideration" supporting old-age pensions was that "industry should take care of its human wastage, whether . . . due to accident or age."[63] Secretary of Labor Frances Perkins agreed. "Unemployment," she contended, "should be regarded as a natural risk of industry, just as workmen's compensation for accidental injuries is regarded as part of the cost of doing business."[64]

The important 1939 amendments to the Social Security Act built still further on the work-accident experience. For one thing, the 1939 amendments reproduced the gendered family wage structure first inscribed into law in the wrongful death statutes of the 1840s and then reincorporated into the compensation statutes of the 1910s. As originally enacted, the Social Security Act tacitly reproduced the family wage model of dependent women and children and male wage earners by limiting old-age pensions to wage earners in certain covered occupations that were overwhelmingly male. Benefits under the 1935 legislation thus typically accrued to women derivatively via their husbands or (in the fledgling Aid to Dependent Children program) through their children.[65]

The 1939 amendments, however, and especially the survivor benefits provisions of those amendments, brought the model of the family wage still further into the social security system, not merely reproducing the family wage but prescribing it. Existing state and federal programs, Roosevelt's 1938 Advisory Council on Social Security explained, failed to provide widows and dependent children with the resources required to "maintain normal family life."[66] Survivor benefits for cases involving the death of a wage earner would remedy this problem. Yet in creating survivor benefits, the council recommended—and Congress enacted—benefits that incorporated precisely the gender asymmetry that American lawmakers had adopted in wrongful death statutes and in workmen's compensation programs. The amendments created "widows' insurance benefits," defined as benefits for "the surviving *wife* of an individual."[67] A widower was therefore unable to claim survivors' benefits under the 1939 amendments, regardless whether he was sixty-five or over, or had in his care young children who had been dependent on his deceased wife's wages.[68]

In various forms, the gender asymmetries drawn from work-accident legislation and introduced to the social security system in 1939 persisted until the mid-1970s, when the U.S. Supreme Court struck them down as part of the first generation of constitutional sex equality cases.[69] By then, the prescriptive model of the family wage had been an important part of American law for well over a century. New Deal lawmakers understood quite clearly whence they derived their ideas about the family wage. "Ample precedent" for the survivors' benefits provisions, the 1939 Senate committee report had explained, "is found in the State workmen's compensation laws."[70]

Perhaps even more striking, Roosevelt and the Congress adopted an insurance strategy that in important ways resembled the cooperative insurance movement of the post–Civil War accident crisis. Roosevelt had insisted that the old-age pensions of the 1935 Social Security Act be self-funded through employer and employee contributions and that each generation of workers pay in advance for its own pensions.[71] In amending the social security system in 1939, Roosevelt and the Congress effectively moved social security to a pay-as-you-go system. Social security—like the cooperative insurance associations before it—had become an intergenerational compact in which younger workers paid for the insurance of older workers. Indeed, as Roosevelt had anticipated in 1931 while still governor of New York, the government had in some respects become a kind of giant cooperative insurance society: a "duly constituted representative of an organized society of human beings—created by them for their mutual protection and well-being." Government, it seemed, was no longer the contract enforcement mechanism envisioned by John Stuart Mill and William Graham Sumner, but rather "the machinery through which . . . mutual aid is achieved." As the committee report to the Senate noted, the process by which this transformation occurred had begun "when small groups of workmen banded together in mutual benefit societies to build up group protection against unforeseen contingencies."[72]

Like so many features of the New Deal state, the Social Security Act went hand-in-hand with a powerful transformation in constitutional law. In *West Coast Hotel Co. v. Parrish*, the famous "switch in time" of 1937, the Supreme Court upheld a state minimum wage statute for women employees, overturning its own decision of fourteen years earlier and bringing to an end the era of constitutional law of which *Ives v. South Buffalo Railway* had been such a controversial part. Two months later, in *Charles C. Steward Machine Co. v. Davis*, the Court adopted the principles advanced in *West Coast Hotel* to uphold the Social Security Act against constitutional attack.[73]

Chief Justice Hughes's opinion in *West Coast Hotel* indicated just how thoroughly the changes associated with work-accident reform had reshaped important features of American law. The *sic utere* principle of classical tort law and of late-nineteenth-century constitutional law had allowed legislatures to regulate where the use of one's property caused harm to another; the logic of *sic utere* was that any other approach effectively required those who suffered injury to subsidize the activities of those who caused them. Now

Hughes suggested that not to have a minimum wage statute would be "to provide what is in effect a subsidy for unconscionable employers."[74] Employers, in other words, were in some sense responsible for the poverty of their employees.

This was just the point that Joseph Cotton of the Wainwright Commission had anticipated in 1909, when he noted that workmen's compensation would "establish the social policy that the industry must keep its workers from poverty." Similarly, Judge William Werner had predicted in *Ives* that if a legislature could make an employer liable for damages under workmen's compensation statutes, it would be "equally competent to visit upon him a special tax for the support of hospitals and other charitable institutions, upon the theory that they are devoted largely to the alleviation of ills primarily due to his business."[75] *West Coast Hotel* now endorsed precisely the "special tax" against which Werner had warned. Hughes's subsidy idea advanced the same notion of statistical causation that underlay the workmen's compensation statutes. In the aggregate, low-wage employment was probabilistically associated with the social ills of poverty. Moreover, Hughes's subsidy idea embraced the managerial engineers' notion that employers and their managers were better thought of as being in a position to remedy the ills associated with an enterprise than the employees themselves. Employers were thus better identified as the presumptive cause of those ills, notwithstanding that at the level of individualized inquiries, certain employees would undoubtedly sometimes be better described as causes of the ills of poverty than their employers.

And, of course, the Court in *West Coast Hotel* did not even stop to ask whether the employment at issue was a dangerous occupation. A decade and a half after *Krinsky v. Ward and Gow*, the dangerous-industries category of late-nineteenth-century constitutional law had disappeared.

As Franklin Roosevelt's description of the state as a mutual benefit society suggested, the rise of workmen's compensation marked a significant reorientation of the relations among everyday Americans, workingmen's organizations, and the state. In the claims that poured into state workmen's compensation boards beginning in the 1910s, everyday American wage earners and their families came to know the workings of the modern administrative state. State compensation commissions edged aside the workingmen's cooperative organizations that had flourished in the late nineteenth century, reorienting the claims of injured wage earners and their dependents from horizontal claims on the voluntary associations of their fellows toward vertical claims on a bureaucratized state apparatus. Workingmen's organizations, in turn, remade themselves as claims brokers in the emerging administrative state.

To be sure, workmen's compensation claims boards were not the first appearance of the administrative state. State rate-making commissions for railroads and public utilities had pioneered in the formation of what would later come to be called the "fourth branch" of government.[76] In 1887, the Interstate Commerce Act created the Interstate Commerce Commission, a critically important early administrative body at the federal level.[77] State factory inspection acts beginning in Massachusetts in 1879 created small cadres of safety inspectors charged with enforcing child labor, safety, and maximum hours laws for women wage earners.[78] Mothers' pension legislation in the 1910s vested local administrative bodies with new authority over programs for poor mothers, usually widows.[79] And beginning in the late nineteenth century, states even experimented with new administrative forms in criminal law, ranging from juvenile courts and eugenicist laboratory adjuncts to the traditional municipal courts, to indeterminate sentences and parole and probation boards.[80]

Yet in terms of the sheer number of people involved, few of these new administrative programs could compete with the workmen's compensation systems enacted around the nation in the 1910s. In New York alone, the State Workmen's Compensation Commission found that "industrial accidents at the rate of approximately 1,000 a day were being reported to the Commission" in the first year of its operation, "about 150 of which each day were found to be compensable."[81] By 1917, seven years after the enactment of the nation's first workmen's compensation statute, 13.3 million American wage earners were covered by the still newly enacted statutes.[82] State industrial commissions waged educational campaigns "to disseminate correct information about the law" and to alert wage earners of their rights under the new compensation systems. Commission officials spoke of the "necessity of a persistent campaign of education to be conducted through circulars, through the press, throughout the plants and in public meetings."[83] By 1916, New York's workmen's compensation officials estimated that their claims hearings were attended by "about 70,000 persons a year."[84] Even a decade later, mothers' pensions provided aid to a relatively meager 93,620 families nationwide.[85]

As states' educational efforts suggest, workmen's compensation claims did not arise spontaneously upon the enactment of compensation legislation. Claims on the compensation systems developed in a dialectic among commission members, workingmen's organizations, employers, and claimants. And in the back-and-forth of commission education efforts and advocacy, on one hand, and claimants' assertions of entitlement on the other, a remarkable process unfolded by which working-class Americans learned to negotiate the interstices of the new administrative state.

The otherwise unremarkable case of Anna and Terence Bennett illustrates the ways in which claimants learned to assert new rights on the state. Anna, Terence, and their infant son Victor lived in the Bronx, where Terence was a lineman in the maintenance department of the New York, Westchester, and Boston Railway. On March 21, 1917, Terence slipped from a catenary post and fell to the ground, fractured his skull, and died. Six days later, the New York State Industrial Commission approached Anna on its own initiative, encouraging her to begin the process of filing her compensation claim. By April 7, the commission had still not heard from Anna. The commission's chief of claims wrote her again: "Perhaps you can find it convenient to call at this office some day next week." Alternatively, a claims officer could "call at your home some time in the afternoon." Finally, a week later, Anna replied to the commission, requesting that the claims officer come to her apartment. By the end of the month, Anna's communications with the commission had taken on a mixed tone of entitlement and deferential petition. The claims officer, she wrote firmly, "told me that I would hear from you before the end of the month as it is now the 30th and no word as yet." Her plaintive conclusion: "you know I have been without a penny, depending on you people to make their payments as my bills are piling way up and I can't meet my creditors." The claims officer met with her once more, and several weeks later the Industrial Commission awarded Anna $9.23 per week plus $100 in funeral expenses. A month and a half later, Anna's distinctive handwriting appears in the files again, this time to upbraid the commission for its failure to take notice of the change of address notification she had sent them; Anna was going to make certain that the commission remedied the problem.[86]

The Bennett case captured the dialectic of needs and rights that took place in workmen's compensation commissions around the country. Workmen's compensation claims officers extended awards to injured workers and their families on the basis of needs. Compensation systems, after all, were designed to replace the rights orientation of the tort system. Lawyers would be eliminated from work-accident disputes, and legal institutions would address need, not entitlement. Claims officers accordingly reached out repeatedly to ensure that potential claimants received the awards they needed. Yet claimants quickly turned extensions of need-based awards to their own ends, appropriating the needs-oriented policies of the commissions and transforming them into claims of entitlement on the state. Indeed, notwithstanding that employers and their insurance companies were technically the defendants in workmen's compensation proceedings, and notwithstanding that employers or their insurance companies would pay any awards, claimants such as Anna Bennett quickly came to see state compensation commissions as institutions on which they could assert claims of entitlement.

The Bennett case appears to have been representative of the way in which the New York compensation commission handled claims. When Petrina Alvettow Caruso's husband Michele was killed in a freak accident in a power mixer at Francesco Longo's bakery on Bleecker Street in Greenwich Village, for example, the commission wrote to Petrina repeatedly in the weeks after the accident in order to get her to file a claim.[87] The commission wrote Philip Koepper's widow Emma no less than six times requesting that she file a claim under the law after her husband had died as a result of injuries suffered in an accident on a freight car in the New York City freight yard.[88] And as in the Bennett case, such need-based awards were eventually appropriated by claimants themselves and re-articulated as claims of right.[89]

Compensation claims often initiated life-long relationships between compensation commission administrators and claimants. Harold Taber's injury in 1917 at the Donner Steel Company in Buffalo, for example, brought him to the compensation commission repeatedly up into the early 1960s.[90] Martha Hall was widowed in November 1915 and left with a small child; the compensation commission closed her file sixty years later upon her death in 1976.[91] Clara Bleich's husband Otto had been killed fighting a fire at a Semet-Solvet Company plant in July 1918. A decade later, Clara was still claiming that her weekly compensation payments of $9.22 should have been higher: "As soon as you hear from the legal department please let me know about it. (And about the Government work my husband done also? before and at the time of his death? And bonus? that he always consider a part of his pay? As I thought there might have been a mistake?)"[92]

Moreover, the very same kinds of workingmen's organizations that had formed the basis for cooperative insurance beginning in the 1860s and 1870s, and which had exhibited some jealous resistance to the development of social insurance programs, began in the 1910s to reorient themselves toward the state. Where once they had functioned as providers of mutual insurance benefits themselves, they now became claims brokers functioning as intermediaries between their membership and the state. This transformation was readily apparent in early compensation cases, for example, in which labor organizations actively advocated on behalf of their members from the 1910s onward.[93] Similarly, by the 1930s workingmen's organizations such as the railroad brotherhoods, many of which had begun as mutual insurance associations, had taken on the new role of representing their members in interactions with the new administrative state.[94] Philippe Nonet has observed the same development in California. In Nonet's account, labor union representation of their members in compensation cases (along with employers' and insurance companies' lawyers) helped to reorganize workmen's compensation proceedings around claims of right (from both sides), rather than claims of need.[95]

The reorientation of workingmen's organizations represented a critically important shift. The cooperative insurance movement had served as one of the most important institutional embodiments of the broad free labor tradition of the American labor movement. The self-sustaining independence of the propertied artisan had become the narrower but still perceptible independence of the cooperatively insured industrial wage earner, whose property in his body and in his insurance certificate would ward off the dependency of poverty in the event of disability or death. Cooperative insurance, in other words, had sought to resuscitate the broad labor movement theory of self-ownership, redescribing it in the form of insurance against the risks associated with wage labor. Moreover, cooperative insurance had seemed to many in the movement to represent only the first in what would be a long line of cooperative enterprises, enterprises that promised to sustain and even restore in a new form the independence of the industrial workingman. By contrast, the workmen's compensation boards transformed reciprocal benefits and cooperative forms into individualized claims of entitlement on the state. The state might be, as in Franklin Roosevelt's formulation, the new cooperative insurer, but social insurance was cooperation on so grand a scale as to abstract away the close relations among members that had sustained the cooperative movement. Insurance against risk had been largely stripped of its linkage to the traditions of free labor independence, of its aspirations to a cooperative commonwealth built on the foundation of the insurance societies.

In workmen's compensation hearings taking place around the country in the 1910s, the free labor ideas that had animated American law and politics from the middle of the nineteenth century onward no longer signified. Lawyers and administrative law judges in such proceedings no longer sought to carve out the boundaries of individuals' respective spheres of free action; aggregates and averages—not corrective justice—were the aims of workmen's compensation systems. Similarly, with the rise of compensation programs came the decline and transformation of those workingmen's insurance organizations that had sought to build a cooperative independence for the industrial workingmen. In the important field of work accidents, cooperative insurance association and torts jurist alike had receded, at least in relative terms, replaced by the interaction of the injured worker or widow with the new administrative apparatus of the state. To be sure, the efficiency strand of the complex of ideas that constituted free labor ideology persisted. But it too had been radically remade, reorganized not around the incentives exerted by free markets in labor, but rather around the engineered efficiency of hierarchically arranged scientific management.

Just as the free labor ideology of Lincoln, Emerson, and Lemuel Shaw had screened out the problem of risk, the new paradigm of risk and insurance screened out many of the problems that had occupied free labor thinking, not so much resolving them as setting them aside. Indeed, among the chief values in the free labor constellation, only the family wage persisted in the law of work accidents with a vigor resembling its mid-nineteenth-century formulation. The family remains to this day an intensely moralized domain in American law. Yet isolated from the array of ideas that had accompanied it, the family wage alone could not carry the weight of the free labor tradition. And so in work accidents, as in the social policies that stand as the legislative legacies of the New Deal, the dialects of free labor gave way to the languages of security and social insurance.

Conclusion

At the opening of the twenty-first century, American lawmakers face a re-newed set of challenges in the field of accidents and personal injury. To be sure, accidents of one sort or another have posed persistent dilemmas throughout the past hundred years. From automobile accidents and products liability to maritime torts and medical malpractice, the law of personal injury has undergone widespread changes. Developments in tort doctrine, for ex-ample, can be characterized broadly as an expansion of liability in tort begin-ning roughly in the 1940s, followed by a more conservative period of re-trenchment beginning in the 1980s and continuing to the present. But in recent years, problems in the law of personal injury have raised dilemmas on the order of those that caused wrenching paradigm changes in our law a cen-tury ago.

For one thing, American tort law outside the work-accident area continues into the early twenty-first century to exhibit significant resistance to the actu-arial models embodied in workmen's compensation. Statistical causation and the allocation of liability among business enterprises on the basis of their mar-ket share, for example, have found their way into contemporary tort law—but only haltingly.[1] As a result, in mass tort cases arising out of asbestos, to-bacco, lead paint, handguns, medical devices, and pharmaceuticals, to name only a few of many examples, actuarial categories and aggregation strategies are pushing once again at boundaries in the American law of accidents that lawmakers first explored 100 years ago.[2]

At the same time, another set of emerging risks seems to press beyond ag-gregation and the actuarial approach. Diverse new risks, including nuclear di-sasters, global warming, genetically modified organisms, and any number of complex systems whose compromise might lead to catastrophic results, pres-ent challenges on a scale that seems to defy even the most innovative acci-dent-law institutions on the contemporary scene. Because we lack aggre-gatable experience with such catastrophes, these new catastrophic risks move beyond the actuarial model that emerged in the work-accident experience.

208

Statistical models of risk like those that animated developments in the law of accidents a century ago simply cannot be assembled in the absence of the requisite time-series data.[3] In this regard, the federal compensation fund set up in the wake of the September 11, 2001 attack on the World Trade Center may be a harbinger of the kinds of departures from traditional practice that we may be compelled to adopt in a world of mass risks and postmodern technologies.[4]

As American lawyers, judges, and policymakers grapple with these renewed challenges, it has become a commonplace that powerful traditions in American law limit the ability of our legal institutions to develop innovative solutions to new problems arising in the law of personal injury. The U.S. Supreme Court, for example, insists that "our deep-rooted historic tradition that everyone should have his own day in court" constrains the use of class actions in mass tort cases.[5] Our historical practices, in other words, are seen as setting bounds on experimentation in accident law. And when American lawyers seek examples of alternative accident-law regimes, we look not to our own history but to the far corners of the earth, to places like Saskatchewan for its early no-fault automobile accident compensation system, adopted in 1946, or even farther away to New Zealand for its 1974 Accident Compensation Act, which replaced common law tort actions in injury cases with a comprehensive administrative compensation scheme.[6] Innovations in accident law thus sometimes seem to be the exotic exports of faraway lands.

This book has described a lost tradition of experimentation in the American law of accidents. In the half-century following the Civil War, workingmen's associations, jurists, scientific managers, and social reformers all converged on the problem of industrial accidents. Their experiments offered a series of plausible alternative paths for the development of American accident-law institutions. Indeed, many of the institutions with which they experimented continue to this day to play important roles in law and social policy. The common law of tort, for example, continues to govern injuries arising out of wide swaths of social life, even if work injuries and certain other limited kinds of injury have been (at least partially) removed from the tort system. Nineteenth-century cooperative insurance organizations found a future in other western nations as the building blocks for social insurance programs; in the United States we carry on the cooperatives' intergenerational compact in our pay-as-we-go social security system. Employee-benefit programs, like those developed by the first generation of human resources managers to provide employee-accident compensation, have become central features of both the employment relation and American social policy, which uses employee benefits to deliver services such as health insurance.[7] And social insurance systems like unemployment insurance and social security, whose beginnings lie in the workmen's compensation statutes of the 1910s, make up approximately half the spending in the $1.8 trillion federal budget. These very different institutions have all had considerable significance over the course of the past century in the United States and elsewhere; any one or more of them might have had a different, perhaps more sustained, significance in the field of American accident law.

That our accident law developed along the paths it did was the contingent result of a number of different factors, including the ideological commitments of common law torts judges; the regulatory framework in which workingmen's insurance operated; judicial review of legislation regulating labor risks; the emergence of the United States's peculiarly strong scientific management movement; and the partial successes of U.S. social insurance advocates in the early part of the twentieth century. This diverse array of considerations does not, to be sure, present a parsimonious account of the development of our law of accidents; the account set out here fails to achieve the conceptual clarity of a formal model. But what it lacks in neatness is hopefully made up for in a narrative that resembles the messy and eclectic—and even accidental—processes by which the practices of human governance change and develop over time.

As I suggested in the introduction, I describe the development of the American law of accidents as accidental in several different senses. Our law of personal injuries has developed along lines that were both unintended and unforeseen by the lawyers, workers, managers, and social reformers who helped create it. To suggest in addition that its development might have been accidental in the sense of not having been determined is to raise more difficult further questions. Could history have been different? Do accidents ever happen, or (as Henry Thomas Buckle's nineteenth-century determinist histories of civilization suggested) are historical events determined by inexorable laws of history and society. That there are no accidents was what I. M. Rubinow implied at the turn of the twentieth century when, with any number of his fellow American students of industrial accidents, he doubted whether the notion of "accident" was a useful way to think about workplace hazards given the inexorable yearly toll of industrial casualties. An "industrial accident," Rubinow wrote in 1913, "is not an accident at all."[8]

At their most theoretical level, such questions of determinism and accident fall within the purview of the philosopher or the student of quantum mechanics rather than the bailiwick of the historian.[9] The historian's contribution to such issues is decidedly less abstract than the contributions of either the philosopher or the physicist. It is to evaluate whether different paths might reasonably have been taken. The historian asks, in other words, whether there were plausible alternatives.[10] In the case of American accident law, the answer seems to be yes. There were alternative institutional directions in which our legal system might have gone, in which other legal systems did go, and with which we seriously experimented a century ago.

The implications of contingency in our accident law are significant. Debates over the desirability of our contemporary accident law are hotly contested on all sides. The goal of corrective justice as between individuals, for example, vies with the goal of economic efficiency for pride of place in the normative framework of tort law.[11] Where some see in tort law an opportunity to create sound incentives for modern enterprises to act reasonably safely, others see an undue tax on the development of new products, pharmaceuticals, and medical procedures. Some see the threat of high damage awards in jury-decided torts cases as a cause of undesirable settlements in frivolous cases. Others focus on the way in which tort law appears to undercompensate the relatively gravely injured, at least in part because the dire needs of many seriously injured people significantly reduce their ability to hold out for better settlement terms.[12]

Evaluating the relative merits and demerits of our tort law, and of various reforms that might be adopted, is an exceedingly difficult endeavor, one on which legal history (absent the additional contributions of such disciplines as moral philosophy and welfare economics) sheds only partial light. The contingency of our contemporary accident-law institutions, however, suggests that there ought to be relatively few presumptions in favor of particular ways of dealing with accidents merely on the ground that they have been adopted by lawyers and jurists before us. Our ways of dealing with accidents have been shaped only loosely by policy successes. They constitute not so much rationally planned systems as an historically assembled hodge podge of programs. Their contours, moreover, are a contingent outcome of contests among a diverse array of competing groups at the turn of the twentieth century—groups that helped to shape the foundations of American accident law from within the institutional structures of late-nineteenth-century American law.

Much the same can be said about those parts of our law and social policy that built on the outcomes of the work-accident experience. That experience occupied a special place in the first generation of American institutions to develop around the risks characteristically addressed by the social policy of modern nation states. Work accidents accordingly had formative consequences for law and policy in a number of important areas, ranging from risks to health, bodily security, and disability, to the risks of unemployment and those attendant on old age. If the law of accidents might have developed differently, so too might other systems of social insurance. Indeed, even the basic terms of our halting paradigm shift from free labor to risk and insurance might have taken on very different textures.

All of this raises the stakes as we turn to deal with the emerging accident-law problems of our own time, whether mass torts and class actions or nonactuarial catastrophic risks. When we struggle for new legal approaches for this new generation of problems, we too are experimenting with more and less plausible alternative futures. The decisions we make in grappling with our own accident problems may prove as consequential for American law in the twenty-first century as decisions made a century ago proved to be in the twentieth.

Notes

Abbreviations

AAAPSS   *Annals of the American Academy of Political and Social Science*

AALLP   American Association for Labor Legislation Papers, Kheel Center for Labor-Management Documentation and Archives, Cornell University, Ithaca, New York

AALLPM   *American Association for Labor Legislation Papers* (Microfilm Edition, Glen Rock, N.J., 1974)

ALLR   *American Labor Legislation Review*

BUSBLS   *Bulletin of the United States Bureau of Labor Statistics*

JMW   Jonathan Mayhew Wainwright Papers, New-York Historical Society

KC   Kheel Center for Labor-Management Documentation and Archives, Cornell University, Ithaca, New York

NYWCBA   New York State Workers' Compensation Board Archives, Albany, New York

RELWCC   *Message of the President of the United States Transmitting the Report of the Employers' Liability and Workmen's Compensation Commission,* Sen. Doc. 338, 62nd Cong., 2nd Sess. (2 vols., 1912)

WCM   *Minutes of Evidence Accompanying the First Report to the Legislature of the State of New York by the Commission Appointed under Chapter 518 of the Laws of 1909 to Inquire into the Question of Employers' Liability and Other Matters, Mar. 16, 1910* (1910)

WCR   *Report to the Legislature of the State of New York by the Commission Appointed under Chapter 518 of the Laws of 1909 to Inquire into the Question of Employers' Liability and Other Matters: First Report, March 19, 1910* (1910), also known as the Wainwright Commission Report

Introduction

1. "Mr. Roosevelt and Georgia Day," *Atlanta Constitution,* June 11, 1907, p. 6; "Georgia's Day at Jamestown Great Success," *Atlanta Constitution,* June 11, 1907, p. 1; "Proud of His Georgian Ancestry," *Washington Post,* June 11, 1907, p. 11.

2. David W. Blight, *Race and Reunion: The Civil War in American Memory* (2001); "The Jamestown Exposition Program," *Independent*, Jan. 10, 1907, p. 110.

3. "Georgia's Day," 2; Albert Castel, "Stephen D. Lee," in 13 *American National Biography* 403–4 (John A. Garraty and Mark C. Carnes eds., 1999); J. Morgan Kousser, *The Shaping of Southern Politics: Suffrage Restriction and the Establishment of the One-Party South, 1880–1910*, pp. 139–45 (1974); Blight, *Race and Reunion*, 281.

4. "Georgia's Day," 2; "The Jamestown Exposition," *Cleveland Journal*, Apr. 6, 1907, p. 4.

5. "Proud of His Georgian Ancestry," 11; "Georgia at Jamestown," *Atlanta Constitution*, June 12, 1907, p. 8.

6. "Proud of His Georgian Ancestry," 11; Theodore Roosevelt, "Sixth Annual Message (December 3, 1906)," in 15 *The Works of Theodore Roosevelt, National Edition: State Papers as Governor and President, 1899–1909*, pp. 342, 360 (1926); Edward A. Moseley, "The Penalty of Progress," *Independent*, June 11, 1908, p. 1340.

7. Frederick Hoffman, "Industrial Accident Statistics," *BUSBLS* no. 157, pp. 5–6, 13 (1915).

8. Mark Aldrich, *Safety First: Technology, Labor, and Business in the Building of American Work Safety, 1870–1939*, pp. 5, 15–16 (1997).

9. *Second Biennial Report of the Bureau of Labor Statistics of the State of Colorado, 1889–1890*, pp. 19–20 (Denver, Collier and Cleaveland 1890).

10. Anthony F. C. Wallace, *St. Clair: A Nineteenth-Century Coal Town's Experience with a Disaster-Prone Industry* 253 (1987).

11. William Graebner, *Coal-Mining Safety in the Progressive Period: The Political Economy of Reform* 117, 1, 3 (1976); Aldrich, *Safety First*, 5. The most dangerous occupations in the 1990s were in logging and timber work.

12. "Proud of His Georgian Ancestry," 11.

13. Id., 11.

14. "Workmen's Compensation Laws of the United States and Foreign Countries," *BUSBLS* no. 126, p. 12 (1914); "Comparison of Workmen's Compensation Laws of the United States and Canada up to January 1, 1920," *BUSBLS* no. 275, p. 6 (1920).

15. Peter H. Schuck, "Equity for All Victims," *New York Times*, Dec. 19, 2001, p. A35; Deborah Jones Merritt and Kathryn Ann Barry, "Is the Tort System in Crisis? New Empirical Evidence," 60 *Ohio St. L.J.* 315, 382 (1999). For various positions in the raging policy debate over tort law, see George L. Priest, "The Current Insurance Crisis and Modern Tort Law," 96 *Yale L.J.* 1521 (1987); Richard L. Abel, "The Real Torts Crisis—Too Few Claims," 48 *Ohio St. L.J.* 443 (1987); Steven P. Croley and Jon D. Hanson, "What Liability Crisis? An Alternative Explanation for Recent Events in Products Liability," 8 *Yale J. on Reg.* 1 (1991); Gary T. Schwartz, "Reality in the Economic Analysis of Tort Law: Does Tort Law Really Deter?" 42 *UCLA L. Rev.* 377 (1994); *Tort Law and the Public Interest: Competition, Innovation, and Consumer Welfare* (Peter H. Schuck ed., 1991); Symposium, "What We Know and Do Not Know about the Impact of

Civil Justice on the American Economy and Polity," 80 *Tex. L. Rev.* 1537 (2002).

16. 3 William Blackstone, *Commentaries* *115–43; John H. Langbein, "Introduction to Book III," in *Commentaries on the Laws of England: A Facsimile of the First Edition of 1765–1769*, vol. 3 (1979).

17. Morton J. Horwitz, *The Transformation of American Law, 1780–1860*, pp. 160–210 (1977) *(Transformation I)*.

18. The literature on nineteenth-century regulation is massive. For recent contributions on the topics mentioned in the text, see Karen Orren, *Belated Feudalism: Labor, the Law, and Liberal Development in the United States* 160–208 (1991); Christopher L. Tomlins, *Law, Labor, and Ideology in the Early American Republic* 232–58 (1993); Reva B. Siegel, "The Modernization of Marital Status Law: Adjudicating Wives' Rights to Earnings, 1860–1930," 82 *Geo. L.J.* 2127, 2133–41 (1994); Carol Rose, "The Comedy of the Commons: Custom, Commerce, and Inherently Public Property," 53 *U. Chi. L. Rev.* 711, 749–53, 771–74 (1986); Hendrik Hartog, *Man and Wife in America: A History* (2000); Ariela R. Dubler, "Governing through Contract: Common Law Marriage in the Nineteenth Century," 107 *Yale L.J.* 1885, 1885–86 (1998). General accounts include William J. Novak, *The People's Welfare: Law and Regulation in Nineteenth-Century America* (1996); Harry N. Scheiber, "Public Rights and the Rule of Law in American Legal History," 72 *Cal. L. Rev.* 217, 225–27 (1984); and James Willard Hurst, *Law and the Conditions of Freedom in the Nineteenth-Century United States* (1956).

19. 2 Max Weber, *Economy and Society* 904–10 (Guenther Roth and Claus Wittich eds., 1978); James Q. Whitman, "At the Origins of Law and the State: Supervision of Violence, Mutilation of Bodies, or Setting of Prices?" 71 *Chi.-Kent L. Rev.* 41, 49–53 (1995); Aristotle, *Nicomachean Ethics* bk. V, ch. 4, in *Introduction to Aristotle* 308, 405 (W. D. Ross trans., Richard McKeon ed., 1947); 2 Frederick Pollock and Frederic William Maitland, *The History of English Law* 450 (2d ed. 1968); 1 Morris Arnold, *Select Cases of Trespass from the King's Courts, 1307–1399* (1985); F. H. Lawson, *Negligence in the Civil Law* 1–29 (1950).

20. Aristotle, *Nicomachean Ethics*, bk. V, ch. 2.

21. Oliver Wendell Holmes Jr., *The Common Law* 84–85 (Boston, Little, Brown 1881), discussing *Brown v. Kendall*, 60 Mass. (6 Cush.) 292 (1850). Building on Holmes's support for the strict-liability theory of *Rylands v. Fletcher*, 1 L.R.-Ex. 265 (1866), David Rosenberg has argued that Holmes's theory of torts is best understood as advocating a foresight-based strict-liability theory that was theoretically consistent with a relatively broad view of enterprise liability for injuries incurred in the course of industrial life. See David Rosenberg, *The Hidden Holmes: His Theory of Torts in History* 135 (1995). But in 1881, as Rosenberg concedes (see id. at 134), Holmes showed little awareness of the possible application of his theory of torts to the accidents of an industrializing era. Instead, he appears to have treated foreseeable but nonnegligent injuries as falling into the category of *damnum absque injuria:* injuries without remedies. See Holmes, *The Common Law*, 115 ("There are certain things which the law allows a man to

do, notwithstanding the fact that he foresees that harm to another will follow from them."); see also id., 77 ("[T]he public generally profits from individual activity. As action cannot be avoided, and tends to the public good, there is obviously no policy in throwing the hazard of what is at once desirable and inevitable upon the actor.").

22. 1 Francis Hilliard, *The Law of Torts, or Private Wrongs* iii (Boston, Little, Brown 1859). Compare 3 Blackstone, *Commentaries* *115–43.

23. "Book Notices," 5 *Am. L. Rev.* 341 (1870). See, e.g., James Barr Ames, *Select Cases on Torts* (Cambridge, 1874); Melville M. Bigelow, *Elements of the Law of Torts for the Use of Students* (Boston, Little, Brown 1878); George Bliss Jr., *The Law of Life Insurance with Chapters upon Accident and Guarantee Insurance* (New York, Baker, Voorhis 1872); Frederick H. Cooke, *The Law of Life Insurance including Accident Insurance and Insurance by Mutual by Benefit Societies* (New York, Baker, Voorhis and Co. 1891); Thomas M. Cooley, *A Treatise on the Law of Torts or the Wrongs Which Arise Independent of Contract* (Chicago, Callaghan 1879); William B. Hale, *Handbook on the Law of Torts* (St. Paul, West 1896); Thomas G. Shearman and Amasa A. Redfield, *A Treatise on the Law of Negligence* (New York, Baker, Voorhis 1869).

24. C. G. Addison, *The Law of Torts, Abridged for Use in the Law School of Harvard University* (Boston, Little, Brown 1870); "The Theory of Torts," 7 *Am. L. Rev.* 652, 659–60 (1873).

25. Oliver Wendell Holmes Jr., "The Path of the Law," 10 *Harv. L. Rev.* 457, 467 (1897).

26. Horwitz, *Transformation I*; Charles O. Gregory, "Trespass to Negligence to Absolute Liability," 37 *Va. L. Rev.* 359 (1951). The strict-liability thesis about the early modern law of accidents has been widely attacked. See, e.g., Peter Karsten, *Heart versus Head: Judge-Made Law in Nineteenth-Century America* 81–85 (1997); Gary T. Schwartz, "Tort Law and the Economy in Nineteenth-Century America: A Reinterpretation," 90 *Yale L.J.* 1717, 1722–34 (1981).

27. Lawrence M. Friedman, *A History of American Law* 299–300 (2d ed. 1985); Horwitz, *Transformation I*, 36; Gregory, "Trespass to Negligence," 361–62; Leon Green, "The Duty Problem in Negligence Cases: II," 29 *Colum. L. Rev.* 255, 255 (1929) ("A feudal economy required a morality of trespass . . .").

28. Friedman, *History of American Law*, 300–2; Horwitz, *Transformation I*, 85–108; Gregory, "Trespass to Negligence," 368, 382. Like the thesis that the eighteenth-century law of torts was characterized by strict liability, the story of the rise of a restrictive negligence principle has also been challenged. See, e.g., Karsten, *Heart versus Head*, 8–15, 79–127; Schwartz, "Tort Law and the Economy," 1727–34.

29. Lawrence M. Friedman and Jack Ladinsky, "Social Change and the Law of Industrial Accidents," 67 *Colum. L. Rev.* 50, 59–60 (1967).

30. Roy Lubove, *The Struggle for Social Security, 1900–1935*, pp. 45–65 (1968); James Weinstein, *The Corporate Ideal in the Liberal State, 1900–1918*, pp. 40–61 (1968); Friedman and Ladinsky, "Social Change," 69–72.

31. G. Edward White, *Tort Law in America: An Intellectual History* 12–19 (1980); Karsten, *Heart versus Head*, 79–127. See also Comment, "The Creation of a

Common Law Rule: The Fellow Servant Rule, 1837–1860," 132 *U. Pa. L. Rev.* 579, 598–600 (1984); Alfred S. Konefsky, "'As Best to Subserve Their Own Interests': Lemuel Shaw, Labor Conspiracy, and Fellow Servants," 7 *Law and Hist. Rev.* 219, 233–35 (1989); Paul Finkelman, "Slaves as Fellow Servants: Ideology, Law, and Industrialization," 31 *Am. J. Legal Hist.* 269, 283–85 (1987); James Barr Ames, "Law and Morals," 22 *Harv. L. Rev.* 97, 98–99 (1908).

32. White, *Tort Law in America*, 4–19.

33. Oliver Wendell Holmes Jr., "The Theory of Torts," 7 *Am. L. Rev.* 652 , 660 (1873); Addison, *Law of Torts*, iii ("The Law of Torts is the law of those rights which avail against persons generally, or against all mankind, as distinguished from the law of those rights which avail against particular persons. . . ."). As Robert Rabin has pointed out, even if late-nineteenth-century lawyers conceived of the negligence principle as attaching universally to social relations, the law of torts was nonetheless shot through with special relational standards, including zones of "no-duty." Robert L. Rabin, "The Historical Development of the Fault Principle: A Reinterpretation," 15 *Ga. L. Rev.* 925, 928 (1981).

34. Randolph E. Bergstrom, *Courting Danger: Injury and Law in New York City, 1870–1910*, pp. 167–96 (1992); Lawrence M. Friedman, *Total Justice* 45–76 (1985); William E. Nelson, "From Fairness to Efficiency: The Transformation of Tort Law in New York, 1920–1980," 47 *Buff. L. Rev.* 117, 130–32 (1999); Daniel Polisar and Aaron Wildavsky, "From Individual to System Blame: A Cultural Analysis of Historical Change in the Law of Torts," 1 *J. Pol'y Hist.* 129 (1989); see also Thomas L. Haskell, *The Emergence of Professional Social Science: The American Social Science Association and the Nineteenth-Century Crisis of Authority* 240–56 (1977).

35. This point is sketched in summary fashion in Robert W. Gordon, "Tort Law in America: An Intellectual History," 94 *Harv. L. Rev.* 903, 907 (1981).

36. For the glimmerings of new approaches to the history of American accident law, see Arthur F. McEvoy, "The Triangle Shirtwaist Factory Fire of 1911: Social Change, Industrial Accidents, and the Evolution of Common-Sense Causality," 20 *Law and Soc. Inquiry* 621 (1995); Christopher L. Tomlins, *Law, Labor, and Ideology in the Early American Republic* (1993); Barbara Young Welke, *Recasting American Liberty: Gender, Race, Law, and the Railroad Revolution, 1865–1920* (2001); Barbara Y. Welke, "Unreasonable Women: Gender and the Law of Accidental Injury, 1870–1920," 19 *Law and Soc. Inquiry* 369 (1994). I rehearse some of the argument in the text in my "Toward a New History of American Accident Law," 114 *Harv. L. Rev.* 625 (2001).

37. Cf. Haskell, *Emergence of Professional Social Science*, 240–56; Thomas L. Haskell, "Capitalism and the Origins of Humanitarian Sensibility, Parts I and II," in *The Antislavery Debate* 107, 107–60 (Thomas Bender ed., 1992).

38. See generally James T. Kloppenberg, *Uncertain Victory: Social Democracy and Progressivism in European and American Thought, 1870–1920* (1986); Daniel T. Rodgers, *Atlantic Crossings: Social Politics in a Progressive Age* (1998).

39. *The Labor Movement: The Problem of Today* 54–59 (George McNeill ed., Boston, A. M. Bridgman 1887).

40. F. W. Taussig, "Workmen's Insurance in Germany," 2 *Q.J. Econ.* 111 (1888);

"An Act Concerning Insurance in Case of Disability and Old Age," 4 *Q.J. Econ.* 103 (1890); B. W. Wells, "Compulsory Insurance in Germany," 6 *Pol. Sci. Q.* 43, 64 (1891); F. W. Taussig, "Workmen's Insurance in Germany," 8 *Forum* 159, 169 (1889); *Seventeenth Annual Report of the Bureau of Labor Statistics of the State of New York for the Year 1899,* pp. 559–60, 1162 (Albany, James B. Lyon 1900); Charles R. Henderson, "Workingmen's Insurance," 4 *Am. J. Soc.* 695, 696 (1899); Edward Cummings, "Workingmen's Insurance," 6 *J. Pol. Econ.* 556, 558 (1898); John Cummings, "Book Review," 6 *J. Pol. Econ.* 556 (1898).

41. *Third Annual Report of the Massachusetts Bureau of Statistics of Labor Embracing the Account of Its Operations and Inquiries from March 1, 1871 to March 1, 1872,* pp. 421–22 (Boston, Wright and Potter 1872); *Fourth Annual Report of the Massachusetts Bureau of Statistics of Labor Embracing the Account of Its Operations and Inquiries from March 1, 1872 to March 1, 1873,* p. 282 (Boston, Wright and Potter 1873); *Fifth Annual Report of the Massachusetts Bureau of Statistics of Labor Embracing the Account of Its Operations and Inquiries from March 1, 1873 to March 1, 1874,* p. 43 (Boston, Wright and Potter 1874); *Fourteenth Annual Report of the Massachusetts Bureau of Statistics of Labor, March, 1883,* pp. 3–52 (Boston, Wright and Potter 1883); John Graham Brooks, *Fourth Annual Special Report of the Commissioner of Labor: Compulsory Insurance in Germany Including an Appendix Relating to Compulsory Insurance in Other Countries in Europe* 11 (Washington, D.C., Gov't Printing Office 1893); William Franklin Willoughby, *Workingmen's Insurance* (New York, Thomas Y. Crowell 1898); William Franklin Willoughby, "The French Workmen's Compensation Act," 12 *Q.J. Econ.* 398 (1898); *Eleventh Annual Report of the Bureau of Statistics of Labor and Industries of New Jersey for the Year Ending Oct. 31, 1888* (Trenton, John L. Murphy 1889); *Seventeenth Annual Report of the Bureau of Labor Statistics of the State of New York,* 559–60; *Thirty-First Annual Report of the Massachusetts Bureau of Statistics of Labor, March 1901,* pp. 65–248 (1901). On Wright, see James Leiby, *Carroll Wright and Labor Reform: The Origin of Labor Statistics* 7–38 (1960).

42. See, e.g., 24 U.S. Department of Labor, *Annual Report of the Commissioner of Labor: Workmen's Insurance and Compensation Systems in Europe* (1909) (2 vols.); Lee K. Frankel and Miles M. Dawson, *Workingmen's Insurance in Europe* (1910) (Russell Sage Foundation study of European social insurance); Ferd. C. Schwedtman and James A. Emery, *Accident Prevention and Relief: An Investigation of the Subject in Europe with Special Attention to England and Germany* (1911) (National Association of Manufacturers study of European accident compensation programs); see also Paul Monroe, "An American System of Labor Pensions and Insurance," 2 *Am. J. Soc.* 501 (1897).

43. Charles Richmond Henderson, *Die Arbeiter-Versicherung in den Vereinigten Staaten von Nord-America* (Berlin, A. Troschel 1907), published in English as Charles Richmond Henderson, *Industrial Insurance in the United States* (1908); August Sartorius von Waltershausen, *The Workers' Movement in the United States, 1879–1885,* pp. 171–219 (David Montgomery and Marcel van der Linden eds., 1998) (1885).

44. Franklin D. Roosevelt, "The Two Hundred and First Press Conference (Excerpts). May 3, 1935," in 4 *Public Papers and Addresses of Franklin D. Roosevelt* 159, 160–6 (1938); *The Autobiographical Notes of Charles Evans Hughes* 153 (David J. Danelski and Joseph S. Tulchin eds., 1973); 1 *RELWCC* (1912); *Report to Legislature of Minnesota Employees' Compensation Commission* 122–23 (1911); George Martin, *Madam Secretary: Frances Perkins* 162–79 (1976); Harry Hopkins to Wm. C. Archer (July 24, 1917), death file no. 818, New York State Workers' Compensation Board Archives, Albany, New York; Alan Brinkley, *Voices of Protest: Huey Long, Father Coughlin, and the Great Depression* 14, 16 (1982).

45. "Workmen's Compensation Laws of the United States and Foreign Countries," *BUSBLS* no. 203, p. 66 (1917); New York State Department of Labor, *Annual Report of the Industrial Commissioner for the Twelve Months Ending December 31, 1930*, p. 7 (1931).

46. Rodgers, *Atlantic Crossings*, 265–66; see also Jacob S. Hacker, "Policy Feedback in the Private Sector: Workplace Benefits and the American Welfare State," paper presented at the American Political Science Association, September 2001.

47. Stephen Jay Gould, *The Structure of Evolutionary Theory* (2002); Stephen D. Krasner, "Approaches to the State: Alternative Conceptions and Historical Dynamics," 16 *Comp. Pol.* 223, 240–44 (1984); Jacob S. Hacker, "The Historical Logic of National Health Insurance: Structure and Sequence in the Development of British, Canadian, and U.S. Medical Policy," 12 *Studies in American Political Development* 57, 77–80 (1998).

48. Mill quoted in Amy Dru Stanley, *From Bondage to Contract: Wage Labor, Marriage, and the Market in the Age of Emancipation* 14 (1998); William Graham Sumner, *What Social Classes Owe to Each Other* 23 (Caldwell, Idaho 1954) (1883).

49. Priestley v. Fowler, 150 Eng. Rep. 1030, 1031 (Ex. 1837); A. W. Brian Simpson, *Leading Cases in the Common Law* 100–34 (1995).

50. Farwell v. Boston and Worcester R.R., 45 Mass. (4 Met.) 49, 56–58 (1842).

51. On the pejarative conception of the term "ideology," see Raymond Williams, *Keywords: A Vocabulary of Culture and Society* 153–57 (rev. ed. 1983). For a leading example of the history of ideology, see Bernard Bailyn, *The Ideological Origins of the American Revolution* (1967).

52. Thomas S. Kuhn, *The Structure of Scientific Revolutions* 23–51 (2d ed. 1970).

53. "Fragment on Free Labor," in 3 *The Collected Works of Abraham Lincoln* 462 (Roy P. Basler ed., 1953); Eric Foner, "Free Labor and Nineteenth-Century Political Ideology," in *The Market Revolution in America* 116 (Melvyn Stokes and Stephen Conway eds., 1996).

54. David Brion Davis, *The Problem of Slavery in the Age of Revolution, 1770–1823*, p. 14 (1975).

55. "Address before the Wisconsin State Agricultural Society, Milwaukee, Wisconsin," in 3 *Collected Works of Abraham Lincoln* 471, 479 (emphasis added).

56. Ralph Waldo Emerson, "Compensation," in *Essays* (1841), reprinted in *The Essential Writings of Ralph Waldo Emerson* 154, 156, 158, 165, 170–71 (Brooks Atkinson ed., 2000).

57. 1 Theodore Roosevelt, *The Roosevelt Policy* 247 (William Griffith ed., 1919); David M. Kennedy, *Freedom from Fear: The American People in Depression and War, 1929–1945,* pp. 245–47 (1999); Franklin D. Roosevelt, "'A Greater Future Economic Security of the American People'—A Message to Congress on Social Security: January 17, 1935," in 4 *Public Papers and Addresses of Franklin D. Roosevelt,* 43–46.

58. Viviana A. Rotman Zelizer, *Morals and Markets: The Development of Life Insurance in the United States* (1983); Geoffrey W. Clark, *Betting on Lives: The Culture of Life Insurance in England, 1695–1775* (1999); Herwitz, *Transformation I,* 226–37.

59. Act for the Relief of Sick and Disabled Seamen, 1 Stat. 605 (1798); Michele L. Landis, "'Let Me Next Time Be "Tried by Fire"': Disaster Relief and the Origins of the American Welfare State, 1789–1894," 92 *Nw. U. L. Rev.* 967 (1998); Theodore Steinberg, *Acts of God: The Unnatural History of Natural Disaster in America* (2000).

60. Kuhn, "Postscript—1969," in *Structure of Scientific Revolution,* 174, 193. David Brion Davis, *Revolutions: Reflections on American Equality and Foreign Liberations* 8 (1990).

61. Grant Gilmore, *The Death of Contract* 94 (1974).

62. Examples of such work include William J. Novak, "The American Law of Association: The Legal-Political Construction of Civil Society," 15 *Stud. Am. Pol. Dev.* 163–88 (2001); Victoria Saker Woeste, *The Farmers' Benevolent Trust: Law and Agricultural Cooperation in Industrial America, 1865–1945* (1998); Risa L. Goluboff, "'Won't You Please Help Me Get My Son Home': Peonage, Patronage, and Protest in the World War II Urban South," 24 *Law and Soc. Inquiry* 777 (1999); Reva B. Siegel, "Text in Contest: Gender and the Constitution from a Social Movement Perspective," 150 *U. Pa. L. Rev.* 297 (2001); William E. Forbath, "Constitutional Welfare Rights: a History, Critique, and Reconstruction," 69 *Fordham L. Rev.* 1821 (2001); Hendrik Hartog, "The Constitution of Aspiration and 'The Rights That Belong to Us All,'" in *The Constitution and American Life* 353 (David Thelen ed., 1988). See generally Robert W. Gordon, "Critical Legal Histories," 36 *Stan. L. Rev.* 57 (1984).

63. E.g., Robert C. Ellickson, *Order without Law: How Neighbors Settle Disputes* (1991); Eric Posner, *Law and Social Norms* (2000).

64. Cf. Bruce H. Mann, "The Death and Transfiguration of Early American Legal History," in *The Many Legalities of Early America* 442, 447 (Christopher L. Tomlins and Bruce H. Mann eds., 2001).

65. Lance Liebman and Kenneth S. Abraham, "Private Insurance, Social Insurance, and Tort Reform: Toward a New Vision of Compensation for Illness and Injury," 93 *Colum. L. Rev.* 75 (1993); Richard B. Stewart, "Crisis in Tort Law? The Institutional Perspective," 54 *U. Chi. L. Rev.* 184 (1987).

66. Thomas D. Morris, *Southern Slavery and the Law, 1619–1850,* pp. 147–58 (1996); Aldrich, *Safety First,* 10–11.

67. Carl Gersuny, *Work Hazards and Industrial Conflict* 56–59 (1981); Claudia Clark, *Radium Girls: Women and Industrial Health Reform, 1910–1935* (1997); Allison L. Hepler, *Women in Labor: Mothers, Medicine, and Occupational Health*

in the United States, 1890–1980 (2000); Leon Stein, *The Triangle Fire* (William Greider ed., 2001) (1962).

68. E.g., W. Page Keeton et al., *Prosser and Keeton on the Law of Torts* § 8, p. 33 (5th ed. 1984).

69. 1A John Alan Appleman and Jean Appleman, *Insurance Law and Practice* § 360, p. 449 (1981).

70. Accident scenarios such as the one in the text have long served as useful hypothetical cases in the philosophy of history. For an erudite recent discussion, see John Lewis Gaddis, *The Landscape of History: How Historians Map the Past* 93–94 (2002).

71. Landress v. Pheonix Mutual Life Ins. Co., 291 U.S. 491, 499 (1934) (Cardozo, J., dissenting), quoting John Milton, *Paradise Lost* bk. II, l. 592 (Scott Elledge ed., 1975) (2d ed. 1674), and Brintons, Ltd. v. Turvey, [1905] A.C. 230, 233 (Halsbury, L.C.).

1. Crippled Workingmen, Destitute Widows, and the Crisis of Free Labor

The chapter epigraph is from 14 *Report of the Industrial Commission on the Relations and Conditions of Capital and Labor* 163 (1901).

1. Horace Herndon Cunningham, *Doctors in Gray: The Confederate Medical Service* 5 (1958); George Worthington Adams, *Doctors in Blue: The Medical History of the Union Army in the Civil War* 3 (1952); James M. McPherson, *Battle Cry of Freedom: The Civil War Era* 854 (1988).

2. Emma E. Edmonds, "July 21, 1861," in *Civil War Medicine: Care and Comfort of the Wounded* 34 (Robert E. Denney ed., 1994).

3. 4 *The Papers of Frederick Law Olmsted, Defending the Union: The Civil War and the U.S. Sanitary Commission, 1861–1863*, p. 363 (Jane Turner Censer ed., 1986).

4. 1 Bernard Bailyn, et al., *The Great Republic: A History of the American People* 616–17 (1992).

5. David W. Blight, *Race and Reunion: The Civil War in American Memory* 21 (2001).

6. U.S. Sanitary Commission, *The Sanitary Commission of the United States Army: A Succinct Narrative of Its Works and Purposes* iii (n.p., 1864).

7. Adams, *Doctors in Blue*, 198–99; see also Frank R. Freemon, *Gangrene and Glory: Medical Care during the American Civil War* 166–80 (1998). On the Confederate army's medical care, which was hamstrung by a lack of resources, see Cunningham, *Doctors in Gray.*

8. Patrick J. Kelly, *Creating a National Home: Building the Veterans' Welfare State 1860–1900*, p. 2 (1997).

9. Theda Skocpol, *Protecting Soldiers and Mothers: The Political Origins of Social Policy in the United States* 109 table 2, 116–30 (1992); Megan J. McClintock, "Civil War Pensions and the Reconstruction of Union Families," 83 *J. Am. Hist.* 456 (1996).

10. *Report of Minnesota Employees' Compensation Commission* 100 (1911).

11. *Thirteenth Annual Report of the Bureau of Statistics of Labor and Industries of New Jersey for the Year Ending Oct. 31, 1890,* p. 367 (Trenton, Trenton Electric 1891).

12. E. H. Downey, *Work Accident Indemnity in Iowa* 11–12 (1912).

13. I. M. Rubinow, *Social Insurance: With Special Reference to American Conditions* 61 (1913).

14. *United Mine Workers' J.,* Feb. 2, 1911, p. 4; see also *The Labor Movement: The Problem of To-day* 490 (George E. McNeill, ed., Boston, A. M. Bridgman 1887).

15. E.g., Lawrence Friedman, *A History of American Law* 467 (2d ed. 1985).

16. Paul Uselding, "In Dispraise of the Muckrakers: United States Occupational Mortality, 1890–1910," 1 *Res. Econ. Hist.* 334, 348–51 (1976); Randolph E. Bergstrom, *Courting Danger: Injury and Law in New York City, 1870–1910,* pp. 40–57 (1992).

17. In some cases, underreporting of accidents resulted from primitive record-keeping practices in nineteenth-century firms, especially in smaller, less sophisticated firms. In other cases, underreporting resulted from employers' incentives to keep state factory inspectors, who could order the installation of expensive safety devices, away from their workplaces. In any event, observers commonly agreed that accidents were vastly underreported. See *Seventeenth Annual Report of the Bureau of Labor Statistics of the State of New York for the Year 1899,* pp. 563–68 (Albany, James B. Lyon 1900).

18. See Adams, *Doctors in Blue,* 176–84; Cunningham, *Doctors in Gray,* 267–73; 4 Allan Nevins, *The War for Union: The Organized War 1863–1864,* pp. 311–14 (1971).

19. Charles E. Rosenberg, *The Care of Strangers: The Rise of America's Hospital System* 122–65 (1987); Lester S. King, *Transformations in American Medicine: From Benjamin Rush to William Osler* 180–81 (1991).

20. Uselding, in concluding that nonindustrial and industrial occupations were equally hazardous, relies on the dubious assumption that the mortality rates of men within a particular occupation reflected the dangerousness of that occupation. His comparison of industrial and nonindustrial occupational death rates does not account for the fact that advances in medical care were likely to be more readily available to industrial workers and workers in urban areas than to nonindustrial or agricultural workers. See Uselding, "In Dispraise of the Muckrakers," 341–49. Similarly, although Bergstrom purports to account for improvements in medical care over time (see Bergstrom, *Courting Danger,* 53), the evidence he advances for the conclusion that "accident rates were not rising" between 1870 and 1910 appears to rest largely on fixed ratios of accidental injuries to accidental deaths (see, e.g., id., 41 table 13).

21. Cornelius Walford, "On the Number of Deaths from Accident, Negligence, Violence, and Misadventure in the United Kingdom and Some Other Countries," 44 *J. Stat. Soc'y London* 444, 450, 452, 464, 476, 485 (1881).

22. Roger Lane, *Violent Death in the City: Suicide, Accident, and Murder in Nineteenth-Century Philadelphia* 36 (2d ed. 1999) (1979).

23. See J. D. B. De Bow, Superintendent, U.S. Census, *Mortality Statistics of the Sev-*

enth Census of the United States, 1850, pp. 17–20 (Washington, D.C., A. O. P. Nicholson 1855). Individual state reports in the 1850 census occasionally listed additional categories such as "explo[sion] . . . steam" (Louisiana), "accident . . . railroad" (Louisiana and Massachusetts), and "accident . . . machinery" (Massachusetts and New York). Id., 99–111, 132–37, 183–87.

24. See Secretary of the Interior, *Statistics of the United States, (Including Mortality, Property, and c.,) in 1860,* pp. 4, 52–55 (Washington, D.C., Gov't Printing Office 1866).

25. Francis A. Walker, Department of the Interior, *Vital Statistics of the United States* xix, 18–21 (Washington, D.C., Gov't Printing Office 1872).

26. I compiled these figures from the published census reports from 1850 to 1880: De Bow,, *Mortality Statistics 1850,* pp. 17–20; Secretary of the Interior, *Statistics of the United States 1860,* pp. 52–55; 2 *Vital Statistics of the United States, Embracing the Tables of Deaths, Births, Sex, and Age, Ninth Census* 20–22 (Washington, D.C., Gov't Printing Office 1872); John S. Billings, *Report on the Mortality and Vital Statistics of the United States as Returned at the Tenth Census (June 1, 1880)* pt. I, pp. 44–53 (Washington, D.C., Gov't Printing Office 1885).

27. In southern states such as Alabama, Louisiana, and South Carolina, accidents accounted for roughly the same percentage of deaths among men aged ten to fifty in 1870 as in 1850, ranging from 5 percent to 9 percent. De Bow, *Mortality Statistics 1850,* pp. 50–53, 99–111, 250–55; 2 *Vital Statistics 1870,* pp. 22–25, 84–87, 164–67. In northern states such as Massachusetts and Pennsylvania, by contrast, accidents accounted respectively for 6 percent and 7 percent of the deaths of men aged ten to fifty in 1850, and 12 percent and 15 percent of such deaths in 1870. De Bow, *Mortality Statistics 1850,* pp. 132–37, 235–39; 2 *Vital Statistics 1870,* pp. 96–99, 156–59. Changes in the 1880 census report make it difficult to calculate state-by-state death figures.

28. See John S. Billings, *Report on Vital and Social Statistics in the United States at the Eleventh Census: 1890, Part I.—Analysis and Rate Tables* 740–45 (Washington, D.C., Gov't Printing Office 1896); Secretary of the Interior, *Statistics of the United States 1860,* pp. 53–55.

29. Carroll W. Doten, "Recent Railway Accidents in the United States," 9 *Publications Am. Stat. Ass'n* 155, 167; Mark Aldrich, *Safety First: Technology, Labor, and Business in the Building of American Work Safety, 1870–1939,* pp. 17, 23, 42 (1997); Gilbert Lewis Campbell, *Industrial Accidents and Their Compensation* 16 (1911); Frederick Hoffman, "Industrial Accident Statistics," *BUSBLS,* March 1915, p. 17; *National Vital Statistics Reports,* July 24, 2000, p. 26 table 8, available at http://www.cdc.gov (97,835 deaths from accidents and adverse effects in the United States in 1998).

30. Hoffman, "Industrial Accident Statistics," 1, 17; Rubinow, *Social Insurance,* 54; Billings, *Report at Eleventh Census,* 980–83; Campbell, *Industrial Accidents and their Compensation,* 11; Aldrich, *Safety First,* 15, 284–85, 300–1; *Report of the [Massachusetts] Bureau of Statistics of Labor . . . From March 1, 1870, to March 1, 1871,* pp. 484–85, 504–5 (Boston, Wright and Potter 1871); *Third Annual Report of the [Massachusetts] Bureau of Statistics of Labor . . . From March 1, 1871, to*

March 1, 1872, pp. 422–23 (Boston, Wright and Potter 1872); Carl Gersuny, *Work Hazards and Industrial Conflict* 24–27, 56 (1981). In 1900, approximately 1 percent of the population fell victim to a work accident resulting in death or disability lasting more than four weeks. By comparison, in the 1990s, work accidents represented only 25 percent of all accidents and less than 1 percent of the population suffered any injury—workplace related or otherwise—requiring medical attention or causing a restriction in activities. See Deborah R. Hensler et al., *Compensation for Accidental Injuries in the United States* 23 (1991); Don Dewees et al., *Exploring the Domain of Accident Law: Taking the Facts Seriously* 3 (1996).

31. P. W. J. Bartrip and S. B. Burman, *The Wounded Soldiers of Industry: Industrial Compensation Policy, 1833–1897,* p. 14 (1983).

32. Chauncey B. Brewster, "Industrial War or Peace," *Independent,* June 29, 1911, p. 1417.

33. Robert W. Bruère, "The Welfare War," *Harper's Mag.,* Oct. 1911, p. 674.

34. F. G. P. Neison, "Analytical View of Railway Accidents," 16 *J. Stat. Soc'y London* 289, 289 (1853). See also F. G. P. Neison, "Analytical View of Railway Accidents," 17 *J. Stat. Soc'y London* 219 (1854).

35. E.g., Doten, "Recent Railway Accidents in the United States," 155; Katharine Pearson Woods, "Accidents in Factories and Elsewhere," 4 *Publications Am. Stat. Ass'n* 303, 303 (1895).

36. William Franklin Willoughby, *Workingmen's Insurance* 7 (New York, Thomas Y. Crowell 1898).

37. Walford, "On the Number of Deaths," 464; *WCR,* 5.

38. James R. Pitcher, "Accidents and Accident Insurance," 12 *Forum* 131, 133 (1891).

39. Id., 136.

40. Charles Francis Adams Jr., *Notes on Railroad Accidents* 1–2, 269 (New York, G. P. Putnam's Sons 1879).

41. *Fourteenth Annual Report of the Massachusetts Bureau of Statistics of Labor, March, 1883,* p. 68 (Boston, Wright and Potter 1883).

42. Rubinow, *Social Insurance,* 52.

43. William Graebner, *Coal-Mining Safety in the Progressive Period: The Political Economy of Reform* 115–23 (1976).

44. See Billings, *Report at Tenth Census,* 455.

45. Aldrich, *Safety First,* 21–22.

46. Graebner, *Coal-Mining Safety,* 139.

47. "Thinks Employers Evade Liability Law," *New York Times,* Oct. 21, 1910, p. 10.

48. "Compensation," *United Mine Workers' J.,* July 21, 1910, p. 4.

49. E. Brandeis, "Labor Legislation," in 3 *History of Labor in the United States, 1896–1932,* pp. 629–42 (John R. Commons ed., 1935); William E. Forbath, *Law and the Shaping of the American Labor Movement* 57 n.99 (1991); Gersuny, *Work Hazards,* 30–31.

50. Aldrich, *Safety First,* 42–46.

51. John M. Gitterman, "The Cruelties of Our Courts," *McClure's Mag.,* June 1910, pp. 151, 161.

52. Henry Carter Adams, "Relation of the State to Industrial Action," in *Relation of the State to Industrial Action and Economics and Jurisprudence: Two Essays by Henry Carter Adams* 57, 89 (Joseph Dorfman ed., 1954). On progressive economists, see Barbara H. Fried, *The Progressive Assault on Laissez Faire: Robert Hale and the First Law and Economics Movement* (1998); Dorothy Ross, *The Origins of American Social Science* 172–218 (1991).

53. Howell Cheney, "Work, Accidents, and the Law," 19 *Yale Rev.* 255, 261 (1910); "Approve Welfare Work," *New York Times*, Nov. 24, 1909, p. 7.

54. *Liability of Employers: Hearings before the Committee on Interstate Commerce of the United States Senate, May 3 to 8, 1906, 59th Cong., 1st Sess.* 151 (1906).

55. Francis H. Bohlen, "A Problem in the Drafting of Workmen's Compensation Acts," 25 *Harv. L. Rev.* 328, 335 (1912).

56. Graebner, *Coal-Mining Safety*, 113.

57. Henry R. Seager, "Outline of a Program of Social Reform," in *Labor and Other Economic Essays* 79, 83 (Charles A. Gulick ed., 1931).

58. "Life in the Railroad Yards," 3 *J. Switchmen's Union of N. Am.* 373, 373–74 (June 1901).

59. Crystal Eastman, *Work-Accidents and the Law* 93–94 (1910).

60. E.g., "America's Lead in Railroad Accidents," 10 *J. Switchmen's Union of N. Am.* 157–66 (Nov. 1907); "Compensation," *United Mine Workers' J.*, July 21, 1910, p. 4.

61. David Brion Davis, *Slavery and Human Progress* (1984).

62. George Fitzhugh, *Cannibals All! or, Slaves without Masters* 32 (C. Vann Woodward ed., Cambridge, Harvard Univ. Press 1960) (1857).

63. Amy Dru Stanley, *From Bondage to Contract: Wage Labor, Marriage, and the Market in the Age of Slave Emancipation* 19–21 (1998); Sean Wilentz, *Chants Democratic: New York City and the Rise of the American Working Class, 1788–1850*, pp. 331–32 (1984); Eric Foner, "Free Labor and Nineteenth-Century Political Ideology," in *The Market Revolution in America* 99–127 (Melvyn Stokes and Stephen Conway eds., 1996).

64. Stanley, *Bondage to Contract*, 21.

65. Eric Foner, *Reconstruction: America's Unfinished Revolution, 1863–1877* (1988); Leon F. Litwack, *Been in the Storm So Long: The Aftermath of Slavery* (1979); Heather Cox Richardson, *The Death of Reconstruction: Race, Labor, and the Politics in the Post–Civil War North, 1865–1901*, pp. 6–40 (2001); Stanley, *Bondage to Contract*.

66. Eric Foner, *Nothing but Freedom: Emancipation and Its Legacy* (1983); William E. Forbath, "The Ambiguities of Free Labor: Labor and the Law in the Gilded Age," 1985 *Wis. L. Rev.* 767.

67. W. D. Howells, "Editorial," 29 *Atlantic Monthly* 124, 126 (1872); David Montgomery, *Beyond Equality: Labor and the Radical Republicans 1862–1872*, pp. 379–80 (1967); Forbath, "The Ambiguities of Free Labor," 786–94.

68. Leon Fink, *Workingmen's Democracy: The Knights of Labor and American Politics* 3–15 (1983); Forbath, "The Ambiguities of Free Labor," 800–11; David Montgomery, *Citizen Worker: The Experience of Workers in the United States with Democracy and the Free Market during the Nineteenth Century* 43–51 (1993); David Montgomery, *The Fall of the House of Labor: The Workplace, the*

State, and American Labor Activism, 1865–1925, pp. 22–44 (1987); Gordon S. Wood, *The Radicalism of the American Revolution* 276–86 (1993).

69. Davis, *Slavery and Human Progress*, 23–32.

70. David Brion Davis, *The Problem of Slavery in Western Culture* 427–31 (1966); Robert William Fogel, *Without Consent or Contract: The Rise and Fall of American Slavery* 72–73 (1989).

71. Quoted in Kenneth M. Stampp, *The Peculiar Institution: Slavery in the Antebellum South* 399 (1956). On Jamaica, see Thomas C. Holt, *The Problem of Freedom: Race, Labor, and Politics in Jamaica and Britain, 1832–1938* (1992). On the question of whether slave labor is necessarily less productive than free labor, see Robert Fogel and Stanley Engerman, *Time on the Cross* (1974); Fogel, *Without Consent or Contract;* and Stampp, *The Peculiar Institution,* 383–418.

72. Jonathan A. Glickstein, "Poverty Is Not Slavery: American Abolitionists and the Competitive Labor Market," in *Antislavery Reconsidered* (Lewis Perry and Michael Fellman eds., 1979).

73. Richardson, *Death of Reconstruction,* 8–12; Foner, "Free Labor," 99–127; Litwack, *Been in the Storm So Long,* 374–447; Julie Saville, *The Work of Reconstruction: From Slave to Wage Laborer in South Carolina, 1860–1870* (1994).

74. John Ashworth, "The Relationship between Capitalism and Humanitarianism," in *The Antislavery Debate: Capitalism and Abolitionism as a Problem in Historical Interpretation* 180, 192–99 (Thomas Bender ed., 1992).

75. Stanley, *Bondage to Contract;* Lawrence B. Glickman, *A Living Wage: American Workers and the Making of Consumer Society* (1997). See also Dana Frank, *Purchasing Power: Consumer Organizing, Gender, and the Seattle Labor Movement, 1919–1929* (1994).

76. Montgomery, *Beyond Equality,* 29–30.

77. *Fourth Annual Report of the Massachusetts Bureau of Statistics of Labor Embracing the Account of Its Operations and Inquiries from March 1, 1872 to March 1, 1873,* p. 440 (Boston, Wright and Potter 1873); see also Stanley, *Bondage to Contract,* 62.

78. I. M. Rubinow, "Labor Insurance," 12 *J. Pol. Econ.* 362, 362 (1904).

79. Stanley, *Bondage to Contract,* 138–74.

80. Id., 218–63; Ruth Rosen, *The Lost Sisterhood: Prostitution in America, 1900–1918* (1982).

81. Martin J. Sklar, *The Corporate Reconstruction of American Capitalism, 1890–1916: The Market, The Law, and Politics* 53 (1988); see also Gabriel Kolko, *The Triumph of Conservatism* (1963); James Weinstein, *The Corporate Ideal in the Liberal State, 1900–1918* (1968).

82. Naomi R. Lamoreaux, *The Great Merger Movement in American Business* (1985); Naomi R. Lamoreaux, Daniel M. G. Raff, and Peter Temin, "Beyond Markets and Hierarchies," 108 *Amer. Hist. Rev.* 404 (2003); Sanford Jacoby, *Employing Bureaucracy: Managers, Unions, and the Transformation of Work in American Industry* (1985); Daniel Nelson, *Managers and Workers: Origins of the New Factory System in the United States, 1880–1920,* pp. 55–78 (1975).

83. Rubinow, *Social Insurance,* 49.

84. Henry Rogers Seager, *Social Insurance: A Program of Social Reform* 17 (1910); John B. Andrews to Henry W. Farnam, Mar. 27, 1909, reel 2, *AALLPM.*

85. *Fourteenth Annual Report of the Bureau of Statistics of Labor and Industries of New Jersey* 214 table 7 (Trenton, Trenton Electric 1892); *Thirteenth Annual Report of the Bureau of Statistics of Labor and Industries of New Jersey*, 407–13.

86. Billings, *Report at Eleventh Census*, 52, 53; *Seventeenth Annual Report of the Bureau of Labor Statistics of the State of New York 1899*, p. 573.

87. *WCR*, 28.

88. For Hine's photographs, see Eastman, *Work-Accidents*, 144, 149, 153, 156.

89. Willoughby, *Workingmen's Insurance*, 282–83, 327–28.

90. *Third Report of the Massachusetts Bureau of Statistics of Labor*, 426; *WCR*, 28.

91. *WCM*, 8 (statement of Edward T. Devine).

92. John Mitchell, *The Wage Earner and His Problems* 42 (1913).

93. Samuel Gompers, "An Address before the Uniform Legislation Conference of the National Civic Federation," 8 *The Samuel Gompers Papers* 31, 33 (Peter J. Albert and Grace Palladino eds., 2001).

94. E.g., Henry R. Seager, "Outline of a Program of Social Legislation with Special Reference to Wage-Earners," in *Labor and Other Economic Essays*, 131.

95. *Seventeenth Annual Report of the Bureau of Labor Statistics of the State of New York*, 1162.

96. *Second Biennial Report of the Bureau of Labor Statistics of the State of Colorado, 1889–1890*, p. 12 (Denver, Collier and Cleveland 1890); *United Mine Workers' J.*, July 21, 1910, p. 4.

97. "Seventh Annual Message (December 3, 1907)," in 15 *The Works of Theodore Roosevelt* 410, 435 (1926).

98. *Report of the Atlantic City Conference on Workmen's Compensation Acts Held at Atlantic City, N.J., July 29–31, 1909*, p. 7 (1909).

99. Leon Stein, *The Triangle Fire* 165 (William Greider ed., 2001) (1962).

100. Nick Salvatore, *Eugene V. Debs: Citizen and Socialist* 61 (1982).

101. "Buying a Man's Arm," *American Mag.*, July 1909, pp. 260, 262.

102. "The Value of a Man," *Independent*, Apr. 30, 1908, p. 991.

103. "Man's Value at 20 and 50," *New York Times*, Nov. 7, 1911, p. 7.

104. Difference between Raw Material and Human Beings, p. 1 (n.d.), reel 68, *AALLPM*.

105. J. W. Brown, "Democracy or Bolshevism," *Labor's Advocate* (Birmingham), Feb. 8, 1919.

106. Kilpatrick v. Choctaw, O. and G. R.R., 121 F. 11, 16 (8th Cir. 1903) (Caldwell, J., dissenting).

107. Gilbert E. Roe, *Our Judicial Oligarchy* 109 (1912).

108. 14 *Report of the Industrial Comm'n on the Relations and Conditions of Capital and Labor* 163 (1901).

109. E.g., "Snipped Finger Exhibit," *New York Times*, Dec. 16, 1910, p. 2 (quoting Albert R. Shattuck of the American Museum of Safety); *Thirteenth Annual Report of the Bureau of Statistics of Labor and Industries of New Jersey*, 367.

110. Alexander Trachtenberg, *The History of Legislation for the Protection of Coal Miners in Pennsylvania, 1824–1915*, p. 19 (1942); Katherine A. Harvey, *The Best-Dressed Miners: Life and Labor in the Maryland Coal Region, 1835–1910*, p. 41 (1969).

111. Miles M. Dawson, Would a Federal Tax to Provide Funds to Compensate Work-

men and Their Dependents for the Consequences of Industrial Accidents Be Constitutional? (n.d.), reel 68, *AALLPM;* "General Discussion," 2 *ALLR* 60, 63–64 (1912) (comments of Miles M. Dawson).

112. Rubinow, *Social Insurance,* 44; "Compensation," *United Mine Workers' J.,* July 21, 1910, p. 4; Stein, *Triangle Fire,* 144.

2. The Dilemmas of Classical Tort Law

The first epigraph in this chapter is from Thomas M. Cooley, *The Elements of Torts* 22 (Chicago, Callaghan 1895); the second is from the Ohio State Bar Association, *Proceedings, Thirty-Fourth Annual Session* 49 (1913).

1. Oliver Wendell Holmes Jr., *The Common Law* 94–95 (Boston, Little, Brown 1881).

2. Id., 84, 96.

3. On Holmes's social Darwinism, see G. Edward White, *Justice Oliver Wendell Holmes: Law and the Inner Self* 151–52, 290–91, 360 (1993); Robert W. Gordon, "Law as a Vocation: Holmes and the Lawyer's Path," in *The Path of the Law and Its Influence: The Legacy of Oliver Wendell Holmes, Jr.* 1 (Steven J. Burton ed., 2000).

4. Farwell v. Boston and Worcester R.R., 45 Mass. (4 Met.) 49 (1842).

5. Brown v. Kendall, 60 Mass. (6 Cush.) 292, 296–97 (1850).

6. Shaw v. Boston and Worcester R.R., 74 Mass. 45, 67 (1857) (emphasis added).

7. Morton J. Horwitz, *The Transformation of American Law, 1780–1860,* pp. 89–99 (1977); G. Edward White, *Tort Law in America: An Intellectual History* 14–15 (1980).

8. Ecclesiastes 11:3 (King James).

9. Atchison v. Steamboat Dr. Franklin, 14 Mo. 63, 67 (1851) (Crockett and Kasson, for the appellants).

10. John Stuart Mill, *On Liberty* 13 (Stefan Collini ed., Cambridge Univ. Press 1989) (1859).

11. Christopher G. Tiedeman, *The Unwritten Constitution of the United States: A Philosophical Inquiry into the Fundamentals of American Constitutional Law* 76 (New York, G. P. Putnam's Sons 1890) ("[T]he doctrine of natural rights may be tersely stated to be a freedom from all legal restraint that is not needed to prevent injury to others"); Francis Lieber, *On Civil Liberty and Self-Government* 39–40 (Theodore D. Woolsey ed., 3d ed., Philadelphia, J. B. Lippincott 1877); Christopher G. Tiedeman, *A Treatise on the Limitations of Police Power in the United States Considered from Both a Civil and Criminal Standpoint* vii (St. Louis, F. H. Thomas 1886) (arguing that individual and minority rights are "free from all lawful control or interference by the majority, except so far as such control or interference may be necessary to prevent injury to others in the enjoyment of their rights"); id., § 30, p. 67 ("No man has a right to make such a use of his liberty as to commit an injury to the rights of others."); see also id., pp. 64–68.

12. 1 Francis Hilliard, *The Law of Torts, or Private Wrongs* 82 (Boston, Little, Brown 1859).

13. Thomas M. Cooley, *The General Principles of Constitutional Law in the United States of America* 226 (Boston, Little, Brown 1880).

14. Thomas M. Cooley, *A Treatise on the Law of Torts, or the Wrongs Which Arise Independent of Contract* 45 (Chicago, Callaghan 1879).

15. Lieber, *On Civil Liberty*, 39–40.

16. See Morton J. Horwitz, *The Transformation of American Law 1870–1960: The Crisis of Legal Orthodoxy* 9–31 (1992); Duncan Kennedy, "Toward an Historical Understanding of Legal Consciousness: The Case of Classical Legal Thought in America, 1850–1940," 3 *Research in Law and Soc.* 3–24 (1980).

17. For examples of this argument in today's tort theory literature, see Jules L. Coleman, *Markets, Morals, and the Law* 174–80 (1988); Jules L. Coleman, *Risks and Wrongs* 229–30 (1992); Guido Calabresi and Alvin K. Klevorick, "Four Tests for Liability in Torts," 14 *J. Legal Stud.* 585, 587–91 (1985). A strict-liability standard for injurers is a negligence rule for victims only if a victim's contributory negligence is a defense to liability for the injuries.

18. C. G. Addison, *The Law of Torts, Abridged for Use in the Law School of Harvard University* 2, 43 (Boston, Little, Brown 1870).

19. 1 Hilliard, *Law of Torts*, 119 ("It is further said, that the maxim, so use your own that you injure not another's property, is supported by the soundest wisdom. But the injury intended is a legal injury; an invasion of some legal right") (footnote omitted); see also id., 119–21 (listing instances of *damnum absque injuria*).

20. See Thomas G. Shearman and Amasa A. Redfield, *A Treatise on the Law of Negligence* (New York, Baker, Voorhis 1869).

21. 1 James Barr Ames and Jeremiah Smith, *A Selection of Cases on the Law of Torts* 56–76 (Cambridge, Harvard Law Review Publishing Association, 2d ed. 1893).

22. See Clarke Butler Whittier, "Mistake in the Law of Torts," 15 *Harv. L. Rev.* 335, 335 (1902).

23. Losee v. Buchanan, 51 N.Y. 476, 484 (1873); see also Ryan v. N.Y. Cent. R.R. Co., 35 N.Y. 210, 216–17 (1866) (arguing that "[i]n a country where wood, coal, gas and oils are universally used," a strict-liability standard would "create a liability which would be the destruction of all civilized society"); Holmes, *Common Law*, 77.

24. 2 Seymour D. Thompson, *The Law of Negligence in Relations Not Resting in Contract* 1234 (St. Louis, F. H. Thomas 1880). For a discussion of Thompson as a legal progressive, see Arnold M. Paul, *Conservative Crisis and the Rule of Law: Attitudes of Bar and Bench, 1887–1895*, pp. 43–44, 54–60 (1960).

25. 2 Thompson, *Law of Negligence*, 1235.

26. E.g., *Losee*, 51 N.Y. at 484.

27. Francis Wharton, *A Treatise on the Law of Negligence* § 66, p. 67 (Philadelphia, Kay and Bro. 1874).

28. Holmes, *Common Law*, 73. Holmes explained that the standard of strict cause-based liability "when [an] act has brought force to bear on another through a comparatively short train of intervening causes, in spite of [an actor's] having used all possible care" required "the same liability, however numerous and unexpected the events between the act and the result." Id., 74. On the development

of new ideas about remote causation, see Horwitz, *Transformation of American Law, 1870–1960,* 51–63; Herbert Hovenkamp, "Pragmatic Realism and Proximate Cause in America," 3 *J. Legal Hist.* 3, 16–18 (1982); Thomas L. Haskell, *The Emergence of Professional Social Science: The American Social Science Association and the Nineteenth-Century Crisis of Authority* 240–56 (1977) (describing changing ideas about causation in late-nineteenth-century America).

29. Holmes, *Common Law,* 77; George P. Fletcher, "The Search for Synthesis in Tort Theory," 2 *Law and Phil.* 63, 69–70 (1983).

30. Shearman and Redfield, *Treatise on the Law of Negligence,* 3.

31. Addison, *Law of Torts,* 2.

32. 1 Edwin A. Jaggard, *Hand-Book of the Law of Torts* 145 (St. Paul, West 1895).

33. 1 Hilliard, *Law of Torts,* 119; see also Victory v. Baker, 67 N.Y. 366, 368 (1876) ("[I]f, in the lawful exercise of [the defendant's property] right, and without negligence on his part, a third person sustains an injury from its use by the owner, the owner is not answerable."); Munger v. Tonawanda R.R. Co., 4 N.Y. 349, 360 (1850) ("[A]s the defendants [a railroad company] were in the lawful exercise and enjoyment of their rights . . . the law did not enjoin it as a duty on the defendants to take care not to injure [the plaintiffs' oxen that had wandered onto the tracks].")*.* The attempt to rest tort decisions on the lawful exercise of one party's rights was especially apparent in landowner liability cases, in which the plaintiff's relationship to the boundaries of the defendant's sphere of sovereign property ownership was the critical factor. See, e.g., Flanagan v. Atl. Alcatraz Asphalt Co., 56 N.Y.S. 18, 21 (App. Div. 1899); Sterger v. Vansicler, 30 N.E. 987, 989 (N.Y. 1892).

34. See Arthur M. Schlesinger Jr., *The Age of Jackson* 177–80 (1945); Whitney R. Cross, *The Burned-Over District: The Social and Intellectual History of Enthusiastic Religion in Western New York, 1800–1850* (1950); Paul E. Johnson, *A Shopkeeper's Millennium: Society and Revivals in Rochester, New York, 1815–1837* (1978).

35. Peter F. Walker, *Moral Choices: Memory, Desire, and Imagination in Nineteenth-Century American Abolition* 337–39 (1978).

36. See Thomas M. Cooley, *A Treatise on the Constitutional Limitations Which Rest upon the Legislative Power of the States of the American Union* (Da Capo Press 1972) (1868); David J. Barron, "The Promise of Cooley's City: Traces of Local Constitutionalism," 147 *U. Pa. L. Rev.* 487, 509–22 (1999).

37. Cooley, *Treatise on the Law of Torts,* 19–20.

38. Id., 80–81.

39. See Shearman and Redfield, *Treatise on the Law of Negligence* §§ 35–52, pp. 35–57. Exceptions were Illinois, Kansas, and Georgia, which in the mid-nineteenth century adopted rules allowing recovery for gross negligence even in the face of relatively slight negligence on the part of the victim. See 2 Thompson, *Law of Negligence,* 1023–24; Cooley, *Treatise on the Law of Torts,* 676–78; Shearman and Redfield, *Treatise on the Law of Negligence* § 37, pp. 37–38. By the latter part of the century, however, the doctrine of contributory negligence emerged in these jurisdictions. See Lawrence M. Friedman, *A History of American Law* 477 (2d ed. 1985). Tennessee appears to have flirted with a comparative negli-

gence standard in which the contributory negligence of a plaintiff was a factor for consideration in the jury's assessment of damages. See Cooley, *Treatise on the Law of Torts,* 677–78.

40. Cooley, *Treatise on the Law of Torts,* 672.

41. A Westlaw search of ("272K!" and DA(AFT 1859 and BEF 1881)), NY-CS database (Dec. 8, 2000), which produces all cases digested under the heading "Negligence" during this time period, yields 968 results. A search of ("272K!" and (contribut! /5 negligen!) and DA(AFT 1859 and BEF 1881)), NY-CS database (Dec. 8, 2000), which produces the subset of cases that raise the issue of contributory negligence, yields 661 results. For examples, see Dexter v. McCready, 5 A. 855 (Conn. 1886); Toledo and W. Ry. Co. v. Goddard, 25 Ind. 185 (1865); Monongahela City v. Fischer, 2 A. 87 (Pa. 1886). Peter Karsten has argued that historians have exaggerated the importance of contributory negligence in the nineteenth century. See Peter Karsten, *Heart versus Head: Judge-Made Law in Nineteenth-Century America* 95–101 (1997). The point here, however, is not to gauge the social consequences of the contributory negligence rule, but rather to place it in the ideological system of late-nineteenth-century tort doctrine.

42. 1 Jaggard, *Hand-Book of the Law of Torts,* 199.

43. Shearman and Redfield, *Treatise on the Law of Negligence* § 94, p. 110.

44. 2 Thompson, *Law of Negligence,* 1108.

45. Id.; see also Shearman and Redfield, *Treatise on the Law of Negligence* § 94, p. 111 ("[W]here the servant's action is founded upon the assumption that the master ought to have known of the defect which caused the injury, it is clearly a sufficient defence to show that the servant had equal means of knowledge," citing Loonam v. Brockway, 28 How. Pr. 472 (N.Y. Sup. Ct. 1864)).

46. Charles W. McCurdy, "The 'Liberty of Contract' Regime in American Law," in *The State and Freedom of Contract* 161, 161–97 (Harry N. Scheiber ed., 1998).

47. 1 Hilliard, *Law of Torts,* x (emphasis removed).

48. Cooley, *Treatise on the Law of Torts,* 1.

49. 1 Hilliard, *Law of Torts,* 83–84.

50. Tapping Reeve, *The Law of Baron and Femme; of Parent and Child; of Guardian and Ward; of Master and Servant; and of the Powers of Courts of Chancery* 63, 201 (New Haven, Oliver Steele 1816); see also Hall v. Nashville and Chattanooga R.R. Co., 1 Tenn. Cases (Thompson) 204, 205 (Tenn. 1859); 3 William Blackstone, *Commentaries* *142–43. See generally John Fabian Witt, "From Loss of Services to Loss of Support: The Wrongful Death Statutes, the Origins of Modern Tort Law, and the Making of the Nineteenth-Century Family," 25 *Law and Soc. Inquiry* 717, 722–31 (2000).

51. 1 Blackstone, *Commentaries* *410.

52. See Elizabeth Blackmar, *Manhattan for Rent, 1785–1850,* pp. 51–60 (1989); Alan Dawley, *Class and Community: The Industrial Revolution in Lynn* 17–18 (1976); Johnson, *Shopkeepers' Millennium,* 43–46; Mary P. Ryan, *Cradle of the Middle Class: The Family in Oneida County, New York, 1790–1865,* p. 25 (1981).

53. Peter W. Bardaglio, *Reconstructing the Household: Families, Sex, and the Law*

in the Nineteenth-Century South (1995); Elizabeth Fox-Genovese, *Within the Plantation Household: Black and White Women of the Old South* (1988).

54. Thomas D. Morris, *Southern Slavery and the Law, 1619–1860*, pp. 147–58 (1996).

55. See, e.g., Johnson, *Shopkeepers' Millennium*, 43–47; Christopher Clark, *The Roots of Rural Capitalism: Western Massachusetts, 1780–1860*, pp. 94–95, 105–6 (1990); Jonathan Prude, *The Coming of Industrial Order: Town and Factory Life in Rural Massachusetts, 1810–1860* (1983).

56. Christopher L. Tomlins, *Law, Labor, and Ideology in the Early American Republic* 301–47 (1993) (discussing Barnes v. Boston and Worcester R.R. (Mass. 1839) (unreported case)); *see, e.g.*, Murray v. S.C. R.R. Co., 26 S.C.L. (1 McMul.) 385 (1841); Farwell v. Boston and Worcester R.R., 45 Mass. (4 Met.) 49 (1842). On the novelty of this line of cases, see A. W. Brian Simpson, "A Case of First Impression: *Priestley v. Fowler* (1837)," in *Leading Cases in the Common Law* 100, 101, 113–29 (1995); and Richard A. Epstein, "The Historical Origins and Economic Structure of Workers' Compensation Law," 16 *Ga. L. Rev.* 775, 777–79 (1982).

57. See Witt, "From Loss of Services to Loss of Support," 730–31.

58. 9 and 10 Vict., ch. 93, §§ 1–2 (1846).

59. An Act Requiring Compensation for Causing Death by Wrongful Act, Neglect, or Default, 1847 N.Y. Laws ch. 450, §§ 1–2, pp. 575–76 (emphasis added).

60. Witt, "From Loss of Services to Loss of Support," 733–37.

61. See Lucas v. N.Y. Central R.R. Co., 21 Barb. 245, 246–47 (N.Y. Sup. Ct., Monroe Cty. 1855); Worley v. Cincinnati Hamilton and Dayton R.R. Co., 1 Handy 481, 490–91 (Ohio Super. Ct., Cincinnati 1855); Dickins v. N.Y. Central R.R. Co., 23 N.Y. 158 (1861); Kramer v. San Francisco Market Street R.R. Co., 25 Cal. 434 (1864); Georgia R.R. and Banking Co. v. Wynn, 42 Ga. 331 (1871); Grosso v. Delaware, Lackawanna and Western R.R. Co., 13 A. 233, 235–36 (N.J. 1888); Shearman and Redfield, *Treatise on the Law of Negligence* § 297, p. 346; 2 Thompson, *Law of Negligence*, 1227. Illinois courts adopted a broad reading of their "next of kin" provision to allow actions by a father for damages resulting from the death of a son. See City of Chicago v. Major, 18 Ill. 349 (1857). New York flirted with a similar reading, see Oldfield v. N.Y. and Harlem R.R. Co., 14 N.Y. 310 (1856); Quin v. Moore, 15 N.Y. 432 (1857); Keller v. N.Y. Cent. R.R. Co., 24 How. Pr. 172, 175 (N.Y. 1861); but quickly abandoned it in *Dickins*, 23 N.Y. at 159–60. For exceptions, see Trafford v. Adams Express Co., 76 Tenn. (8 Lea) 96 (1881) (holding that the term "widow" in the Tennessee statute embraced widowers as well as widows); Steel v. Kurtz, 28 Ohio St. 191 (Ohio 1875) (husband is next of kin for purposes of wrongful death statute in Ohio).

62. Grosso v. Delaware Lackawanna and Western R.R. Co., 13 A. 233, 236 (N.J. 1888).

63. Georgia R.R. and Banking Co. v. Wynn, 42 Ga. 331, 333 (1871).

64. Western Union Tel. Co. v. McGill, 57 F. 699, 703 (8th Cir. 1893).

65. Commonwealth v. Boston and Albany R.R. Co., 121 Mass. 36, 38 (1876).

66. Witt, "From Loss of Services to Loss of Support," 736–46.

67. See Prude, *Coming of Industrial Order,* 36–64. The "family system" was also used in Pennsylvania textile mills. See Anthony F. C. Wallace, *Rockdale: The Growth of an American Village in the Early Industrial Revolution* 180 (1978).

68. Robert F. Dalzell Jr., *Enterprising Elite: The Boston Associates and the World They Made* 33 (1987).

69. Teresa Anne Murphy, *Ten Hours' Labor: Religion, Reform, and Gender in Early New England* 20 (1992); see also Dalzell, *Enterprising Elite,* 31–36.

70. Philip Scranton, "Varieties of Paternalism: Industrial Structures and the Social Relations of Production in American Textiles," 36 *Am. Q.* 235 (1984); see also Philip Scranton, *Proprietary Capitalism: The Textile Manufacture at Philadelphia, 1800–1885,* pp. 247–51 (1983).

71. Herman Melville, *Moby-Dick* 287 (Arion Press 1979) (1851) ("For, when the line is darting out, to be seated then in the boat, is like being seated in the midst of the manifold whizzings of a steam-engine in full play, when every flying beam, and shaft, and wheel, is grazing you."); see also Carl Gersuny, *Work Hazards and Industrial Conflict* 24–28 (1981).

72. George E. McNeill, *A Study of Accidents and Accident Insurance* 129 (1900).

73. On the increasing prevalence of the family-based approach in the Lowell mills as the labor market for young single native women declined, see Thomas Dublin, *Women at Work: The Transformation of Work and Community in Lowell, Massachusetts, 1826–1860,* p. 138 (1979). By 1831 about two out of three workers in Slater-owned mills in Massachusetts and Rhode Island had a family member working in the same mill. Prude, *Coming of Industrial Order,* 43, 87.

74. Dublin, *Women at Work,* 59; Cynthia J. Shelton, *The Mills of Manayunk: Industrialization and Social Conflict in the Philadelphia Region, 1787–1837,* pp. 100–1 (1986).

75. Tamara K. Hareven and Randolph Langenbach, *Amoskeag: Life and Work in an American Factory-City* 11 (1978). Worker deference to the company was a complex combination of sincerely held affective bonds, on the one hand, and, on the other, rational calculation as to the power of the company over workers' lives.

76. E.g., Peter Way, *Common Labour: Workers and the Digging of North American Canals, 1780–1860,* pp. 148–51 (1993).

77. Hareven and Langenbach, *Amoskeag,* 133.

78. Crystal Eastman, *Work-Accidents and the Law* 156 (1910).

79. Even a cursory glance at treatises on tort law readily suggests the importance of railroad cases and the extreme paucity of mining cases. By another measure, the West Publishing Company digested only six mining-related personal injury cases before 1900 in the mining state of Pennsylvania as compared with 203 railroad cases involving injuries to persons on or near the tracks—a category that excluded passenger and work accidents. Search of Westlaw, PA-HN-ALL database (Dec. 2, 2000) (search of cases containing "260w118" or "320x(G)" in the TOPIC field and "BEF 1900" in the DATE field). See also Katherine A. Harvey, *The Best-Dressed Miners: Life and Labor in the Maryland Coal Region 1835–1910,* pp. 41–42 (1969).

80. Ronald C. Brown, *Hard-Rock Miners: The Intermountain West, 1860–1920,* pp. 13, 128 (1979).

81. Elizabeth Jameson, *All That Glitters: Class, Conflict, and Community in Cripple Creek* 53–59 (1998).

82. John S. Spratt Sr., *Thurber, Texas: The Life and Death of a Company Coal Town* xix, 6, 13 (Harwood P. Hinton ed., 1986).

83. Mildred Allen Beik, *The Miners of Windber: The Struggles of New Immigrants for Unionization, 1890s–1930s,* p. 18 (1996); John H. M. Laslett, *Nature's Noblemen: The Fortunes of the Independent Collier in Scotland and the American Midwest, 1855–1889,* pp. 42–43 (1983); Priscilla Long, *Where the Sun Never Shines: A History of America's Bloody Coal Industry* 80 (1989); Crandall A. Shifflett, *Coal Towns: Life, Work, and Culture in Company Towns of Southern Appalachia, 1880–1960,* pp. 145–61 (1991).

84. Wallace, *Rockdale,* 258–61.

85. Anon. [Sir Jeffrey Gilbert], *The Law of Evidence* 86–87 (photo. reprint 1979) (1754).

86. E.g., Starr v. Tracy, 2 Root 528, 529 (Conn. Super. Ct. 1797); Connor v. Bradey, 1 Ant. N.P. Cas. 99, 99–100 (N.Y. Sup. Ct. 1809); see also Zephaniah Swift, *A Digest of the Law of Evidence, in Civil and Criminal Cases, and a Treatise on Bills of Exchange and Promissory Notes* 44–73 (Hartford, Oliver D. Cooke 1810).

87. See John H. Langbein, "Historical Foundations of the Law of Evidence: A View From the Ryder Sources," 96 *Colum. L. Rev.* 1168, 1174–75 (1996); William E. Nelson, *Americanization of the Common Law: The Impact of Legal Change on Massachusetts Society, 1760–1830,* pp. 24–25, 156 (1975).

88. Nelson, *Americanization,* 60, 156.

89. See Langbein, "Historical Foundations," 1174.

90. Clyde J. Crobaugh and Amos E. Redding, *Casualty Insurance* 495 (1928).

91. Nelson, *Americanization,* 156–57; Hunscom v. Hunscom, 15 Mass. (14 Tyng) 184, 184 (1818).

92. An Act to Prevent Excessive and Deceitful Gaming, ch. 46, 1801 N.Y. Laws 70; An Act to Prevent Usury, ch. 430, 1837 N.Y. Laws 486.

93. 22 Mich. Rev. Stat. ch. 102, § 99 (1846); Conn. Rev. Stat. tit. I, ch. x, § 141 (1849); *First Report of the Commissioners on Practice and Pleadings: Code of Procedure* §§ 344, 351, pp. 242, 246 (Albany, Charles Van Benthuysen 1848); George Fisher, "The Jury's Rise as Lie Detector," 107 *Yale L.J.* 575, 710 (1997); John Fabian Witt, "Making the Fifth: The Constitutionalization of American Self-Incrimination Doctrine, 1791–1903," 77 *Tex. L. Rev.* 825, 864–66 (1999).

94. Nelson, *Americanization,* 157; Fisher, "Jury's Rise," 673–74, 709–11.

95. C. J. W. Allen, *The Law of Evidence in Victorian England* 14 (1997); Langbein, "Historical Foundations," 1194, 1201; 1 Frank S. Rice, *The General Principles of the Law of Evidence* § 211, p. 367 (Rochester, Lawyers' Co-Operative 1892).

96. Fed. R. Evid. 801(d)(2)(D); see also 4 John Henry Wigmore, *Evidence in Trials at Common Law* § 1078, p. 162 (James H. Chadbourn ed., 1976).

97. See, e.g., *McCormick on Evidence* § 262, p. 774 (John William Strong ed., 4th ed. 1992).

98. 4 Wigmore, *Evidence* § 1078, p. 166 n.2 (quoting Slifka v. Johnson, 161 F.2d

467, 469 (2d Cir. 1947)); Koninklijke Luchtvaart Maatschappij N.V. KLM Royal Dutch Airlines Holland v. Tuller, 292 F.2d 775, 782–85 (D.C. Cir. 1961).

99. 1 Rice, *General Principles* § 212, p. 375; Gandy v. Humphries, 35 Ala. 617, 624 (1860).

100. McCormick on Evidence § 259, p. 454; Simon Greenleaf, *A Treatise on the Law of Evidence,* § 113, pp. 145–46 (Isaac E. Redfield ed., 12th ed., Boston, Little, Brown 1866).

101. E.g., Salem India Rubber Co. v. Adams, 40 Mass. (23 Pick.) 256, 265 (1839).

102. E.g., Lincoln Coal Mining Co. v. McNally, 15 Ill. App. 181, 184–85 (1884) (declarations of defendant coal mine's servants inadmissible because not forming part of the *res gestae* of the accident); Patterson v. Wabash, St. Louis and Pac. Ry. Co., 19 N.W. 761, 765–66 (Mich. 1884) (post-accident statement of railroad company servant inadmissible); Forsee v. Ala. Great S. R.R. Co., 63 Miss. 66, 72 (1885) (post-accident declaration of a railroad ticket agent inadmissible); Meyer v. Va. and Truckee R.R. Co., 16 Nev. 341, 344–46 (1881) (post-fire statements of the defendant's agent inadmissible because not part of the *res gestae*); Erie and W. Va. R.R. Co. v. Smith, 17 A. 443, 445–47 (Pa. 1889) (post-accident declaration of a defendant railroad corporation's servants as to character of engine inadmissible).

103. Greenleaf, *Law of Evidence* § 113, p. 134; see also 1 Rice, *General Principles* § 230, p. 449.

104. McDermott v. Hannibal and St. Joseph R.R. Co., 73 Mo. 516, 518–19 (1881).

105. "The Res Gestae of an Accident," 4 *Wkly. L. Bull.* 872, 872 (1878); see also "The Res Gestae of an Accident," 10 *Cent. L.J.* 23, 23 (1880) (citing Mobile and Montgomery R.R. Co. v. Ashcraft, 48 Ala. 15 (1872)); id. (statement of stage driver that coach was overloaded inadmissible as evidence for the plaintiff) (citing Maury v. Talmadge, 16 F. Cas. 1182, 1184 (D. Ohio 1840) (No. 9315)); id. (declarations of boat pilot) (citing Ready v. Steamboat Highland Mary, 20 Mo. 264 (1855)).

106. "The Res Gestae of an Accident" (1880), 24; "Case Note," 41 *Cent. L.J.* 397, 397 (1895) (citing St. Louis Iron Mountain and S. Ry. Co. v. Kelley, 31 S.W. 884, 884–85 (Ark. 1895)); see also "Evidence," 40 *Cent. L.J.* 166, 166–67 (1895) (discussing Barker v. St. Louis Iron Mountain and S. Ry. Co., 28 S.W. 866, 866–67, 126 Mo. 143 (1894) (holding a conductor's declaration made eight to ten minutes after accident not admissible as not within the *res gestae*)); "The Res Gestae of an Accident" (1878), 872.

107. Vicksburg and Miss. R.R. Co. v. O'Brien, 119 U.S. 99 (1886).

108. "Notes of Recent Decisions," 30 *Cent. L.J.* 2, 3 (1890) (citing Carroll v. E. Tenn., Va. and Ga. Ry. Co., 10 S.E. 163 (Ga. 1889)). The mid- and late-nineteenth-century doctrine appears to have limited the scope of agents' admissions to "spontaneous exclamation[s]," which constitute a specific hearsay exemption today. See "Note," 40 *Cent. L.J.* 167, 167–68 (1894) ("If . . . the court is satisfied that the agent, without time to premeditate, expressed truly and spontaneously his thoughts in regard to a fact within his knowledge and in issue . . . the evidence would be admissible."); see also 6 Wigmore, *Evidence* §§ 1756a–1757,

pp. 234–37 (discussing confusion in the early case law between *res gestae* and spontaneous exclamations).

109. "Res Gestae—Admissibility of Declarations as a Part of—Railroad Accidents," 36 *Cent. L.J.* 170, 172 (1893) (citing Louisville and Nashville R.R. Co. v. Pearson, 12 So. 176, 179 (Ala. 1893)).

110. 1 Rice, *General Principles* § 212, p. 377; see also id., 384 ("Apparent abuses resulting from receiving descriptive declarations of pain in negligence cases, has led to a reconsideration of the rule; and the better opinion now is that a party seeking to recover damages on account of his own suffering cannot give in evidence, in his own behalf, his own descriptive declarations of suffering, as distinguished from apparently spontaneous manifestations of the distress.").

111. Randolph E. Bergstrom, *Courting Danger: Injury and Law in New York City, 1870–1910,* p. 20 table 4 (1992).

112. Robert A. Silverman, *Law and Urban Growth: Civil Litigation in the Boston Trial Courts, 1880–1900,* p. 105 (1981). See also George Fisher, "Plea Bargaining's Triumph," 109 *Yale L.J.* 857, 995–1001 (2000).

113. E. Parmalee Prentice, "The Speculation in Damage Claims for Personal Injuries," 164 *N. Am. Rev.* 199, 199 (1897); Eli Shelby Hammond, "Personal Injury Litigation," 6 *Yale L.J.* 328, 332 (1897); Elon R. Brown, "Some Faults of Legal Administration," in New York State Bar Association, *Proceedings of the Thirty-First Annual Meeting Held at New York, January 21, 24–25, 1908,* pp. 136, 142 (1908).

114. A change in 1910 in the way the category of "lawyer" was defined (removing semiprofessionals such as notaries, abstractors, and justices of the peace) makes comparisons between pre- and post-1910 census information difficult. For statistical treatments of the legal profession, see Richard L. Abel, *American Lawyers* 249–318 (1989); Terence C. Halliday, "Six Score Years and Ten: Demographic Transitions in the American Legal Profession, 1850–1980," 20 *Law and Soc'y Rev.* 53 (1986). The data presented here are compiled from the published reports of the U.S. Census Bureau cited in the note accompanying Table 2.1.

115. Figures in this paragraph are derived from the sources cited in Table 2.1. The extremely high growth rate of lawyers in Manhattan suggests a qualification of Bergstrom's claim that "after 1880 the population grew at an even faster pace than the number of lawyers." Bergstrom, *Courting Danger,* 88.

116. Andrew J. Hirschl, "The Plaintiff's Standpoint," 1 *Ill. L. Rev.* 16, 17, 19 (1906).

117. See, e.g., In re Clark, 77 N.E. 1, 5–6 (N.Y. 1906) (disbarring an attorney who, among other things, sold the claims of his own clients for $25 each); In re Newell, 174 A.D. 94, 98–99 (N.Y. App. Div. 1916) (per curiam) (disbarring an attorney for paying an employee of the New York Central Railroad Company to monitor the company's telegraphic communications and notify him of accidents—and thus potential clients).

118. See the interesting but sensationalist and decidedly one-sided Ken Dornstein, *Accidentally, on Purpose: The Making of a Personal Injury Underworld in America* 53–191 (1997).

119. *Clark,* 77 N.E. at 5.

120. Bergstrom, *Courting Danger,* 101–12; see generally Edward A. Purcell Jr., *Litigation and Inequality* (1992).

121. Bergstrom, *Courting Danger,* 99–100.

122. Edward A. Purcell, "The Action Was Outside the Courts: Consumer Injuries and the Uses of Contract in the U.S., 1875–1945," in *Private Law and Social Inequality in the Industrial Age* 505, 513–21 (Willibald Steinmetz ed., 2000).

123. E.g., Silverman, *Law and Urban Growth,* 99–100.

124. E.g., In re O'Neill, 171 N.Y.S. 514, 515 (App. Div. 1918) (attorney used runners to generate accident claims that otherwise appear unlikely to have been brought).

125. E.g., "To Establish Rules of Professional Ethics: A Proper Function of the Association," in New York State Bar Association, *Reports.—Vol. III: Proceedings of the Third Annual Meeting of the Association* 74, 78–79 (Albany, Argus 1880) (observing that many lawyers in the association viewed contingent fees as "disreputable, unworthy, demoralizing and tending to degrade the profession and impair the administration of justice").

126. Id., 78–79.

127. Brown, "Some Faults," 142.

128. Irving G. Vann, *Contingent Fees: Address in Hubbard Course on Legal Ethics Delivered at Commencement of Albany Law School* 10–12 (1905) (internal quotation marks omitted).

129. "The Contingent Fee Business," 24 *Alb. L.J.* 24, 25–26 (1881) (quoting Thomas Cooley).

130. Fishback and Kantor's statistical studies of late-nineteenth- and early-twentieth-century tort law support Cooley's suspicions: common law doctrines appear to have had some influence on the "probability and level of accident payments, but they were clearly not the only influence and sometimes not even the dominant influence." Price V. Fishback and Shawn Everett Kantor, *A Prelude to the Welfare State: The Origins of Workers' Compensation* 45 (2000).

131. *Fourteenth Annual Report of the Massachusetts Bureau of Statistics of Labor, March, 1883,* p. 68 (Boston, Wright and Potter 1883).

132. *Seventeenth Annual Report of the Bureau of Labor Statistics of the State of New York for the Year 1899,* p. 559 (Albany, James B. Lyon 1900).

133. An Act to Create a Co-Operative Insurance Fund, 1902 Md. Laws 593, 593–94, ch. 412.

134. Don D. Lescohier, "Industrial Accidents and Employers' Liability in Minnesota," in *Part II of the Twelfth Biennial Report of the Bureau of Labor, Industries and Commerce of the State of Minnesota 1909–1910,* p. 156 (1910).

135. E. H. Downey, *History of Work Accident Indemnity in Iowa* 2 (1912).

136. Eastman, *Work-Accidents,* 86. It is worth noting that the argument here reverses the standard account of the shift in attribution of blame in the late nineteenth century. Lawrence Friedman suggests—drawing on the Samuel Clemens / Mark Twain story of a steamboat accident in the novel *The Gilded Age* (a story modeled on the steamboat explosion that killed Clemens's brother)—that the mid-nineteenth century was a period in which the law held "Nobody to Blame" for accidents causing injury and death. Friedman, *History of American Law,* 470

(quoting Samuel Clemens and Charles Dudley Warner, *The Gilded Age* 52 (Hartford, American Publishing 1883)). I prefer the interpretation of the passage from *The Gilded Age* offered by Nan Goodman's *Shifting the Blame: Literature, Law, and the Theory of Accidents in Nineteenth-Century America* 65–97 (1998). In Goodman's view, the story of the steamboat accident reflects the crisis of causal attribution in the mechanized United States in the final decades of the century. As I have tried to suggest here, the law at midcentury generally had little difficulty attributing negligence to either the defendant or the plaintiff, though it attributed blame to the injured far more often than we do today. Toward the end of the century, however, the increase in apparently blameless accidents created real difficulties for the law of torts.

137. Ohio State Bar Association, *Proceedings of the Thirty-First Annual Session* 63 (1910) (comments of Judge Robertson).

138. Ohio State Bar Association, *Proceedings of the Thirty-Second Annual Session* 94 (1911).

139. Compare Friedman, *History of American Law,* 475–76, 485, with Gary T. Schwartz, "The Character of Early American Tort Law," 36 *UCLA L. Rev.* 641, 664–70 (1987); and Gary T. Schwartz, "Tort Law and the Economy in Nineteenth-Century America: A Reinterpretation," 90 *Yale L.J.* 1717, 1759–65 (1981). See also Karsten, *Heart versus Head,* 99, 255–91.

140. Marc Galanter, "Real World Torts: An Antidote to Anecdote," 55 *Md. L. Rev.* 1093, 1099–1102 (1996).

141. In New York, for example, work-accident cases brought by employees against their employers represented, by my count, only 10 percent (18 out of 180) of all personal injury cases among reported Court of Appeals decisions between 1860 and 1880, even though the best estimate suggests that work accidents represented one-third of accidental deaths and one-half of all accidental injuries during the period. In the trial courts, Randolph Bergstrom has found that no work-accident cases were filed in New York City in 1870. Bergstrom, *Courting Danger,* 21; see also Lawrence M. Friedman, "Civil Wrongs: Personal Injury Law in the Late 19th Century," 1987 *Am. B. Found. Res. J.* 351, 361 (finding that work-accident suits against employers made up 12 percent of the personal injury caseload of state courts in Alameda County, California from 1880 to 1900); Lawrence M. Friedman and Thomas D. Russell, "More Civil Wrongs: Personal Injury Litigation, 1901–1910," 34 *Am. J. Legal Hist.* 295, 299 (1990) (finding that personal injury suits between employees and employers accounted for 17.6 percent of trial court personal injury filings in Alameda County Superior Court between 1901 and 1910).

142. Thomas D. Russell, "Blood on the Tracks: Turn-of-the-Century Streetcar Injuries, Claims, and Litigation in Alameda County, California, (paper presented at the Annual Meeting of the American Society for Legal History, Minneapolis, October 1997). Fishback and Kantor's study of compensation in work-accident cases similarly concludes that in fatal-accident cases compensation was "relatively meager"; a substantial proportion of workers' families in their samples (ranging from 24.4 percent in Minnesota to 67.9 percent among Illinois coal miners) received no compensation at all, and more than half of those families re-

ceiving any compensation from the decedent's employer received less than half of one year's earnings. Fishback and Kantor, *Prelude to the Welfare State,* 34–39. Fishback and Kantor's analysis of nonfatal work-accident cases is somewhat more difficult to interpret, but again substantial percentages of workplace accident victims (ranging from 9.1 percent in Minnesota to 72.9 percent in Kansas City, Missouri) received no compensation at all from the employer, and in most of the samples used, workers who did recover some compensation received too little to compensate them fully for their economic losses. Id., 39–42.

143. Ohio State Bar Association, *Proceedings of the Thirty-Fourth Annual Session* 49 (1913).

144. See, e.g., Weber v. N.Y. Cent. and Hudson River R.R. Co., 67 N.Y. 587, 587–88 (1876) (finding that the mere fact that the railroad had rung its warning bell and carried a light on the train was not enough to absolve it of negligence and liability when the plaintiff had not been contributorily negligent); Roach v. Flushing and N. Side R.R., 58 N.Y. 626, 626 (1874) (affirming the denial of a railroad's motion for a nonsuit when evidence suggested that the wind had been blowing "so as to carry sound in a direction contrary to that in which the train was going"); Eaton v. Erie Ry., 51 N.Y. 544, 551–52 (1873) (upholding a negligence verdict against a railroad for backing up over the plaintiff's wagon at a railroad crossing).

145. See, e.g., McGrath v. N.Y. Cent. and Hudson River R.R. Co., 59 N.Y. 468, 473 (1875) (reversing a verdict for the plaintiff and rejecting the proposition that the railroad's failure to post a flagman excused the plaintiff's carelessness in crossing the tracks); Culhane v. N.Y. Cent. and Hudson River R.R. Co., 60 N.Y. 133, 137–38 (1875) (observing that absent negligence on the defendant's part, "[a] collision taking place at noonday . . . must have been in part if not wholly the result of carelessness on the part of the servant in charge of the plaintiff's team [of horses]"); Calligan v. N.Y. Cent. and Hudson River R.R. Co., 59 N.Y. 651, 651 (1874) ("A traveller has no right to omit the exercise of proper care in crossing a railroad track, upon the assumption that a train is being run precisely in obedience to a city ordinance [limiting the speed of the train]."); Reynolds v. N.Y. Cent. and Hudson River R.R. Co., 58 N.Y. 248, 252 (1874) (reversing a jury verdict for the plaintiff on the ground that a reasonable jury would have had to find contributory negligence in a case in which the victim "would have saved his life, so far as can be seen from the evidence," by looking before he went out on the railroad tracks); McCall v. N.Y. Cent. R.R. Co., 54 N.Y. 642 (1873) (finding contributory negligence where the victim did not know of a railroad crossing at a particular point on the highway but had passed by it earlier that same day and thus should have known of it); Wilds v. Hudson River R.R., 29 N.Y. 315 (1864) (affirming a nonsuit for the defendant railroad where the plaintiff crossed the tracks in the path of an oncoming train, despite the presence of a factual issue as to the excessive speed of the train).

146. As the New York Court of Appeals explained in 1869, in railroad crossing cases "the guide of duty on either hand assumes that, if each party is duly careful, neither will be injured." Grippen v. N.Y. Cent. R.R., 40 N.Y. 34, 44 (1869).

147. For example, in cases involving obstructions near the tracks that hindered vic-

tims' views of an oncoming train, the New York Court of Appeals consistently held that in the absence of contributory negligence on the victim's part, the railroad company's conduct was unreasonably dangerous. See, e.g., Kissenger v. N.Y. and Harlem R.R., 56 N.Y. 538, 542–43 (1874) (upholding a jury verdict when boxcars obstructed the plaintiff's view of the tracks); Beisiegel v. N.Y. Cent. R.R., 34 N.Y. 622, 632–33 (1866) (reversing a nonsuit for the defendant when idle freight cars blocked the plaintiff's view of a backing-up train). Cf. Cordell v. N.Y. Cent. and Hudson River R.R., 70 N.Y. 119, 124 (1877) (ruling that obstructions placed by the railroad on tracks go to a determination of the victim's contributory negligence and not the railroad's negligence); Salter v. Utica and Black River R.R., 59 N.Y. 631, 633 (1874) (holding that the question whether a railroad owned an obstruction that blocked a victim's view of the tracks was not relevant to the issue of the railroad's negligence).

148. 1 Hilliard, *Law of Torts,* 128; see also Shearman and Redfield, *Treatise on the Law of Negligence* § 12, pp. 10–11.

149. See Kearney v. London, Brighton and S. Coast Ry. Co., 5 L.R.-Q.B. 411 (1870), *aff'd,* 6 L.R.-Ex. 759 (1871) (involving an injury by a brick falling from a railroad bridge soon after the passing of a train); Byrne v. Boadle, 159 Eng. Rep. 299, 300 (Ex. Ch. 1863) (finding, in a case involving a barrel of flour that fell from a window of the defendant's building and injured the plaintiff on the sidewalk below, that "[t]here are certain cases of which it may be said res ipsa loquitur, and this seems one of them"). The *Byrne* case appears to have been the first *res ipsa* case; from Baron Pollock's "casual utterance, dignified and magnified by the cloak of the learned tongue, there has grown by a most extraordinary process the 'doctrine' of res ipsa loquitur." William L. Prosser, "Res Ipsa Loquitur in California," 37 *Cal. L. Rev.* 183, 183 (1949).

150. *Kearney,* 6 L.R.-Ex. at 761–62; see also *Byrne,* 159 Eng. Rep. at 300.

151. Gleeson v. Va. Midland Ry. Co., 140 U.S. 435, 441–42 (1891) (landslide); Lowery v. Manhattan Ry. Co., 1 N.E. 608, 611 (N.Y. 1885) (cinders); Volkmar v. Manhattan Ry. Co., 31 N.E. 870, 871 (N.Y. 1892) (bolts); Thomas v. W. Union Tel. Co., 100 Mass. 156, 157 (1868) (telegraph wires); Sheridan v. Foley, 33 A. 484, 485 (N.J. 1895) (bricks); Mullen v. St. John, 57 N.Y. 567, 569–70 (1874) (building); Flynn v. Gallagher, 52 N.Y. Super. 524, 525 (N.Y. Super. Ct. 1885) (scaffold); Griffin v. Manice, 59 N.E. 925, 927–28 (N.Y. 1901) (elevator); Eagle Packet Co. v. Defries, 94 Ill. 598, 602 (1880) (gangway); Grimsley v. Hankins, 46 F. 400, 401 (S.D. Ala. 1891) (boiler); Illinois Cent. R.R. Co. v. Phillips, 55 Ill. 194, 201 (1870) (boiler); Blanton v. Dold, 18 S.W. 1149, 1151 (Mo. 1892) (machinery). The application of the *res ipsa loquitur* doctrine was extraordinarily haphazard. For every case applying the doctrine, another refused to apply it despite similar circumstances. See, e.g., Robinson v. Charles Wright and Co., 53 N.W. 938, 940 (Mich. 1892) (refusing to apply *res ipsa* in the case of the sudden malfunction of properly constructed machinery); Kirby v. President of Del. and Hudson Canal Co., 62 N.Y.S. 1110, 1111 (App. Div. 1900) (finding that an explosion of hot water apparatus did not fall under the *res ipsa* doctrine); Piehl v. Albany Ry., 51 N.Y.S. 755, 756–57 (App. Div. 1898), *aff'd,* 57 N.E. 1122 (N.Y. 1900) (reaching the same conclu-

sion as the *Robinson* court); May v. Berlin Iron-Bridge Co., 60 N.Y.S. 550, 553 (App. Div. 1899) (refusing to apply *res ipsa* in a case involving falling iron trusses).

152. Shearman and Redfield, *Treatise on the Law of Negligence* § 266, pp. 296–97.

153. 1 Hilliard, *Law of Torts,* 87.

154. Id., 126.

155. Id., 127 (citing Scott v. Bay, 3 Md. 431 (1853)).

156. Cooley, *Treatise on the Law of Torts,* 328–29.

157. Id., 329, 337–50.

158. Bradford Glycerine Co. v. St. Marys Woolen Mfg. Co., 54 N.E. 528, 530–31 (Ohio 1899).

159. Berger v. Minneapolis Gaslight Co., 62 N.W. 336, 337–38 (Minn. 1895).

160. Mears v. Dole, 135 Mass. 508 (1883).

161. Frost v. Berkeley Phosphate Co., 20 S.E. 280, 283–84 (S.C. 1894).

162. Cooley, *Treatise on the Law of Torts,* 570–71.

163. See Fletcher, "Search for Synthesis," 66–67; Mark Kelman, "The Necessary Myth of Objective Causation Judgments in Liberal Political Theory," 63 *Chi.-Kent L. Rev.* 579 (1987); Stephen R. Perry, "The Impossibility of General Strict Liability," 1 *Canadian J.L. and Jurisprudence* 147, 154–59 (1988).

164. Kelman, "Necessary Myth," 586.

165. 1 Arthur Larson and Lex K. Larson, *Larson's Workers' Compensation Law* § 2.05, pp. 2–7 to 2–9 (2002); Lawrence M. Friedman and Jack Ladinsky, "Social Change and the Law of Industrial Accidents," 67 *Colum. L. Rev.* 50 (1967); Federal Employers' Liability Act, 34 Stat. 232 (1906); Federal Employers' Liability Act, 35 Stat. 65 (1908).

166. *Ticket cases:* N.Y. Cent. R.R. Co. v. Lockwood, 84 U.S. 357 (1873) (discussing a contractual waiver of liability for injury to a drover accompanying livestock); Chi., Rock Island and Pac. Ry. Co. v. Hamler, 74 N.E. 705, 705–6 (Ill. 1905) (reviewing a waiver of liability for porters employed by the Pullman Company); Ohio and Miss. Ry. Co. v. Selby, 47 Ind. 471, 474–75 (1874) (reviewing a waiver of liability for carrying a stockman); Doyle v. Fitchburg R.R. Co., 44 N.E. 611, 611 (Mass. 1896) (reviewing a waiver of liability for paying employees); Bates v. Old Colony R.R. Co., 17 N.E. 633, 638 (Mass. 1888) (reviewing a waiver of liability for carrying an express messenger); Ill. Cent. R.R. Co. v. Crudup, 63 Miss. 291 (1885) (reviewing a waiver of liability for carrying a mail agent); Bissell v. N.Y. Cent. R.R. Co., 25 N.Y. 442, 446–47 (1862) (reviewing a waiver of liability for injuries to paying passengers); Cleveland, Painesville, and Ashtabula R.R. Co. v. Curran, 19 Ohio St. 1, 2–3 (1869) (stockman); Pa. R.R. Co. v. Henderson, 51 Pa. 315, 316 (1865) (paying passengers). *Releases:* Hissong v. Richmond and Danville R.R. Co., 8 So. 776, 776 (Ala. 1891); Kan. Pac. Ry. Co. v. Peavey, 29 Kan. 169, 174–75 (1883); Purdy v. Rome, Watertown, and Ogdensburgh R.R. Co., 26 N.E. 255, 255 (N.Y. 1891). *Contractual limitations periods:* Mumford v. Chi., Rock Island and Pac. Ry. Co., 104 N.W. 1135, 1137 (Iowa 1905). *Safety regulation waivers:* Chi. and Erie R.R. Co. v. Lawrence, 82 N.E. 768 (Ind. 1907); D. H. Davis Coal Co. v. Polland, 62 N.E. 492 (Ind. 1902); Lassiter v. Raleigh and Gaston R.R. Co., 49 S.E. 93 (N.C.

1904). *Medical examination requirements:* Galveston, Houston and San Antonio Ry. Co. v. Hughes, 91 S.W. 643 (Tex. Civ. App. 1905).

167. Shearman and Redfield, *Treatise on the Law of Negligence* § 274, p. 308.

168. 2 Thompson, *Law of Negligence,* 1025.

169. See McCurdy, "'Liberty of Contract,'" 161–97.

170. N.Y. Cent. R.R. Co. v. Lockwood, 84 U.S. 357, 378–79 (1873).

171. Cleveland, Painesville and Ashtabula R.R. Co. v. Curran, 19 Ohio St. 1, 14 (1869); see also Ill. Cent. R.R. Co. v. Beebe, 50 N.E. 1019, 1022 (Ill. 1898) (refusing to enforce a waiver on the ground that a stockman cannot waive liability rules rooted in "public policy"); Doyle v. Fitchburg R.R. Co., 44 N.E. 611, 612 (Mass. 1896) (voiding a waiver of liability between a railroad and a paying passenger on the ground that the passenger could not waive the railroad's "public" duties to take care); Lake Shore and Mich. S. Ry. v. Spangler, 8 N.E. 467, 470 (Ohio 1886) (holding a waiver of employer liability unenforceable on grounds that "[s]uch liability is not created for the protection of the employees simply"); McCurdy, "'Liberty of Contract,'" 177–79.

172. See McCurdy, "'Liberty of Contract,'" 178.

173. Runt v. Herring, 21 N.Y.S. 244, 246 (Ct. Comm. Pl. 1892) (voiding an employee-plaintiff's agreement to hold an employer harmless even for injuries suffered because of the employer's negligence).

174. 2 Thompson, *Law of Negligence,* 1008.

175. See, e.g., Greenleaf v. Dubuque and Sioux City R.R. Co., 33 Iowa 52, 58 (1871); Kroy v. Chi., Rock Island and Pac. R.R. Co., 32 Iowa 357, 361 (1871); Crutchfield v. Richmond and Danville R.R. Co., 78 N.C. 300, 302 (1878); 2 Thompson, *Law of Negligence,* 1008. Courts split on this point, however. See Karsten, *Heart versus Head,* 112–27.

176. De Young v. Irving, 38 N.Y.S. 1089, 1092 (App. Div. 1896). *De Young* was a truly astounding decision. A New York factory law provided, inter alia, that no woman under twenty-one years of age "shall be allowed to clean machinery while in motion." Ch. 673, § 8, 1892 N.Y. Laws 1376. The defendant angrily ordered his employee (the plaintiff, a woman under twenty-one years of age) to clean the machinery in a crinoline machine even though it was in motion. The plaintiff complied and caught her hand in the machinery, inflicting a severe burn. The plaintiff based her subsequent tort action against her employer on the latter's violation of the factory law. The appellate division, however, affirmed the dismissal of her case on the ground that the "plaintiff knowingly entered upon the forbidden task, and thereby waived the benefit of the statute." *De Young,* 38 N.Y.S. at 1092.

177. Peterson v. Seattle Traction Co., 63 P. 539, 547–48 (Wash. 1900).

178. See, e.g., Cleveland, Cincinnati, Chi. and St. Louis Ry. Co. v. Henry, 83 N.E. 710, 712 (Ind. 1908).

3. The Cooperative Insurance Movement

The chapter epigraph is from the *Fraternal Monitor,* Dec. 1, 1894, p. 7.

1. Walter Basye, *History and Operation of Fraternal Insurance* 9–10 (1919); see

also M. W. Sackett, *Early History of Fraternal Beneficiary Societies in America: Original Growth 1868–1880,* p. 27 (1914).

2. Mary Ann Clawson, *Constructing Brotherhood: Class, Gender, and Fraternalism* 139–44 (1989); Leon Fink, *Workingmen's Democracy: The Knights of Labor and American Politics* (1983).

3. See Basye, *History and Operation;* Sackett, *Early History.*

4. See J. Owen Stalson, *Marketing Life Insurance: Its History in America* 816 (1942).

5. See David T. Beito, *From Mutual Aid to Welfare State: Fraternal Societies and Social Services, 1890–1967,* p. 14 (2000); B. H. Meyer, "Fraternal Beneficiary Societies in the United States," 6 *Am. J. Soc.* 646–47 (1901) (estimating that one in fifteen Americans belonged to a cooperative insurance society at the turn of the century).

6. Eric Hopkins, *Working-Class Self-Help in Nineteenth-Century England: Responses to Industrialization* 9–10 (1995); Stalson, *Marketing Life Insurance,* 447; Sean Wilentz, *Chants Democratic: New York City and the Rise of the American Working Class, 1788–1850,* pp. 220–27 (1984); James M. Lynch, "Trade Union Sickness Insurance," 4 *ALLR* 82, 82–83 (1914); Richard de Raismes Kip, *Fraternal Life Insurance in America* 32–35 (1953); Henry Hansmann, *The Ownership of Enterprise* 265–86 (1996); *Fourth Biennial Report of the Bureau of Labor Statistics of the State of California for the Years 1889–1890,* p. 143 (Sacramento, State Printing Office 1890).

7. Morton Keller, *The Life Insurance Enterprise, 1885–1910: A Study in the Limits of Corporate Power* 6–7 (1963).

8. *Fourth Biennial Report of the Bureau of Labor Statistics of the State of California,* 142; see also Keller, *The Life Insurance Enterprise,* 52.

9. W. A. Dinsdale, *History of Accident Insurance in Great Britain* 52–58 (1954); George E. McNeill, *A Study of Accidents and Accident Insurance* 12–15 (1900); Clyde J. Crobaugh and Amos E. Redding, *Casualty Insurance* 28, 31 (1928); James R. Pitcher, "Accidents and Accident Insurance," *Forum,* Sept. 1891–Feb. 1892, p. 133.

10. See "Accident Insurance," 7 *Am. L. Rev.* 585, 597–98 (1873). For accounts of the inexperience of the early companies and their difficulties in mastering the "many varying factors, the control of which rested with the assured, such as moral qualities, cooperation in the treatment, and so forth, which greatly influenced the business," see Crobaugh and Redding, *Casualty Insurance,* 29; see also McNeill, *A Study of Accidents,* 9 (describing the susceptibility of early accident insurance companies to fraudulent claims).

11. "Accident Insurance," 598. For railway worker cases involving the ill-fated Provident, see Provident Life Ins. and Inv. Co. v. Martin, 32 Md. 310 (1869); Perry v. Provident Life Ins. and Inv. Co., 99 Mass. 162 (1868).

12. "Accident Insurance," 48 *Cent. L.J.* 280, 280 (1896); see also "Accident Insurance," 3 *University L. Rev.* 264, 264 (1897).

13. "Accident Insurance," 3 *Cent. L.J.* 651, 651–52 (1876).

14. Herbert Bruce Fuller, *The Law of Accident and Employers' Liability Insurance* 128–41 (1913); McNeill, *A Study of Accidents,* 98.

15. McNeill, *A Study of Accidents*, 98.
16. Fuller, *The Law of Accident*, 260; see McNeill, *A Study of Accidents*, 100.
17. See generally Fuller, *The Law of Accident*, 87–288 (including, inter alia, injuries sustained on a railroad bed or bridge and those sustained from inhaling gas; entering, leaving, or standing on moving cars; bodily infirmities; and disease); McNeill, *A Study of Accidents*, 98–100.
18. McNeill, *A Study of Accidents*, 100.
19. Id., 105.
20. Mark Twain, "Speech at the Hartford Accident Insurance Company, Hartford, Conn. (Oct. 12, 1874)," in *Mark Twain Speaking* 89, 91 (Paul Fatout ed., 1976); Nan Goodman, *Shifting the Blame: Literature, Law, and the Theory of Accidents in Nineteenth-Century America* 91 (1998).
21. Malvin E. Davis, *Industrial Life Insurance in the United States* 3–24 (1944).
22. Stalson, *Marketing Life Insurance*, 809.
23. Robert Coit Chapin, *The Standard of Living among Workingmen's Families in New York City* 191 (1909); see also Charles Richmond Henderson, *Industrial Insurance in the United States* 150 (1909) (estimating the average policy value in 1899 at slightly more than $100).
24. Chapin, *The Standard of Living*, 191.
25. Maurice Taylor, *The Social Cost of Industrial Insurance* 54–56 (1933).
26. Kenneth S. Abraham, *Distributing Risk: Insurance, Legal Theory, and Public Policy* (1986); Tom Baker, "On the Genealogy of Moral Hazard," 75 *Tex. L. Rev.* 237, 239–40 (1996).
27. August Sartorius von Waltershausen, *The Workers' Movement in the United States, 1879–1885*, p. 197 (David Montgomery and Marcel van der Linden eds., 1998)(1885).
28. See James B. Kennedy, *Beneficiary Features of American Trade Unions* 9–10 (1908).
29. *Twenty-Third Annual Report of the Commissioner of Labor: Workmen's Insurance and Benefit Funds in the United States* 23, 29–30 (1909).
30. Waltershausen, *The Workers' Movement*, 198; *Twenty-Third Annual Report of the Commissioner of Labor*, 23.
31. Kennedy, *Beneficiary Features of American Trade Unions*, 9–10.
32. The Cigar Makers' Union created a death benefit program in 1867, as did the Iron Molders' Union in 1870 and the Granite Cutters' Union in 1877. After 1880 a number of trade unions established similar death benefit programs; by 1904, 53 of 117 national unions affiliated with the American Federation of Labor provided death benefits for their membership. 24 *Proceedings of the Annual Convention of the American Federation of Labor* 46 (1904). In these nonrailway union programs, the death benefit seldom exceeded the cost of burial. Kennedy, *Beneficiary Features of American Trade Unions*, 53 n.12.
33. Terence V. Powderly, *Thirty Years of Labor: 1859 to 1889*, p. 453 (Columbus, Ohio, Rankin and O'Neal 1890); Nick Salvatore, *Eugene V. Debs: Citizen and Socialist* 112 (1982); Kennedy, *Beneficiary Features of American Trade Unions*, 72.
34. Salvatore, *Eugene V. Debs*, 20; Walter Licht, *Working for the Railroad: The Organization of Work in the Nineteenth Century* 242–43 (1983).

35. Kennedy, *Beneficiary Features of American Trade Unions*, 49.
36. Id.; Emory R. Johnson, "Railway Relief Departments," in 8 *Bulletin of the United States Department of Labor* 39, 39 (Washington, D.C., Gov't Printing Office 1897).
37. Johnson, "Railway Relief Departments," 78; Kennedy, *Beneficiary Features of American Trade Unions*, 41.
38. *Twenty-Third Annual Report of the Commissioner of Labor*, 32.
39. Benefits Recordbook, Brotherhood of Railroad Trainmen Papers, box 22, KC.
40. *Twenty-Third Annual Report of the Commissioner of Labor*, 79.
41. Switchmen's Union of North America Papers, folder 5, box 163; folder B-4, box 163; and book 1, box 269, KC.
42. For a discussion of the membership numbers, see Kennedy, *Beneficiary Features of American Trade Unions*, 20–29. For the total numbers of railroad workers in the late nineteenth and early twentieth centuries, see 1 Bureau of the Census, U.S. Department of Commerce, *Historical Statistics of the United States, Colonial Times to 1970*, p. 139 (1975).
43. For a discussion of the seven great railway brotherhoods, see Kennedy, *Beneficiary Features of American Trade Unions*, 19.
44. *Twenty-Third Annual Report of the Commissioner of Labor*, 48, 50.
45. Stalson, *Marketing Life Insurance*, 818–19.
46. Id., 819. This $6.6 billion figure accounts for Stalson's estimate of 20 percent underreporting by fraternal societies.
47. See 72 *Ann. Rep. Superintendent of the Ins. Dep't of the State of N.Y.*, pt. II, p. xxiii (1931). State insurance reports provide only a partial state-by-state picture of fraternal insurance association membership before the turn of the century.
48. Meyer, "Fraternal Beneficiary Societies in the United States," 647.
49. Id.; see also Kip, *Fraternal Life Insurance in America*, 15 (estimating 6.5 million members in 1910). The number of life insurance company policyholders kept pace, doubling to over 6 million by 1910. See *Ann. Rep. N.Y. Superintendent*, xxiii.
50. E.g., *Fourth Biennial Report of the Bureau of Labor Statistics of the State of California*, 102; "Insurance Law as a Specialty," 2 *Yale L.J.* 145, 145 (1893).
51. *Seventh Annual Report of the Bureau of Labor Statistics of the State of Connecticut for the Year Ending Nov. 30, 1891*, at 113 (Hartford, Fowler and Miller 1892) *(Connecticut Report)*.
52. The study found that 118,613 of 126,613 members were men. Id., 68.
53. David Beito concludes that during the late nineteenth century one in three adult males participated in fraternal cooperative insurance societies nationwide. See David T. Beito, "Thy Brother's Keeper: The Mutual Aid Tradition of American Fraternal Orders," 70 *Pol'y Rev.* 55, 56 (1994).
54. See *Connecticut Report*, 109, 111, 113.
55. George Emery and J. C. Herbert Emery, *A Young Man's Benefit: The Independent Order of Odd Fellows and Sickness Insurance in the United States and Canada, 1860–1929*, pp. 50–51 (1999).
56. See, e.g., Hutchinson v. Supreme Tent of Maccabees of the World, 22 N.Y.S. 801, 801–4 (Gen. Term 1893) (describing the $2,000 life insurance benefit and

$1,000 permanent disability benefit of the Maccabees of the World); *Connecticut Report,* 169 (describing the $1,000 life insurance benefit of the Knights of Columbus); R. C. Hill, "The Evolution of an Idea," *Fraternal Monitor,* Aug. 1, 1890, p. 2 (describing the $2,000 life insurance benefit of the Ancient Order of United Workmen).

57. See 1 *Historical Statistics of the United States,* 168 (estimating average annual wages in manufacturing and railroad occupations in 1890 at $439 and $560, respectively).

58. Emery and Emery, *Young Man's Benefit,* 52–53; Beito, *From Mutual Aid to Welfare State,* 12.

59. *Connecticut Report,* 168 (describing the $5 per week disability benefits offered through the local lodges of the Knights of Columbus); id., 231 (describing the $2 to $5 disability benefits offered through the local lodges of the Ancient Order of United Workmen); *Fourth Biennial Report of the Bureau of Labor Statistics of the State of California,* 117, 128, 131.

60. *Fourth Biennial Report of the Bureau of Labor Statistics of the State of California,* 122.

61. See *Twenty-Third Annual Report of the Commissioner of Labor,* 17–18; *Connecticut Report;* Waltershausen, *The Workers' Movement in the United States,* 192, 205–18.

62. *Connecticut Report,* 85.

63. Randolph J. Brodsky, "The Advisability of Fraternal Insurance as a System of Workingmen's Insurance," *Fraternal Monitor,* Sept. 1910, pp. 16, 17.

64. Peter Roberts, *Anthracite Coal Communities* 252 (1904); Mildred Allen Beik, *The Miners of Windber: The Struggles of New Immigrants for Unionization 1890s–1930s* (1996); Joe William Trotter Jr., *Coal, Class, and Color: Blacks in Southern West Virginia, 1915–1932* (1990).

65. *Constitution and By-Laws of the Bricklayers' and Plasterers' Benevolent and Protective Union* 12 (New Haven, Pettle, Morehouse and Taylor 1868).

66. See David Montgomery, *Beyond Equality: Labor and the Radical Republicans 1862–1872,* appendix D, p. 467 (1967); 15 *American National Biography* 170, 170–71 (John A. Garraty and Mark C. Carnes eds., 1999); 12 *Dictionary of American Biography* 150, 150–51 (Dumas Malone ed., 1933).

67. 15 *American National Biography,* 171.

68. Co-Operative Association of America, *National Co-Operative Conference at Lewiston, Maine, June 20–24, 1902* (Pamphlets in American History: Cooperative Societies, Microfilming Corp. of America 1980) (handbill listing George McNeill, "'the grand old man'" of the labor movement, as the lead speaker).

69. *The Labor Movement: The Problem of Today* 455, 466, 468, 463 (George McNeill ed., Boston, A. M. Bridgman 1887).

70. See McNeill, *A Study of Accidents,* 47. More than four of every ten accidents reported to the association by its members were work-related, as compared to only 1.5 of every ten for the next largest category, accidents "about house and grounds."

71. Clawson, *Constructing Brotherhood,* 100–1.

72. Beito, *From Mutual Aid to Welfare State,* 220.

73. Historians of nineteenth-century fraternal associations have emphasized the fraternals' middle-class membership. These studies, however, have been preoccupied with the elite associations of the fraternal world, whose records are often more complete than those of the cooperative fraternal insurance associations of the working class. E.g., Mark C. Carnes, *Secret Ritual and Manhood in Victorian America* 3–4 (1989); Clawson, *Constructing Brotherhood*, 87–110; Lynn Dumenil, *Freemasonry and American Culture, 1880–1930*, p. 9 (1984); Daniel Greenberg, "Worker and Community: Fraternal Orders in Albany, New York, 1845–1885," 8 *Maryland Historian* 38, 43 (1977); Roy Rosenzweig, "Boston Masons, 1900–1935: The Lower Middle Class in a Divided Society," 6 *J. Voluntary Action Res.* 119, 124 (1977).

74. *Connecticut Report*, 12; see also *Twenty-Third Annual Report of the Commissioner of Labor*, 15; Henderson, *Industrial Insurance in the United States*, 117; Waltershausen, *The Workers' Movement in the United States*, 171–230.

75. *Connecticut Report*, 105.

76. "The Order of the World," *Fraternal Monitor*, Aug. 1, 1890, p. 12; see also National Fraternal Congress, *Journal of Proceedings, Nov. 21, 1888*, pp. 15–16 (Chicago, National Fraternal Congress 1889); *Constitution of the Universal Workmen's Sick and Death Benefit Fund of the United States of North America* 3–4 (New York, John Oehler, Steam Book and Job Printer 1893) *(Sick and Death Benefit Fund); General Laws, Rules and Regulations of the Beneficiary Degree, Junior Order of United American Mechanics* 10 (1905).

77. E.g., *Sick and Death Benefit Fund*, 5.

78. "Legal Environments," *Fraternal Monitor*, Oct. 1, 1890, p. 14.

79. *Sick and Death Benefit Fund*, 5–7.

80. People ex rel. Doyle v. N.Y. Benevolent Soc'y of Operative Masons, 6 Thompson and Cook 85, 86–89 (N.Y. Sup. Ct. 1875) (requiring a society to reinstate a member after his expulsion without notice and a hearing, but suggesting that such an expulsion would be allowable in the event of proper notice and a hearing); Cartan v. Father Matthew United Benevolent Soc'y, 3 Daly 20, 20–22 (N.Y. Ct. Comm. Pl. 1869) (holding that a society's refusal to pay disability benefits on the ground that the member was delinquent in paying dues was unreasonable); St. Mary's Beneficial Soc'y v. Burford, 70 Pa. 321, 323–25 (1872) (upholding a denial of benefits because the member's intemperance caused his death).

81. *Connecticut Report*, 232–35.

82. E.g., *Bricklayers' and Plasterers' Constitution*, 7; Carnes, *Secret Ritual and Manhood in Victorian America*, 104–7; Theo. A. Ross, *Odd Fellowship: Its History and Manual* 575–87 (New York, M. W. Hazen 1888); Albert C. Stevens, *The Cyclopaedia of Fraternities* (New York, Hamilton 1899).

83. See William Morse Cole, "Co-Operative Insurance and Endowment Schemes," 5 *Q.J. Econ.* 466, 469–70 (1891).

84. Hill, "The Evolution of an Idea," 2 (calculating the average annual number of assessments in the Ancient Order of United Workmen between 1875 and 1890 as seventeen).

85. Cole, "Co-Operative Insurance and Endowment Schemes," 471.

86. Id.
87. Insurance Research and Review Service, *Fraternal Life Insurance* 30 (1938).
88. *Connecticut Report,* 119.
89. Stevens, *The Cyclopaedia of Fraternities,* 128.
90. See, e.g., id. 123, 137, 141 (discussing the American Legion of Honor, the Home Palladium, and the Independent Order of Mechanics).
91. Stevens, *The Cyclopaedia of Fraternities,* 131; see also M. S. Stuart, *An Economic Detour: A History of Insurance in the Lives of American Negroes* 11–34 (1969); Monroe N. Work, "Secret Societies as Factors in the Social and Economical Life of the Negro," in *Democracy in Earnest: Southern Sociological Congress, 1916–1918,* p. 342 (James E. McCulloch ed., 1969) (1918).
92. A black beneficiary organization called the Improved Benevolent and Protective Order of Elks existed until 1912, when the Benevolent and Protective Order of the Elks, a white association, obtained an order restraining the black association from using the elk as its namesake. Arthur Preuss, *A Dictionary of Secret and Other Societies* 324–28 (1924). White associations strictly prohibited their members from fraternizing with members of the parallel black organizations. "The Negro Odd Fellows," wrote one Catholic lawyer, "are not recognized by the white lodges of the same name and a member of one of these white lodges who might visit a colored lodge, if indeed he could, would be expelled." Id., 327.
93. Elsa Barkley Brown, "Womanist Consciousness: Maggie Lena Walker and the Independent Order of Saint Luke," 14 *Signs* 610, 616 (1989); Anne Firor Scott, "Most Invisible of All: Black Women's Voluntary Associations," 56 *J.S. Hist.* 3 (1990).
94. Stuart, *An Economic Detour,* 19–20.
95. Juliet E. K. Walker, *The History of Black Business in America: Capitalism, Race, Entrepreneurship* 166, 187, 411 nn.26–30 (1998).
96. Id., 188.
97. See Glenda Elizabeth Gilmore, *Gender and Jim Crow* 165–66 (1996); Alexa Benson Henderson, *Atlanta Life Insurance Company: Guardian of Black Economic Dignity* 3–19 (1990); Walker, *History of Black Business,* 189–90; Walter B. Weare, *Black Business in the New South: A Social History of the North Carolina Mutual Life Insurance Company* (1973).
98. See W. E. B. Du Bois, *The Philadelphia Negro: A Social Study* 221–25 (Schocken Books 1970) (1899); Nick Salvatore, *We All Got History: The Memory Books of Amos Webber* 59–67 (1996).
99. Charles W. Ferguson, *Fifty Million Brothers: A Panorama of American Lodges and Clubs* 301–3 (1937).
100. See Daniel Soyer, *Jewish Immigrant Associations and American Identity in New York, 1880–1939* (1997); Beik, *The Miners of Windber,* 125–26.
101. I borrow the terms "thin" and "thick" from the political theory literature on the difference between "thin" or minimalist theories of justice, on one hand, which require few substantive commitments to particular notions of the good and take persons as prior to the rich particularities that constitute their ends, and "thick" or full theories of justice, on the other hand, which entail more significant com-

mitments to particular conceptions of the good and take persons as necessarily encumbered by a rich set of social attachments. See John Rawls, *A Theory of Justice* 396–99 (1971); John Rawls, *Political Liberalism* 178 (1993); Michael J. Sandel, *Liberalism and the Limits of Justice* 50–65, 120–21 (1982).

102. Philip Green Wright and Elizabeth Q. Wright, *Elizur Wright: The Father of Life Insurance* 1 (1937). For accounts of the New England antebellum reformers, see generally Robert H. Abzug, *Cosmos Crumbling: American Reform and the Religious Imagination* (1994); Lawrence J. Friedman, *Gregarious Saints: Self and Community in American Abolitionism, 1830–1870* (1982); Peter F. Walker, *Moral Choices: Memory, Desire, and Imagination in Nineteenth-Century American Abolition* (1978); Ronald G. Walters, *The Antislavery Appeal: American Abolitionism after 1830* (1976).

103. Lawrence B. Goodheart, *Abolitionist, Actuary, Atheist: Elizur Wright and the Reform Impulse* 44 (1990). On human perfectibility and abolitionism, see David Brion Davis, *The Problem of Slavery in Western Culture* 333–64 (1966).

104. Goodheart, *Abolitionist, Actuary, Atheist,* 41.

105. Id., 103.

106. Id., 103–4, 117, 124.

107. R. Carlyle Buley, *The American Life Convention, 1906–1952: A Study in the History of Life Insurance* 57–59 (1953); Stalson, *Marketing Life Insurance,* 232–34; Wright and Wright, *The Father of Life Insurance,* 220–39. Many others were led to life insurance by commercial tragedies in the form of bankruptcy. See Edward Balleisen, *Navigating Failure: Bankruptcy and Commercial Society in Antebellum America* (2001).

108. Goodheart, *Abolitionist, Actuary, Atheist,* 148.

109. Id., 145.

110. For discussion of the eighteenth-century background for the perceived relationship between life insurance and gambling, see generally Buley, *The American Life Convention, 1906–1952,* pp. 13–26; Geoffrey Clark, *Betting on Lives: The Culture of Life Insurance in England, 1695–1775* (1999); Viviana Zelizer, *Morals and Markets: The Development of Life Insurance in the United States* (1979).

111. Goodheart, *Abolitionist, Actuary, Atheist,* 176. For Wright's response to the persistent gambling critique of life insurance, see Stalson, *Marketing Life Insurance,* 151–52.

112. See Goodheart, *Abolitionist, Actuary, Atheist,* 165.

113. See id., 208.

114. See *Connecticut Report,* 66.

115. "Paternalism," *Fraternal Monitor,* Feb. 1, 1891, p. 12.

116. Walter S. Waldie, *American Co-Operative Labor Social Economy vs. Monarchial Labor Degrading Social Economy* 24 (Philadelphia, Sherman 1871).

117. J. M. Bloomer, *The Cooperative Educator: A Key to the Mines of Wealth Accessible to Honest Producers Who Think and Act for Themselves* 2 (Toledo, News Publ'g Co. 1888).

118. Waldie, *American Co-Operative Labor Social Economy.*

119. Bloomer, *The Cooperative Educator,* 9.

120. William Haller, *The New Idea: Universal Co-operation and Theories of Future Government* 8 (Cincinnati, H. Watkin, n.d.).

121. Franklin Henry Giddings, *Twelve Principles of Cooperation* (New York, Sociologic Soc'y (1887).

122. *Labor Movement: The Problem of Today,* 490.

123. McNeill, *A Study of Accidents,* 65.

124. John Fabian Witt, Note, "The Transformation of Work and the Law of Workplace Accidents, 1842–1910," 107 *Yale L.J.* 1467, 1481–82, 1482 n.79 (1998). In New York in the 1850s, labor activists advocated land reform, mechanics' lien laws, minimum wage legislation for public works, maximum hours legislation, and repeal of the law of labor conspiracy, but not employers' liability reform. See "The Congress of Trades," *N.Y. Herald,* July 26, 1850, p. 1; "The New-York City Industrial Congress," *N.Y. Daily Trib.,* Sept. 25, 1850, p. 8.

125. See 9 *A Documentary History of American Industrial Society* 224 (John R. Commons and John B. Andrews eds., 1910).

126. Robert Asher, "Failure and Fulfillment: Agitation for Employers' Liability Legislation and the Origins of Workmen's Compensation in New York State, 1876–1910," 24 *Labor Hist.* 198, 202–3 (1983); Witt, "The Transformation of Work," 1482 n.79.

127. Salvatore, *Eugene V. Debs,* 42–43.

128. William Graebner, *Coal-Mining Safety in the Progressive Period: The Political Economy of Reform* 128 (1976).

129. David Montgomery, *Workers Control in America* (1979); David Montgomery, *The Fall of the House of Labor: The Workplace, the State, and American Labor Activism, 1865–1925* (1987); Walter Licht, *Industrializing America: The Nineteenth Century* (1995); John K. Brown, *The Baldwin Locomotive Works 1831–1915,* pp. 125, 130–32 (1995); John Buttrick, "The Inside Contract System," 12 *J. Econ. Hist.* 205 (1952); Ernest J. Englander, "The Inside Contract System of Production and Organization: A Neglected Aspect of the History of the Firm," 28 *Lab. Hist.* 429 (1987); Charles F. Sabel and Jonathan Zeitlin, "Historical Alternatives to Mass Production: Politics, Markets and Technology in Nineteenth-Century Industrialization," 108 *Past and Present* 133 (1985).

130. Antonio Gramsci, *Selections from the Prison Notebooks* 247 (Quintin Hoare and Geoffrey Nowell Smith eds. and trans., International Publishers 1971) (1948); see also Eugene Genovese, *Roll, Jordan, Roll: The World the Slaves Made* 27 (1974); Witt, "The Transformation of Work," 1480 and n.74.

131. Clawson, *Constructing Brotherhood,* 100–1; Montgomery, *Beyond Equality,* 218.

132. Nelson Booth, *Experiences as Co-Operators* 6 (n.p., n.d.).

133. *Prospectus of the American Workers' Alliance for the Advancement of Educational, Industrial, Cooperative, and Social Reform* 6 (Washington, The Alliance 1879).

134. William Nelson Black, *Ultimate Finance: A True Theory of Co-operation,* appendix, p. 42 (New York, Humboldt 1888).

135. Waltershausen, *The Workers' Movement in the United States,* 198. The editors very likely referred to the passage in which Marx argued that wages were set according to the labor time necessary to sustain and reproduce the workforce but

observed that the minimum necessities of any given workforce are themselves inevitably "products of history, and depend therefore . . . on the habits and expectations with which, the class of free workers has been formed." 1 Karl Marx, *Capital* 275 (Ben Fowkes trans., Penguin Books 1990) (1867).

136. Waltershausen, *The Workers' Movement in the United States,* 198; see also "Tim's Plan," *United Mine Workers' J.,* Jan. 10, 1895, p. 1.

137. Waltershausen, *The Workers' Movement in the United States,* 198. This Marxian theory of charging employers "for the care of their victims" via increases in wage levels resembles in certain respects the contemporary law and economics theory that parties to contracts will freely contract around liability rules so long as transaction costs are sufficiently low, see R. H. Coase, "The Problem of Social Cost," 3 *J.L. and Econ.* 1 (1960). The Marxian approach, however, goes one step beyond the law and economics theory to posit an account of the construction of the parties' norms, expectations, and preferences.

138. *Fraternal Monitor,* Dec. 1, 1894, p. 7.

139. Abb Landis, "Life Insurance by Fraternal Orders," 24 *AAAPSS* 475, 487–88 (1904).

140. "The Co-Operative Association of America," *Co-operator,* Nov. 1891, p. 4.

141. E.g., Davis v. Supreme Lodge Knights of Honor, 54 N.Y.S. 1023, 1024 (App. Div. 1898) (upholding a claim for benefits where an association alleged that the decedent had misrepresented his family's history of consumption).

142. E.g., Foley v. Royal Arcanum, 45 N.E. 456, 457 (N.Y. 1896).

143. Cole, "Co-Operative Insurance and Endowment Schemes," 470.

144. Henderson, *Industrial Insurance in the United States,* 117.

145. Cole, "Co-Operative Insurance and Endowment Schemes," 474.

146. *Fraternal Monitor,* Nov. 1, 1894, p. 9.

147. William C. Niblack, *The Law of Voluntary Societies and Mutual Benefit Insurance* § 162, p. 191 (Chicago, Callaghan 1888).

148. Meyer, *Fraternal Beneficiary Societies in the United States,* 655–56.

149. 26 *Ann. Rep. Superintendent of the Ins. Dep't of the State of N.Y.,* pt. II, p. xi (Albany, Weed, Parsons 1885); 27 *Ann. Rep. Superintendent of the Ins. Dep't of the State of N.Y.,* pt. II, pp. xviii–xix (Albany, Argus 1886); 29 *Ann. Rep. Superintendent of the Ins. Dep't of the State of N.Y.,* pts. II, III, p. xxviii (n.p., Troy Press 1888); *31 Ann. Rep. Superintendent of the Ins. Dep't of the State of N.Y.,* pts. II, III, p. xxv (Albany, J. B. Lyon 1890); 46 *Ann. Rep. Superintendent of the Ins. Dep't of the State of N.Y.,* pts. III, IV, pp. xxii–xxvi (Albany, J. B. Lyon 1905).

150. See "Contracts of Insurance," 3 *University L. Rev.* 297, 297 (1897). Commercial policies denied claims on a variety of grounds, including voluntary assumption of increased risk, self-inflicted wounds, failure to maintain "sober and temperate habits," and death or disability from any number of causes that either posed risks of moral hazard or suggested the possibility of an undisclosed preexisting condition. George Bliss Jr. *The Law of Life Insurance with Chapters upon Accident and Guarantee Insurance* 134–80 (New York, Baker, Voorhis 1872); see Dexter Reynolds, *Treatise on the Law of Life Assurance* 85–113 (Albany, Gould, Banks 1853); William Reynolds Vance, *Handbook of the Law of Insurance* 524–27 (1904); see also Spencer L. Kimball, *Insurance and Public Policy: A*

Study in the Legal Implementation of Social and Economic Public Policy, Based on Wisconsin Records, 1835–1959, p. 211 (1960) (noting that company lawyers viewed contract drafting as a game to be played against the courts).

151. Frederick H. Cooke, *The Law of Life Insurance including Accident Insurance and Insurance by Mutual Benefit Societies* § 3, pp. 3–4 (New York, Baker, Voorhis 1891); Vance, *Handbook of the Law of Insurance*, 429–30.

152. Lawrence M. Friedman, *Contract Law in America: A Social and Economic Case Study* (1965); Lawrence M. Friedman, *A History of American Law* 545–49 (2d ed. 1985).

153. Frederick H. Bacon, *A Treatise on the Law of Benefit Societies and Incidentally of Life Insurance* § 78, at 94 (St. Louis, F. H. Thomas 1888) (explaining that "Benefit Societies doing a Life Insurance Business are like other Life Insurance Corporations" and that "[t]he contracts of all [cooperative or assessment companies] must be judged by the laws applicable to all similar contracts of other corporations"). See also id., § 468, pp. 704–5; Cooke, *The Law of Life Insurance* § 3, pp. 3–4.

154. See "Insurance Law as a Specialty," 147–48 (ascribing high rates of cooperative insurance litigation to the cooperatives' reliance on lay persons to draft policies). Consider the example of the Maccabees' persistently frustrated policy-drafting. In 1887 the Maccabees amended the disability provision of their bylaws. Under the new provision, a member was entitled to disability benefits if he became "unable to direct or perform the kind of business or labor which he has always followed, and by which alone he can thereafter earn a livelihood." Notwithstanding this restrictive language, at least one court required payment of disability benefits to a member who lost the fingers of his right hand while coupling railroad cars. Hutchinson v. Supreme Tent of Knights of Maccabees of the World, 22 N.Y.S. 801, 801–4 (Gen. Term 1893). In response the Maccabees amended the disability provision again to provide disability benefits only to members unable "to perform *or direct any kind* of labor or business." Beach v. Supreme Tent of Knights of Maccabees of the World, 77 N.Y.S. 770, 771 (App. Div. 1902) (quoting the defendant's bylaws) (emphasis added). Once again, however, courts defeated the Maccabees' own interpretation of their disability provision and held in favor of disabled members. Id., 772, 775 (requiring payment of disability benefits to a member who lost the use of his right arm in a workplace sawmill accident, even though he could still direct and supervise work in the sawmill).

155. On rules versus standards, see Duncan Kennedy, "Form and Substance in Private Law Adjudication," 89 *Harv. L. Rev.* 1685 (1976).

156. "Amendment by a Mutual Benefit Society of Its Contract of Insurance," 37 *Cent. L.J.* 86, 87 (1893); see Bacon, *A Treatise on the Law of Benefit Societies* § 92, pp. 109–10. The leading cases on retroactive amendment of benefits provisions were disability insurance cases, in which moral hazard issues were likely to be more of a problem than in life insurance cases. See id.

157. "Expulsion of Members of Corporations and Societies," 24 *Am. L. Rev.* 537, § 4, pp. 539–41 (1890); see also Bacon, *A Treatise on the Law of Benefit Societies* §§ 95–111, pp. 113–40.

158. E.g., Sheppard Homans, *Limitations of Assessment Insurance* (New York, Spectator 1895); Francis B. Forbes, "Notes on Fraternal Beneficiary Corporations Doing Business in Massachusetts," 8 *Publications Am. Stat. Ass'n* 1, 2–3 (1902) (calling for greater state oversight of the cooperative insurance societies). Some of the criticism of fraternals came from commercial insurance companies, which rightly perceived fraternals as competitors in the life insurance market. See Keller, *The Life Insurance Enterprise*, 71.

159. E.g., "Editorial," *Fraternal Monitor*, Sept. 1, 1890, p. 8; see also "Annual Report of the Committee on Statistics and Good of the Orders," *Fraternal Monitor*, Aug. 1, 1911, pp. 16–18.

160. See Frank P. Bennett, "The 'Endowment' Craze in Massachusetts," 1892 *Am. J. Pol.* 514; Cole, "Co-Operative Insurance and Endowment Schemes," 487–93.

161. "A Good Illustration," *Fraternal Monitor*, Sept. 1, 1890, p. 14.

162. Advertisement, "The Iron Hall," *Fraternal Monitor*, Sept. 1, 1890, p. 1; "A Good Illustration," 14; Advertisement, "The Anti-Poverty Association of the Age," *Fraternal Monitor*, Oct. 1, 1890, p. 19; Cole, "Co-Operative Insurance and Endowment Schemes," 488; see also Bennett, "The 'Endowment' Craze in Massachusetts," 515.

163. 23 *Ann. Rep. Superintendent of the Ins. Dep't of the State of N.Y.*, pt. I, pp. lx–lxi (Albany, Weed, Parsons 1882); 26 *Ann. Rep. Superintendent of the Ins. Dep't of the State of N.Y.*, pt. II, p. xxx (Albany, Weed, Parsons 1885).

164. Glines v. Supreme Sitting of Order of Iron Hall, 21 N.Y.S. 543, 544 (Gen. Term 1892); 1894 Mass. Acts 367; "A Fraternal Beneficiary Society," *Fraternal Monitor*, Jan. 1, 1895, p. 7; New York State Department of Labor, *Annual Report of the Bureau of Industries and Immigration* 100 (1911).

165. Werner Pfennigstorf with Donald G. Gifford, *A Comparative Study of Liability Law and Compensation Schemes in Ten Countries and the United States* 158 (1991); George L. Priest, "Compensation for Injury in the United States," in *Compensation for Personal Injury in Sweden and Other Countries* 127, 138 (Carl Oldertz and Eva Tidefelt eds., 1988); Deborah R. Hensler et al., *Compensation for Accidental Injuries in the United States* 101 (1991); *Report of the Royal Commission on Civil Liability and Compensation for Personal Injury* 13 table 4 (1978); Richard A. Posner, "Explaining the Variance in the Number of Tort Suits across U.S. States and between the United States and England," 26 *J. Legal Stud.* 477, 478–79 (1997).

166. See generally P. H. J. H. Gosden, *Self-Help: Voluntary Associations in the 19th Century* (1973); P. H. J. H. Gosden, *The Friendly Societies in England, 1815–1875* (1961); Eric Hopkins, *Working-Class Self-Help in Nineteenth-Century England* (1995).

167. Geoffrey Finlayson, *Citizen, State, and Social Welfare in Britain, 1830–1990*, pp. 80–88, 166–67, 176 (1994); E. P. Hennock, *British Reform and German Precedents: The Case of Social Insurance 1880–1914*, p. 195 (1987).

168. See A. I. Ogus, "Great Britain," in *The Evolution of Social Insurance 1881–1981: Studies of Germany, France, Great Britain, Austria, and Switzerland* 150, 185 (Peter A. Köhler and Hans F. Zacher eds., with Martin Partington, 1982). The fact that, by 1910, many friendly societies were employer-managed relief funds

rather than workingmen's self-insurance cooperatives somewhat complicates the story of the implementation of friendly societies into the national insurance scheme. See J. R. Hay, "Employers' Attitudes to Social Policy and the Concept of 'Social Control,' 1900–1920," in *The Origins of British Social Policy* 107, 119 (Pat Thane ed., 1978).

169. See Ogus, "Great Britain," 150, 185.

170. Bentley B. Gilbert, *The Evolution of National Insurance in Great Britain: The Origins of the Welfare State* 316–43 (1966); Ogus, "Great Britain," 150, 185; J. G. Crownhart, *Sickness Insurance in Europe* 69 (1938); W. A. Dinsdale, *History of Accident Insurance in Great Britain* 19–21 (1954).

171. Gerhard A. Ritter, *Social Welfare in Germany and Britain* 56–58, 69 (1983); Hennock, *British Reform and German Precedents*, 202–3.

172. I. M. Rubinow, *Social Insurance: With Special Reference to American Conditions* 240 (1913).

173. I. M. Rubinow, "Labor Insurance," 12 *J. Pol. Econ.* 362, 362–63 (1904); Henderson, *Industrial Insurance in the United States*, 83.

174. National Fraternal Congress, *Journal of Proceedings* (1888), 1–3.

175. Id., 38.

176. See National Fraternal Congress, *Report of the Special Commission on Rates* 2–8 (1899); Meyer, *Fraternal Beneficiary Societies in the United States*, 652.

177. See Beito, *From Mutual Aid to Welfare State*, 137; National Fraternal Congress, *Uniform Bill Relating to Fraternal Beneficiary Associations* 8–9 (1905).

178. "One National Organization," *Fraternal Monitor*, Apr. 1, 1912, p. 18.

179. A. I. Vorys, "National Supervision," *Fraternal Monitor*, Aug. 1, 1911, pp. 23, 23–27; "Editorial," *Fraternal Monitor*, Oct. 1, 1911, p. 10; Olin Bryan, "National Insurance Supervision—Its Objections and Disadvantages," *Fraternal Monitor*, Oct. 1, 1911, p. 13.

180. National Fraternal Congress, *Report of John J. Hynes, President* 7–8 (1911).

181. Beito, *From Mutual Aid to Welfare State*, 142.

182. E.g., "Paternalism," *Fraternal Monitor*, Feb. 1, 1891, p. 12.

183. E.g., *Fraternal Monitor*, Aug. 1, 1911, p. 18.

184. E.g., *Fraternal Monitor*, Nov. 1, 1911, p. 6.

185. Gilbert, *Evolution of National Insurance*, 160–88; Hennock, *British Reform and German Precedents*.

186. E.g., 15 *The Works of Theodore Roosevelt* 501 (1926) (Dec. 8, 1908 annual message to Congress).

187. 1 *Twenty-Fourth Annual Report of the Commissioner of Labor, 1909: Workmen's Insurance and Compensation Systems in Europe* 3 (1911).

188. See generally John Bodnar, *The Transplanted: A History of Immigrants in Urban America* 120–30 (1985); Oscar Handlin, *The Uprooted: The Epic Story of the Great Migrations That Made the American People* 170–201 (1952).

189. Lizabeth Cohen, *Making a New Deal: Industrial Workers in Chicago, 1919–1939*, pp. 64–72 (1990); Soyer, *Jewish Immigrant Associations and American Identity*, 81–112.

190. Hill, "The Evolution of an Idea," 2. In 1890 the Ancient Order of United Workmen estimated that $2,000 in fraternal insurance cost $21 yearly. Id.

191. *WCR,* 26; see also Chapin, *The Standard of Living,* 191–92, 307–10 (making similar findings in local studies of New York City and Buffalo). The Wainwright Commission study of 211 industrial fatalities from Erie County and Manhattan in 1907 and 1908 found that 57 percent of decedents earning less than $16 per week received no insurance payments at all, whereas 70 percent of decedents earning $16 per week or more received insurance payments of some kind. Even within the high-wages group, however, almost half the decedents' families received less than $500 in insurance payments.
192. Cohen, *Making a New Deal,* 65–66.
193. Crystal Eastman, *Work-Accidents and the Law* 134 (1910).
194. Cohen, *Making a New Deal,* 65.
195. Witt, "The Transformation of Work," 1469–84.
196. Today's accident-law literature commonly makes the point that first-party or social insurance approaches require supplementary command-and-control deterrence and safety regulations. E.g., Guido Calabresi, *The Costs of Accidents: A Legal and Economic Analysis* 284–85 (1970).
197. See, e.g., P. Tecumseh Sherman to Jonathan Mayhew Wainwright (Dec. 8, 1909), folder for July to December 1909, box 6, JMW; Graebner, *Coal-Mining Safety in the Progressive Period,* 72–111; folder for Factory Inspection, 1914–1930, box 3, AALLP. The highly successful 1893 federal legislation requiring automatic couplers was a rare exception to the general failure of regulatory control. See Mark Aldrich, *Safety First: Technology, Labor, and Business in the Building of American Work Safety, 1870–1939,* p. 37 (1997). Other federal railroad safety requirements had mixed effects on railroad accident rates; air brakes, for example, allowed railroad companies to increase the length and speed of their trains. See id. 38.
198. Donald W. Rogers, "From Common Law to Factory Laws: The Transformation of Workplace Safety Law in Wisconsin before Progressivism," 39 *Am. J. Legal Hist.* 177, 196–208 (1995).
199. See R. Rudy Higgens-Evenson, "From Industrial Police to Workmen's Compensation: Public Policy and Industrial Accidents in New York, 1880–1910," 39 *Lab. Hist.* 365, 369–70 (1998); *WCR,* 61–62.
200. *Report of the Employers' Liability and Workmen's Compensation Commission for the State of Iowa* 19 (1912); Carl Gersuny, *Work Hazards and Industrial Conflict* 31 (1981); *Industrial Accident Prevention: An Address by R. W. Cambpell, Chairman of Committee of Safety, Illinois Steel Co.* 1 (1911).
201. James R. Pitcher, "Accidents and Accident Insurance," 12 *Forum* 131, 134 (1891).
202. Woods, "Accidents in Factories and Elsewhere," 316–17; *WCR,* 7; Joint Conference of the Central Labor Bodies of the City of New York, Brief in Favor of a Compensation Act 7 (1910), folder for Workmen's Compensation 1908–1910, box 11, AALLP; P. Tecumseh Sherman to Jonathan Mayhew Wainwright (Dec. 8, 1909), folder for July to December 1909, box 6, JMW.
203. Randolph J. Brodsky, "The Advisability of Fraternal Insurance as a System of Workingmen's Insurance," *Fraternal Monitor,* Sept. 1910, pp. 16, 17.
204. Figures derive from Table 3.1.

205. See Stalson, *Marketing Life Insurance,* 819 table B.

206. I arrived at these amounts by dividing the total dollar amount of life insurance by the number of certificates for each year, see Stalson, *Marketing Life Insurance,* 807 app. 19, and then adjusting for price inflation using the Douglas price index, see 1 *Historical Statistics of the United States,* 213.

4. From Markets to Managers

The epigraph is from Will Irwin, "The Awakening of the American Business Man," *Century Magazine,* May 1911, p. 118.

1. Howard Gillman, *The Constitution Besieged: The Rise and Demise of Lochner Era Police Powers Jurisprudence* 33–45 (1993); Stanley I. Kutler, *Privilege and Creative Destruction: The Charles River Bridge Case* (1971).

2. 1 Karl Marx, *Capital* 899 (Ben Fowlkes trans., Penguin Books 1990) (1867).

3. Id., 425.

4. For examples, see David Brion Davis, *The Problem of Slavery in the Age of Revolution* 358 (1975).

5. Adam Smith, *An Inquiry into the Nature and Causes of the Wealth of Nations* bk. 3, ch. 2, p. 165 (Richard F. Teichgraeber III, abridged ed. 1985) (1776); Benjamin Franklin, "Observations Concerning the Increase of Mankind," in 4 *The Papers of Benjamin Franklin* 229–30 (1961); Amy Dru Stanley, *From Bondage to Contract* 21 (1998); David Brion Davis, *Slavery and Human Progress* 113 (1984).

6. Thomas K. McCraw, *Prophets of Regulation* 38–39, 60–61 (1984); Gabriel Kolko, *Railroads and Regulation 1877–1916,* pp. 7–29 (1965); Gabriel Kolko, *The Triumph of Conservatism: A Reinterpretation of American History, 1900–1916,* pp. 26–56 (1963).

7. C. F. Adams Jr., *Railroads: Their Origins and Problems* 186–90 (New York, G. P. Putnam and Sons 1887).

8. Kolko, *The Triumph of Conservatism,* 30–39; Martin J. Sklar, *The Corporate Reconstruction of American Capitalism, 1890–1916: The Market, the Law, and Politics* 54–57 (1988); T. S. Bentley, "Neglected Factors in Machine-Shop Economics," 22 *Engineering Mag.* 514, 514 (1901–2); Charles M. Schwab, "Competition—Its Uses and Abuses," in *Year Book of the American Iron and Steel Institute 1912,* p. 47 (1912) ("We must avoid destructive competition.").

9. David A. Wells, *Recent Economic Changes* 78–80 (New York, D. Appleton 1889).

10. Daniel Nelson, *Managers and Workers: Origins of the New Factory System in the United States, 1880–1920,* pp. 34–54 (1975); see also Herbert Gutman, *Work, Culture, and Society in Industrializing America* 3–78 (1977); Jonathan Prude, *The Coming of Industrial Order: Town and Factory Life in Rural Massachusetts, 1810–1860,* pp. 82–84, 129–31 (1983); Anthony F. C. Wallace, *Rockdale: The Growth of an American Village in the Early Industrial Revolution* 178–79 (1978); David A. Zonderman, *Aspirations and Anxieties: New England Factory Workers and the Mechanized Factory System 1815–1850,* pp. 144–62 (1992); E. P. Thompson, "Time, Work-Discipline, and Industrial Capitalism," 38 *Past and Present* 56, 79–95 (1967).

11. Christopher Tomlins, *Law, Labor, and Ideology in the Early American Republic* (1993); Karen Orren, *Belated Feudalism: Labor, the Law, and Liberal Development in the United States* (1991); Arthur McEvoy, "Freedom of Contract, Labor, and the Administrative State," in *The State and Freedom of Contract* 198 (Harry N. Scheiber ed., 1998); Robert J. Steinfeld, *Coercion, Contract, and Free Labor in the Nineteenth Century* (2001); John Fabian Witt, "Rethinking the Nineteenth-Century Employment Contract, Again," 18 *Law and Hist. Rev.* 627 (2000).

12. Charles F. Sabel and Jonathan Zeitlin, "Historical Alternatives to Mass Production: Politics, Markets and Technology in Nineteenth-Century Industrialization," 108 *Past and Present* 133 (1985); Philip Scranton, *Proprietary Capitalism: The Textile Manufacture at Philadelphia, 1800–1885* (1983).

13. John K. Brown, *The Baldwin Locomotive Works 1831–1915,* p. 95 (1995); Walter Licht, "Studying Work: Personnel Policies in Philadelphia Firms, 1850–1950," in *Masters to Managers* 43, 65–66 (Sanford Jacoby ed., 1991).

14. Philip Scranton, "'Have a Heart for the Manufacturers!': Production, Distribution, and the Decline of American Textile Manufacturing," in *World of Possibilities: Flexibility and Mass Production in Western Industrialization* 310, 313 (Charles F. Sabel and Jonathan Zeitlin eds., 1997).

15. Brown, *The Baldwin Works,* 115–19; Dan Clawson, *Bureaucracy and the Labor Process: The Transformation of U.S. Industry, 1860–1920,* pp. 71–125 (1980); Licht, *Industrializing America,* 129–30; Nelson, *Managers and Workers,* 36–37; John Buttrick, "The Inside Contract System," 12 *J. Econ. Hist.* 205 (1952); Ernest J. Englander, "The Inside Contract System of Production and Organization: A Neglected Aspect of the History of the Firm," 28 *Lab. Hist.* 429 (1987).

16. David Montgomery, *The Fall of the House of Labor: The Workplace, the State, and American Labor Activism, 1865–1925,* pp. 9–19 (1987).

17. David Brody, *Workers in Industrial America* 3–4 (1980); James Whiteside, *Regulating Danger: The Struggle for Coal Mine Safety in the Rocky Mountain Coal Industry* 43–44 (1990); David Montgomery, *Workers' Control in America* (1979).

18. Montgomery, *Workers' Control in America.*

19. Sanford M. Jacoby, *Employing Bureaucracy: Managers, Unions, and the Transformation of Work in American Industry, 1900–1945,* pp. 13–37, 43 (1985); Nelson, *Managers and Workers,* 11–54.

20. Thomas C. Holt, *The Problem of Freedom: Race, Labor, and Politics in Jamaica and Britain, 1832–1938* (1992).

21. Gerald Jaynes, *Branches without Roots: Genesis of the Black Working Class in the American South, 1862–1882,* p. 13 (1986).

22. Philip S. Foner, *The Great Labor Uprising of 1877* (1977); Montgomery, *Fall of the House of Labor,* 36–57; Nell Irvin Painter, *Standing at Armageddon: The United States, 1877–1919* (1987); Kenneth Warren, *Triumphant Capitalism: Henry Clay Frick and the Industrial Transformation of America* 84–97 (1996); Heather Cox Richardson, *The Death of Reconstruction: Race, Labor, and Politics in the Post–Civil War South, 1865–1901,* xiii–xiv, 211 (2001).

23. Walter Adams, "The Steel Industry," in *The Structure of American Industry: Some Case Studies* 145–49 (Walter Adams ed., 1950); see also Kolko, *Triumph of*

Conservatism; Kolko, *Railroads and Regulation,* 64; Naomi R. Lamoreaux, *The Great Merger Movement in American Business, 1895–1904* (1985); McCraw, *Prophets of Regulation,* 48–49; Sklar, *Corporate Reconstruction of American Capitalism,* 10–11, 16–17; Warren, *Triumphant Capitalism,* 118–40; James Weinstein, *The Corporate Ideal in the Liberal State 1900–1918,* p. 63 (1968); Robert H. Wiebe, *The Search for Order, 1877–1920,* pp. 151–55 (1967).

24. Kolko, *Triumph of Conservatism,* 12–14.
25. Alfred D. Chandler Jr., *The Visible Hand: The Managerial Revolution in American Business* (1977); see also Sanford M. Jacoby, *Modern Manors: Welfare Capitalism since the New Deal* 12–13 (1997); Sanford M. Jacoby, "American Exceptionalism Revisited: The Importance of Management," in *Masters to Managers: Historical and Comparative Perspectives on American Employers* 173, 173–200 (Sanford M. Jacoby ed., 1991); Joel Rogers, "In the Shadow of the Law: Institutional Aspects of Postwar U.S. Union Decline," in *Labor Law in America: Historical and Critical Essays* 283, 287 (Christopher L. Tomlins and Andrew J. King eds., 1992).
26. Nelson, *Managers and Workers,* 48–54; David F. Noble, *America by Design: Science, Technology, and the Rise of Corporate Capitalism* 36 (1977).
27. O. M. Becker, "The Square Deal in Works Management I: The Common Sense of the Management of Men," 30 *Engineering Mag.* 536, 537, 542 (1905–6); see also William B. Dickson, "Betterment of Conditions in the Steel Industry," in *Proceedings of the American Iron and Steel Institute* 56 (1910).
28. Becker, "Square Deal I," 542; Jacoby, *Employing Bureaucracy,* 99–101.
29. E.g., "The Premium Plan for Paying Labor," 26 *Engineering News* 63, 63 (1891).
30. "Editorial: New Shop Methods a Corollary of Modern Machinery," 19 *Engineering Mag.* 368, 368 (1900); John H. Patterson, "Altruism and Sympathy as Factors in Works Administration," 20 *Engineering Mag.* 577, 577 (1900–1); see also John B. C. Kershaw, "The Promotion of Industrial Efficiency and National Prosperity," 25 *Engineering Mag.* 329, 329 (1903); "The Maintenance of Machine Shop Personnel," 25 *Engineering Mag.* 750, 750 (1903).
31. See Robert Kanigel, *The One Best Way: Frederick Winslow Taylor and the Enigma of Efficiency* 234 (1997). The best account of the relationship between Taylor and the management engineering movement generally is Daniel Nelson, *Frederick W. Taylor and the Rise of Scientific Management* (1980).
32. See David Brion Davis, *The Problem of Slavery in Western Culture* 291–332 (1966).
33. Cf. R. Keith Aufhauser, "Slavery and Scientific Management," 33 *J. Econ. Hist.* 811, 823 (1973).
34. Frederick Winslow Taylor, *The Principles of Scientific Management* 19–21 (1911).
35. On the results of Taylor's experiments in metal-cutting, see Kanigel, *One Best Way,* 173–80.
36. Taylor, *Principles of Scientific Management,* 25, 31–32, 112, 5.
37. Id., 114.
38. Frederick Winslow Taylor, "Taylor's Testimony before the Special House Com-

mittee," in *Scientific Management* 40, 89 (1947); see also Montgomery, *Fall of the House of Labor,* 9 ("The manager's brain under the workman's cap").

39. Nelson, *Managers and Workers,* 56.

40. Licht, "Studying Work," 43, 70–72; Daniel Nelson, "Scientific Management and the Workplace, 1920–1935," in *Masters to Managers,* 74, 74–89; Taylor, *Principles of Scientific Management,* 28.

41. 3 U.S. House of Representatives, *Hearings before Special Committee of the House of Representatives to Investigate the Taylor and Other Systems of Shop Management* 1387 (1912).

42. Taylor, "Shop Management," in *Scientific Management,* 119–20, 198; 14 *Report of the Industrial Commission on the Relations and Conditions of Capital and Labor Employed in Manufactures and General Business* 352 (1901).

43. Lewis A. Kornhauser, "A Guide to the Perplexed Claims of Efficiency in the Law," 8 *Hofstra L. Rev.* 591, 592–97 (1980).

44. Leicester Allen, "Economy of Heating and Ventilating the Machine Shop," 21 *Engineering Mag.* 75, 80 (1901).

45. *Rereading Frederick Jackson Turner: "The Significance of the Frontier in American History" and Other Essays* (John Mack Faragher ed., 1994); Samuel P. Hays, *Conservation and the Gospel of Efficiency* 122–27 (1959); 1 *Report of the National Conservation Commission (February 1909): Special Message from the President of the United States Transmitting a Report of the National Conservation Commission, with Accompanying Papers,* Sen. Doc. No. 676, 60th Cong., 2d Sess. (1909); Gifford Pinchot, *The Fight for Conservation* 3 (1910). See also Charles Richard Van Hise, *The Conservation of Natural Resources in the United States* (1910).

46. Frank Koester, *The Price of Inefficiency* xiii (1913); see also Day Allen Whitney, "Mining Accidents," 39 *Cassier's Mag.* 232, 240 (1910–11) (predicting that the benefits of increased attention to safety in mines "will be increasingly important as American resources become scarcer and less equal to the larger and larger demands of a growing nation with expanding commerce").

47. Koester, *The Price of Inefficiency,* 44–46.

48. H. H. Stock, "First-Aid Movement in the Anthracite Region of Pennsylvania," 37 *Engineering Mag.* 321, 321 (1909).

49. Van Hise, *Conservation of Natural Resources,* 364, 369–70.

50. S. W. Robinson, "Railroad Economics," 2 *Transactions of the American Society of Mechanical Engineers* 524, 525 (1881). Issues of the *Engineering News* illustrate the point well. The 1874 opening issue (published as *Engineer and Surveyor*) included no reference to accidents as a subject for the journal. Only in 1877 and 1878 did the *News* include index entries for accidents: one in the New York post office, another arising out of the building of a caisson, and another on a railroad bridge. By 1890, recounting the details of accidents on railroads and railroad bridges had become a major part of the *News*'s mission. Each issue of the magazine covered the week's major accidents, and the index for the year included dozens of entries under the heading "accident."

51. George Ethelbert Walsh, "Accident Prevention Devices in America: An American Criticism," 28 *Cassier's Mag.* 223, 226 (1905).

52. Day Allen Willey, "Safety in American Railway Travel," 28 *Cassier's Mag.* 55, 55 (1905).
53. Walsh, "Accident Prevention Devices," 223; see also "English Railway Accidents," 12 *Engineering Mag.* 705, 705–6 (1896–97).
54. Herbert T. Wade, "The American Museum of Safety Devices," 35 *Engineering Mag.* 329, 330 (1908).
55. Clarence Hall and Walter O. Snelling, "The Waste of Life in American Coal Mining," 34 *Engineering Mag.* 721, 721 (1908).
56. "Editorial," 18 *Cassier's Mag.* 441, 441 (1900).
57. E.g., Adna Weber, "Employers' Liability and Accident Insurance," 17 *Pol. Sci. Q.* 256, 259–60 (1902). See also note 144 below.
58. E.g., Bentley, "Neglected Factors in Machine-Shop Economics," 514.
59. Id.
60. See J. A. Holmes, "Coal Mining Accidents in the United States and their Prevention," 37 *Cassier's Mag.* 374, 375 (1910). On the effects of competition in the coal mining industry on safety conditions in the mines, see William Graebner, *Coal-Mining Safety in the Progressive Period* (1976).
61. Holmes, "Coal Mining Accidents," 375.
62. See Aldrich, *Safety First*, 42. Fatality rates in the anthracite mines typical of eastern Pennsylvania declined dramatically from their heights in the 1850s and 1860s to approximately three workers in every thousand per year by 1890. By 1900, fatality rates in bituminous and anthracite mines were roughly the same.
63. Aldrich, *Safety First*, 41–60; Graebner, *Coal-Mining Safety*, 8; "Mining and Metallurgy," 12 *Engineering Mag.* 347, 349 (1897).
64. Aldrich, *Safety First*, 64; Whiteside, *Regulating Danger*, 33.
65. Robert Asher, "The Limits of Big Business Paternalism: Relief for Injured Workers in the Years before Workmen's Compensation," in *Dying for Work* 19, 21 (David Rosner and Gerald Markowitz eds., 1989).
66. Id., 21.
67. See William Franklin Willoughby, *Workingmen's Insurance* 307 (New York, Thomas Y. Crowell 1898); *Third Annual Report of the Interstate Commerce Commission* 360–61 (Washington D.C., Gov't Printing Office, 1890). Willoughby described the Lehigh system as follows: "The system is briefly this: A fund is accumulated by the voluntary contributions on the part of employés to the amount of one day's wages or less, but in no case to exceed three dollars, as called for by the administration of the fund, to meet demands for the payment of benefits. The company on its part makes a contribution equal in amount to the total contributions of the employés. Benefits are only paid in the case of accidents, and to employés who responded to the last call for contributions. The value of the daily benefit is equal to three-fourths of the amount contributed by the injured member on the last call, during a period not exceeding nine months. In case of death, $50 is immediately paid for funeral expenses, and subsequently to the family of the deceased, during two years, the accident benefit to which the deceased would have been entitled." Willoughby, *Workingmen's Insurance,* 307.
68. See Emory R. Johnson, "Railway Relief Departments," in *Bulletin of the Department of Labor, No. 8,* pp. 39, 42–43 (Washington, D.C., Gov't Printing Office

1897); "The Baltimore and Ohio Relief Department," *Massachusetts Labor Bulletin,* Oct. 1897, pp. 19–32.

69. *Third Annual Report of the ICC,* 342–82. The twelve railroads were the Atchison, Topeka, and Santa Fe Company; the Baltimore and Ohio Railroad Company; the Central Vermont Railroad Company; the Chicago, Burlington, and Quincy Railroad Company; the Cincinnati, Hamilton, and Dayton Railroad Company; the Delaware and Hudson Canal Company; the Lehigh Valley Railroad Company; the Northern Pacific Railroad Company; the Pennsylvania Railroad Company; the Philadelphia and Reading; the Pittsburgh, Cincinnati, and St. Louis Railway Company (also known as the Pennsylvania Line West of Pittsburgh); and the Utah Central Railway Company. See id.

70. Johnson, "Railway Relief Departments," 42–43; Charles Richmond Henderson, *Industrial Insurance in the United States* 212–13 (1909).

71. Asher, "Limits of Big Business Paternalism," 21; Nuala McGann Drescher, "The Workmen's Compensation and Pension Proposal in the Brewing Industry, 1910–1912: A Case Study in Conflicting Self-Interest," 24 *Ind. and Lab. Rel. Rev.* 32, 36 (1970); *Twenty-Third Annual Report of the Commissioner of Labor, 1908: Workmen's Insurance and Benefit Funds in the United States* 429–39 (Washington, D.C., Gov't Printing Office 1909); William B. Gates Jr., *Michigan Copper and Boston Dollars: An Economic History of the Michigan Copper Mining Industry* 109 (1951); Willoughby, *Workingmen's Insurance,* 284.

72. Paul Monroe, "An American System of Labor Pensions and Insurance," 2 *Am. J. Soc.* 501, 507 (1897).

73. Henderson, *Industrial Insurance,* 200–5. There was a slight increase in the establishment of accident-relief funds in the 1880s. *Twenty-Third Annual Report of the Commissioner of Labor,* 387; Stuart Brandes, *American Welfare Capitalism, 1880–1940,* pp. 95–96 (1976); Henderson, *Industrial Insurance,* 195.

74. *Twenty-Third Annual Report of the Commissioner of Labor,* 387.

75. E. M. Atkin and H. M. Edwards, *Compensation to Injured Employees: Plan of the New York Edison Company* (1910); Henderson, *Industrial Insurance,* 190–211, 345–76; Ferd. C. Schwedtman and James Emery, *Accident Prevention and Relief: An Investigation of the Subject in Europe with Special Attention to England and Germany* 415–26 (1911); see also *A Conference of the Representatives of the Several Death and Accident Funds of the Pittsburgh Coal Company Held at the General Offices of the Company, 232 Fifth Avenue, Pittsburgh, Pennsylvania, Thursday, the Sixth Day of February, Nineteen Hundred and Two* (1902); *Constitution and By-Laws of the Pittsburgh Lamp, Brass and Glass Company Employees' Beneficial Association, Organized August 2, 1904* (1906); *Constitution of the Allis Mutual Aid Society, Milwaukee, Wisconsin, Revised March 12, 1907* (1907).

76. Atkin and Edwards, *Compensation to Injured Employees,* 5–6.

77. *Constitution of the Allis Mutual Aid Society,* 4, 12.

78. *Twenty-Third Annual Report of the Department of Labor,* 387.

79. Don D. Leschohier, "Working Conditions," in 3 *History of Labor in the United States* 3, 320 (John R. Commons ed., 1935). Several historians have interpreted the Department of Labor's 1908 report on 461 establishment funds covering some 640,000 member employees as an estimate of the national total. E.g.,

Brandes, *American Welfare Capitalism*, 96; Asher, "The Limits of Big Business Paternalism," 27. The report appears instead to have been a self-consciously partial survey of representative firms. See *Twenty-Third Annual Report of the Department of Labor*, 387.

80. Crystal Eastman, *Work-Accidents and the Law* 158 (1910). A 1910 survey of members of the National Association of Manufacturers showed that 17 percent of the NAM's membership operated a system of accident relief of one kind or another. Schwedtman and Emery, *Accident Prevention and Relief*, 381.

81. Henderson, *Industrial Insurance*, 192–201, 375; *Twenty-Third Annual Report of the Department of Labor*, 274.

82. Willoughby, *Workingmen's Insurance*, 316.

83. Johnson, "Railway Relief Departments," 42.

84. In 1908, 33 of 36 railroad relief funds had optional membership rules combined with age and physical condition requirements for membership. See *Twenty-Third Annual Report of the Department of Labor*, 272. Only 70 of the 458 nonrailroad firms' employee accident relief programs surveyed made membership a condition of employment. See id., 394; see also Willoughby, *Workingmen's Insurance*, 286.

85. *Third Annual Report of the ICC*, 375 (statement of Mr. A. A. McLeod, vice president and general manager of the Philadelphia and Reading Railroad Co.).

86. *Industrial Accident Department of International Harvester Company and Associated Companies* (1910); Robert Ozanne, *A Century of Labor-Management Relations at McCormick and International Harvester* 71–95 (1967); C. W. Price, "Employees' Benefit Association of the International Harvester Company," 33 *AAAPSS* 246 (1909).

87. Charles A. Gulick, *Labor Policy of the United States Steel Corporation* 141, 154–55 (1924).

88. *Twenty-Third Annual Report of the Department of Labor*, 637.

89. Eastman, *Work-Accidents and the Law*, 162.

90. Raynal C. Bolling, Assistant General Solicitor, United States Steel Corp., "Rendering Labor Safe in Mine and Mill," in *Year Book of the American Iron and Steel Institute 1912*, pp. 106, 107–9 (1912).

91. Gulick, *Labor Policy of the United States Steel Corporation*, 182–83.

92. Dickson, "Betterment of Conditions," 56, 61.

93. Id., 63.

94. William B. Schiller, President, National Tube Company, Pittsburgh, Pa., "Welfare Work in the Steel Industry," in *Year Book of the American Iron and Steel Institute 1912*, 119, 120. Also see Bolling, "Rendering Labor Safe," 106, 107–9.

95. Historians generally see scientific management and employee welfare programs before the 1920s as two competing strands in the development of modern managerial techniques. E.g., Nelson, *Managers and Workers*, 78; Jacoby, *Employing Bureaucracy*, 54–56. Management engineers' ideas about employer accident-relief policies suggest that the antinomy of scientific management and welfare work was not especially sharp.

96. "The Baltimore and Ohio Railroad Relief Department," 11 *Engineering Mag.* 347, 348 (1896); Thomas L. Green, "Railways," 6 *Engineering Mag.* 244, 245–

46 (1893–94); see also "Editorial," 28 *Engineering News* 276, 276 (1892–93); Miles M. Dawson, "Employers' Liability Insurance," 7 *Industrial Engineering and the Engineering Dig.* 449, 452 (1910); Louis A. Boettiger, *Employee Welfare Work: A Critical and Historical Study* 106 (1923).

97. O. M. Becker, "The Square Deal I," 30 *Engineering Mag.* 536, 537 (1905–6); O. M. Becker, "The Square Deal in Works Management," 30 *Engineering Mag.* 823 (1905–6); *Constitution and By-Laws of the Minneapolis Street Railway Company Employees' Mutual Benefit Association Pension System* 2 (ca. 1915); Emory R. Johnson, "Railway Departments for the Relief and Insurance of Employes," 6 *AAAPSS* 64, 67 (1895).

98. See Walter Licht, *Working for the Railroad: The Organization of Work in the Nineteenth Century* 207–11 (1983). On the railroad strikes of the late nineteenth century, see Foner, *Great Labor Uprising of 1877;* Painter, *Standing at Armageddon;* Nick Salvatore, *Eugene V. Debs: Citizen and Socialist* (1982).

99. Asher, "The Limits of Big Business Paternalism," 23. On welfare capitalism as a strategy to undermine labor organizations, see Irving Bernstein, *The Lean Years: A History of the American Worker, 1920–1933* (1960); Brandes, *American Welfare Capitalism;* Montgomery, *Fall of the House of Labor;* Willoughby, *Workingmen's Insurance,* 317.

100. Slason Thompson, "Railway Accidents in England and America," 28 *Engineering Mag.* 981, 983 (1904).

101. Farwell v. Boston and Worcester R.R., 45 Mass. (4 Met.) 49, 57 (1842).

102. Id., 59.

103. E.g., "Boiler Accidents," 11 *Cassier's Mag.* 166, 166–67 (1896–97); "Experimental Mechanics," 2 *Transactions of the American Society of Mechanical Engineers* 58, 61 (1881) ("[T]here are three principal causes of steam-boiler explosions . . . : the first is ignorance, the second is carelessness, and the third is utter recklessness.").

104. Cf. H. D. Emerson, "Railroad Accidents in America," 28 *Engineering Mag.* 833, 835 (1904). Historian David Moss and I have developed much the same point in parallel, comparing Shaw's view of risk in the workplace to the early-twentieth-century way of thinking about such risks. See David A. Moss, *When All Else Fails: Government as the Ultimate Risk Manager* 233 (2002); John Fabian Witt, "The Transformation of Work and the Law of Workplace Accidents, 1842–1910," 107 *Yale L.J.* 1467 (1998).

105. Economic historian Mark Aldrich describes this shift among American businesses from blaming accidents on employee carelessness to blaming accidents on managerial failure in the safety movement of the 1910s. See Aldrich, *Safety First,* 116–17. The point here is that safety engineers had been making the same claim for several decades.

106. The leading contemporary account along these lines is Guido Calabresi, *The Costs of Accidents* (1970).

107. John G. Burke, "Bursting Boilers and the Federal Power," 7 *Technology and Culture* 1 (Winter 1966).

108. Aldrich, *Safety First,* 79–80.

109. E.g., "Current Topics," 26 *Cassier's Mag.* 333, 333–34 (1904); "The Uncer-

tainty of Cast Iron Steam Pipe," 11 *Cassier's Mag.* 334, 334 (1896–97); Fred H. Daniels, Member of the American Society of Mechanical Engineers, "A Peculiar Explosion of a Boiler," 3 *Cassier's Mag.* 123, 123–24 (1892–93); "A Boiler Explosion," 2 *Engineering Mag.* 548, 548 (1891–92); William Barnet Le Van, "The Lifetime or Age of Steam Boilers," 2 *Transactions of the American Society of Mechanical Engineers* 503, 503–25 (1881); "A Warning," 27 *Cassier's Mag.* 337, 337–38 (1904–5); "With All the Disastrous Steam Pipe Accidents . . . ," 9 *Cassier's Mag.* 78, 78 (1895–96); "Steam Boilers," 16 *Cassier's Mag.* 704, 704 (1899).

110. "Danger Signals about the Boiler," 1 *Engineering Mag.* 158, 158–59 (1891).

111. J. M. Allen, "Steam Boiler Explosions," 1 *Cassier's Mag.* 191, 191 (1891–92).

112. Arthur Herschmann, "The Protection of Steam Pipes from Accident," 34 *Engineering Mag.* 456, 456–62 (1907–8); R. S. Hale, "Boiler Design and Boiler Explosions," 27 *Engineering Mag.* 232, 232–46 (1904).

113. F. B. Allen, "The Protective Value of Boiler Inspection," 4 *Transactions of the American Society of Mechanical Engineers* 142, 142–48 (1883); see also W. A. Carlile, "Boiler Insurance and Inspection," 11 *Cassier's Mag.* 65, 65, 73 (1896–97); "Regarding Boiler Accidents," 1 *Cassier's Mag.* 115, 115 (1891–92).

114. Carlile, "Boiler Insurance and Inspection," 73.

115. F. W. Haskell, "Causes of Accidents on American Railways," 28 *Engineering Mag.* 321, 322 (1904–5).

116. E.g., Robinson, "Railway Economics," 525–60; "Safety Devices on Railroad Cars," 4 *Cassier's Mag.* 239, 239–40 (1893); "Air Brake Pump Performance," 5 *Cassier's Mag.* 152, 152–53 (1893–94).

117. E.g., "The Prevention of Railway Accidents," 34 *Engineering Mag.* 817, 817 (1907–8).

118. "Current Topics," 27 *Cassier's Mag.* 260, 260 (1904–5).

119. Haskell, "Causes of Accidents," 323.

120. E.g., Charles Hansel, "Safety in Railway Travel," 16 *Engineering Mag.* 599, 604 (1898–99); Julian A. Hall, "The Causes of Railroad Accidents," 9 *Engineering Mag.* 720, 726 (1895).

121. E.g., "Electricity," 4 *Engineering Mag.* 285, 286 (1892–93); "Editorial," 28 *Engineering News* 12, 12 (1892).

122. Hall, "Causes of Railroad Accidents," 725.

123. "Editorial," 26 *Engineering News* 34, 34 (1891).

124. See id.; "Editorial," 28 *Engineering News* 12, 12 (1892); Emerson, "Railroad Accidents in America," 834–35; Hansel, "Safety in Railway Travel," 605; "Railways," 6 *Engineering Mag.* 897, 897 (1893–94); "Prevention of Railway Accidents," 819; Charles T. Howard, "Safety in American Railway Transport," 34 *Cassier's Mag.* 3, 3–9 (1908).

125. Aldrich, *Safety First*, 174–75, 20–21, 178, 169. A chief cause of the increase in collisions after 1897, ironically, appears to have been the introduction of air brakes, which encouraged faster speeds.

126. "Current Topics," 28 *Cassier's Mag.* 327, 327 (1905).

127. "Editorial," 28 *Engineering News* 12, 12 (1892).

128. Thompson, "Railway Accidents," 983.

129. "Current Topics," 33 *Cassier's Mag.* 304, 304–6 (1907–8); William Wallace Christie, "Safety Appliances in the Engine Room," 32 *Cassier's Mag.* 333, 333–49 (1907); R. W. Raymond, "Blasting in Large Cities," 30 *Cassier's Mag.* 561, 561–62 (1906); "The Physiological Effects of Working under Compressed Air," 30 *Cassier's Mag.* 285, 285–86 (1906); "Mining and Metallurgy," 1 *Engineering Mag.* 264, 264–65 (1891); "Mining and Metallurgy," 2 *Engineering Mag.* 265, 265–66 (1891–92); "Learning the Danger of Blasting in Fiery Pits," 11 *Engineering Mag.* 583, 583–84 (1896); "The Handling of High Explosives in Coal Mines," 17 *Engineering Mag.* 841, 841–42 (1899); C. M. Percy, "Colliery Ventilating Machinery," 22 *Cassier's Mag.* 394 (1902); Robinson, "Railroad Economics," 524–59; W. M. Mitchell, "The Safety Car-Coupler Problem," 5 *Engineering Mag.* 519, 519–23 (1893).

130. Harold Vinton Cox, "Can Railroad Collisions Be Reduced to a Theoretical Minimum," 34 *Engineering Mag.* 632, 632 (1907–8).

131. Leschohier, "Working Conditions," 366.

132. Gulick, *Labor Policy of the United States Steel Corporation,* 138.

133. Id., 139.

134. Aldrich, *Safety First,* 127.

135. Dodge Mutual Relief Association, Indiana, folder marked Health Insurance, 1909–14, box 3, AALLP.

136. "Blame for Accidents Is Laid to Employers," *Labor's Advocate* (Birmingham), Oct. 30, 1914. Note the archaic spelling in the original.

137. Economic historian Mark Aldrich has described this as a kind of "creative tension" between engineering ideas of efficiency and profit maximization. Aldrich, *Safety First,* 109.

138. Compare W. and Atl. R.R. v. Strong, 52 Ga. 461 (1874) (enforcing waiver), with Consolidated Coal Co. v. Lundak, 63 N.E. 1079 (Ill. 1902) (waivers of employers' common law duties are unenforceable); and Wagner v. Boston Elevated Ry., 74 N.E. 919 (Mass. 1905) (waivers of employers' common law duties unenforceable under state statute barring such waivers). See generally George E. Beers, "Contracts Exempting Employers from Liability for Negligence," 7 *Yale L.J.* 352 (1898); Charles W. McCurdy, "The 'Liberty of Contract' Regime in American Law," in *The State and Freedom of Contract* 161, 161–97 (Harry N. Scheiber ed., 1998).

139. Compare Chicago B. and Q. R.R. v. Bell, 62 N.W. 314 (Neb. 1895) (enforcing bar on tort actions by employees accepting accident-relief benefits); Pittsburgh, C., C. and St. L. Ry. v. Cox, 45 N.E. 641 (Ohio 1896) (same); and Leas v. Pennsylvania Co., 37 N.E. 423 (Ind. App. 1894) (same), with Chicago, B. and Q. R.R. v. Miller, 76 F. 439 (8th Cir. 1896) (election of remedy scheme unenforceable where it provides an enforceable contract right as against the employer for the value of the accident benefits); and Chicago, B. and Q. R.R. v. Healy, 111 N.W. 598 (Neb. 1907) (receipt of accident benefits by widow does not bar widow's wrongful death action on behalf of decedent's minor children). See generally Beers, "Contracts Exempting Employers," 359–61.

140. See Chicago, B. and Q. R.R. v. McGuire, 219 U.S. 549 (1911) (upholding constitutionality of Iowa statute enacted in 1898); Sturgess v. Atl. Coast Line R.R.,

60 S.E. 939 (S.C. 1908) (considering state statute barring employers from using acceptance of relief benefits as a bar to tort actions).

141. An Act Concerning Carriers Engaged in Interstate Commerce and their Employees, 30 Stat. 424, 428 § 10 (1898).

142. *WCR*, 160.

143. See Bolling, "Rendering Labor Safe," 106, 107–9 (estimating a cost of $2 million per year in 1912).

144. Econometric studies yield varying answers to the questions whether employees in dangerous industries earned a wage premium, and whether employees receiving increases postinjury compensation paid for such increases through reduced wages. See generally Price V. Fishback and Shawn Everett Kantor, *A Prelude to the Welfare State: The Origins of Workers' Compensation* 48–49 (2000). The question is an exceedingly difficult one, at least in part because strong correlations of job risks with any number of job characteristics for which employees might demand compensation—noise, repetition, lack of worker discretion, etc.—make it exceedingly difficult to separate out wage differentials attributable specifically to risk premiums. We can say with some confidence, however, that regardless whether wages did or did not actually adjust to compensate for risk or for post-accident-compensation benefits, many employers at the turn of the twentieth century appear to have believed (along with progressive economists) that employee wages did not reflect underlying accident risks or expected post-accident compensation. Indeed, few, if any, employers around the turn of the century seriously entertained the idea that workers made meaningful risk calculations, or that accident risk and post-accident benefits were reflected in wage adjustments. Employers like Howell Cheney of Connecticut complained that compensation legislation was an attempt "to artificially raise a class of wages," the costs of which would inevitably have to be passed through to the consumer, not to the employee. Similarly, in legislative hearings on workmen's compensation, firms fought bitterly for joint employer–employee contributions to workmen's compensation insurance funds. And both unions and employers struggled to push benefit levels in directions that they believed favored them. If employers had believed that wages adjusted to reflect either the risk of accidents or the value of post-accident-compensation benefits, these positions would have made little sense. Progressive reformers also put little stock in the theory of wage premiums. Adna Weber contended in the *Political Science Quarterly* that the notion of wage adjustments was a "legal fiction" with "no basis in fact." "In theory," President Roosevelt observed in a 1908 message to Congress on employers' liability, workingmen would act as "experienced businessmen" and would exact a wage allowance for the risk of injury just as sophisticated lenders incorporated a risk premium into rates of interest. "But as a matter of fact," he argued, "it is not practical to expect that this will be done by the great body of employees." Judge Learned Hand of the Southern District of New York concurred; a "theoretical justice," he wrote in 1909, "might be accomplished if by a higher wage [the workingman] could insure himself." But the difficulty was that "even that would not answer the practical objection that actually he does not do it." The Wainwright Commission report summed up this thinking when it concluded simply

that the "laissez faire" theory of wages and risk "does not work out." Howell Cheney, "Work, Accidents, and the Law," 19 *Yale Rev.* 255, 257–58 (1910); *WCM*, 93–94, 98; Adna Weber, "Employers' Liability and Accident Insurance," 17 *Pol. Sci. Q.* 256, 259–60 (1902); Theodore Roosevelt, "The Employers' Liability Law," in 2 *The Roosevelt Policy: Speeches, Letters and State Papers, Relating to Corporate Wealth and Closely Allied Topics, of Theodore Roosevelt, President of the United States* 699, 702 (1908); Letter from Learned Hand to J. M. Wainwright (Nov. 17, 1909), printed in *WCR*, 74–75; *WCR*, 7; see also Henry R. Seager, "Outline of a Program of Social Reform," in *Labor and Other Economic Essays* 79, 83 (Charles A. Gulick ed., 1931).

145. J. Mayhew Wainwright to Francis Lynde Stetson (Apr. 4, 1911), 1911 folder, box 6, JMW; see also Eastman, *Work-Accidents and the Law*, 164.

146. Luther Anderson, *Workmen's Compensation: An Address before the West Virginia Bar Association, White Sulpher Springs, West Virginia, July 14, 1910* (1910), available in folder marked Workmen's Compensation 1908–10, box 12, AALLP.

147. Colleen A. Dunlavy, *Politics and Industrialization: Early Railroads in the United States and Prussia* 189–90 (1993).

148. "Workers Insurance," *Labor Advocate* (Birmingham), May 12, 1911; Drescher, "Workmen's Compensation and Pension Proposal," 32–36.

149. Henry Carter Adams, "Relation of the State to Industrial Action," in *Relation of the State to Industrial Action and Economics and Jurisprudence: Two Essays by Henry Carter Adams* 57, 89 (Joseph Dorfman ed., 1954); John B. Andrews, "Legal Protection for Workers in Unhealthful Trades," 2 *ALLR* 356, 357 (1912).

150. David A. Moss, *Socializing Security: Progressive Era Economists and the Origins of American Social Policy* 21 (1996).

151. Leicester Allen, "Mechanics," 4 *Engineering Mag.* 605, 605 (1892–93); "Liability of Employers for Injuries to Workmen," 10 *Engineering Mag.* 134, 134–35 (1895–96); "Insurance of Labor in Italy," 33 *Engineering Mag.* 105 (1907); "Insurance of Labor in Germany," 33 *Engineering Mag.* 625 (1907); "Labor Insurance in the United States," 39 *Engineering Mag.* 411 (1910); "Industrial Accidents and Liability of Employers," 41 *Engineering Mag.* 721 (1911).

5. Widows, Actuaries, and the Logics of Social Insurance

The epigraph is from William Hard, "The Law of the Killed and Wounded," 19 *Everybody's Magazine* 361, 371 (1908).

1. Clarke A. Chambers, *Paul U. Kellogg and the Survey: Voices for Social Welfare and Social Justice* 36–37 (1971); Sylvia Law, "Crystal Eastman: NYU Law Graduate," 66 *N.Y.U. L. Rev.* 1963 (1991); Blanche Wiesen Cook, "Introduction," in *Crystal Eastman on Women and Revolution* 6–7 (Blanche Wiesen Cook ed., 1978); Crystal Eastman, *Work-Accidents and the Law* 6–7 (1910); Roy Lubove, *Twentieth-Century Pittsburgh* 4–19 (1969); Maurine W. Greenwald, "Visualizing Pittsburgh in the 1900s: Art and Photography in the Service of Social Reform," in *Pittsburgh Surveyed: Social Science and Social Reform in the Early Twentieth Century* 124, 144–46 (Maurine W. Greenwald and Margo Anderson

eds., 1996); John A. Fitch, *The Steel Workers* (1910); Margaret F. Byington, *Homestead: The Households of a Mill Town* (1910).

2. Eastman, *Work-Accidents and the Law*, 188.

3. Id., 133–34, 153–64.

4. Edward Bunnell Phelps, *Workmen's Compensation* 1 (1912); Durand Halsey Van Doren, *Workmen's Compensation and Insurance* 18 (1918); WCR, 1; An Act to Amend the Labor Law in Relation to Workmen's Compensation in Certain Dangerous Employments, ch. 674, 1910 N.Y. Laws 1945; "Comparison of Workmen's Compensation Laws of the United States and Canada up to January 1, 1920," BUSBLS no. 275, pp. 5–18 (1920); *Report to the Special Committee on Industrial Insurance, Wisconsin Legislature 1909–1910*, p. 50 (1911) *(Wisconsin Report)*.

5. Eastman, *Work-Accidents and the Law*, 185.

6. E.g., National Industrial Conference Board, *Workmen's Compensation Acts in the United States: The Legal Phase* 22 (1917); Walter F. Dodd, *Administration of Workmen's Compensation* 1–26 (1936).

7. See Roy Lubove, *The Struggle for Social Security, 1900–1935*, pp. 45–65 (2d ed. 1986); James Weinstein, *The Corporate Ideal in the Liberal State, 1900–1918* (1968); James Weinstein, "Big Business and the Origins of Workmen's Compensation," 8 *Lab. Hist.* 156 (1967); Eliza K. Pavalko, "State Timing of Policy Adoption: Workmen's Compensation in the United States, 1909–1929," 95 *Am. J. Soc.* 592, 596 (1989).

8. See Edward Berkowitz and Kim McQuaid, *Creating the Welfare State: The Political Economy of Twentieth-Century Reform* 37 (1980); Theda Skocpol, *Protecting Soldiers and Mothers: The Political Origins of Social Policy in the United States* 286 (1992); Lubove, *The Struggle for Social Security, 1900–1935;* David Moss, *Socializing Security* (1996); Hace Sorel Tishler, *Self Reliance and Social Security 1870–1917* (1971).

9. See Price V. Fishback and Shawn Everett Kantor, *A Prelude to the Welfare State: The Origins of Workers' Compensation* (2000); Richard Epstein, "The Historical Origins and Economic Structure of Workers' Compensation Law," 16 *Ga. L. Rev.* 775 (1982). The bargain theory of workmen's compensation as a quid pro quo trade among competing interests groups has a long history in the literature. See, e.g., Robert Asher, "Business and Workers' Welfare in the Progressive Era: Workmen's Compensation Reform in Massachusetts, 1880–1911," 43 *Bus. Hist. Rev.* 452 (1969); Robert Asher, "Failure and Fulfillment: Agitation for Employers' Liability Legislation and the Origins of Workmen's Compensation Legislation in New York State, 1876–1910," 24 *Lab. Hist.* 198 (1983); Robert E. Wesser, "Conflict and Compromise: The Workmen's Compensation Movement in New York, 1890s–1913," 11 *Lab. Hist.* 345 (1971).

10. These problems are analyzed in more detail in John Fabian Witt, "Workmen's Compensation and the Logics of Social Insurance," Columbia Law School, Pub. Law Research Paper No. 02–41, Apr. 2002, Social Science Research Network, available at *http://papers.ssrn.com/sol3/papers.cfm?abstract_id=311582*.

11. "Thinks Employers Evade Liability Law," *New York Times*, Oct. 12, 1910, p. 10; Ferd. C. Schwedtman and James Emery, *Accident Prevention and Relief: An Investigation of the Subject in Europe with Special Attention to England and*

Germany 131–34, 152–53 (1911); *First Report of the Industrial Accident Board of the State of California* 3 (1913); *Proceedings of the Conference of Commissions on Compensation for Industrial Accidents* 7 (1910); *WCR,* 132, 147, 163; Aetna Life Insurance Co., *New York Employers' Liability and Compensation Laws* 10 (1910); Frank E. Law, Letter to the Editor, *New York Times,* Aug. 30, 1910, p. 6; *Report of the Workmen's Compensation Commission to the Fifty-Ninth General Assembly of Tennessee* 13 (1916), box 12, folder 8–17, AALLP *(Tennessee Report); First Biennial Report of the Industrial Commissioner to the Governor of the State of Iowa* 17 (1914); State of Connecticut, *Report of the Committee Appointed to Investigate and Report regarding Legislation to Regulate the Liability of Employers* 15 (1909) *(Connecticut Report).*

12. Act of June 25, 1910, ch. 674, 1910 N.Y. Laws 1945. The corporate-liberal and (especially) the bargain theory also cannot account for the decision to enact workmen's compensation schemes rather than merely to legislate the enforceability of welfare-capitalist employment contract terms waiving the right to sue in return for certain-but-limited insurance benefits.

13. I. M. Rubinow, quoted in Roy Lubove, "Workmen's Compensation and the Prerogatives of Voluntarism," 8 *Lab. Hist.* 254, 255 (1967).

14. E.g., Deborah A. Stone, *Policy Paradox and Political Reason* 154–55 (1988); Deborah A. Stone, "Causal Stories and the Formation of Policy Agendas," 104 *Pol. Sci. Q.* 281, 289 (1989).

15. Amy Dru Stanley, *From Bondage to Contract: Wage Labor, Marriage, and the Market in the Age of Slave Emancipation* 138 (1998); Eastman, *Work-Accidents and the Law,* 185.

16. Quoted in Cook, "Introduction," 4. On the contradictions of the family wage, see Ariela R. Dubler, "In the Shadow of Marriage," 112 *Yale L.J.* 1641 (2003).

17. Law, "Crystal Eastman," 1994; Academic Transcript of Catherine Crystal Eastman, Columbia University, June 8, 1904; William L. O'Neill, *The Last Romantic: A Life of Max Eastman* (1978); Cook, "Introduction," 4–6; Crystal Eastman, "Now We Can Begin," in *Crystal Eastman on Women and Revolution,* 52–57; Crystal Eastman, "Who Is Dora Black?," in *Crystal Eastman on Women and Revolution,* 114–18.

18. Eastman, *Work-Accidents and the Law,* 223, 119–20, 137–38. See also Greenwald, "Visualizing Pittsburgh," 144–46; S. J. Kleinberg, "Seeking the Meaning of Life: The Pittsburgh Survey and the Family," in *Pittsburgh Surveyed,* 88–105. Hine was virtually unknown when Paul Kellogg gave him the assignment to do the photos for the Pittsburgh Survey. See Chambers, *Paul U. Kellogg,* 36.

19. Mary K. Conyngton, "Effect of Workmen's Compensation Laws in Diminishing the Necessity of Industrial Employment of Women and Children," *BUSBLS* no. 217 (1918).

20. Don D. Lescohier, "Industrial Accidents and Employers' Liability in Minnesota," *Part II of the Twelfth Biennial Report of the Bureau of Labor, Industries and Commerce of the State of Minnesota 1909–10,* p. 160 (case 2) (1910); *Wisconsin Report,* app. IIA, p. 70.

21. *WCR,* 28; see also Francis H. McLean, "Industrial Accidents and Dependency in New York State," 19 *Charities and the Commons* 1205 (1907).

22. For an expanded version of the argument advanced about the wrongful death

statutes, see John Fabian Witt, "From Loss of Services to Loss of Support: Wrongful Death, the Origins of Modern Tort Law, and the Making of the Nineteenth-Century Family," 25 *Law and Soc. Inquiry* 717 (2000).

23. 1910 N.Y. Laws ch. 674, § 219a.

24. Witt, "From Loss of Services to Loss of Support"; see also Chapter 2.

25. Rough Draft Amendment to Employers' Liability Act Legalizing Compensation Plan (n.d.), folder for 1909–12, box 6, JMW (early draft compensation act with gender-symmetrical death benefits); *WCR*, 54 (March 1910 draft compensation act with gender-asymmetrical death benefits).

26. "Workmen's Compensation Laws of the United States and Foreign Countries," *BUSBLS* no. 126 (1914). The six preclusive asymmetrical statutes were Arizona (1913), Illinois (1913), New Hampshire (1911), New York (1910 (compulsory) and 1910 (elective)), and U.S. government employees (1908). Presumptions of dependency appeared in California, New Jersey and Ohio. Asymmetrical invalidity requirements appeared in New York (1913), Oregon (1913), Washington (1911), and West Virginia (1913). Minnesota's 1913 statute provided widowers with lower benefits than it provided to widows. Important industrial states such as Massachusetts, Michigan, Pennsylvania, and Wisconsin enacted statutes that made no distinction between widows and widowers.

27. 59 Stat. 232 (1906). The second Federal Employers' Liability Act dropped the gendered asymmetry of the first act's death-benefit scheme. See 60 Stat. 65 (1908).

28. 60 Stat. 556, 556–57 (1908).

29. See Employers' Liability Act, S. Rep. 553, pt. 2, 62d Cong., 2d Sess., p. 9 (1912) (reporting on S. 5382, passed May 6, 1912); H.R. 20487, 62d Cong., 2d Sess. (Feb. 20, 1912). See also S. 959, 63d Cong. (Apr. 15, 1913), which failed passage, reprinted in *Workmen's Compensation Laws of the United States and Foreign Countries* 451, 460 (1914) (Bulletin of the U.S. Bureau of Labor Statistics, Whole No. 126, Workmen's Insurance and Compensation Series No. 5), and the draft legislation sent to the Senate by the Employers' Liability and Workmen's Compensation Commission, printed in 1 *RELWCC* 120 (1912).

30. 69 Stat. 1424, 1425, 1430 (1927).

31. Chretien v. Amoskeag Mfg. Co., 180 A. 254, 255 (N.H. 1935).

32. Wengler v. Druggists' Mut. Ins. Co., 446 U.S. 142 (1980).

33. In re Jacobs, 98 N.Y. 98 (N.Y. 1885); Lochner v. New York, 198 U.S. 45 (1905); Ritchie v. People, 40 N.E. 454 (Ill. 1895).

34. Melvin I. Urofsky, "State Courts and Protective Legislation during the Progressive Era: A Reevaluation," 72 *J. Am. Hist.* 63 (1985); Charles Warren, "The Progressiveness of the United States Supreme Court," 13 *Colum. L. Rev.* 294 (1913).

35. Henry W. Farnham, "Practical Methods in Labor Legislation," 1 *ALLR* 5, 8 (June 1911).

36. The *sic utere* principle had a long history in common law and civil law traditions and in liberal political theory, going back to Locke, Kant, and Blackstone. Its great nineteenth-century exponent was John Stuart Mill. See John Stuart Mill, *On Liberty* 13 (Stefan Collini ed., Cambridge University Press 1989) (1859);

John Locke, *Two Treatises of Government* bk. II, § 6 (Peter Laslett ed., 1988) (1690); Immanuel Kant, *The Philosophy of Law: An Exposition of the Fundamental Principles of Jurisprudence as the Science of Right* 46 (W. Hastie trans., reprint ed. Augustus M. Kelley, Clifton, N.J. 1974) (1887); 2 J. J. Burlamaqui, *The Principles of Natural and Politic Law in Two Volumes* § XVI, p. 19 (Thomas Nugent trans., Philadelphia, Carey and Lea, 7th ed. 1830); 3 William Blackstone, *Commentaries* *217; *William Aldred's Case*, 77 Eng. Rep. 816 (K.B. 1611); see also Slaughter-House Cases, 83 U.S. 36, 62 (1873); Commonwealth v. Alger, 61 Mass. (7 Cush.) 53 (1851) (Shaw, C.J.).

37. Thomas Cooley, *A Treatise on the Constitutional Limitations Which Rest upon the Legislative Power of the States of the American Union* 577 (Boston, Little, Brown 1868); Christopher G. Tiedeman, *A Treatise on the Limitations of Police Power in the United States: Considered from Both a Civil and Criminal Standpoint* vii (St. Louis, F. H. Thomas 1886); William P. Prentice, *Police Powers Arising under the Law of Overruling Necessity* 42–43 (Albany, Banks and Brothers 1894); Willis Reed Bierly, *Police Power: State and Federal* 9 (1907).

38. Mass. Gen. Laws ch. 85, § 1 (1840); 1887 Missouri Laws 101; Iowa Code of 1873, § 1289; 1881 Conn. Pub. Acts ch. 92; S.C. Code of 1902, § 2135; 1907 Ark. Acts 336; 1907 S.D. Laws ch. 215; 1911 Ind. Acts 186; see also Mass. Gen. Laws ch. 226 (1837) (shifting the burden of proof on the use of due caution to railroad defendants in spark cases); Grand Trunk R.R. Co. v. Richardson, 91 U.S. 454, 456, 472 (1875) (Vermont statute doing same); Conn. Stat. ch. 26 (1840) (making communication of a fire from a railway locomotive prima facie evidence of negligence).

39. St. Louis and S.F. Ry. Co. v. Mathews, 165 U.S. 1 (1897); Rodemacher v. Milwaukee and St. P. Ry. Co., 41 Iowa 297 (1875); Grissell v. Housatonic R.R. Co., 9 A. 137 (Conn. 1886); Brown v. Carolina Midland Ry. Co., 46 S.E. 283 (S.C. 1903); St. Louis and S.F. Ry. Co. v. Shore, 117 S.W. 515 (Ark. 1909); Jensen v. South Dakota Cent. Ry., 127 N.W. 650 (S.D. 1910); Pittsburgh, Cincinnati, Chicago, and St. Louis Ry. Co. v. Home Ins. Co., 108 N.E. 525, 527 (Ind. 1915); Pittsburgh, Cincinnati, Chicago and St. Louis Ry. Co. v. Chappell, 106 N.E. 403, 405 (Ind. 1914). See also Lyman v. Boston and Worcester R.R., 58 Mass. (4 Cush.) 288 (1849) (upholding judgment for the plaintiff in an action under a strict-liability fire statute without reaching constitutional question).

40. *Mathews*, 165 U.S. at 19.

41. Ohio and Miss. Ry. Co. v. Lackey, 78 Ill. 55, 57 (1875).

42. Denver and Rio Grande Ry. Co. v. Outcalt, 31 P. 177, 180 (Colo. App. 1892); see also Oregon Ry. and Navigation Co. v. Smalley, 23 P. 1008 (Wash. 1890); Bielenberg v. Montana Union Ry. Co., 20 P. 314, 315 (Mont. 1889).

43. Atchison and Neb. R.R. Co. v. Baty, 6 Neb. 37 (1877); Ziegler v. S. and N. Ala. R.R. Co., 58 Ala. 594 (1877); Bielenberg v. Montana Union Ry. Co., 20 P. 314 (Mont. 1889); Jensen v. Union Pac. Ry. Co., 21 P. 994 (Utah 1889); Cottrel v. Union Pac. Ry. Co., 21 P. 416 (Idaho 1889); Oregon Ry. and Navigation Co. v. Smalley, 23 P. 1008 (Wash. 1890); Denver and Rio Grande Ry. Co. v. Outcalt, 31 P. 177 (Colo. App. 1892); Wadsworth v. Union Pac. Ry. Co., 33 P. 515

(Colo. 1893); Schenck v. Union Pac. Ry. Co., 40 P. 840 (Wyo. 1895). Some southern courts upheld the statutes by interpreting them as merely shifting the burden of proof on negligence to the railroads. See Little Rock and Ft. S. R.R. Co. v. Payne, 33 Ark. 816 (1878); Tilley v. St. Louis and S.F. Ry. Co., 6 S.W. 8 (Ark. 1887); Macon and Augusta R.R. Co. v. Vaughn, 48 Ga. 464 (1873); Mobile and Ohio R.R. Co. v. Williams, 53 Ala. 595 (1875); Nashville and Chattanooga R.R. Co. v. Peacock, 25 Ala. 229 (1854). Moreover, legislatures could accomplish the desired end by imposing a duty on railroads to fence their rights of way, default on which led to liability for injured animals. See Thorpe v. Rutland and Burlington R.R. Co., 27 Vt. 140 (1855); Gorman v. Pac. R.R., 26 Mo. 441 (1858); Indianapolis and Cincinnati R.R. Co. v. Kercheval, 16 Ind. 84 (1861).

44. *Baty,* 6 Neb. at 44; *Outcalt,* 31 P. at 179.
45. *Report of the Minnesota Employees' Compensation Commission, Appointed Pursuant to Chapter 286, General Laws of Minnesota, 1909,* pp. 119–20 (1911) *(Minnesota Report).*
46. George E. Barnett, "The Maryland Workmen's Compensation Act," 16 *Q.J. Econ.* 591 (1902); George E. Barnett, "The End of the Maryland Workmen's Compensation Act," 19 *Q.J. Econ.* 320, 321 (1905).
47. First Employers' Liability Act Cases, 207 U.S. 463 (1908).
48. Isaac M. Rubinow, *Social Insurance* 172 (1913).
49. Lindley D. Clark, "Constitutionality and Construction of Workmen's Compensation Laws," *BUSBLS* no. 203, p. 165 (1917). See also *[Iowa] Employers' Liability Commission: Majority and Minority Reports and Bills* 4, folder 8–8, box 12, AALLP.
50. *Wisconsin Report,* 53; *Connecticut Report,* 18; *Proceedings, Third National Conference: Workmen's Compensation for Industrial Accidents, Chicago, June 10–11, 1910,* pp. 28, 35 (1910); *Report of the Employers' Liability Commission of the State of Illinois* 72–73 (1910) *(Illinois Report).*
51. Henry R. Seager, *Labor and Other Economic Essays* 260 (1931). See also *New York Times,* Mar. 25, 1911, p. 3 (Assemblyman Phillips describing workmen's compensation as falling within a kind of "judicial shadowland"); *Proceedings, Third National Conference,* 17–18. Governor Charles Evans Hughes had noted the constitutional problems in his call for a commission to study the work-accident problem. See *Report to the Legislature of the State of Ohio . . . Part I, January, 1911,* p. xx (1911) *(Ohio Report).*
52. Gilbert L. Campbell, *Industrial Accidents and Their Compensation* 96 (1911).
53. Wainwright Commission Hearings, Executive Chamber, Albany, N.Y., May 20, 1910, p. 30, reel 20, *The John Mitchell Papers, 1885–1919* (Glen Rock, N.J. Microfilming Corp. 1974). Crystal Eastman is often identified as the primary drafter of the New York statute, but this seems unlikely. J. Mayhew Wainwright credited Cotton as the statute's primary drafter in public hearings held on May 20, 1910 in Albany. And in the time she worked for the commission, Eastman was extremely busy preparing her *Work-Accidents and the Law* for publication. At one point, she even wrote to Wainwright explaining her need to reduce her time commitments to the work of the commission. See Crystal Eastman to J.

Mayhew Wainwright, Nov. 13, 1909, folder for 1909–12, box 6, JMW. That Eastman was nonetheless closely involved in the drafting of the statute is suggested by the fact that an early rough draft of the statute (located in the papers of Jonathan Mayhew Wainwright at the New York Historical Society) would have provided death benefits on a gender-neutral basis. (See the "Rough Draft Amendment" cited above in note 25.) How the statute ultimately enacted came to be revised to provide death benefits to widows but not to widowers is unclear.

54. Seager, *Labor and Other Economic Essays,* 260.

55. *Illinois Report,* 72–73; *Wisconsin Report,* 13.

56. In *Holden v. Hardy,* 169 U.S. 366 (1898), for example, the U.S. Supreme Court upheld a Utah statute setting maximum hours of labor for employees working in mines or in smelting, reducing, or refining ores or metals. The Court had upheld employers' liability law reform legislation on such "dangerousness" grounds since the 1880s. See Mo. Pac. Ry. Co. v. Mackey, 127 U.S. 205 (1888); Minneapolis and St. Louis Ry. Co. v. Herrick, 127 U.S. 210, 211 (1888); Chicago, K. and W. R.R. Co. v. Pontius, 157 U.S. 209, 211 (1895); Tullis v. Lake Erie and W. R.R. Co., 175 U.S. 348, 351 (1899); Minn. Iron Co. v. Kline, 199 U.S. 593, 597–98 (1905).

57. 1910 N.Y. Laws ch. 674, § 215.

58. "Worker Shot Skyward from under River Bed," *New York Times,* Mar. 28, 1905, p. 1. See the similar incident recounted in Colum McCann's 1998 novel, *This Side of Brightness,* which draws on a 1916 blow-out that threw a sandhog named Marshall Mabey out of the East River. Adam Fifield, "The Underground Men," *New York Times,* Jan. 12, 2003, § 14, p. 1.

59. Edward T. Devine, *Misery and Its Causes* 21–22 (1909).

60. "Worker Shot Skyward," p. 2.

61. *Minnesota Report,* 4; "Employers' Liability, Workmen's Compensation and Insurance," 1 *ALLR* 87, 96 (Oct. 1911); "Accident Liability Reform Advocated," *New York Times,* Apr. 9, 1911, p. 8 (Walter George Smith of Philadelphia, president of the Conference of Commissioners on Uniform State Laws); Joseph Tripp, "An Instance of Labor and Business Cooperation: Workmen's Compensation in Washington State," 17 *Lab. Hist.* 532, 550 (1976). See also A. Maurice Low, "Shifting the Burden," *N. Am. Rev.,* July 19, 1907, p. 651; Jeremiah Smith, "Sequel to Workmen's Compensation Acts," 27 *Harv. L. Rev.* 233, 233 (1914); J. Walter Lord, *Employers' Liability and Workmen's Compensation Laws: An Address Delivered at the Seventeenth Annual Meeting of the Maryland Bar Association, July, 1912,* p. 10 (1912); John Mitchell, "The Wage Earners," *United Mine Workers' J.,* Oct. 5, 1911, p. 2; Campbell, *Industrial Accidents and their Compensation,* 62.

62. Ian Hacking, "Nineteenth-Century Cracks in the Concept of Determinism," 44 *J. Hist. Ideas* 455, 458–59 (1983).

63. Ian Hacking, *The Taming of Chance* 2 (1990); Ian Hacking, *The Emergence of Probability: A Philosophical Study of Early Ideas about Probability, Induction and Statistical Inference* (1975); Gerd Gigerenzer et al., *The Empire of Chance: How Probability Changed Social Science and Everyday Life* 2–10, 38–45 (1989); Theodore M. Porter, *The Rise of Statistical Thinking, 1820–1900,* pp. 40–70 (1986);

Stephen M. Stigler, *The History of Statistics: The Measurement of Uncertainty before 1900,* pp. 161–220 (1986).

64. Ian Hacking, "Prussian Numbers, 1860–1882," in 1 *The Probabilistic Revolution: Ideas in History* 377–94 (Lorenz Krüger et al. eds., 1987).

65. Francois Ewald, "Insurance and Risk," in *The Foucault Effect: Studies in Governmentality* 197, 202 (Graham Burchell, Colin Gordon, and Peter Miller eds., 1991); see also Francois Ewald, "The Return of Descartes's Malicious Demon: An Outline of a Philosophy of Precaution," in *Embracing Risk: The Changing Culture of Insurance and Responsibility* 273, 277–81 (Tom Baker and Jonathan Simon eds., 2002).

66. Morton J. Horwitz, *The Transformation of American Law, 1780–1860,* pp. 226–37 (1977); Patricia Cline Cohen, *A Calculating People: The Spread of Numeracy in Early America* 176 (1999); see also Margo J. Anderson, *The American Census: A Social History* 1–82 (1988). On early statistical thinking in North America, see James H. Cassedy, *Demography in Early America: Beginnings of the Statistical Mind, 1600–1800* (1969).

67. Oliver Wendell Holmes Jr., "The Path of the Law," 10 *Harv. L. Rev.* 457, 467, 469 (1897).

68. Louis Menand, *The Metaphysical Club* (2001); G. Edward White, *Justice Oliver Wendell Holmes: Law and the Inner Self* 92–93 (1993).

69. Robert W. Bruère, "The Welfare War," *Harpers' Monthly,* Oct. 1911, p. 674.

70. *Illinois Report,* 9; see also Peter Roberts, *The Anthracite Coal Industry* 170 (1901).

71. *WCR,* 5.

72. J. P. Cotton Jr., "The Work of the New York State Commission on Employers' Liability," memorandum presented to the National Civic Federation, Nov. 22, 1909, folder for 1909–12, box 6, JMW.

73. Hard, "The Law of the Killed and Wounded," 361.

74. Rubinow, *Social Insurance,* 49.

75. Eugene Wambaugh, "Workmen's Compensation Acts: Their Theory and Their Constitutionality," 25 *Harv. L. Rev.* 129, 134 (1911).

76. E. H. Downey, *Work Accident Indemnity in Iowa* 14 (1912).

77. *Report of Commission Appointed by Governor M. E. Hay to Investigate the Problems of Industrial Accidents and to Draft a Bill on the Subject of Employes' Compensation to Be Submitted to the 1911 Session of the Washington Legislature* 32–33 (1910), in folder 8–3, Workers' Compensation 1908–10, box 11, AALLP.

78. Academic Transcript of Catherine Crystal Eastman, Columbia University, June 8, 1904.

79. F. H. Hankins, "Franklin Henry Giddings, 1855–1931: Some Aspects of His Sociological Theory," 37 *Am. J. Soc.* 349, 359 (1931); see also Franklin H. Giddings, *Studies in the Theory of Human Society* 144–53 (1922); Clarence H. Northcott, "The Sociological Theories of Franklin H. Giddings," 24 *Am. J. Soc.* 1 (1918).

80. Eastman, *Work-Accidents and the Law,* 12–13.

81. Quotations from Hacking, "Nineteenth-Century Cracks," 470; see also Porter, *The Rise of Statistical Thinking,* 151–92.

82. Eastman, *Work-Accidents and the Law*, 84, 188, 218; Porter, *The Rise of Statistical Thinking*, 52–54.

83. Hacking, *Taming of Chance*, 115.

84. George W. Alger, *Moral Overstrain* 15 (1906).

85. Managers of firms were what late-twentieth-century tort lawyers would come to call the "cheapest cost avoider." See Guido Calabresi, *The Costs of Accidents* 135–73 (1970).

86. Eastman, *Work-Accidents and the Law*, 29.

87. E. H. Downey, *Workmen's Compensation* 122 (1924).

88. Morris F. Tyler, "Workmen's Compensation Acts," *Yale Rev.*, Feb. 1899, pp. 421, 428; Theodore Roosevelt, quoted in Edward A. Moseley, "The Penalty of Progress," *Independent*, June 11, 1908, p. 1340.

89. "Scientific Accident Prevention," 1 *ALLR* 14, 14, 22 (1911).

90. On this point, see Chapter 4.

91. Fishback and Kantor, *A Prelude to the Welfare State*, 108; *Proceedings of the Conference of Commissions*, 19; *Post Express*, Mar. 25, 1911, scrapbook, William E. Werner Papers, Rush Rhees Library, University of Rochester; George W. Anderson, "Progress in Legislation concerning Industrial Accidents," 38 *AAAPSS* 205 (1911). At International Harvester, it was only when compulsory legislation of some sort was sure to be enacted—when the firm could "see the 'handwriting on the wall'" such that competitors would bear increased accident costs as well—that management decided it could afford to establish a voluntary accident-relief plan. 2 *RELWCC* 800.

92. *WCR*, 160, 148; Ferd. C. Swedtman, "Voluntary Indemnity for Injured Workmen," 1 *ALLR* 49, 49 (1911).

93. David A. Moss, *Socializing Security: Progressive-Era Economists and the Origins of American Social Policy* 21 (1996); see also Eastman, *Work-Accidents and the Law*, 164; John B. Andrews, "Legal Protection for Workers in Unhealthful Trades," 2 *ALLR* 356, 357 (1912).

94. See Charles Richmond Henderson, "The Logic of Social Insurance," 33 *AAAPSS* 265, 277 (1909).

95. Ulrich Beck, *Risk Society: Toward a New Modernity* 28 (Mark Ritter trans., 1992).

96. *Hearings before the Committee on the Judiciary, House of Representatives, Sixty-Second Congress, on H.R. 20487 (S. 5382) (Federal Accident Compensation Act)* 53 (1913) (statement of Hon. William G. Brantley).

97. *WCR*, 109–10.

98. Lubove, *Struggle for Social Security*, 56.

99. Digest of Minutes Taken at Public Sessions of the Commission on Employers' Liability and Causes of Industrial Accidents, Unemployment, and Lack of Farm Labor (n.d.), pp. 668–82, folder for 1909–1912, box 6, JMW.

100. Joseph Cotton to J. Mayhew Wainwright (Sept. 27, 1909), folder for July–December 1909, box 6, JMW.

101. "Courts Usurp Power, Declares Gompers," *New York Times*, Nov. 15, 1910, p. 3.

102. "Testimony before the Committee on the Judiciary of the U.S. House of Repre-

sentatives," in 8 *The Samuel Gompers Papers: Progress and Reaction in the Age of Reform, 1909–1913,* pp. 442, 443–446 (Peter J. Albert and Grace Palladino eds., 2001).

103. *WCM,* 94.

104. The openness of actuarial and managerial categories to many different kinds of politics is often obscured in the sociological literature on the emergence of risk as a cultural preoccupation in twentieth-century western nations. Following Michel Foucault, this literature sees in actuarial techniques "new strategies of social control" that "imply a particular view of individuals and their communities" in which individuals are "stripped of a certain quality of belongingness." Actuarial approaches to risk, on this theory, thus "mark[ ] a change in the way power is exercised on individuals by the state and other large organizations." Jonathan Simon, "The Ideological Effects of Actuarial Practices," 22 *Law and Soc'y Rev.* 771, 772, 774 (1988). Actuarial techniques and managerial categories were in fact open to a wide array of political ends, many of them considerably more egalitarian and democratic than the sociology of insurance literature might suggest. As Nikolas Rose has suggested, there is "no necessary political complexion" to statistical politics. Nikolas Rose, *Powers of Freedom: Reframing Political Thought* 210 (1999). On the indeterminacy of statistical approaches to risk, see Tom Baker and Jonathan Simon, "Embracing Risk," in *Embracing Risk,* 1, 20–21.

105. Ernst Freund, "Constitutional Status of Workmen's Compensation," 2 *ALLR* 43, 48–49 (1912). See also Ewald, "Return of Descartes's Malicious Demon," 277–81.

106. *Ohio Report,* xv.

107. *Tennessee Report,* 9; *Ohio Report,* xv; *Report to the Legislature of the State of New York by the Commission Appointed under Chapter 518 of the Laws of 1909 to Inquire into the Question of Employers' Liability and Other Matters: Third Report, Employment and Lack of Farm Labor* (1911) *(Third Report of the Wainwright Commission);* see also Extract of the Message of Governor of Wisconsin to the Legislature of 1917, reel 68, AALLPM; Extract of the Message of Governor of Nevada, reel 68, AALLPM.

108. Typescript dated July 20, 1918, reel 68, AALLP.

109. Excerpt from the Proceedings of the Minnesota State Federation of Labor Convention, July, 1917, folder marked "Health Insurance, 1917," box 3, AALLP; Report of the Committee on Health Insurance [Pennsylvania Federation of Labor], folder marked "Health Insurance, 1917," box 3, AALLP; Health Insurance [Utah Federation of Labor], folder marked "Health Insurance, 1919," box 3, AALLP; Endorsements of Health Insurance, folder marked "Health Insurance, 1916," box 3, AALLP; Resolution 55, Massachusetts State Federation of Labor, Sept. 1917, folder marked "Health Insurance, 1917," box 3, AALLP.

110. Platform of the Progressive Party, reel 62, AALLPM; Preliminary Report of the American Medical Association Committee to the Social Insurance Committee, Jan. 31, 1916, folder marked "Health Insurance, 1916," box 3, AALLP; Ronald L. Numbers, *Almost Persuaded: American Physicians and Compulsory Health Insurance, 1912–1920* (1978); Paul Starr, *The Social Transformation of American*

Medicine: The Rise of a Sovereign Profession and the Making of a Vast Industry 243–49 (1982).

111. William Hard, "Unemployment as a Coming Issue," 2 *ALLR* 93, 98 (1912); *Third Report of the Wainwright Commission;* J. Mayhew Wainwright to Charles R. Miller, Esq. (Nov. 2, 1911), folder for 1911, box 6, JMW.
112. Charles Nagel, "Introductory Address," 2 *ALLR* 91, 92 (1912).
113. Chauncey B. Brewster, "Industrial War or Peace, I: Employers' Liability," *Independent,* June 29, 1911, pp. 1417, 1420.
114. Smith, "Sequel to Workmen's Compensation," 233, 348.
115. Chas. R. Otis to J. Mayhew Wainwright (Feb. 20, 1911), folder for 1911, box 6, JMW.
116. E. H. Downey, *Work Accident Indemnity in Iowa* 19 (1912); "Social Insurance," *Illinois Med. J.,* Dec. 1916, folder marked "Health Insurance, 1916," box 3, AALLP.
117. Downey, *Workmen's Compensation,* 1; Rubinow, *Social Insurance,* 61; "Employers' Liability," *New York Times,* July 17, 1910, p. 8; Moseley, "Penalty of Progress," 1343; Hard, "Law of the Killed and Wounded," 371; "Mitchell's Letter," *United Mine Workers' J.,* Aug. 18, 1904, p. 1.
118. *WCM,* 233; Skocpol, *Protecting Soldiers and Mothers.*
119. "Reward for Insured in All Industries," *New York Times,* Dec. 23, 1910, p. 2; "Health Insurance: A Paper Read before the Health Service Section of the National Safety Council, Detroit, Oct. 18, 1916," folder marked "Health Insurance, 1916," box 3, AALLP.
120. J. P. Cotton Jr., "The Work of the New York State Commission on Employers' Liability," memorandum presented to the National Civic Federation, Nov. 22, 1909, folder for 1909–12, box 6, JMW.
121. Louis D. Brandeis, "From the Standpoint of the Lawyer," in William Hard et al., *Injured in the Course of Duty* 113–21 (1910).
122. *New York State Bar Association Proceedings 1911,* p. 442 (1911).
123. Ernst Freund, "Constitutional Status of Workmen's Compensation," 6 *Ill. L. Rev.* 432, 432 (1912).

6. The Passion of William Werner

The epigraph is from Samuel B. Horovitz and Josephine H. Klein, "The Constitutionality of Compulsory Workmen's Compensation Acts," *United States Department of Labor Division of Labor Standards Bulletin No. 26,* p. 13 (1938).

1. Act of June 25, 1910, ch. 674, 1910 N.Y. Laws 1945; Ives v. S. Buffalo Ry. Co., 94 N.E. 431 (N.Y. 1911).
2. Note, "Judicial Acceptance of Workmen's Compensation," 29 *Harv. L. Rev.* 199, 200 (1915); J. Mayhew Wainwright, "Employers Liability and the Decision of the New York Court of Appeals . . . April 8, 1911," box 6, JMW; N.Y. Cent. R.R. Co. v. White, 243 U.S. 188 (1917); Harry Shulman et al., *Cases and Materials on the Law of Torts* 1–15 (3d ed. 1976); William G. Ross, *A Muted Fury: Populists, Progressives, and Labor Unions Confront the Courts* (1994); see

generally Hace Sorel Tishler, *Self-Reliance and Social Security, 1870–1917,* pp. 120–22 (1971); Roy Lubove, *The Struggle for Social Security, 1900–1935,* pp. 57–58 (1986); David A. Moss, *Socializing Security: Progressive-Era Economists and the Origins of American Social Policy* 125–26 (1996); Theda Skocpol, *Protecting Soldiers and Mothers: The Political Origins of Social Policy in the United States* 258–59 (1992); Louis Michael Seidman and Mark V. Tushnet, *Remnants of Belief: Contemporary Constitutional Issues* 29–30 (1996).

3. H. L. A. Hart and Tony Honoré, *Causation in the Law* 26–61 (2d ed. 1985); Howard Margolis, *Dealing with Risk* 49–69 (1996); Howard Margolis, *Paradigms and Barriers: How Habits of Mind Govern Scientific Beliefs* (1993); see also Clifford Geertz, "Common Sense as a Cultural System," in *Local Knowledge: Further Essays in Interpretive Anthropology* 73–93 (3d ed. 2000); Arthur F. McEvoy, "The Triangle Shirtwaist Fire of 1911: Social Change, Industrial Accidents, and the Evolution of Common-Sense Causality," 20 *Law and Soc. Inquiry* 621 (1995).

4. Ronald Coase, "The Problem of Social Cost," 3 *J.L. and Econ.* 1 (1960); Guido Calabresi, *The Costs of Accidents* 133–235 (1970).

5. Thomas Reed Powell, "The Workmen's Compensation Cases," 32 *Pol. Sci. Q.* 542, 546 (1917).

6. William E. Werner, "Lincoln the Liberator," in Speeches by Hon. William E. Werner, vol. 2, box 7, William E. Werner Papers, Rush Rhees Library, University of Rochester; Memorial Scrapbook, 1916, Werner Papers; King v. Masonic Life Ass'n, 34 N.Y.S. 563 (Sup. Ct. 1895); Zangen v. Krakauer Young Men's Ass'n, 56 N.Y.S. 1052 (Sup. Ct. 1899); Bull v. Case, 59 N.E. 301, 303 (N.Y. 1901); Shipman v. Protected Home Circle, 67 N.E. 83 (N.Y. 1903); Sneck v. Travellers' Ins. Co., 34 N.Y.S. 545 (Sup. Ct. 1895).

7. Kuehn v. Syracuse Rapid Transit Ry. Co., 76 N.E. 589 (N.Y. 1906); In re Speranza, 78 N.E. 1070 (N.Y. 1906); N.Y. Cent. and Hudson River R.R. Co. v. Auburn Interurban Elec. R.R. Co., 70 N.E. 117, 119 (N.Y. 1904).

8. See Letters of William E. Werner to Lillie Boller, box 1, Caroline Werner Gannett Papers, Cornell University Library Rare and Manuscripts Collections.

9. "Judge Werner," *Seneca County Courier,* June 12, 1902, in Scrapbook, box 3, Werner Papers; Memorial Scrapbook, 1916, Werner Papers; "Judge Werner," *Bench and Bar,* March 1916, at 477. In John Cawelti's typology of ideas of the self-made man, Werner (like the characters in Horatio Alger's novels) represented a late-nineteenth-century revival of the seventeenth- and eighteenth-century Puritan tradition of the self-made man as paragon of diligence and frugality. See John G. Cawelti, *Apostles of the Self-Made Man* (1965). I thank Robert Ferguson for bringing Cawelti's ideas to my attention.

10. "Judge Werner," Scrapbook, box 3, Werner Papers; Memorial Scrapbook, 1916, Werner Papers; William E. Werner to Lillie Boller (Sept. 5, 1888), folder 1, box 1, Caroline Werner Gannett Papers; Marriage Announcement, Mar. 7, 1889, Caroline Werner Gannett Papers.

11. Memorial Scrapbook, 1916, Werner Papers.

12. Scrapbook, box 3, Werner Papers; "The Movement for Judge Werner," *Wayne County Rev.,* May 15, 1902, in Scrapbook, box 3, Werner Papers.

13. William E. Werner, "Republican Party," p. 13, box 6, Werner Papers.
14. Werner, "Lincoln the Liberator," box 7, Werner Papers.
15. Werner, "Republican Party," p. 13.
16. Memorial Scrapbook, 1916, Werner Papers; Albert Hall Harris to William E. Werner (Nov. 5, 1913), folder 8, box 1, Werner Papers; Rudolph Hofheinz to William E. Werner (Nov. 8, 1913), folder 8, box 1, Werner Papers; "In Honor of A. S. Weston: Dinner on Saturday Night at Standard Brewery," *Rochester Union and Advertiser,* Sept. 1895, available at *http://wnyrails.railfan.net/news/c0000037.htm.//enottxt//.*
17. William E. Werner to Lillie Boller Werner (Mar. 7, 1897), and WEW to LBW (Mar. 8, 1897), folder 4, box 1, Caroline Werner Gannett Papers.
18. William E. Werner, "The Evolution of the Corporation," *The American Legal News,* Jan. 1902, pp. 5, 12; People v. Bowen, 74 N.E. 489, 493 (N.Y. 1905) (Werner, J., dissenting).
19. Scrapbook, box 3, Werner Papers.
20. *Sunday Star,* May 27, 1894, and "The Movement for Judge Werner," *Wayne County Rev.,* May 15, 1902, Scrapbook, box 3, Werner Papers.
21. William E. Werner to Lillie Boller (Oct. 30, 1888), and WEW to LB (Oct. 2, 1888), folder 1, box 1; WEW to LBW (Sep. 30, 1889), unnumbered folder, box 1; WEW to LB (Jan. 16, 1889), folder 2, box 1, Caroline Werner Gannett Papers; "Justice William E. Werner," *Leslie's Illustrated Weekly Newspaper,* Mar. 18, 1897, p. 175.
22. "First Round for Werner," *New York Herald,* June 12, 1894, Scrapbook, box 3, Werner Papers; "Disgraceful Scene," *Rochester Union and Advertiser,* June 12, 1894, Scrapbook, box 3, Werner Papers.
23. "Seventh Judicial District," *New York Times,* Sept. 15, 1894.
24. "Judge Werner as a Candidate," *New York Times,* July 20, 1902; Francis Bergan, *The History of the New York Court of Appeals, 1847–1932,* pp. 225–26, 229 (1985); New York State Constitutional Convention Commission, *New York State Constitution Annotated, Part II,* p. 128 (1915).
25. William E. Werner, "Address at the New York County Lawyers' Association Annual Bar Dinner" (Feb. 28, 1911), in *New York County Lawyers' Association Year Book* 141 (1911); Scrapbook, box 3, Werner Papers.
26. William E. Werner to Louis Wiley (Oct. 30, 1909), folder 3, box 1, Werner Papers; Scrapbook, box 2, Werner Papers; Robert F. Wesser, *Charles Evans Hughes: Politics and Reform in New York, 1905–1910,* pp. 290–92 (1967); *The Autobiographical Notes of Charles Evans Hughes* 159–61 (David J. Danelski and Joseph S. Tulchin eds., 1973); William E. Werner to Louis Wiley (Nov. 5, 1909), folder 3, box 1, Werner Papers.
27. William E. Werner, "Judge Haight" (Dec. 21, 1912), p. 9, box 6, Werner Papers.
28. William E. Werner to Lillie Boller (Jan. 29, 1888), folder 1, box 1; WEW to LBW (Sept. 23, 1889), unnumbered folder, box 1; WEW to LBW, n.d., folder 4, box 1; WEW to LB (Nov. 19, 1888), WEW to LB (Nov. 20, 1888), and WEW to LB (Nov. 22, 1888), folder 1, box 1; WEW to LB (Dec. 27, 1888), folder 2, box 1, Caroline Werner Gannett Papers. See also WEW to LB (Nov.

27, 1888), folder 1, box 1; WEW to LBW (May 23, 1890), and WEW to LBW (Mar. 3, 1890), unnumbered folder, box 1; WEW to LBW (Feb. 25, 1889), and WEW to LBW (Feb. 27, 1889), folder 2, box 1, Caroline Werner Gannett Papers.

29. Werner, "Judge Haight," 9.

30. William E. Werner, "Changes in Our Profession," p. 10, n.d., Werner Papers.

31. Werner, "Judge Haight," 11.

32. William E. Werner, "Address before the New York Bar Association," p. 5, Jan. 28, 1908, box 6, Werner Papers.

33. Louis Menand, *The Metaphysical Club* 67 (2001).

34. Wright v. Hart, 75 N.E. 404, 406 (N.Y. 1905).

35. William E. Werner, "Address at Dinner Given by Mr. Watson," p. 126, n.d., in Speeches by William E. Werner, vol. 2, box 7, Werner Papers.

36. Werner, "Address before the New York Bar Association," 5–6.

37. Werner, "Address at the New York County Lawyers' Association Annual Bar Dinner," 146.

38. William E. Werner, "Address at the Buffalo Bar Association Dinner," p. 142, Dec. 21, 1912, in Speeches by William E. Werner, vol. 2, box 7, Werner Papers.

39. Memorial Scrapbook, 1916, Werner Papers.

40. King v. N.Y. Cent. and Hudson River R.R. Co., No. 67, May 1, 1888, box 5, Werner Papers.

41. Lechner v. Village of Newark, 44 N.Y.S. 557 (N.Y. Sup. Ct. 1896). In Werner's hands, the focus on the lawful boundaries of actors' liberty had a perceptible tendency to favor defendants in accident cases; where the parties had not departed from their rightful sphere of action (where, in other words, the accident involved the classic nonfaulty plaintiff and nonnegligent defendant), Werner declined to intervene to reallocate their resources. The status quo bias implicit in this approach may explain why out of all his personal injury suit opinions, Werner wrote thirty-one opinions in favor of defendants and nineteen in favor of plaintiffs. The ratio of defendant victories was not out of the mainstream, but Werner was consistently among the judges on the Court of Appeals most likely to side with defendants in such cases.

42. On conditional injunctions, see Boomer v. Atl. Cement Co., 257 N.E. 2d 870 (N.Y. 1970); Guido Calabresi and A. Douglas Melamed, "Property Rules, Liability Rules, and Inalienability: One View of the Cathedral," 85 *Harv. L. Rev.* 1089 (1972).

43. Story v. N.Y. Elevated R.R. Co., 90 N.Y. 122 (N.Y. 1882); Louise A. Halper, "Nuisance, Courts and Markets in the New York Court of Appeals, 1850–1915," 54 *Alb. L. Rev.* 301, 341–54 (1990).

44. Whalen v. Union Bag and Paper Co., 101 N.E. 805 (N.Y. 1913). Market-rate compensation in eminent-domain-like proceedings will not always involve redistributive consequences. The initial owner's refusal to sell may stem from a desire to hold out for strategic gains over and above the market valuation, rather than from an idiosyncratic above-market valuation. As Werner might have responded, in practice it is virtually impossible to distinguish strategic hold-outs from idiosyncratic valuations.

45. Complaint at 5, Ives v. S. Buffalo Ry. Co., 94 N.E. 431 (N.Y. 1911), New York State Library, Albany (hereinafter "Ives Complaint").

46. Ives Complaint at 6; "Union Scale of Wages and Hours of Labor, 1907–1912," *BUSBLS* no. 131, pp. 20–21 (1913).

47. Gertrude Beeks to P. Tecumseh Sherman (Jan. 17, 1911), National Civic Federation Papers, New York Public Library; "Wainwright Act's Legality Tested," *New York Times,* Jan. 17, 1911, p. 9; "Fighting Judge-Made Laws," *Philadelphia North American,* Oct. 8, 1913, Scrapbook 1913–39, Werner Papers; Robert L. Bloom, *The Philadelphia North American: A History, 1839–1925,* pp. 534–40 (1952) (Ph.D. diss., Columbia University).

48. Earl Ives v. The South Buffalo Railway Co., Papers on Appeal, pp. 5–11, 15–22, New York State Library, Albany (hereinafter "Ives Papers on Appeal").

49. Ives Complaint at 7.

50. *Birdseye's New York Revised Statutes, Codes, and General Laws of the State of New York* § 542, p. 2660 (1901). The compensation statute, it should be noted, barred tort actions by any injured workman who "shall avail himself" of the compensation statute by "beginning proceedings" under the statute. 1910 N.Y. Laws ch. 674, § 218. A tort claim might therefore have been dismissed as waived by the compensation claim. Nonetheless, it would be an awfully harsh reading of the statute to refuse to allow the first plaintiff under the compensation act to file a back-up, or conditional, tort claim on the chance that the act would be held unconstitutional. Other than the election of remedies provision, there was no obstacle to alleging negligence in a compensation case; the compensation statute applied both to injuries caused by the inherent risks of employment and to injuries caused by negligent acts. See § 217.

51. "Wainwright Act's Legality Tested," *New York Times,* Jan. 17, 1911, p. 9.

52. "Workers' Compensation," *Labor's Advocate* (Birmingham), Jan. 6, 1911; "Help for Toilers," *Labor's Advocate* (Birmingham), Nov. 25, 1910 (reprinting from *St. Paul Dispatch*).

53. "Industrial Accidents and their Prevention—Discussion," 38 *AAAPSS* 262, 269 (1911).

54. *Ives,* 94 N.E. at 436–37, 439–40; William E. Werner to Louis Wiley (Mar. 27, 1911), quoted in Tishler, *Self-Reliance and Social Security,* 122.

55. *Ives,* 94 N.E. at 440; id. at 449 (Cullen, C.J., concurring).

56. Ohio and Miss. Ry. Co. v. Lackey, 78 Ill. 55 (1875).

57. *Ives,* 94 N.E. at 439.

58. E.g., Ernst Freund, "Constitutional Status of Workmen's Compensation," 6 *Ill. L. Rev.* 432, 433–34 (1912).

59. People v. Bowen, 74 N.E. 489, 493 (N.Y. 1905) (Werner, J., dissenting).

60. Note, "The New York Workmen's Compensation Act as Due Process of Law," 24 *Harv. L. Rev.* 647, 651 (1911); Jeremiah Smith, "Sequel to Workmen's Compensation Acts," 27 *Harv. L. Rev.* 235, 246 (1914).

61. Eugene Wambaugh, "Workmen's Compensation Acts: Their Theory and Their Constitutionality," 25 *Harv. L. Rev.* 129, 134 (1911); Note, "The Constitutionality of New York's Workingmen's Compensation Act," 10 *Colum. L. Rev.* 751, 753–54 (1911).

62. *Ives,* 94 N.E. at 440, 444.

63. E.g., Oliver Wendell Holmes Jr., *The Common Law* 92–95 (Boston, Little, Brown 1881).

64. Hart and Honoré, *Causation in the Law,* 29–35; Richard W. Wright, "Causation in Tort Law," 73 *Cal. L. Rev.* 1735 (1985).

65. Brief for the Appellant, pp. 41–43, Ives Papers on Appeal; *Ives,* 94 N.E. at 436, 443.

66. White v. Atl. City Press, 313 A.2d 197 (N.J. 1973); Tedesco v. Gen. Elec. Co., 114 N.E.2d 33 (N.Y. 1953).

67. 1 Arthur Larson and Lex K. Larson, *Larson's Workers' Compensation Law* §§ 3.02–3 (2001).

68. Morton J. Horwitz, *The Transformation of American Law, 1870–1960: The Crisis of Legal Orthodoxy* 54–55 (1992) *(Transformation II);* Francis Wharton, *A Suggestion as to Causation* 10 (Cambridge, Riverside Press 1874).

69. Morris F. Tyler, "Workmen's Compensation Acts," *Yale Rev.,* Feb. 1899, p. 429.

70. *Ives,* 94 N.E. at 440.

71. Walter S. Nichols, "An Argument against Liability," 38 *AAAPSS* 159–65 (1911); Tyler, "Workmen's Compensation Acts," 433; Brief for the New York Dock Company, Intervenor on Behalf of the Defendant-Appellant, p. 28, Ives Papers on Appeal.

72. Farwell v. Boston and Worcester R.R. Corp., 45 Mass. (4 Met.) 49 (1842).

73. Brief for the Appellant, pp. 30–31.

74. *Ives,* 94 N.E. at 444; id. at 449 (Cullen, C.J., concurring).

75. Werner, "Evolution of the Corporation," 8.

76. Menand, *Metaphysical Club,* 344–46; Nicholas St. John Green, "Proximate and Remote Cause," in *Essays and Notes on the Law of Tort and Crime* 16 (1933); Horwitz, *Transformation II,* 59; Oliver Wendell Holmes Jr., "The Path of the Law," 10 *Harv. L. Rev.* 457, 467, 469 (1897).

77. E.g., The T. J. Hooper, 60 F.2d 737 (2d Cir. 1932) (L. Hand, J.); Texas and Pac. Ry. v. Behymer, 189 U.S. 468, 470 (1903) (Holmes, J.) ("What is usually done may be evidence of what ought to be done, but what ought to be done is fixed by a standard of reasonable prudence whether it is usually complied with or not."). The custom rule in tort means that the "reasonable man" test is in fact *not* an average. In this respect, Menand's *The Metaphysical Club* (see pp. 344–47) has it slightly wrong.

78. Werner, "Judge Haight," 5–6; *Ives,* 94 N.E. at 450 (Cullen, C. J., concurring); Nichols, "Argument against Liability," 159–65; Tyler, "Workmen's Compensation Acts," 429.

79. Louis Marshall to William E. Werner (Apr. 1, 1911), in 2 *Louis Marshall: Champion of Liberty* 1004 (Charles Reznikoff ed., 1957); Louis Marshall to William E. Werner (Nov. 8, 1913), folder 8, box 1, Werner Papers.

80. Henry R. Seager, *Labor and Other Economic Essays* 162 (1931); Note, "The Business of the Supreme Court of the United States—A Study in the Federal Judicial System," 39 *Harv. L. Rev.* 1046, 1053 (1926); Charles H. Betts, *The Betts–Roosevelt Letters* 92 (1912); "Bar Association Meetings," 23 *Green Bag* 492, 496 (1911); Isaac M. Rubinow, *Social Insurance* 174 (1913).

81. "Employers' Liability, Workmen's Compensation and Insurance," 1 *ALLR* 87, 98 (Oct. 1911).

82. Hal H. Smith, "Worker's Compensation in Michigan," 10 *Mich. L. Rev.* 278, 280 (1912); John Mitchell, "The Wage Earners," *United Mine Workers' J.,* Oct. 5, 1911, p. 2.

83. Leon Stein, *The Triangle Fire* 139 (William Greider ed., 2001) (1962); McEvoy, "Triangle Shirtwaist Factory Fire"; Tishler, *Self-Reliance and Social Security,* 120.

84. "Court Decisions," *Labor Advocate* (Birmingham), Apr. 21, 1911, p. 1; "Court Invalidates New Liability Law," *New York Times,* Mar. 25, 1911, p. 3.

85. Edmund Morris, *Theodore Rex* 504–9 (2001); Employers' Liability Cases, 207 U.S. 463 (1908).

86. "Roosevelt Defiant to Gov. Baldwin," *New York Times,* Jan. 27, 1911; Theodore Roosevelt to Simeon Eben Baldwin (Nov. 2, 1910), in 7 *The Letters of Theodore Roosevelt* 149, 151 (Elting E. Morison ed., 1954); Hoxie v. N.Y., New Haven and Hartford R.R. Co., 73 A. 754 (Conn. 1909).

87. Betts, *Betts–Roosevelt Letters,* 9–10, 16; Theodore Roosevelt to Charles Dwight Willard (June 20, 1911), in 7 *The Letters of Theodore Roosevelt,* 290, 291.

88. George E. Mowry, *The Era of Theodore Roosevelt, 1900–1912,* pp. 268–72 (1958); George E. Mowry, *Theodore Roosevelt and the Progressive Movement* 215–19 (1947). The election of Woodrow Wilson, the first southern-born president since the Civil War, was a result of Roosevelt's defeat.

89. George F. Canfield, "Book Review," 14 *Colum. L. Rev.* 363, 365 (1914) (reviewing Frederic R. Coudert, *Certainty and Justice* (1913)); Roscoe Pound, "The End of Law as Developed in Legal Rules and Doctrines," 27 *Harv. L. Rev.* 195, 197 (1913).

90. Rubinow, *Social Insurance,* 165; N.Y. Const. art. I, § 19 (adopted Nov. 2, 1913).

91. Jensen v. S. Pac. Co., 109 N.E. 600 (N.Y. 1915).

92. Powell, "The Workmen's Compensation Cases," 552; Note, "Constitutional Law: Workmen's Compensation Act," 4 *Cal. L. Rev.* 60, 63 (1915); see also Montgomery v. Daniels, 340 N.E.2d 444, 461 (N.Y. 1975) (upholding a no-fault automobile insurance statute and describing *Ives* as long "relegated to obscurity").

93. "Advance to Werner Followed by Attack," *New York Times,* Oct. 2, 1913, p. 1; "Mr. Roosevelt and the Courts," *New York Times,* Oct. 6, 1913, p. 6; Scrapbook, 1913–39, Werner Papers.

94. Werner, "Judge Haight," 6–8; Fitzwater v. Warren, 99 N.E. 1042 (N.Y. 1912) (overruling Knisley v. Pratt, 42 N.E. 986 (N.Y. 1896) (holding that a female employee had assumed the risk of her employer's violation of the state factory safety laws)). It also seems possible that Werner arranged through his friend Louis Wiley of the *New York Times* to have the *Times* editorial page feature a minor proplaintiff personal injury opinion written by Werner in January 1912. See "Rights afoot at Crossing," *New York Times,* Jan. 13, 1912, which emphasizes Werner's role as author of the opinion and is about an otherwise inconsequential accident case. For Werner's dinner speech, see Werner, "Address at Dinner Given by Mr. Watson," 128–30.

95. "Mr. Barnes Habitual Liar, Says Theodore Roosevelt," *New York Herald,* Oct. 3, 1913, Scrapbook, 1913–39, Werner Papers; "Fighting Judge-Made Laws," *Philadelphia North American,* Oct. 8, 1913, Scrapbook, 1913–39, Werner Papers; William E. Werner to Judge Otto Kempner (Sept. 15, 1913), folder 7, box 1, Werner Papers; William E. Werner to Cyrus W. Phillips (Sept. 28, 1913), folder 7, box 1, Werner Papers.

96. "Advance to Werner Followed by Attack," 1; Scrapbook, 1913–39, Werner Papers.

97. Gerald Gunther, *Learned Hand: The Man and the Judge* 234–36 (1994); "Progressives Aid Tammany," *Jamestown Morning Post,* Sept. 29, 1913, Scrapbook, 1913–39, Werner Papers; *New York Tribune,* Nov. 7 1913, Scrapbook, 1913–39, Werner Papers; "Werner Elected by Narrow Margin," *New York Times,* Nov. 7, 1913; Nicholas Murray Butler to William E. Werner (Nov. 7, 1913), folder 8, box 1, Werner Papers; Bartlett Family Diary, Jan. 1, 1913, box 24, Willard Bartlett Papers, Columbia University; "Bartlett Is Elected," *New York Times,* Nov. 15, 1913, p. 8; Bergan, *History of the New York Court of Appeals,* 246–47.

98. William E. Werner to Caroline Werner (Nov. 11, 1913), and WEW to CW (Nov. 19, 1913), folder 6, box 1, Caroline Werner Gannett Papers.

99. William E. Werner to Tracy Chatfield Becker (May 20, 1914), folder 10, box 1, Werner Papers; William E. Werner to Tracy Chatfield Becker (Apr. 18, 1914), folder 10, box 1, Werner Papers; William E. Werner to Archibald Robinson Watson (Dec. 3, 1914), folder 14, box 1, Werner Papers; "Justice Werner Rapidly Recovering," *New York Times,* Oct. 11, 1915; Willam E. Werner to Willard Bartlett (Feb. 8, 1916), Willard Bartlett Papers; "Judge Werner," *New York Times,* Mar. 2, 1916; Benjamin Cardozo to Mrs. William E. Werner (Mar. 1, 1916), folder 19, box 1, Werner Papers.

100. Klein v. Maravelas, 114 N.E. 809, 810 (N.Y. 1916).

101. N.Y. Cent. R.R. Co. v. White, 243 U.S. 188 (1917); Mountain Timber Co. v. State of Washington, 243 U.S. 219 (1917); Hawkins v. Bleakly, 243 U.S. 210 (1917); Coppage v. State of Kansas, 236 U.S. 1 (1915); Hitchman Coal and Coke Co. v. Mitchell, 245 U.S. 229 (1917); Duplex Printing Press Co. v. Deering, 254 U.S. 443 (1921).

102. Werner, "Judge Haight," 11.

103. Seager, *Labor and Other Economic Essays,* 165–66; Moss, *Socializing Security,* 125–29; Ohio Const. art. 2, § 35 (adopted Sept. 3, 1912, effective Jan. 1, 1913); Cal. Const. of 1879, art. 20, § 21 (added Oct. 10, 1911); Wyo. Const. art. 10, § 4 (ratified Nov. 3, 1914); Vermont Const. ch. 2, § 70 (adopted as amendment 35, Apr. 8, 1913).

104. 1 *RELWCC* 12.

105. Note, "The Business of the Supreme Court of the United States—A Study in the Federal Judicial System," 39 *Harv. L. Rev.* 1046, 1055 (1925–26); W. F. Dodd, "The United States Supreme Court as the Final Interpreter of the Federal Constitution," 6 *Nw. U. L. Rev.* 289, 292–93, 297, 309–10 (1911–12); *Iowa Employees' Liability Commission: Majority and Minority Reports and Bills* 12–13 (1912), folder 8–7, box 12, AALL Papers, Kheel Center, Cornell University; *Report of the Workmen's Compensation Commission to the Fifty-Ninth General Assembly of Tennessee* pp. 33 ff. (1916), folder 8–17, box 12, AALL Papers.

106. Brief for the Appellant at 34–35; Cunningham v. Northwestern Improvement Co., 119 P. 554 (Mont. 1911).

107. Raynal C. Bolling, "Workmen's Compensation," 23 *Green Bag* 367, 367 (1911); see also "Workmen's Compensation," 23 *Green Bag* 266, 267 (1911); Ernst Freund, "Constitutional Status of Workmen's Compensation", 6 *Nw. U. L. Rev.* 432, 438 (1911–12).

108. 1 *RELWCC* 63; Jensen v. S. Pac. Co., 109 N.E. 600, 603 (N.Y. 1915).

109. 2 *RELWCC* 16.

110. Jas. Harrington Boyd, "Important Constitutional Questions, New in Form, Raised by the Texas Workmen's Compensation Act," 25 *Yale L.J.* 100, 121 (1915–16); "Workmen's Compensation," 23 *Green Bag* 266, 267 (1911); 1 *RELWCC* 63; Powell, "Workmen's Compensation Cases," at 557; N.Y. Cent. R.R. Co. v. White, 243 U.S. 188, 197 (1917).

111. Arizona Copper Co. v. Hammer, 250 U.S. 400, 423 (1919).

112. *Jensen,* 109 N.E. at 603.

113. 1911 Nev. Laws 362, ch. 183, § 11; 1913 Nev. Laws 137, ch. 111, § 3; 1911 N.H. Laws 181, ch. 163, § 4; 1947 N.H. Laws 402, ch. 266, § 10; Lubove, *Struggle for Social Security,* 56–57; Note, "Elective Provisions in Workmen's Compensation Acts," 60 *Harv. L. Rev.* 1131, 1133 (1947).

114. Cass Sunstein makes a similar point about a number of areas of early-twentieth-century constitutional law, pointing in particular to the Supreme Court's reasoning (quoted above in the text) in *New York Central R.R. v. White,* 243 U.S. 188, 197 (1917). See Cass R. Sunstein, *The Partial Constitution* 48, 361 n.8 (1993); Cass R. Sunstein, "Lochner's Legacy," 87 *Colum. L. Rev.* 873, 879 and n.30 (1987). The *White* reasoning is best understood as the outcome of a process set in motion by *Ives.*

115. *Proceedings of the Third National Conference on Workmen's Compensation for Industrial Accidents, Chicago, June 10–11, 1910,* p. 11 (1910); Subcommittee Memorandum, n.d., folder for 1909–12, box 6, JMW; Durand Halsey Van Doren, *Workmen's Compensation and Insurance* 59 (1918); Moss, *Socializing Security,* 125–26; 1911 N.J. Laws ch. 95, §§ 7–10. Only Ohio, California, Washington, and Nevada enacted compulsory statutes during this period, the first two after amending their state constitutions, and the last on the same day the *Ives* decision was handed down. Rubinow, *Social Insurance,* 175–81.

116. Rubinow, *Social Insurance,* 180; E. H. Downey, *Workmen's Compensation* 148 (1924); Roy Lubove, "Workmen's Compensation and the Prerogatives of Voluntarism," 8 *Lab. Hist.* 254, 269 (1967).

117. N.Y. Cent. R.R. Co. v. White, 243 U.S. 188, 203 (1917).

118. Id. at 197.

119. Arizona Copper Co. v. Hammer, 250 U.S. 400, 423 (1919). As Tom Green has pointed out to me, Pitney's actuarial causation reasoning nicely hid the ways in which workmen's compensation statutes worked hand-in-hand with assertions of new managerial power in the workplace. In Pitney's account, the statutes described a workplace of equal power among managers and workers alike. "Both parties," Pitney insisted, were "responsible" for the employment "since they voluntarily engage in it as coadventurers." *White,* 243 U.S. at 205. Interestingly, Justice Pitney also never completely abandoned the older language of rights and

justice for the categories of actuarial science. The constitutional validity of quid
pro quo compensation statutes, he wrote, was "plain . . . on grounds of *natural
justice.*" Id. at 203 (emphasis added).
120. *White,* 243 U.S. at 205.
121. *Jensen,* 100 N.E. at 603; Freund, "Constitutional Status of Workmen's Compensation," 438.
122. Samuel B. Horovitz and Josephine H. Klein, "The Constitutionality of Compulsory Workmen's Compensation Acts," *United States Department of Labor
Division of Labor Standards Bulletin No. 26,* pp. 3–4, 13 (1938).
123. Hearing on Mills Health Insurance Bill—Before N.Y. Senate Judiciary Committee, March 7, 1917, box 3, AALLP.
124. "Slap at Roosevelt in Barnes Reply," *New York Times,* Oct. 6, 1913, p. 5.
125. Mountain Timber Co. v. Washington, 243 U.S. 219, 265 (1917); id. at 266
(quoting Stertz v. Indus. Ins. Comm'n, 158 P. 256, 263 (Wash. 1916)).
126. Edward S. Corwin, "Social Insurance and Constitutional Limitations," 26 *Yale
L.J.* 431, 432 (1917).

7. The Accidental Republic

The epigraphs are from Franklin Delano Roosevelt, "Presidential Statement Signing
the Social Security Act. August 14, 1935," in *The Report of the Committee on Economic Security of 1935 and Other Basic Documents Relating to the Social Security
Act* 145 (1985); and Fleming James Jr., "The Columbia Study of Compensation for
Automobile Accidents: An Unanswered Challenge," 59 *Colum. L. Rev.* 408 (1959).
  1. I draw heavily in this paragraph on Mark Aldrich's very useful "cliometric" study
of the history of American work safety. See Mark Aldrich, *Safety First: Technology, Labor, and Business in the Building of American Work Safety, 1870–1939,*
pp. 129, 211, 284, 310 (1997). Aldrich reports that railroad employee nonfatal-
injury rates appear to have increased throughout the period, and actually stayed
above their 1890s levels until the 1930s. There is considerable difficulty here,
however, in controlling for increased accident reporting as injury compensation
increased. For a summary of the econometric literature on the impact of workmen's compensation on work safety, see Price V. Fishback and Shawn Everett
Kantor, *A Prelude to the Welfare State: The Origins of Workers' Compensation* 77–
82 (2000). It should be noted that alongside declines in the rates of work accidents, twentieth-century American industry also witnessed a migration south-
ward of the worst industrial hazards. See, e.g., David Barstow and Lowell Bergman, "At a Texas Foundry, An Indifference to Life," *New York Times,* Jan. 8,
2003, p. A1; David Barstow and Lowell Bergman, "A Family's Fortune, a Legacy of Blood and Tears," *New York Times,* Jan. 9, 2003, p. A1; David Barstow
and Lowell Bergman, "Deaths on the Jobs, Slaps on the Wrist," *New York
Times,* Jan. 10, 2003, p. A1.
  2. Aldrich, *Safety-First,* 122–67; Walter Licht, *Working for the Railroad: The Organization of Work in the Twentieth Century* 207–12 (1983); Christopher C.
Sellers, *Hazards of the Job: From Industrial Disease to Environmental Health Sci-*

ence 107–40 (1997). For "human resources," see William Hard, preface to William Hard et al., *Injured in the Course of Duty* (1910); John G. Park, "The Public Service of the Future Lawyer," 8 *Mich. L. Rev.* 122, 127 (1910).

3. See Judith Resnik, "Trial as Error, Jurisdiction as Injury," 113 *Harv. L. Rev.* 924, 953 (2000); Judith Resnik, "'Uncle Sam Modernizes His Justice': Inventing the Federal District Courts of the Twentieth Century for the District of Columbia and the Nation," 90 *Geo. L.J.* 607, 619–21, 662–63 (2002); Paul R. Verkuil, "Reflections upon the Federal Administrative Judiciary," 39 *UCLA L. Rev.* 1341 (1992).

4. Verkuil, "Reflections upon the Federal Administrative Judiciary," 1341; see, e.g., New York Compilation of Rules and Regulations tit. 15, ch. I, subch. I (Administrative Adjudication of Traffic Violations).

5. Walter F. Dodd, *Administration of Workmen's Compensation* 338–407 (1936); Henry D. Sayer, *Workmen's Compensation in New York: Its Development and Operations* 39–42 (1953); Crowell v. Benson, 285 U.S. 22 (1932); John Dickinson, "*Crowell v. Benson:* Judicial Review of Administrative Determinations of Questions of 'Constitutional Fact,'" 80 *U. Penn. L. Rev.* 1055 (1932); Comment, "Administrative Tribunals—Workmen's Compensation—The Scope of Federal Judicial Review under Longshoremen's and Harbor Workers' Compensation Act," 30 *Mich. L. Rev.* 1312 (1932); Comment, "*Crowell v. Benson:* Inquiries and Conjectures," 46 *Harv. L. Rev.* 478 (1933); Comment, "Administrative Law—Workmen's Compensation—Scope of Federal Judicial Review under Longshoremen's and Harbor Workers' Act," 32 *Colum. L. Rev.* 738 (1932); Note, "Judicial Review of Administrative Findings: *Crowell v. Benson,*" 41 *Yale L.J.* 1037 (1932). See generally Grant Gilmore and Charles L. Black Jr., *The Law of Admiralty* § 6–47 (2d ed. 1975); Henry P. Monaghan, "Constitutional Fact Review," 85 *Colum. L. Rev.* 229 (1985); Henry P. Monaghan, "Marbury and the Administrative State," 83 *Colum. L. Rev.* 1 (1983).

6. 35 Stat. 65, § 1 (1908).

7. *Liability of Employers: Hearings before the Committee on Interstate Commerce of the United States Senate, . . . May 3 to 8, 1906,* 59th Cong., 1st Sess., pp. 181, 11 (1906).

8. Lester P. Schoene and Frank Watson, "Workmen's Compensation on Interstate Railways," 47 *Harv. L. Rev.* 389, 398 (1934).

9. Erie R.R. v. Collins, 253 U.S. 77 (1920) (water); Delaware, L. and W. R.R. v. Vurkonis, 238 U.S. 439 (1915) (coal).

10. Compare Baltimore and Ohio Southwestern R.R. v. Burtch, 263 U.S. 540 (1924) (unloading interstate goods is interstate commerce), with Lehigh Valley R.R. v. Barlow, 244 U.S. 183 (1917) (unloading interstate goods seventeen days after their arrival is not interstate commerce).

11. Compare Atchison, T. and S.F. Ry. v. Industrial Accident Comm., 220 P. 342 (Cal. 1923) (guarding interstate train is interstate commerce), with Chicago and Alton R.R. v. Industrial Comm., 125 N.E. 378 (Ill. 1919) (looking for a place to hide from which to guard an interstate train is not interstate commerce), and Alabama and Great S. R.R. v. Bonner, 75 So. 986 (Ala. 1917) (pursuit of bandits who plundered interstate train is not interstate commerce). It should be noted

that the Court several times explained that the field of application for the FELA was narrower than the full extent of Congress's domain of authority under the Commerce Clause. See Illinois Cent. R.R. v. Behrens, 233 U.S. 473, 477 (1914); Chicago and Northwestern Ry. v. Bolle, 284 U.S. 74, 78 (1931); Railroad Retirement Bd. v. Alton R.R. Co., 295 U.S. 330, 388–89 (1935) (Hughes, C.J., dissenting).

12. Schoene and Watson, "Workmen's Compensation on Interstate Railways," 398. See also Rufus E. Foster, "The Federal Employers' Liability Act as Construed by the Supreme Court," 1 *So. L.Q.* 230, 235 (1916); "Federal Employers' Liability Act—When Is an Employee Engaged in Interstate Commerce," 63 *U. Pa. L. Rev.* 900, 900–1 (1915).

13. McLeod v. Threlkeld, 319 U.S. 491, 495 (1943).

14. Santa Cruz Fruit Packing Co. v. NLRB, 303 U.S. 453, 467–68 (1938).

15. Carl Hookstadt, "Comparison of Workmen's Compensation Laws in the United States up to December 31, 1917," BUSBLS no. 240, pp. 6, 28 (1918); New York State Department of Labor, *Annual Report of the Industrial Commission for the Twelve Months Ended June 30, 1917*, p. 138 (1918).

16. Jeremiah Smith, "Sequel to Workmen's Compensation Acts," 27 *Harv. L. Rev.* 235, 344 (1914).

17. Mountain Timber Co. v. Washington, 243 U.S. 219, 239, 242 (1917); New York Cent. R.R. v. White, 243 U.S. 188, 202–3 (1917) ("[I]t is important to be observed that the act applies only to . . . hazardous employment. . . ."); see also Arizona Copper Co. v. Hammer, 250 U.S. 400, 417 (1919).

18. National Industrial Conference Board, *The Workmen's Compensation Problem in New York State* 13–15 (1927); 1916 N.Y. Laws 2035, ch. 622, §§ 2 and 3.4; 1917 N.Y. Laws 2267, ch. 705, §§ 2 and 3.4; 1918 N.Y. Laws 2017, ch. 634, § 2.

19. *Proceedings, Third National Conference, Workmen's Compensation for Industrial Accidents, Chicago, June 10–11, 1910*, pp. 44–48 (1910); "Eighth Annual Message (1908),"15 *The Works of Theodore Roosevelt* 489, 502 (1926).

20. Ward and Gow v. Krinsky, 259 U.S. 503, 513 (1922).

21. Holden v. Hardy, 169 U.S. 366 (1898).

22. Lochner v. New York, 198 U.S. 45, 58–60 (1905).

23. Long hours among women workers, argued Brandeis and Goldmark in the famous 1908 Brandeis Brief, for example, were dangerous to the workers' health and safety. Brief for Defendant in Error, Muller v. Oregon, 208 U.S. 412 (1908) (October Term, 1907, no. 107).

24. *Krinsky,* 259 U.S. at 514–15.

25. Id. at 529 (McReynolds, J., dissenting).

26. On the many systems that make up the American law of accident compensation, see Kenneth S. Abraham and Lance Liebman, "Private Insurance, Social Insurance, and Tort Reform: Toward a New Vision of Compensation for Illness and Injury," 93 *Colum. L. Rev.* 75 (1993).

27. State of Wisconsin Industrial Commission to J. Mayhew Wainwright (Sept. 20, 1911), folder for 1911, box 6, JMW.

28. Southern Pac. Co. v. Jensen, 244 U.S. 205 (1917) *(Jensen II),* rev'g Jensen v. Southern Pac. Co., 109 N.E. 600 (N.Y. 1915).

29. Knickerbocker Ice Co. v. Stewart, 253 U.S. 149 (1920); Washington v. W. C. Dawson and Co., 264 U.S. 219 (1924); see also Gilmore and Black, *The Law of Admiralty*, § 6–45; Barry Cushman, "Lochner, Liquor, and Longshoremen: A Puzzle in Progressive Era Federalism," 32 *J. Maritime Law and Commerce* 1 (2001).

30. New York Cent. R.R. v. Winfield, 244 U.S. 205 (1917).

31. "Workmen's Compensation Legislation of the United States and Canada as of January 1, 1929," *BUSBLS* no. 496, pp. 6–8 and n.2 (1929).

32. Longshoremen and Harbor Workers Compensation Act, 44 Stat. 1424 (1927); Gilmore and Black, *Law of Admiralty*, § 6–46 et seq.; Federal Employees' Workmen's Compensation Act, 35 Stat. 556 (1908).

33. 35 Stat. 65 (1908); Jones Act, 41 Stat. 1007 (1920); Gilmore and Black, *Law of Admiralty*, § 6–20 et seq.

34. William G. Thomas, *Lawyering for the Railroad: Business, Law, and Power in the New South* 226–39 (1999); 2 *RELWCC* 141, 161, 635.

35. E.g., "Let the Pendulum Swing Free," *United Mine Workers' J.*, Jan. 20, 1910; William Green, "Law Interests Are Opposed to Compensation," *United Mine Workers' J.*, Oct. 22, 1912, p. 1.

36. Chas. R. Otis to Jonathan Mayhew Wainwright, Feb. 20, 1911, folder for 1911, box 6, JMW; *Report by the Committee to Study Compensation for Automobile Accidents to the Columbia University Council for Research in the Social Sciences* 18–20 (1932).

37. Arthur A. Ballantine, "A Compensation Plan for Railway Accident Claims," 29 *Harv. L. Rev.* 705 (1916); Weld A. Rollins, "A Proposal to Extend the Compensation Principle to Accidents in the Streets," 4 *Mass. L.Q.* 392 (1919); Ernest C. Carman, "Is a Motor Vehicle Accident Compensation Act Advisable?" 4 Minn. L. Rev. 1 (1919); Wayland H. Elsbree and Harold Cooper Roberts, "Compulsory Insurance against Motor Vehicle Accidents," 76 *U. Pa. L. Rev.* 690 (1928)

38. *Report by the Committee to Study Compensation for Automobile Accidents,* 134; Young B. Smith, Austin J. Lilly, and Noel T. Dowling, "Compensation for Automobile Accidents: A Symposium," 32 *Colum. L. Rev.* 785 (1932); Simon, "Driving Governmentality," 567–75.

39. Frank P. Grad, "Recent Developments in Automobile Accident Compensation," 50 *Colum. L. Rev.* 300, (1950); Fleming James Jr., "The Columbia Study of Compensation for Automobile Accidents: An Unanswered Challenge," 59 *Colum. L. Rev.* 408, 423 (1959); see also Simon, "Driving Governmentality," 585; Crandall Melvin, *Compulsory Compensation Insurance for Automobiles: Discussion . . . before the Federation of Bar Associations of the Fifth Judicial District . . . Oswego, N.Y.* (1932); P. Tecumseh Sherman, "Grounds for Opposing the Automobile Accident Compensation Plan," 3 *Law and Contemp. Probs.* 598 (1936). Sherman was an insurance defense lawyer and veteran of the workmen's compensation movement. After serving as an informal, behind-the-scenes advisor to the Wainwright Commission, he bitterly opposed the enactment of further social insurance or compensation-like programs.

40. Philippe Nonet, *Administrative Justice: Advocacy and Change in Government Agencies* 66–103 (1969).

41. "Your Guide to ATLA," available at http://www.atla.org/info/guide.ht (vis-

ited July 30, 2002); Robert A. Kagan, *Adversarial Legalism: The American Way of Life* (2001); Robert A. Kagan, "American Lawyers, Legal Culture, and Adversarial Legalism," in *Legal Culture and the Legal Profession* 7, 36–37 (Lawrence M. Friedman and Harry Scheiber eds., 1996).

42. Southern Pac. Co. v. Jensen, 244 U.S. 205, 221 (1917) (Holmes, J., dissenting).

43. Orin Kramer and Richard Briffault, *Workers' Compensation: Strengthening the Social Compact* (1991); David Rosner and Gerald Markowitz, *Deadly Dust: Silicosis and the Politics of Occupational Disease in Twentieth-Century America* 77–86 (1991); Price-Anderson Act of 1957, 42 U.S.C.A. § 2210 (West 2002); Federal Coal Mine Health and Safety Act of 1969, 30 U.S.C.A. §§ 901 et seq. (West 2002); National Childhood Vaccine Injury Act of 1986, 42 U.S.C.A. §§ 300aa-10 to 300aa-33 (West 2002).

44. At the end of the 1990s, twenty-six U.S. jurisdictions had no-fault automobile compensation statute, twenty-four states plus the District of Columbia and Puerto Rico. Two states—Nevada and Georgia—enacted no-fault schemes but subsequently repealed them. Robert H. Joost, *Automobile Insurance and No-Fault Law 2d* § 1:2 (1992). On automobile no-fault statutes, see Robert E. Keeton and Jeffrey O'Connell, *Basic Protection for the Traffic Victim: A Blueprint for Reforming Automobile Insurance* (1965).

45. Robert L. Rabin, "Some Reflections on the Process of Tort Reform," 25 *San Diego L. Rev.* 13, 22 (1988). Other tort reform measures have included shortening the period after the injury in which a suit may be brought (statute of limitations reform), and allowing tortfeasors to set off against damages awards any collateral benefits—e.g., health or disability insurance benefits—received by a plaintiff (collateral source rule reform). See generally Marc A. Franklin and Robert L. Rabin, *Tort Law and Alternatives* 787–92 (7th ed. 2001).

46. Wex S. Malone, "Damage Suits and the Contagious Principle of Workmen's Compensation," 9 *National Ass'n of Claimants' Compensation Attorneys L.J.* 20 (1952).

47. K. N. Llewellyn, "The Effect of Legal Institutions upon Economics," 15 *Am. Econ. Rev.* 665, 678–80 (1925); see also David A. Moss, *When All Else Fails: Government as the Ultimate Risk Manager* 231 (2002).

48. Peter Huber, *Liability: The Legal Revolution and Its Consequences* (1990); see also George L. Priest, "The Invention of Enterprise Liability: A Critical History of the Intellectual Foundations of Modern Tort Law," 14 *J. Leg. Stud.* 461 (1985).

49. John Fabian Witt, "Speedy Fred Taylor and the Ironies of Enterprise Liability," 103 *Colum. L. Rev.* 1 (2003).

50. Different accident-law schemes often address the very different kinds of legal and policy problems arising in diverse areas such as work accidents, automobile injuries, and medical malpractice. On the other hand, diversity among accident-law schemes often seems to give rise to morally arbitrary distinctions between otherwise similarly situated plaintiffs and defendants. A motor vehicle driver seriously injured in an automobile accident arising out of no one's negligence, for example, will generally have great difficulty recovering lost wages or pain and

suffering. Yet an employee injured in a similarly nonnegligent work accident will recover medical costs and a percentage of lost wages in the workers' compensation system. On the systemlessness of American accident law, see Abraham and Liebman, "Private Insurance, Social Insurance, and Tort Reform."

51. Arthur J. Altmeyer, *The Formative Years of Social Security* 14–15, 19–21 (1966); Edwin E. Witte, *The Development of Social Security* 100 (1963); Railroad Retirement Bd. v. Alton R.R. Co., 295 U.S. 330 (1935).

52. E.g., Robert C. Lieberman, *Shifting the Color Line: Race and the American Welfare State* (1998).

53. Jacob S. Hacker, *The Divided Welfare State: The Battle over Public and Private Social Benefits in the United States* (2002); Daniel T. Rodgers, *Atlantic Crossings: Social Politics in a Progressive Age* 265–66 (1998).

54. Sanford M. Jacoby, "Employers and the Welfare State: The Role of Marion B. Folsom," 80 *J. Am. Hist.* 525 (1993); Edward D. Berkowitz and Kim McQuaid, *Creating the Welfare State* 6–66, 92–97 (rev. ed. 1992); Colin Gordon, *New Deals: Business, Labor, and Politics in America, 1920–1935*, pp. 240–79 (1994); Steve Fraser, "The 'Labor Question,'" in *The Rise and Fall of the New Deal Order* 55–84 (Steve Fraser and Gary Gerstle eds., 1989); Nelson, *Unemployment Insurance*, 32–33, 142.

55. Alexander Keyssar, *Out of Work: The First Century of Unemployment in Massachusetts* 292–93 (1986).

56. William Greider, introduction to Leon Stein, *The Triangle Fire* x (William Greider ed., 2001) (1962); Frances Perkins, *The Roosevelt I Knew* 54–60 (1946); George Whitney Martin, *Madam Secretary, Frances Perkins* 141–50, 163–79, 204–16 (1976).

57. Witte, *Development of the Social Security Act*, xiv–xv.

58. Id., 23; John R. Commons, *Myself: The Autobiography of John R. Commons* 141 (1964) (1934); J. Mayhew Wainwright to Charles R. Miller, Esq. (Nov. 2, 1911), folder for 1911, box 6, JMW; *Third Report to the Legislature of the State of New York by the Commission Appointed . . . to Inquire into the Question of Employers' Liability and Other Matters: Unemployment and Lack of Farm Labor, April 26, 1911* (1911).

59. Commons, *Myself*, 156; Altmeyer, *Formative Years*, 3–42; Alice Kessler-Harris, *In Pursuit of Equity: Women, Men, and the Quest for Economic Citizenship in Twentieth-Century America* 79–82 (2001); David A. Moss, *Socializing Security: Progressive-Era Economists and the Origins of American Social Policy* 65 (1996); Daniel Nelson, *Unemployment Insurance: The American Experience* 13, 192–222 (1969).

60. Moss, *Socializing Security*, 65; Nelson, *Unemployment Insurance*, 13, 192–222.

61. Michael J. Graetz and Jerry L. Mashaw, *True Security: Rethinking American Social Insurance* 189 (1999); see also Moss, *Socializing Security*, 158–65; Nelson, *Unemployment Insurance*, 192–222.

62. "Two-Hundred and First Press Conference (Excerpts), May 3, 1935," in 4 *The Public Papers and Addresses of Franklin D. Roosevelt* 159, 160–61 (1938); "A Radio Address to the Young Democratic Clubs of America, August 24, 1935," in 4 *Public Papers and Addresses*, 336, 341; *Report to the President of the Com-*

mittee on Economic Security v (1935); "A Greater Future Economic Security of the American People"—A Message to the Congress on Social Security. January 17, 1935," in 4 *Public Papers and Addresses*, 43, 43.

63. Railroad Retirement Bd. v. Alton R.R. Co., 295 U.S. 330, 384 (1935) (Hughes, C.J., dissenting).
64. Perkins, *The Roosevelt I Knew*, 290.
65. Gwendolyn Mink, *The Wages of Motherhood: Inequality in the Welfare State, 1917–1942*, p. 130 (1995); Kessler-Harris, *In Pursuit of Equity*, 117–30; Linda Gordon, *Pitied but Not Entitled: Single Mothers and the History of Welfare, 1890–1935*, pp. 253–85 (1994).
66. Advisory Council on Social Security, *Final Report, December 10, 1938*, S. Doc. 4, 76th Cong., 1st Sess., p. 18 (1939); see also Kessler-Harris, *In Pursuit of Equity*, 130–42; Mink, *Wages of Motherhood*, 135–37.
67. Social Security Act Amendments of 1939, H.R. Rep. 728, 76th Cong., 1st Sess., pp. 86, 94 (June 2, 1939) (emphasis added); 53 Stat. 1360, §§ 202(d), 209(i), and 209(j) (1939).
68. Subsequent amendments to the survivors' benefit provisions in 1950 allowed aged widowers to collect survivors benefits, but only if they could establish that they had been supported by their wife's wages—a requirement, like those found in a number of state workmen's compensation statutes, that widows did not face. 64 Stat. 483, 485 (1950).
69. Weinberger v. Wiesenfeld, 420 U.S. 636 (1975); Califano v. Goldfarb, 430 U.S. 199 (1977); Kessler-Harris, *In Pursuit of Equity*, 167–69.
70. Social Security Act Amendments of 1939, S. Rep. 734, 76th Cong., 1st Sess., p. 11 (1939).
71. Witte, *Development of the Social Security Act*, 149.
72. Kennedy, *Freedom from Fear*, 99–100; Social Security Act Amendments of 1939, S. Rep. 734, 76th Cong., 1st Sess., p. 6 (July 7, 1939).
73. West Coast Hotel Co. v. Parrish, 300 U.S. 379 (1937); Chas. C. Steward Machine Co. v. Davis, 301 U.S. 548 (1937). For particularly important recent contributions to the vast literature on the "switch in time," see Barry Cushman, *Rethinking the New Deal Court: The Structure of a Constitutional Revolution* (1998); Bruce Ackerman, *We the People II: Transformations* 255–311 (1998).
74. West Coast Hotel 300 U.S. at 399.
75. J. P. Cotton Jr., The Work of the New York State Commission on Employers' Liability, memorandum presented to the National Civic Federation, Nov. 22, 1909, folder for 1909–12, box 6, JMW; Ives v. S. Buffalo Ry., 94 N.E. 431, 440 (1911).
76. Thomas K. McCraw, *Prophets of Regulation: Charles Francis Adams, Louis D. Brandeis, James M. Landis, Alfred E. Kahn* 57–79 (1984); Peter L. Strauss, "The Place of Agencies in Government: Separation of Powers and the Fourth Branch," 84 *Colum. L. Rev.* 573 (1984).
77. An Act to Regulate Commerce, 24 Stat. 379 (1887).
78. Elizabeth Brandeis, "Labor Legislation," in 3 *History of Labor in the United States, 1896–1932*, pp. 397, 629 (John R. Commons ed., 1935).
79. Gordon, *Pitied but Not Entitled*, 37–66; Mink, *Wages of Motherhood*, 49–50.
80. Michael Willrich, "The Two Percent Solution: Eugenic Jurisprudence and the

Socialization of American Law, 1900–1930," 16 *Law and Hist. Rev.* 63 (1998); David J. Rothman, "Behavior Modification in Total Institutions: An Historical Overview," in *American Law and the Constitutional Order* 293 (Lawrence M. Friedman and Harry N. Scheiber eds., enlarged ed. 1984); Jonathan Simon, *Poor Discipline: Parole and the Social Control of the Underclass, 1890–1990* (1993); Lawrence M. Friedman, *Crime and Punishment in American History* 413–17 (1993).

81. New York State Department of Labor, *Annual Report of the Industrial Commission for the Twelve Months Ending September 30, 1915*, p. 10 (1916).

82. "Workmen's Compensation Laws of the United States and Foreign Countries," *BUSBLS* no. 203, p. 66 (1917).

83. New York State Department of Labor, *Annual Report of the Industrial Commission . . . 1917*, p. 121.

84. New York State Department of Labor, *Annual Report of the Industrial Commission for the Nine Months Ended June 30, 1916*, p. 115 (1917).

85. "Workmen's Compensation Laws of the United States and Foreign Countries," 66; Gordon, *Pitied but Not Entitled*, 49.

86. Case 3778, Terence E. Bennett, NYWCBA.

87. Case 226337, Michele Caruso (1919), NYWCBA. Caruso had been cleaning the dough mixer while the power was on. His arm was apparently caught in the mixer, and while trying to extricate himself, Caruso caught his leg in the mixer as well. Both the arm and the leg were crushed and Caruso died on the scene as a result of his injuries.

88. Case 277041, Philip Koepper (1919), NYWCBA. The state Industrial Commission also pushed at the boundaries of the compensation scheme so as to make awards to needy families in any number of borderline cases.

89. E.g., Case 2640, John Welch (1918), NYWCBA.

90. Case B3149, Harold Taber (1917), NYWCBA.

91. Case 198, George H. Hall (1915), NYWCBA.

92. Case 10230, Otto N. Bleich (1918), NYWCBA. See also Case 114, Harry Natanblut (1915), NYWCBA; Case 812169, Antonio Gattuso (1922), NYWCBA; Case 822378, Joe Ponessa (1922), NYWCBA.

93. E.g., Case 12903, John E. Harry (1919), NYWCBA (International Association of Machinists); Case 350571, Vincenzo Scotto (1918), NYWCBA (International Longshoremen's Association). On the relationship between individual rights claims and community organizations, see Risa L. Goluboff, "'Won't You Please Help Me Get My Son Home': Peonage, Patronage, and Protest in the World War II Urban South," 24 *Law and Soc. Inquiry* 777 (1999).

94. E.g., folder marked "Workmen's Compensation Law and Correspondence," box 230, Brotherhood of Locomotive Firemen and Enginemen Papers, KC.

95. Nonet, *Administrative Justice*, 66–97.

Conclusion

1. Compare Sindell v. Abbott Lab., 607 P.2d 924 (Cal. 1980) (market share liability in DES litigation), and Herskovitz v. Eli Lilly and Co., 539 N.E.2d 1069 (N.Y. 1989) (same), with Santiago v. Sherwin Williams Co., 3 F.3d 546 (1st Cir.

1993) (rejecting market share liability in lead paint litigation), and Goldman v. Johns-Manville Sales Corp., 514 N.E.2d 691 (Ohio 1987) (rejecting market share liability in asbestos litigation).

2. Deborah R. Hensler et al., *Class Action Dilemmas: Pursuing Public Goals for Private Gain* (2000); Samuel Issacharoff, "Governance and Legitimacy in the Law of Class Actions," 1999 *Sup. Ct. Rev.* 337; David Rosenberg, "The Causal Connection in Mass Exposure Cases: A 'Public Law' Vision of the Tort System," 97 *Harv. L. Rev.* 849 (1984).

3. Anthony Giddens, *The Third Way and Its Critics* 135–39 (2000); Anthony Giddens, *Modernity and Self-Identity: Self and Society in the Late Modern Age* 121–24 (1991); Charles Perrow, *Normal Accidents: Living With High-Risk Technologies* (1984).

4. Air Transportation Safety and System Stabilization Act, Pub. L. No. 107–42, 115 Stat. 230, §§ 401 et seq. (2001); 28 C.F.R. §§ 104.1 et seq. (2002).

5. Ortiz v. Fibreboard Corp., 527 U.S. 815, 846 (1999) (Souter, J.) (quoting Martin v. Wilks, 490 U.S. 755, 762 (1989) (quoting 18 C. Wright et al., *Federal Practice and Procedure* § 4449, p. 417 (1981))).

6. E.g., Robert Keeton and Jeffrey O'Connell, *Basic Protection for the Traffic Victim* 140–48 (1965); Marc A. Franklin and Robert L. Rabin, *Tort Law and Alternatives* 858–60 (7th ed. 2001).

7. Jacob S. Hacker, *The Divided American Welfare State: Public and Private Benefits* (2002); Christopher Howard, *The Hidden Welfare State: Tax Expenditures and Social Policy in the United States* (1997); Jennifer Klein, *For All These Rights: Business, Labor, and the Shaping of America's Public-Private Welfare State* (2003).

8. I. M. Rubinow, *Social Insurance* 49 (1913).

9. E.g., Robert Nozick, "Choice and Indeterminism," in *Agents, Causes, and Events: Essays on Indeterminism and Free Will* (Timothy O'Connor ed., 1995).

10. See John Lewis Gaddis, *The Landscape of History: How Historians Map the Past* 91–109 (2002); Niall Ferguson, "Virtual History: Towards a 'Chaotic' Theory of the Past," in *Virtual History: Alternatives and Counterfactuals* 1, 83–85 (Niall Ferguson ed., 1997)

11. Compare Ernest J. Weinrib, *The Idea of Private Law* (1995), with Guido Calabresi, *The Costs of Accidents: A Legal and Economic Analysis* (1970).

12. For an introduction to the policy debates over tort law, see Donald Dewees et al., *Exploring the Domain of Accident Law: Taking the Facts Seriously* (1996).

Acknowledgments

I have looked forward for some time to writing these acknowledgments for the opportunity they afford to thank friends, teachers, and colleagues for the extraordinary generosity that has made this book much better than it would have been had I gone it alone. *The Accidental Republic* began as a history dissertation at Yale University, where I was exceedingly fortunate to have a dissertation committee consisting of Glenda Gilmore in the history department and Peter Schuck in the law school, and chaired by Robert W. Gordon, whose nimble mind seems to evade all disciplinary bounds and whose seemingly offhand remarks shaped the project's most basic directions.

At Columbia Law School, colleagues have provided warm encouragement and robust intellectual exchange. Ariela Dubler's contributions are to be found on virtually every page of this book. Barbara Black, Robert Ferguson, Lance Liebman, Gillian Metzger, and Peter Strauss read early drafts of a number of chapters, though they may barely recognize the final version thanks to incisive responses that caused me to rethink any number of points. Cindy Estlund, Katherine Franke, Victor Goldberg, David Leebron, Subha Narisimhan, Andrzej Rapaczynski, Chuck Sabel, Bill Sage, and Cathy Sharkey provided enormously helpful readings of parts of the manuscript at critically important junctures in the process, as did Alan Brinkley of the university's history department.

I am grateful to Bill Nelson for shepherding this work along in his capacity as overseer of the Golieb Fellowship in Legal History at the New York University School of Law. Willy Forbath provided an initially anonymous outside review that became the point of departure for an immensely stimulating series of conversations. Mark Brilliant, Guido Calabresi (who introduced me to the *Ives* case), Risa Goluboff, Tom Green, Henry Hansmann, Dirk Hartog, and Viviana Zelizer each read and offered generous comments on parts of the project. Scott Messinger helped shape the title of the book, which I use with apologies to the great mid-twentieth-century critic Michael Harrington, whose book *The Accidental Century* predates mine by over thirty-five years. Audiences at NYU's Legal History Colloquium, the American Society for Legal History meetings, the Columbia Institutions Workshop run by Ira Katznelson, the Columbia Law School Faculty Retreat, the Boston University Legal History Workshop, and the University of Michigan Legal History Workshop helped me to work through many of the finer points in the narrative.

Kent McKeever and the Columbia Law School Library's excellent reference librarians and circulation staff—especially Duncan Alford, Whitney Bagnall, Simon Canick, Christine Cipollone, Charles Cronin, Marc Hasen, and Dana Neacsu—responded with expert knowledge and unflagging enthusiasm to my often unreasonable requests. Reference librarians at the New-York Historical Society, the New York Public Library, NYU School of Law, Yale Law School, the Kheel Center at Cornell, Rush Rhees Library at the University of Rochester, and the New York State Library in Albany provided invaluable assistance on discrete parts of the project.

Molly Biklen, Huy Chu, Jim Downes, Bryan Kessler, Jason Parkin, Colleen Shanahan, and David Tice provided superb research assistance. Important financial assistance has been provided at various stages of the process by the Richard J. Franke and John F. Enders fellowships at Yale; a Littleton-Griswold grant from the American Historical Association; a John M. Olin summer fellowship from the Yale Law School Center for Law and Economics; a Hackman Research Residency grant from the New York State Archives Partnership; and the Samuel Golieb Fellowship at NYU School of Law. A timely grant from the Bernard H. Kayden Faculty Research Fund at Columbia made completion of the book possible.

Early versions of Chapters 2 and 3 appear in "Toward a New History of American Accident Law," 114 *Harv. L. Rev.* 625 (2001). The argument about gender in American accident law and social insurance that appears in Chapters 2, 5, and 7 draws on ideas that first appeared in "From Loss of Services to Loss of Support: The Wrongful Death Statutes, the Origins of Modern Tort Law, and the Making of the Nineteenth-Century Family," 25 *Law & Soc. Inquiry* 717 (2000). Some of the material in Chapter 4 appears in "Speedy Fred Taylor and the Ironies of Enterprise Liability," 103 *Colum. L. Rev.* 1 (2003).

No one has had to live with this book as Annie Murphy Paul has had to virtually every day for the past three years. Annie has taken time from her own book to contribute extraordinary editorial acumen and analytic rigor to mine. I am the lucky one.

Index

Milton Keynes UK
Ingram Content Group UK Ltd.
UKHW021808260124
436770UK00006B/492